QUOTH THE MAVEN

QUOTH THE MAVEN

William Safire

Illustrations by Keith Bendis

Random House
New York

Grateful acknowledgment is made to *The New York Times* for permission
to reprint 75 "On Language" columns by William Safire, published
in *The New York Times* between April 3, 1988, and December 31, 1989.
Copyright © 1988, 1989 by The New York Times Company.
Reprinted by permission.

Illustrations by Keith Bendis

Library of Congress Cataloging-in-Publication Data
Safire, William
Quoth the maven / William Safire.—1st ed.
p.   cm.
A collection of the author's weekly columns "On language"
from The New York Times Magazine.
Includes index.
ISBN 0-679-42324-9
1. English language—Usage. 2. English language—Style.
I. Title.
PE1421.S233   1993
428—dc20   92-34206

Manufactured in the United States of America

24689753

FIRST EDITION

For the members of "olbom," which stands for On Language's Board of Octogenarian Mentors. They are:

Jacques Barzun
Alistair Cooke
Fred Cassidy
Allen Walker Read

These giants of linguistics and usage might agree that an acronym of more than four letters is lowercased— olbom, not OLBOM—or they might not.

CREDITS

Acknowledgments is a word that, to me, connotes grudging admission of the need to say thanks, or a sneaky way to avert charges of plagiarism, or a regal wave from a limousine window. Besides, the snooty word has a fake Latin prefix; hell with it.

What follows are *credits* to people who support my work either because they want to or because they must. Among them are the leading lexies: Fred Mish of Merriam-Webster and Sol Steinmetz of Random House, on the descriptive side, and Anne Soukhanov of the *American Heritage Dictionary,* who is a tad more prescriptive. For current etymology (an oxymoron), I'm often indebted to John Algeo and Cynthia Barnhart, who head the Phrasedick Brigade, as well as James D. McCawley on grammar and Robert L. Chapman and Richard A. Spears on slang.

The quotation anthologist Len Safir, my late brother, knocked himself out tracking obscure quotes on my behalf; Justin Kaplan of *Bartlett's Familiar Quotations* is also a valuable resource. Jeanne Smith at the Library of Congress does more for the taxpayers than any research aide in Washington. At Random House, where this compilation is produced, I am indebted to Kate Medina, Jonathan Karp, Camille Capozzi, Beth Pearson, Margaret Wimberger, and Patricia Abdale.

At the *New York Times* bureau in Washington, D.C., I am propped up by Jeffrey McQuain, destined to be general editor of the next edition of *Safire's Political Dictionary. New York Times Magazine* editors Warren Hoge and (since 1993) Jack Rosenthal, Harvey Shapiro, and Michael Molyneux stand resolutely at the dividing line between with-it coverage of slang and the limits of good taste. The copy editors of my political column, Steve Pickering and Linda Cohen, often contribute useful ideas for my language column as they save me from countless embarressments (that's not how you spell *embarrass*); our chief librarian, Barclay Walsh, and librarians Monica Borkowski and

Marjorie Goldsborough are more than helpful, for which I reciprocate by never using the word *morgue*. Ann Elise Rubin, my assistant, and Rebecca Lawrence keep me in touch with the Lexicographic Irregulars, who—from the eyries of the Poetic Allusion Watch to the heights of glee reached by the Gotcha! Gang—empower my prose and enliven my life.

INTRODUCTION

This is a book that draws together some seventy-five columns that appear under the heading "On Language" in *The New York Times Magazine,* enlivened with emendations, corrections and objections from members of a far-flung group of language lovers called the Lexicographic Irregulars. Before presenting this book to the reader, the author must ask himself: "What am I?"

Not "*Who* am I?"—a sense of self is not a problem with me—but "*What* am I?" What is my role in this writer-reader communications symbiosis, and how do I properly explain my calling in an instant, without going into a labored job description?

The language has developed a way to signal a person's position. It has been hailed as a time-saving device and derogated as "bogus titling." Let us, at the outset, examine this shorthand identifier and reach a conclusion about its use, thereby illustrating the approach to language throughout this book.

Ready? The language maven William Safire is about to take a stand in the controversy over bogus titling.

Why does the previous sentence begin with the word *the*? Because if it started with the words *language maven,* that would be construed as a title, and the style arbiters of the best publications have long said it's bad form to throw false titles around.

But if I had dared to write *Language Maven William Safire,* without the *the,* would I have been trying to give myself airs? Of course not; if I wanted to assume a title, I'd have tried Lord Safire, which sounds grander than anything we have in the language dodge.

The purpose of the noun phrase used attributively before the name is not to confer rank but to help the reader recognize the subject. The controversy centers on this: Should the identification of the subject be placed after the name, to be in gentle apposition, or before the name, to be fused tightly to it?

Apposition uses two nouns in succession to refer to the same thing. *Bill*

Clinton, the President is an example; the second noun repeats the meaning of the first. However, when you adopt the loyal apposition, you seem to be saying something else as well: "Not Bill Clinton, the haberdasher down the street who objects to being confused with the famous Bill Clinton." With a famous person, the repetition in apposition is unnecessary.

Just to avoid the problem of bogus titling, the stylebooks create the problem of conferring too much renown. *The* can be a powerful isolator, especially in print, where no emphasis in pronunciation is shown: *Safire, the language maven* suggests that I am the one and only language maven, and the legions of the Gotcha! Gang are ready to hoot at that thought. On the other hand, *a* is a relentless equalizer: *Safire, a language maven* is a put-down, suggesting that I am an anonymous crank and nobody at all knows my attempts to free mankind from the clutches of obsolete stylebooks.

When *the* is too singular and *a* or *an* is too general, you've run out of articles; the vocabulary bin is empty. What to do? Our resilient language scrambles around for a way out, and as always, the lingo will prevail.

The answer of usage: Take that appositive identifier following the name and stick it up front without any article at all. Voilà: *Language maven Safire.* Neither a big shot nor a pipsqueak; just right.

Because this encapsulation of reputation was pioneered by journalists, my fellow grammarians have sniffed at it as "journalese"—a sorry trade of inelegance for the sake of compression. But we are not merely saving three spaces on a tight line or, in Garrick Utley's case of "the beating of motorist Rodney King," a whole second; consider the differentiation value of the front-end identifier in the case of three people.

James Jones wrote *From Here to Eternity* (a title taken from "The Whiffenpoof Song"). Another James Jones, known better as Jim, led a cult to mass suicide. And James Earl Jones is the actor who was the voice of Darth Vader and who announces the station breaks of CNN.

Not only does *the author James Jones* sound stilted, but that restrictiveness may also make him seem like the only author. *James Jones, a cult leader* suggests that the reader has already forgotten who he was. *James Earl Jones, an actor* or *the actor* slights his genuine renown. How much clearer and less judgmental are *author James Jones, cult leader James Jones, actor James Earl Jones.*

Editors recognize this difference, and are sensitive to distortions of meaning by copy editors on the front lines, who try to play by the book. When I referred to a colleague as *reporter R. W. Apple*—better to my eye than *Apple, the reporter* (we have a few others) or *Apple, a reporter* (he'd kill me)—an editor trying to squeeze me onto the team changed it to *the reporter R. W. Apple.*

This addition created nonsense, according to the pooh-bah of style at my newspaper, Allan M. Siegal. "The 'the' form can be used only where we're discussing someone of at least modest renown: 'the soprano Emma Kirkby,' for example," he advised. "With lesser mortals—including my friend

Apple—some form of apposition has to be used: '. . . told a reporter, Joe Doakes,' or 'told Joe Doakes, a reporter.' In brief, writing should read like the work of a writer, not an editor."

I'm for that. Henceforth, on first mention, full frontal identification will be my style. In deference to traditionalists now staring decisively at me, I will eschew cliché bogus titles like *consumer advocate Ralph Nader,* and will refrain from capitalizing the attributive noun phrase, thus making it seem less like an official title. When it does not appear that way in the paper, and you see instead *the language maven Safire,* it is only because I do not own the paper. Be patient; the stylebooks will come around.

Having zigged to conform to linguistic reality, let us now zag to avert compresspeak. Beware *the Chinese hamster syndrome.*

In a recent polemic, I referred to George Bush's "1,400-word, hastily slapped together and ill-rehearsed speech in the guise of a statement to a news conference." David J. Jacobs of Stephentown, New York, who coaches sportswriters at the Springfield *Union-News* in Massachusetts, refers to this space-saving habit as *noun-clustering;* he fears that it has spread, "like the blob from an outer-space horror movie thing," from sports pages to pristine Op-Ed pages.

Sportswriting coach Jacobs (better than *Jacobs, the sportswriting coach*) cites such recent usages as "mobster-turned-informant Jack Johns" and "reputed Mafia underboss William P. 'The Wild Guy' Grasso" in the *Union-News.* He also cites "the 6,718-yard, par-70 Oakland Hills Country Club course," on which Ben Hogan won with "a remarkable five-under-par 65," phrases that appeared in *The Times* and are topped only by this newspaper's "after his two-walk, six-strikeout, 14-fly-ball-outs of dominance."

Out-of-hand noun-clustering leads to crammed prose. Put that sentence less tightly: The clustering of nouns, when it gets out of hand, jam-packs five pounds of words into a two-pound bag.

The newsletter of the New England Medical Writers Association cites the classic clustering of nouns: "*The Chinese Hamster ovary/hypoxanthine guanine . . . mammalian cell forward gene mutation* assay was used to evaluate uforia." The words in italics all modify the noun *assay.*

Taking a deep breath, Mr. Jacobs calls this "the 'from single nouns as adjectives, to the occupational and false titles, to the strings of attributive nouns called noun clusters or stacked modifiers, to the whereinhell is this thing going' locution."

Like the modern person, modern prose needs a little space. Titular encapsulation, within reason, saith language maven Safire, is useful; however, the acceptance of rampant sentence-compressing clustering could suck us all into the black hole of terminological implosion. ("Noun clusters that compress sentences beyond comprehensibility" is more easily understood than "sentence-compressing clustering.") Today's message: Loosen up. Take all the *the*'s saved from apposition and sprinkle 'em around.

QUOTH THE MAVEN

Ahead of the Vanguard

The actor Jack Nicholson said three years ago that he would "like to play people that haven't existed yet, a future something, a *cusp* character." So he wound up playing the Joker character in *Batman,* the movie based on the old comic book.

"*Cusp* bears watching," wrote Robert Meier of Bethesda, Maryland, when he sent in that citation back in 1986. He noted that in *The New York Times Magazine* Ron Rosenbaum had written of Mr. Nicholson that he was "on the *cusp* of 50," and that a *Washington Post* reporter, Paul Taylor, predicted we may be "at the *cusp* of a major national mood swing."

Somewhere in the attic of my mind was a quotation from Winston Churchill about being "at the *cusp* of history"; I slammed around my memories and noodled through the anthologies, raising a cloud of braindust but no Churchill on the cusp.

Good word, though; it means "tip, pointed end, peak," and in astronomy "the projection formed by the convergence of curves, as in 'the cusps of a crescent moon.'" Rooted in the Latin *cuspis,* "point," the English word got its start in astrology; in the 1585 edition of Thomas Lupton's *A Thousand Notable Things of Sundrie Sorts,* which sounds like a kind of Renaissance *Book of Lists,* the word *cusp* was used with the sense of "the beginning or entrance of a 'house.' " (Presumably, Nancy Reagan explains the astrological term in her forthcoming book.)

Mathematicians picked up the word, using it in geometry to mean "a point at which two branches of a curve meet and stop, with a common tangent." Architects liked it, too, for the projecting points between the small arcs in Gothic arches. Dentists grabbed it to mean a protuberance or projection of the crown of a tooth, which remains with us in *bicuspid.* (No, there is no connection to *cuspidor,* rooted in the unrelated Latin *spuere,* "to spit"; I point that out to avert a flock of queries.)

For three years now, I have been collecting *cusp* usages, against the day the word would make it to prime-time network television. Last year, *The Times Magazine,* whose editors seem curiously attracted to the word, used it in large type to describe the actor Dennis Quaid as one who "rocks on the *cusp* of stardom," perhaps taking the idea from a phrase in Michael Norman's piece calling him "the man on the *cusp.*"

Finally, the useful little extended metaphor made it. On CBS, Dan Rather spoke of Hungary as being a nation "on the *cusp* of freedom and democracy." That did it; *cusp* will now be included in all the dictionaries with its new sense, of "cutting edge."

But where did this modern usage begin? P. J. McKenna, a professor of mathematics at the University of Connecticut, who has also been watching this word for years, suggests it may have evolved from catastrophe theory.

"In the late Nixon and Carter years of malaise in the 70's, appropriately enough," he writes, "catastrophe theory was the mathematical rage. It purposed to explain why things would suddenly jump discontinuously from one state to another. I think the usage of *cusp* has evolved from the two-dimensional surface of the same name in catastrophe theory."

(Professor McKenna also notes that the latest mathematical vogue term to describe the erratic behavior of nonlinear systems is *chaotic.* We will see if this crosses over into street slang as an approving "Man, that's *chaotic!*")

Do you realize what the emergence of *cusp* as the most avant-garde term for "vanguard" means? It means that *cutting edge* is no longer on the cutting edge.

I'd better download my file on *cutting edge* before it becomes a synonym for "lagging indicator." The phrase, in its original sense of a sharp border of a blade, goes back to 1825, but began being used in its metaphoric sense in the early 1950's. "I suspect that it may be related to the much earlier *leading edge,*" reported Stuart Berg Flexner of Random House, "which dates back to 1877. That term began in reference to a ship's propeller, then in 1912 to airplanes and by the mid-40's to impulses in electronics and radar research. That may have led into the technical use of *cutting edge.*"

Now the term means "forefront, vanguard, lead" or, as the military would say about the soldier in the most advanced and dangerous position of an advancing squad, "on the point." In its heyday in 1985, the phrase was found in *Cutting Edges,* the title of a book by Charles Krauthammer, but the phrase has been used in titles before and since; a weekly health column in *The Washington Post* carries the title "The Cutting Edge," though it may seem to some as too suggestive of surgery. Here's a *TV Guide* ad for Geraldo Rivera's talk show: "Geraldo keeps you at the *cutting edge* of what's happening with today's kids."

The aforesaid *what's happening* was once the phrase for "*au courant,* with-it, up-to-date"; now it needs a boosting slice from *cutting edge* to bring it sharply up to date.

Cutting edge replaced the oldest, creakiest phrase in this lexicon of leadership: *state of the art.* That began in 1889 in a photography publication: "The illustrations give a good idea of the present status of the art. . . ." *Status* was then changed to *state,* and in 1910 a gas-turbine expert was writing of "the present *state of the art.*" George Lowell Cabot, a shipper of carbon black, wrote the Interstate Commerce Commission in 1920 to hail the efforts of the railroad industry to "advance the *state of the art*" (a citation submitted by Arthur P. Bloom of New York City).

Now *state-of-the-art* is often used adjectivally, just as it was by the pioneering *Journal of the Royal Aeronautics Society* in 1955, "where automatic flying could be fitted into a consistent *state-of-the-art* picture." But it is losing its modern zing.

That's what has to happen to the words used to describe the most advanced thinking, the latest thing. Who says *the latest thing* anymore? A few traditionalist designers, maybe. When the Scottish *at the forefront* and the French *in the vanguard* and the British *of the state of the art* gave way to *on the cutting edge* (note the wide range of prepositions), it was only a matter of time before a replacement would be demanded.

Contrariwise, such words as *decrepit, archaic, backward, old-fashioned, fusty, outmoded* all keep their freshness. They don't need to keep up with the latest locutions.

Enjoy being *on the cusp* for a few years. Then be careful how you use that pointed word, for it will date you. See those poor old codgers with their *state-of-the-art cutting edges*? They thought they were out front in their day.

Android's Revenge

Witness a word with its meaning being stretched.

David S. Broder, the *Washington Post* reporter and pundit, went before the National Press Club recently to deplore the too-frequent crossing of the

political/media street. In his mind, the practice of politics was over on that side, and the profession of news gathering was here on this side. "But," he told the press assembled to honor him, "there's a developing pattern—encouraged most, perhaps, by television but visible also in the print media—to create a new hybrid creature, an androgynous blending of politician and journalist called The Washington Insider."

I took issue with my colleague in columny in a piece entitled "Color Me Tainted," arguing that political experience enriches a commentator's understanding of the "contrivance and manipulation" that goes on. Where you stand depends on where you sit, goes the political adage, and having sat in the seat of power helps the observer understand what goes into the taking of a political stand.

But in summarizing his view, I wrote that Mr. Broder took a pop at the "androgenous analyst," thereby misspelling *androgynous*. (*Androgenous* is a different word, meaning "producing only male offspring," and has nothing to do with this discussion.) The error prompted this doggerel from Richard P. Hunt of New York City:

> You ain't tainted
> And you ain't sainted
> But as a speller
> You ain't stellar.
> It's androgYnous!

The word combines the Greek *andros,* "man," and *gyne,* "woman," to produce the meanings of "both masculine and feminine" and "neither masculine nor feminine." It's the kind of haircut everybody gets at a unisex barbershop.

Viewed from the outside, the adjective means "of indeterminate sex" or, from within, "of ambiguous sexual identity." *Androgynous* is synonymous with, but not the same as, *bisexual* because it describes only a state of being or appearing rather than an activity. "The next time you need a word meaning 'endowed with the characteristics of both sexes,' " writes Louis Jay Herman of New York City, ". . . you might try *epicene* or *hermaphroditic.*"

Back in 1628, when the word first surfaced, the meaning was clearly pejorative: "effeminate," applied to unmanly males. But astrologers picked it up to categorize planets as "masculine, feminine, androgynous," and botanists applied it to plants with stamens and pistils in the same cluster of flowers. Grammarians seized upon it, too, to label those words in some languages with gender wavering between male and female. Sailors preferred another term for half-and-half, neither-this-nor-that, or goes-both-ways: a *hermaphrodite brig* was a double-masted vessel square-rigged forward and schooner-rigged aft.

Wait a minute—sex was not in the mind of Mr. Broder when he spoke of "an androgynous blending of politician and journalist." Nor was it in mine when I wrote about the "androgenous [misspelled] analyst." What we both had in mind was *interchangeable.*

That's how the meaning of a word grows. *Androgynous* is a word in vogue, as rock stars and fashion designers erase the outward differences in the appearance of men and women. *Androgynous* is exciting because it is sexy, while *interchangeable* is dull because it is mechanistic, most often associated with *parts.* But until recently, no synonym was available for *interchangeable,* which is a word to fall asleep over. You could try *transposable,* but that connotes "reversible," or change of order in position; *transferable* loses the exchange function, and *exchangeable* has come to mean you can't get your money back when you bring in the sweater, but how about this snazzy tie?

Writers need arterial words, pumping blood through their copy; when the only available word loses its force, writers will look around for other, similar words—and will stretch their meanings or extend their metaphors to cover the old word. The new meaning, though not in the dictionary, is not incorrect; it's being tested, and may vanish as a nonce word or take root as a synonym.

What we now have in this trivial altercation between Mr. Broder and me over political/media fence-jumping is a significant tryout of the extended meaning of *androgynous*. Will it last? Who knows? Language, like political attraction, is a mystery, and experts and -ologists can point and comment with certitude but can never be sure which way the flow will go.

At the moment (for the nonce), one sense of the volatile and voguish adjective *androgynous* has been made interchangeable with the adjective *interchangeable*, although the unchanging *interchangeable* is not as readily interchangeable with *androgynous*. If you don't like either, find something else mutually substitutable.

Re your column of this date, and the lack of a synonym for interchangeable; try fungible.

> Christopher J. Vann
> Peoria, Illinois

The word you want is fungible. *It means interchangeable and has no connotations of sex.*

> H. Wolf
> Teaneck, New Jersey

Androgynous *is a word in vogue far less because of unisex barbers and costumes than because it is an important concept in feminist theory, where it means "having female and male characteristics in one"—that is, a combination of the mental and emotional characteristics "usually" attributed to the two genders separately. The word does* not, *in this usage, carry the connotations of the terms you used to define it, "ambiguous" sexual identity or "bisexual" sexual orientation. It does* not *mean, as you put it, "interchangeable" nor does it imply shifting back and forth between two modes of being; it means transcending that separateness by integrating the two.*

Mr. Broder's and your attempt to preempt androgynous *in order to describe people (men, no doubt) who move back and forth between media work and political appointments sounds to me like a male attempt to neutralize an important concept by neutering the term which describes it.*

> Annette Chappell
> Towson, Maryland

Your ancient Greek is not up to Shakespearean standards. The word for "man" is anar; andros is the genitive singular form. Students have been caned for less.

Harvey Fried
Queens College
Flushing, New York

You describe a hermaphrodite brig as being "schooner-rigged aft." Actually "schooner-rigged" refers not to the fore and aft aftermast mainsail but to all the rigging on a schooner. That is, two masts with the aft mast about mid-ship and the fore and aft mainsail you wrote about larger than the sails forward.

I think you meant to say "square rigged foreword and fore and aft rigged aft."

William Baumrucker
Marblehead, Massachusetts

The term hermaphrodite brig is something of a bastard since the function of the rig whether square rigged or schooner is the same. Sails propel the vessel. The sex organs of plants or animals even when mounted on one individual are highly specialized and of totally different function. A case could be made, however, that the function of sex organs wherever they are located, whatever their form, is to propel the species toward its genetic destiny. But here we are only speaking of individuals, whether ships, earthworms or flowers. What we have in this case is undoubtedly what a forlorn sailor might imagine after long periods at sea: an androgyny of sails.

The centerboard and its slot would more effectively define the androgyny of a sailboat. Other examples could easily be found (the rudder or bows plunging through effulgent seas, for example) but why labor needlessly with the mariner's excessive metaphor?

Pursuing the dictionary further stretches the imagination. An androgen is a substance that promotes male characteristics while epicene, meaning androgynous or hermaphroditic also means effeminate or unmanly. Seems to me if we were to continue a pursuit of the meaning of sex related possibly interchangeable terms, we will quickly end up like our lonely sailor giving stretched notions of sexuality to his craft.

Roy H. Sagarin
St. Petersburg, Florida

You used the adage "Where you stand depends on where you sit," without attribution to its author, Rufus E. Miles, Jr. I believe Professor Miles is still alive and well and living in Princeton.

Ned Pattison
Troy, New York

You quoted a maxim of mine, without realization of its source. The maxim is: "Where you stand depends on where you sit." It occurs to me that you might like to know more about its origin.

I formulated this maxim in 1948 when I was in the Bureau of the Budget in Washington (the predecessor of the Office of Management and Budget). It spread by word of mouth among the officialdom of Washington to such a degree that I did not consider it necessary to copyright it.

I am enclosing a photocopy of a page from a book by Elliot Richardson (The Creative Balance, 1976), referring to his frequent use of this maxim when we worked together in HEW in the late 1950s, and a piece by Allen Otten in The Wall Street Journal, dated February 22, 1973, both of which may be of use in authenticating my authorship.

Rufus E. Miles, Jr.
Ithaca, New York

Behalf-Truths

In titling a book, an author or editor can get in trouble with gritty grammarians. *On Our Own Behalf* is a new collection by feminist women writers (no, that's not redundant, and is better than "female feminist writers"), edited by Kathleen McNerney.

On behalf of means "representing, acting as agent of," as in "I'm speaking, Your Honor, on behalf of my client, the defendant." *In behalf of* means "for the advantage or benefit of," as in "I'm copping this plea in behalf of my client."

Dictionaries split on preserving the distinction. I'm for holding on to the difference between the two locutions because it sharpens meanings. You act *on behalf of* someone else for whatever selfish or selfless purpose, and *in behalf of* others only for their benefit, whether they want your help or not.

Did the title writer mean "*In* Our Own Behalf," as in "for our own benefit," or "*On* Our Own Behalf," representing themselves with no outside or masculine help? Hard to tell. Ambiguity is sometimes profound, sometimes confused.

This brings us to the related solecism, *on behalf of myself.* "I would appreciate it," writes the comedian Steve Allen of Burbank, California, "if you could use your public influence to get people to stop using the absurd phrase *on behalf of myself.*"

Absurd it is: You speak for yourself, and never on behalf of yourself. (*Behalf* is rooted in "by the side of," and you cannot be beside yourself, unless you're really furious.) The trouble comes when the speaker refers to himself and somebody else.

"On behalf of myself and my colleagues," said the bank regulator M. Danny Wall to a banking committee wondering where the $100 billion went, "we are pleased to be here." What he means is "Speaking both for myself and on behalf of my colleagues . . ."

That's the trick: Make someone else the person on whose behalf you are speaking. When President Reagan welcomed President Gorbachev with "On behalf of myself and Mrs. Reagan," he was in error; he should have said, "Speaking for myself and on behalf of Mrs. Reagan . . ."

"In the 1940's," concludes Mr. Allen, "a popular radio warm-up joke was 'On behalf of the National Broadcasting Company—and I'd like to be half of the National Broadcasting Company. . . .' But this 'on behalf of myself' nonsense has to stop."

The variant in behalf of *is used in American (and Canadian) English, but not in British English. Thus, the difference that you describe does not exist in British English or in the varieties close to it. See the* BBI Combinatory Dictionary of English *(page 22) or the* Longman Dictionary of Contemporary English *(page 82) or the* Collins English Dictionary *(page 138), etc.*

> Morton Benson
> Havertown, Pennsylvania

When you changed "On behalf of myself and my colleagues, we are pleased to be here" to "Speaking both for myself and on behalf of my colleagues . . ." you repaired the grammar but failed to eliminate the pretentiousness. Surely the proper way for Mr. Wall to have introduced his group to the banking committee would have been "My colleagues and I are pleased to be here."

> Bruce E. Altschuler
> Oswego, New York

"Ambiguity is sometimes profound, sometimes confused," you sinfully asseverate. Alas! Anything we read can be confus<u>ing</u>, only the reader who tries to comprehend becomes conf<u>used</u>, enraged or indifferent.

Would you eat or rather be eaten?

Romuald Orlowski, M.D.
Jackson, Michigan

Beware of Greeks Wearing Lifts

At a clandestine meeting of the Attention-Getting Headline Writers Society, the subject of Michael Dukakis was discussed in detail (PUNCHY HEADSCRIBE GANG SECRET CONFAB TARGETS DUKE, as one of them reported to me in his characteristic patois).

What phrases playing on any Greek candidate's ethnic background can we expect in coming months? What lines will run across the corner of newsmagazines to titillate our curiosity, replacing the tried-and-true "Crisis of Confidence"? Here is the first cut of the Headline Writers Society's list of references for Dukakis stories.

GREEK TO ME, VOTERS SAY is to be used whenever pollsters find that the candidate addresses complex issues without sufficient oversimplification.

This saying is from Act I, Scene 2, of Shakespeare's *Julius Caesar.* After reporting that Cicero commented in Greek on Caesar's refusal of a crown, Casca tells Cassius: ". . . those that understood him smil'd at one another, and shook their heads; but for mine own part, it was Greek to me."

GREEK TRAGEDY will be used whenever a minor mishap befalls the campaign. This refers to the period in the 5th century B.C. in which Greek drama (stories about behind-the-scenes staff battles will be headed GREEK DRAMA) flourished in Athens. Secondary allusions to Aeschylus, Sophocles and Euripides will be found in subheads or the text of the story, but the headscribes were warned to stay away from Aristophanes, unless the campaign commits enough errors to be described as a GREEK COMEDY. (If some skeleton is found in the Dukakis closet, or some fact surfaces that had been long hidden, it may be described as an ATTIC TRAGEDY, but few readers will catch the double meaning).

SMALL LATIN AND LESS GREEK will be held for stories about the Dukakis position on Central America. It's from Ben Jonson's comment on Shakespeare's learning, in the competing playwright's posthumous poetic tribute for the First Folio of 1623: "And though thou hadst small Latine, and lesse Greeke . . ."

GREEK FIRE is a surefire headline for any Dukakis appearance in which the candidate becomes impassioned. Greek fire was an incendiary mixture of materials in ancient and medieval warfare; it was primarily used by the Greeks of Byzantium. The mixture's composition is unknown, but was said to have burst into flames upon wetting; if the candidate becomes infuriated after being inundated at a rainy rally, this phrase is almost certain to be used.

BEWARE OF GREEKS BEARING GIFTS will be the standard Republican riposte to any promises of new entitlements.

This saying, meaning "Don't trust all acts of apparent kindness," comes from a line in Book II of Virgil's Latin epic, *Aeneid,* in which the hero Aeneas escapes the fall of Troy. After having besieged Troy for more than nine years because their admired Helen was a captive there, the Greeks pretended to abandon their quest and left the Trojans a "gift" of a wooden horse; once the horse was taken within the walls of Troy, Greek soldiers poured out of its hollow interior and destroyed the city.

The Latin line *Quidquid id est, timeo Danaos et dona ferentis* is translated as "Whatever it is, I fear Greeks even when they bear gifts." *Greeks bearing gifts* is now a phrase recalling "enemy infiltration" and is an imputation of treachery or trickiness.

Because Governor Dukakis stands five feet eight inches tall, and Vice President Bush is six feet two inches, cruel Republicans are already playing on the ancient phrase with "Beware of Greeks wearing lifts." Mr. Dukakis, not noted for his skill with one-liners, has responded with "My opponent is the only candidate who ever had a league named after him." The Headscribe Gang is ecstatic: It's going to be a rough campaign.

"Greeks Wearing Lifts" is wicked but wonderful. Toward the end, though, there is a run of little slips to amend when reprinting: it's dona ferentes, not -tis. Then Helen was not a captive in Troy; she eloped voluntarily with Paris, a beautiful youth favored by Aphrodite. What the Greeks really wanted was "Helen and all her wealth"—a phrase repeated by Homer. In Troy she was a sort of Princess of Wales, greatly admired by the old men loungers as she strutted about. Finally, it is a question whether Greek fire was particularly effective, though it had scare value—a sort of fireworks.

Best regards.
Jacques [Barzun]
New York, New York

"It's Greek to me" was used at least twice before Shakespeare, by George Gascoigne in 1573 and by Robert Greene in 1598. Gascoigne was translating a play by Ariosto, written in 1509. Interestingly, the Greek equivalent of the phrase is "It's Hebrew to me."

Mac E. Barrick
Shippensburg, Pennsylvania

Virgil wrote, "timeo Danaos et dona ferentes," not "ferentis." As I recall my Latin from a half century ago, "ferentes" modifies "Danaos," and is the plural form of the participle "ferens."

Incidentally, Bartlett has another appropriate quotation for your attention-getting headline writers: "Put not thy faith in any Greek." This is from Gilbert Murray's translation of Iphigenia in Tauris, written by a Greek, Euripides. He should know.

V. T. Boatwright
Stonington, Connecticut

The Big Renouncement

Deeds, not words, are what count, we are repeatedly reminded. And Shakespeare's Hamlet, with his sighing dismissal of "Words, words, words," gave the word *words* a cast of inaction if not meaninglessness.

Yet a word can count for plenty. Ask the Palestine Liberation Organiza-

tion's Yasir Arafat, whose reluctant adoption of a key verb opened a channel of diplomatic communication with the United States.

The verb was *renounce,* as in "renounce terrorism." This was one of the three conditions the United States government placed on official contact with the organization that masterminded assassinations of Israelis and moderate Palestinians throughout the Middle East and Europe.

For years Mr. Arafat has been willing to *condemn* terrorism, and to the United Nations in Geneva—in a speech that fell short of United States requirements—he said that the Palestine National Council had "reaffirmed its *rejection* of terrorism." But for substantive reasons of policy, he could not get the word *renounce* past his lips.

What was the big semantic deal? Aren't *condemn* and *reject* as severely censorious as *renounce*?

No, not in a strictly diplomatic sense, and the difference in meaning carries weight. *Reject,* from the Latin *jacere,* "to throw," means "to throw back; to refuse to accept, hear or admit." Thus it is possible to reject without ever having accepted something—in this case, the verb *reject* was presumably chosen by Mr. Arafat because it contained no acknowledgment that the P.L.O. had ever engaged in terrorism. That was not good enough for the United States, because it meant that the P.L.O. could feel free to continue the past activities that it may not have considered terrorism.

Condemn did not fill the bill either. Like *damn,* it is ultimately rooted in the

Latin *damnare,* "to damage, hurt," and now means "to criticize severely, blame, reprehend, denounce," or more damagingly, "to convict, doom, sentence." The verb is powerful enough—"the freedom with which Dr. Johnson condemns whatever he disapproves is astonishing," wrote the novelist Fanny Burney about the opinionated lexicographer in 1778—but the disapprobation is directed outward, containing no hint of admission or confession.

Renounce, however, usually conveys the sense of giving up an activity in which one has been engaged. The *nounce* part is rooted in the Latin for "report"—a *nuncio* once was a messenger—from which we get *announce,* "to make known"; *pronounce,* "to say clearly"; *denounce,* "to report against," and *renounce,* "to give up, cast off, repudiate."

You may *condemn* or *reject* a position you've never accepted, but *renounce* implies giving up a position or an activity you've formerly accepted. In law, it is an intransitive verb referring to the giving up of a right.

You *renounce* a royal crown that you have worn, or a claim you have been making; in that sense, synonyms are *abdicate* and *resign.* You also *renounce* a belief, with synonyms such as *recant* and *retract.* (Some of the Gotcha! Gang demand more of me, to the point of *abjure,* which is abandoning under oath, but that's when I'm really off base.) You can also *deny, disavow* and *disown* in the course of renouncement, but the unique meaning persists: You are promising not to do again what you once did.

When Sir Francis Bacon confessed in 1621 that "I am guilty of corruption," he added, "and do renounce all defense." When the essayist Matthew Arnold wrote in 1869 that "I am a Liberal," he added a defensive "yet I am a Liberal tempered by experience, reflection and renouncement," the last word implying the abandonment of an excess of liberalism.

So Mr. Arafat, by accepting the hated word *renounce,* promised to cut out what his organization had been doing in the past. "We totally and absolutely renounce all forms of terrorism," he told a press conference, "including individual, group and state terrorism." (Unfortunately, he mispronounced the word *terrorism* in English, making it sound like *tourism.* Many harried air travelers long ago renounced tourism, and may have found themselves agreeing with the P.L.O. leader, but this was inadvertent.)

I have been using the English meaning of *renounce,* and Mr. Arafat was forced to use that specific English word. In Arabic, a close term would be *'astankir,* "I renounce," but its meaning ranges from "I disapprove" to "I reject" to "I loathe." The essence of the English *renounce*—stopping a previous action or policy—isn't as clear when the word is translated back into Arabic. That may turn out to be a problem.

Translation disputes are not new to U.N.-ese. In the famous Resolution 242, which contains the phrase "withdrawal of Israeli armed forces from territories occupied," there was a great struggle over whether to place the article *the* before the word *territories.* The Arabs wanted "from *the* territories," because that could be easily construed as meaning "from all the territories"; the Israelis wanted "from territories," because that might mean "from part of the territories."

In English, the Israeli and American position prevailed. Many Israelis now say that the return of the Sinai to Egypt meant that its troops have been withdrawn from 90 percent of the territories, fulfilling the U.N. resolution's call; however, Arabs point to the French translation, *"le retour des territoires occupés,"* in which *des* can be construed to mean "of the," more inclusive than the English version.

When next you hear a dismissive "That's just splitting hairs" on a wrangle about the meaning of a word or the placement of an article, remember the Middle East. Some disputes can be caused by disagreements over the meaning of words; other disputes can be finessed by adopting different translations of words; still others can be resolved by insisting on a verb like *renounce.*

I was taken aback by your calling <u>renounce</u> *an intransitive verb in legal usage. Surely some object or right is always implied even if the attorney stands up and says "I renounce." It isn't like "I demur" or "the defence rests," which are true intransitives.*

> Jacques [Barzun]
> New York, New York

The Bloopie Awards

A sinister force for solecism exists on Madison Avenue. It is the work of the copywrongers.

Copywrongers are copywriters who make mistakes in grammar on purpose; in this way, they pander to the most common, even substandard, usage.

The guiding light of the copywrongers was the Winston cigarette advertisement: ". . . tastes good *like* a cigarette should," instead of *as;* thus, a generation of Americans learned to use *like* as a conjunction. (Not *like* a preposition.)

This year's chief copywronger, who works for *Newsweek* magazine or its ad agency, came up with the slogan "No One Reports It Like *Newsweek* Reports It." Sounds crisp. Tough. The way hard-nosed people talk, and to blazes with the schoolmarms and their stodgy good-English pretensions.

But the rule is still "Never use *like* as a conjunction before a clause—use *like* when it introduces a noun not followed by a verb," and *Newsweek*'s flub

illustrates it perfectly. "No One Reports It Like *Newsweek*" would be correct, because the noun, *Newsweek*, is not followed by a verb; but when the copywronger adds the second verb "Reports," *like* becomes wrong.

Perhaps this grabber of a slogan was taken from *People* magazine's "Nothing grabs people like *People*," but in that case, *like* is correct, because "*People*" is not followed by a verb.

The reader who is alert (as are you all—who could be idly studying grammar?) will note another similarity in these two slogans: The *else* is missing. The meaning of *Newsweek*'s phrase is "no one *else* reports it the way *Newsweek* does," and *People* magazine wants you to know that "Nothing *else* grabs people . . ."

I am not making a fuss about the elided *else,* because that is an omission so common as to be readily accepted. The missing *else* is not worth fighting for; *else* in these cases is "understood"—that is, taken to be present even though it is not.

But *like* as a conjunction where a verb is lurking remains taboo. Thus, to the promotion department of *Newsweek* goes this year's first Bloopie Award.

And now for the category we call redundancy in direct mail advertising. (The Direct Mail Advertising Association has changed its name to the Direct Marketing Association, presumably because "mail" has not been delivering for them lately.) The envelope, please.

The winner is the National Council of Teachers of English for offering a "15 percent off discount" on its member-nomination form. That's one layer too thick. It's either *off* or *discount;* together, they're a case for the Squad Squad.

Worse, the widely mailed form states: "I understand neither me, nor any of the colleagues I've recommended above, are obligated to accept NCTE membership." That is not the sort of sentence we want to hold up as an example to our pupils. Try "I understand *that* neither *I* nor *any colleague* I've recommended *is* obligated . . ." (Oh, they'll get even with me for this.)

The award for redundancy in general advertising is shared this year by Citibank for its repeated *free gift* (rarely do the folks at Citi use the correct "special gift") and by the Acura Legend automobile for its "2-DR Coupe." Since 1834, the French *coupé*—from the verb *couper,* "to cut," its pronunciation Anglicized of late to *coupe,* like the Surgeon General—has meant "carriage for two." Its current meaning is "closed two-door automobile." A two-door coupe should sell for a 15 percent off discount.

The Bloopie for punctuation goes to Jaguar, which should send its copy back to the factory for a handful of hyphens.

Attributive noun phrases, as well as other phrases used as adjectives, should be hyphenated. When Jaguar writes with pride but without hyphens of its "high speed responsiveness," "four wheel independent suspension," "three year/36,000 mile limited warranty" in a car "as elegant as a 400 year-old manor house," the advertiser leaves us unguided about its modifiers; those phrases cry out for hyphenation. I'm not sure what "double overhead cams" are, but if "double overhead" is a single modifying phrase, it could take a hyphenation job, too, while it's in the shop.

Runner-up in the punctuation category is Corvo wines for "The difference between having dinner, and dining with pleasure."

Between is a preposition that takes two objects, usually connected by the conjunction *and;* three or more objects require the preposition *among.* Corvo's wine makers are correct in their use of *between* with two objects, but sloshily wrong in their use of an unnecessary comma between them.

For creative spelling, who gets this year's coveted Bloopie? (Awards from peer groups are always, like thy neighbor's wife, *coveted,* a word rooted in the Latin *cupiditas,* source of the related *cupidity,* or "greed.")

The winner is Macy's. That chain of stores, in selling computer equipment, found a way to avoid the *processor/processer* problem. (Why am I using a virgule? Must be my three year/36,000 mile limited warranty.) They advertise the "Epson word processing system"; I would go ahead and use *processor,* on the analogy of *professor* and *confessor.*

But le tout New York was agog at these additional programs: "Personal correspondance" and "Business correspondance." That has been the French spelling since the fourteenth century, but since the word's first appearance in English in 1413, corresponding to its root in the Latin verb *correspondere,* we have been spelling it *correspondence.* So, Macy's—shall we *-dence?*

So, as used in the preceding sentence, is a colloquial conjunction, meaning "in sum" or "therefore" but with a triumphant lilt. However, *so* is used all too often as an arch intensifier. ("Arch intensifier" sounds like a foot-support ad, while I have in mind the use of *arch* as an adjective meaning "coy." Change that to: *So* is too often used archly, as an intensifier.)

When *so* is followed by *that*—even a silent, understood *that*—it works fine. CBS does not get a Bloopie for its *Beauty and the Beast* ad, which reads: "so romantic you can feel it." However, Keri Lotion has announced that "Keri is so very"; presumably, this is to make three two-syllable lines with the first and third rhyming—Keri/is so/very—but that use of *so* is just too icky for words. Give Keri a so-so Bloopie.

Shall we return to spelling? An entry that almost qualifies as the work of a copywronger is the *National Enquirer*'s invitation to readers to "Enquire Within." This is not incorrect, and if I were an *Enquirer* man with my job on the line, I would choose that spelling, but the preferred form to the rest of us is *inquire,* as in the newspaper called by residents of Philadelphia "The Fluffya Inkwire."

Thank you for bringing to light what you believe was an unnecessary comma in the Corvo wine ad. The offending copy line was, "The difference between having dinner, and dining with pleasure."

First, as the author of the ad, I'm delighted that you actually read it. The client and our marketing people will be pleased to know that the ad is being read by the kind of people for whom it was intended.

Second, as a student of language, I assure you that I received an excellent education well grounded in the rules of grammar. However, as an advertising writer, I believe that punctuation marks have stronger powers of communication than the rules of grammar tolerate. Therefore, I occasionally find it necessary to break the rules to ensure that my words are read in precisely the way I want them to be read.

To me words are like music. So in the same way that an orchestra conductor may interpret the values of tempo and dynamic indications in a musical score in order to enhance the mood of a passage, I choose to interpret the values of punctuation marks to enhance the impact of my words. In the Corvo ad I felt a pause between the words dinner and and was needed to add what I can only describe as drama. It's an intangible and subtle addition—perhaps imperceptible to many—but important nonetheless.

I try to keep my grammatical transgressions to a minimum, though our proofreader wishes I'd keep them to myself.

Steve Coppola
Ketchum/Mandabach &
Simms
Chicago, Illinois

Between you and me and the lamppost, I cannot let you get away with erroneous dogma. Between is not, never has been, and must never be—as long as freedom shall flourish—restricted to couples. It rejoices in threesomes and foursomes, just between all us fellows and girls, and delights in even moresomes. If you want to know why, just look it up in Fowler or even the OED (now in non-book form for your computer's delight).

Your schoolmarm's approach to between can only keep lawyers, nice fellows and careful about words, captive in the hobbles of dicta such as yours which they think compel them to talk about agreements among seven or eight parties, leaving the agreements they define precisely in hundreds of pages vague, loose and ambling, not disciplined as they would be if their drafters simply wrote what comes natural to the language and its speakers and writers, between.

Please, save us all, retract, bite your tongue. Between and with your teeth, of course.

Myles Slatin
Department of English
State University of New York
at Buffalo
Buffalo, New York

Re: placing the blame for the first ad-world solecism on "Winstons taste good like a cigarette should." You are correcter than you know. My father was creative head of BBDO (as well as president in those palmy days) when the decision was reached to go ungrammatical. It was his, and his alone. As a former high school English teacher, he did agonize over the choice, but yielded gracefully to Common Usage—as the ad would never have worked with "as." The proper grammar, ironically, would have sounded both high-falutin' and dumb.

Brock Brower
Princeton, New Jersey

As an inveterate "copywronger," I defend the heinous practice of murdering traditional grammar on the grounds of simple pragmatism. Hey, buddy, it works. It works when the proper construction won't. Improper usage often serves to convey just the right innuendo to the majority, where no grammatically correct wording would do as well.

The fellow who wrote, "No one reports it like Newsweek reports it" probably couldn't care less whether masters of English usage recoil in horror. He simply devised the phrase that he felt would have the better impact on the greatest percentage of his magazine's readers. And all the analyses by all the experts in the world won't change that.

We'll grant a boon in some of your examples. Only a pure dunce would have written "15 percent off discount." Such juvenile ignorance is no more tolerated here than in your quarter. Same goes for ". . . neither me, nor any . . . are . . ." And spelling errors are simply tidbits of illiteracy peeking through.

But your dissertation on the usage of "coupe" is rather moot, since eighty years of such misuse by the auto industry should by now have established an accepted form. And your argument for hyphens can be nullified by the pragmatist who might state, "99–44/100 percent of the reading public will know exactly what it means, with or without proper hyphens, despite your misguidance about modifiers." Incidentally, a "double overhead cam" is a double cam, the entire assembly of which is of the overhead type, hence "double overhead" is by no means a single modifier.

Finally, your fault with the comma in "The difference between having dinner, and dining with pleasure." You should at least have given some credence to the intentional use of "pause for effect" commas commonly inserted by the skillful "copywronger." Subtle! This writer might have used three dots rather than a comma, but to each his own. When you're selling to the general public, a little drama often helps. In a commercial script, that comma would be preferred!

Having composed this letter, I now know what your award should be titled: "The Grammarian's Tempest in a Teapot Award."

Jon W. DeFrees
Anthony, Florida

You wondered if "processor" or "processer" were the correct spelling. You chose the former, because "professor" and "confessor" ended in "or."

However, my eighth grade German teacher, Dr. Richards, and I believe that because "process" is a Latinate word, its agent noun should take the more Latinate ending, "-or." "Profess" and "confess" are also Latinate, so they take the same ending.

If the verb were Saxon, like "jog" and "run," one would use the more Saxon ending, "-er."

Marc Pollak
New Rochelle, New York

You neglected to mention the slogan The Wall Street Journal uses in its advertisements: The Wall Street Journal—the Daily Diary of the American Dream. How about a "doubly redundant" award?

Erik Warga
Vienna, Virginia

Bracket Racket

"Get your Truth Squad on the road," the Bush campaign was exhorted by supporters who felt that Democratic candidate Michael Dukakis was making unchallenged claims.

Republican Senator John S. McCain 3d of Arizona was promptly dispatched into cities where Mr. Dukakis was scheduled to appear. His task was to present questions about the candidate's record. Presumably, Senator McCain or another surrogate for Mr. Bush would remain to rebut his remarks until the Democrat had left.

"Calling the technique 'bracketing,' " reported *The Washington Post*, "he [a Bush aide] said the campaign intended to 'be in front' of Dukakis 'until the last day' of the campaign."

The marks around the phrase "a Bush aide" in the preceding sentence are called *brackets*. That word was originally used in architecture in the sixteenth century to describe supports projecting from a wall to bear the weight of a shelf or cornice. In mathematics, the squared parentheses have been used to indicate that the numbers or letters enclosed are to be treated as a unit. The word also has meaning in shipbuilding, gunnery, and gossip columning.

What's the etymology? The new *Random House II Dictionary* says it's of "obscure origin," but the *Oxford Dictionary of English Etymology* says it comes from the French *braguette,* diminutive of *brague,* a word that pops up in English as *breeches.* (Why *breeches,* a synonym of *trousers*? Simple: *Braguette* means "codpiece," which *Random House* fearlessly defines as "a flap or cover for the crotch in men's hose or tight-fitting breeches.")

In punctuation, the marks are used to indicate an interpolation by the writer within another's quotation. Here's a double example in which a long-time Dukakis supporter recently made public a letter, written by the candidate, that included a grammatical error: "You have done so much for me since then [1978] and Kitty and me [*sic*] can never adequately thank you."

In the political participle *bracketing,* we may have one of the first neologisms (and perhaps the first new campaign device) of the 1988 presidential campaign.

The predecessor term was *Truth Squad.* I was never able to pinpoint the origin of that phrase; it may have been coined on the analogy of "Poison Squad," an intrepid group of Agriculture Department untouchables whose self-experimentation led to the Pure Food and Drug Act of 1906. The earliest citation, according to the *Oxford English Dictionary* supplement, is from the *Tuscaloosa* (Alabama) *News* of November 3, 1952: "The Republican 'Truth Squad,' after trailing President Truman across the country on his campaign trips, passed down its final verdict today that the President was 'guilty of over 100 lies, half-truths and distortions.' "

In the 1956 Eisenhower campaign, Adlai Stevenson, mildly nettled by having his steps dogged by "correcting" Republicans, said, "A truth squad bears the same relationship to 'truth' as a fire department does to 'fire.' "

In the 1960 campaign, the Nixon forces assigned a team led by Pennsylvania Senator Hugh Scott called "the Truth Squad" to bedevil John F. Kennedy, but that group appeared in a town only after the Democratic candidate had left. In its 1988 form, apparently the technique is to supply pointed questions in advance and to make rebuttal afterward—thereby *bracketing* the opposition candidate's appearance.

"Call it *bracketing,*" scoffed Stephen Rosenfeld, a Dukakis campaign aide, "*surrogating, working with skyhooks*—they are trying everything except building a strong position for George Bush."

We will monitor that word, however. If it makes it in the parlance of politics, this year's campaign will not have been a linguistic loss.

Cajun Talk

Acadia—originally *Archadia,* the explorer Verrazano's name for "place of rural peace"—is a region that includes Canada's maritime provinces as well as parts of Quebec and the state of Maine; when some of its French Catholic inhabitants sought refuge in Louisiana in the late eighteenth century, these Acadians were called *Cajuns,* in a pronunciation shift on the analogy of Indians and *Injuns.*

As a result, tourists in New Orleans stuff their faces with "blackened redfish," an invention of the chef Paul Prudhomme, which they assume to be the star attraction of "Cajun cooking." Other restaurateurs, from those of Brennan's in the French Quarter to the Upperline in the Garden District, include that dish but point out that it is relatively new to the cuisine.

People who talk Cajun-style call themselves *Yats,* derived from "Where y'at?" (short for "Where are you at?"). A primer published in the New Orleans *Times-Picayune* defined *po-boy* as "a sandwich on French bread known elsewhere as a hero, sub or grinder" and *dressed* as "How you order your po-boy. It means with lettuce, tomato and mayonnaise, pronounced my-nez."

The Cajun word that might be most useful for the general language is *lagniappe,* pronounced "lan-yap" and meaning "small bonus" or, as Northern banks would put it, "free gift." The word originated in the Quechua language of Peru as *yapa,* "overweight." It was borrowed by the Spanish and changed to *ñapa,* then Frenchified in Louisiana to its present state.

When a merchant hands a customer's child a lollipop, or a baker tosses a thirteenth beignet (square doughnut without the hole) into a bag and charges for only a dozen, that's a *lagniappe*. Although *tip* or *gratuity* is sometimes given as a synonym, that misses the special sense that is not yet covered by an English word. *Lagniappe* means "unexpected benefit" or "small surprise bonus," and this nice way of thanking a customer for his or her patronage sure beats the much-promised and redundant "free gift."

You are to be congratulated for your comments on Cajuns, a group of people whose culture is very often misunderstood and misrepresented. You err, however, when you state that "People who talk Cajun-style call themselves Yats, *derived from 'Where y'at?' (short for 'Where are you at?').'" You are certainly correct in the derivation of the word. It is not, however, Cajun at all, but rather a localized New Orleans expression.*

For the most part, those "who talk Cajun-style" still live either along the bayous south of New Orleans or on the prairies in the western part of the state. Many Cajuns have, of course, moved into the city over the years, but they have generally lost their "Cajun-style" language.

"Yats," on the other hand, are New Orleanians who live, for the most part, in the Ninth Ward in the eastern part of the city where a heavy settlement of Irish and Italians in the last century produced a unique dialect that bears some similarities, as linguists are fond of pointing out, to Brooklynese. If they read your article and later meet you, their comments to you might be, "Where y'at, man? We ain't no Cajuns."

W. Kenneth Holditch
Professor of English
University of New Orleans
New Orleans, Louisiana

The earliest derivation of "lagniappe" is from the French, not the Cajun, language.

With due credit to Professor Eldon Elder (who in 1966 demanded strict attention to historical detail in our Advanced Costume Design course at Brooklyn College), a "lagniappe" is the end piece of the hood commonly worn by men in fourteenth-century France. Visualize a court jester, if you will (as depicted by Danny Kaye, in the motion picture of the same name, or the traditional Punch puppet), notice the end piece of the hood, that's a "lagniappe." They could be short or long, accessorized with tassels, bells, or other adornments. The length of the "lagniappe" could designate the measure of one's sense of humor, or, more practically, the longer "lagniappe" could be wrapped around the neck or face as protection against cold weather.

> *Eleanor Weintraub Layfield*
> *Brooklyn, New York*

The Acadians did not "seek refuge" in Louisiana. They were deported, under the aegis of Admiral Sir Peter Warren (no relation), whose name is immortalized on an apartment house in Greenwich Village: some Acadians found their way back to Nova Scotia, where they were soon joined by British loyalists both White and Black, fleeing persecution in the newly independent United States of America. Some of the Blacks then emigrated to Freetown in West Africa, where they called themselves "Creoles."

> *Peter B. Warren*
> *Roosevelt, New Jersey*

I've always understood po-boy to be a corruption of the French pourboire, which my Webster's defines as "for to drink" or drinking money given someone (a panhandler?) or in other words a tip or gratuity. During hard times in old French-speaking New Orleans street urchins would gather at the kitchen entrances of restaurants, hold out their hands, and whine pourboire or po-boy. The kitchen helper split a French roll and filled it with whatever was at hand. By further logical extension this became the poorboy sandwich.

So the New Orleans restaurant backdoor handout was both a pourboire and a lagniappe.

> *Brooke Nihart*
> *McLean, Virginia*

People who talk Cajun are not called "yats"; that term is generally used to refer to middle- and working-class individuals from the New Orleans area who speak with an accent that has been described as Brooklynesque. Many of these individuals are of Irish and Italian origin, which some offer as explanation of the similarities between the New Orleans (pronounced "Noo Awlins") accent and that of urban areas in the Northeast.

A lumping together of the Cajun and New Orleans cultures is rampant these days, despite the fact that the language, food and music of these two areas are dramatically different.

Here is a quick primer on the differences between the two cultures. Crawfish ettouffee is Cajun; po-boys are New Orleans. Cajuns say "Comment ça va?" when they see someone, or perhaps "Quoi ça dit?" New Orleanians say, "Where y'at, man." Michael Doucet, Zachary Richard and Dewey Balfa are Cajun musicians; the Neville Brothers, (the late) Professor Longhair and Dr. John play New Orleans funk.

Of course, there are overlaps. Everybody eats gumbo. Both areas are predominantly Catholic. And the term "lagniappe" is used by Cajuns and New Orleanians alike, although more frequently by the latter. (By the way, I have never heard of an item being referred to as "a lagniappe"; it's always just "lagniappe" or perhaps "some lagniappe.")

Richard E. Baudouin Jr.
Editor, The Times
Lafayette, Louisiana

Verrazano may well have used the term Acadia or Archadia in reference to Canada's Maritimes. You imply, however, that he coined the word, which must upset the Micmacs, whose Akade became Acadie under the French.

Growing up in the '30's in suburban Philadelphia, a rare treat was to have dinner at the Arcadia Chios restaurant in Narberth. (Printed letters to the Editor of The Times and The Wall Street Journal usually render it Narbeth. Merion, where we lived, frequently comes out Marion, but that is another matter.) Mr. Chios, having been of Greek descent, suggested strongly that Arcadia's source was to be found there, which of course it is. Webster's Second New International says of Arcadia, "a mountainous and picturesque district of Greece, inhabited by a simple, pastoral people, distinguished for contentment and rural happiness. Hence, fig., any region or scene of simple pleasure, rustic innocence, and untroubled quiet."

Richard S. McQuillen
New York, New York

Call Off the Dogs

George Bush proudly described himself and his running mate, Dan Quayle, as "a couple of pit bulls." In a headline, *Time* magazine labeled the campaign so far as "pit-bull politics."

Lest political rhetoric go to the dogs, let's focus on the meaning of this vogue term.

The pit bull terrier gained its name and fierce reputation from being used in cruel and bloody dogfights in a pit that protected spectators. It is a generic term for a cross between a bulldog and a terrier, and is not a breed. Although the American pit bull terrier has been recognized by the United Kennel Club, a similar dog, recognized by the larger American Kennel Club, is called the American Staffordshire terrier.

"It's unfair that the term *pit bull* is being used," says Andy Johnson of the United Kennel Club, "to make the dogs suffer from adverse publicity." He estimates a pit bull population of more than 200,000 in the United States today. "Just as with any breed, some may be dangerous, but that's not true of the majority," he says.

The *pit* has long been the place where animals are made to fight. In Shakespeare's time, one form of competition for the Globe Theatre was the Bear Garden, which featured fights between chained bears and dogs; such fights were not outlawed in England until 1835.

The use of the phrase in politics and political reporting is an unfair slur on the animals. It's not the dogs, but the low-blow campaigning, that is the pits.

Thank you for citing the inappropriate use of the term "pit bulls" in current political rhetoric. The unfortunate American Pit Bull suffers greatly because of unthinking and ignorant reporting.

Last April, I found an American Pit Bull, collarless and lost, on Madison Avenue at 55th Street in Manhattan. "Madison," as he has become known, was only 9 months old. My husband and I live in midtown with 3 cats and a dog from the streets of New York; therefore it was necessary to house Madison in a kennel, we thought—temporarily. In the car on the way to a kennel, Madison put his head on my shoulder and slept. He has now spent 6 months of his puppyhood in a kennel. It looks as though he'll be there a lot longer. Because of sensational headlines and blood-and-guts stories about "pit bulls," we have found no one to adopt this gentle, loving creature. The owner of the kennel in which Madison lives says, "There isn't a mean bone in this dog's body, he loves everyone."

Although it probably won't help Madison, we are delighted that you took the time and the space in your column to cite writers who are either too lazy or uncreative to think beyond the current hype.

Mary Hoffman
Friends of Animals
New York, New York

Child's Garden of *Vs.*

How do you pronounce the *v.* in *Roe v. Wade*? Beyond that, where do you stand on the entire abbreviation issue of *v.* versus *vs.*?

"It is the policy of NBC News," speaks its person, Dom Giofre, "to use the abbreviation *v.* for *versus.*" Sure—then how does he explain the title of the NBC program *Roe vs. Wade,* with the two-letter abbreviation *vs.* appearing in television listings and on video promos throughout the land? Ask an NBC newsperson about a news-ish program produced in the network's entertainment division and you get the sort of look a Frenchman gives you when asked about American wines: "It is our policy to use *v.* regardless of whether the entertainment division puts out a film it calls *Roe vs. Wade.*"

The Associated Press and the *Los Angeles Times* both disagree with NBC: their stylebooks call for *vs.,* never *v. The New York Times* takes a sophisticated straddle: *v.* is reserved for the names of court cases and legal proceedings, *vs.* is used for nonlegal contexts (next week it's Leonard vs. Hearns) and the word is spelled out in ordinary use, as in "It was cowboy versus steer, and the steer won."

Let's go to the top; how does the Supreme Court stand on this? "In writing," says Kathy Arberg, a spokeswoman for the Court, "*v.* is always used in Supreme Court cases." That's the easy part: Nobody disputes that lawyers abbreviate *versus* with a single letter, though the Associated Press will blithely correct them in wire copy. But how do the Justices pronounce the word from the bench? " 'Versus' is most often used when the case name is spoken," she reports, "but the abbreviation has also been pronounced as 'vee.' "

In law schools, according to Norman Dorsen, president of the American Civil Liberties Union, professors often like to substitute *and* when referring to cases: Marbury and Madison, you know. Ira Robbins, a professor of law at American University, has heard this informal use, too: "You will occasionally hear 'the case of Smith and Jones.' It's not necessarily incorrect, but I regard it as an affectation."

Which is the correct abbreviation—*v.* or *vs.*? Answer: both. Comment on answer: That's silly. We ought to be able to decide on an abbreviation; indeed, we should, since the pronunciation of the two abbreviations differs.

To review the state of play: Lawyers use *v.*, and pronounce it mostly "versus," occasionally "vee" if they're swingers; laymen and journalists mostly use *vs.*, pronouncing it "versus," except when referring to court cases, when they pick up the lawyer's *v.*, and pronounce it "vee."

The etymology is no help in this decision: The Latin *vertere* means "to turn," and is also the root of *revert, version* and the well-turned *verse* (as well as *animadvert*, "to comment on with disapproval," one of my favorite verbs). *Versus* means "against" or "turned to face toward," at which point the person facing you is your *adversary.* Both abbreviations have been in use for centuries.

O.K., we're going to clear it up today. Abbreviations exist to save space— e.g. (short for *exempli gratia,* "for example, and it won't cost you a thing"), *R.S.V.P.,* for the French *Répondez s'il vous plaît,* which now means "Get back to us by Friday or we'll invite somebody else." The speaker, who is not concerned with space, must decide: Do I want to pronounce the abbreviation or the word for which the abbreviation is saving space?

The trend, I think, is toward pronouncing the abbreviation, thereby saving time, the speaker's equivalent of space. (If you understand quantum theory, this is a snap.) Let's go with that irresistible flow; since the written *v.* has become immutable in law, its pronunciation should be "vee"; nobody suggests *vs.* be pronounced "viz" (which would then be confused with *viz.,* from *videlicet,* "that is, namely").

Others can do what they like—some purists will even do *as* they like—and

I hate to give up the chance to overturn the Supreme Court, but I'm going with *v.* in all cases, legal and general. I'll pronounce the abbreviation "vee"; when I want to use the whole word *versus*—for emphasis, as in "It's me versus the world," as so often it is—I'll simply spell it out and pronounce it with both syllables, no matter how much space it occupies or split seconds it takes.

This elitist fiat has the added advantage of removing the confusion from the abbreviation of *verse,* which is and should remain *vs.* That's it; remanded to the boondocks for usage.

You recommend that we abbreviate the word "versus" with a single "v.," and that we pronounce the abbreviation "vee," instead of saying the word. I respectfully dissent.

As for writing, The Times's *policy is absolutely correct. There is no more reason for laymen to adopt the lawyer's abbreviation than for them to adopt "id." for "ibid.," "3d" for "3rd," or "eleemosynary" for "charitable." All these are legal usages, proper in legal writing, but jargon elsewhere.*

As for saying the word or the abbreviation, the best-educated lawyers and fight announcers all say the whole word. Lawyers who say "Smith vee Jones" are sniggered at. If you don't want to say "versus," say "against," as moot-court contestants in law school are instructed to do. Saying "vee" is like pronouncing "&" as "et," or even "ampersand."

You mention that nobody has suggested that we pronounce "vs." the same way we pronounce "viz." This is quite understandable, since "viz." is always *pronounced "namely."*

James D. Crutchfield
Norfolk, Virginia

The use of "and" as the spoken translation of "v." is an import from England, where it is the customary usage of English lawyers. This use of "and" by American lawyers seems to me to have become more common in the last couple of years. At least it has the virtue of sidestepping the issue discussed in your column. In practice, lawyers usually avoid the v. anyway by referring to cases with a single name—as in "the Roe case" or just "Roe."

Many of the problems posed by abbreviations in foreign languages can be eliminated by using unabbreviated English. "For example" is more readable than "e.g.," "that is" more comprehensible than "i.e.," and "Please Reply" more direct than "R.S.V.P." Abbreviations save little space and confuse many intelligent people. I have often seen i.e. used where "for example" was meant;

and surely no one should have to endure <u>ibid.</u> or <u>id.</u> <u>V.</u> and <u>vs.</u> (and <u>versus</u>, too, for that matter) should be spoken—and written—as "against."

> *David Dasef*
> *Washington, D.C.*

Your injection of the quantum theory into the discussion of the use of the word "versus" and its abbreviations had not a particle of logic in it. In fact, you introduced an element of uncertainty into the whole matter that shows that, in this respect, you have no principle at all.

> *H. Douglas Midkiff*
> *Rochester, New York*

When discussing the landmark Supreme Court decision, we use <u>Roe v. Wade</u>.
When discussing George Washington's dilemma when approaching the Delaware River, we use <u>Roe versus Wade</u>.

> *James M. Neville*
> *St. Louis, Missouri*

If you must insist on remanding, please use the customary and proper form of judicial authority!

> *"That's it; remanded to the boondocks for usage <u>not inconsistent with this opinion</u>."*

This is a special leave to the lower court to apply as it sees fit the appellate court's decision. It also sometimes bespeaks a lazy appellate court that is unwilling to apply the principles of its decision to a particularly nasty tangle of facts.
If you had used this form you would have given your readers a little more leeway in applying your decision, which may be hard to take retroactively.

> *Ward C. Stoneman*
> *Attorney at Law*
> *Berkeley, California*

My attention was drawn to your quotation from Professor Robbins: "You will occasionally hear 'the case of Smith and Jones.' It's not necessarily incorrect, but I regard it as an affectation." I enclose a copy of a reference to indicate that in England this is the only correct way of speaking the title of a civil case. That is also the practice in Canada and, I suspect, in most of the Commonwealth.

Therefore, the <u>and</u> usage is not, I venture to think, even in the United States an affectation, but rather a reflection of the English tradition from which American law is derived.

> The Honourable Mr. Justice
> Mark R. MacGuigan
> Federal Court of Canada
> Ottowa, Canada

Many times I have thought of writing to you to ask that you discuss the military's misuse of the word "vice." They use it when they intend to convey the notion "as opposed to," "versus," or "vis à vis." Then today I opened my copy of the <u>International Herald Tribune</u> and found "Chapter and Versus: Some Case Law."

Would you supplement your "Chapter and Versus" column with one on "Versus Isn't Vice"?

> Carolsue Holland
> Professor of International
>   Relations & Public Affairs
> Troy State University
> APO, New York

Cloud-Cuckoo-Land

The notion of the Republicans to halve the capital-gains tax while proposing an expensive child-care plan was an idea, charged Governor Dukakis, that belonged in "financial Cloud-Cuckoo-Land."

The man knows his Greek roots. This is from *Nephelokokkygia,* a name given the dream world built by flying creatures in Aristophanes' *Birds.* The first English translation was *Cuckoocloudland* in 1824, but the English journalist Richard Whiteing wrote of a character in his 1899 novel, *No. 5 John Street:* "All his thinking processes fade off into the logic of Cloud Cuckoo Land."

Now usually hyphenated, *Cloud-Cuckoo-Land* means "a fanciful realm in which foolish behavior flourishes." Synonymy: more bookish than *cloud nine,* sillier than *utopia,* more far-out and less ideologically freighted than *left field.*

The common European species of the cuckoo is a grayish-brown bird with the habit of laying its eggs in the nests of other birds, which then hatch them and take care of the young. This has given the cuckoo a reputation of being confused or crackbrained, but may show a predisposition to the liberating advantages of child care that human politicians are just beginning to explore.

The cuckoo does not use the nests of other birds because it can't remember where its own nest is or what it looks like; rather, the cuckoo builds no nest at all and parasitizes other birds to raise its young. In the process, the offspring of the host bird are often killed. There are 126 species of cuckoos, and some of them are so adept at this process—known as "brood parasitism"—that they lay eggs that so closely resemble those of the host species that the host female cannot tell the difference.

Call this behavior parasitic or opportunistic; call it the quintessence of sur-vival-of-the-fittest; call it cruel or insensitive, but whatever you call it, it is hardly "confused or crackbrained."

It is obvious that the confusion arose because of the sound made by the cuckoo, replicated in the cuckoo clock, and having no association whatever with the behavior of the real bird.

Richard Ellis
Director, Shark and Cuckoo
Division
Biological Irregulars
New York, New York

Coiners' Corner

The greatest thrill a man can experience, Winston Churchill was reported to have said, is to be shot at and missed. (If that quotation cannot be found in his works, I have taken a shot at the source and missed.)

For a writer, the big thrill is to coin a word or phrase that fills a linguistic void and becomes part of the history of the era. The widespread adoption of Churchill's blockbuster phrase *Iron Curtain* must have been profoundly satis-fying to him as a historian as well as a statesman; never mind that earlier uses of the phrase were found. In the same way, the ghost of Teddy Roosevelt must smile when a modern pol denounces his *lunatic fringe*.

In this century, newspaper columnists have made great contributions to

phrasemaking. In the Coinage Hall of Fame, we find Arthur Krock's *government by crony* (which the *New York Times* pundit gave to Interior Secretary Harold Ickes); Herbert Swope's *cold war* (which he gave to Bernard Baruch, and Walter Lippmann then tried to steal it from him); Stewart Alsop's *egghead* and, in collaboration with Charles Bartlett, *hawks and doves;* Joseph Kraft's *Middle American,* and Joseph Alsop's *Southern strategy.*

Speechwriters have a ghostly place in this pantheon. The other day, a picture appeared in *The New York Times* of Theodore Sorensen, working on the Democratic platform under the light of a tilted lampshade in a lonely hotel room. Though he steadfastly rejects the credit, his was the hand that penned *New Frontier* and *Ich bin ein Berliner;* was he trying to cook up a ringing phrase for this year's no-offense platform that the candidate can make his own? Of course he was.

But it's hard. At meetings of the Judson Welliver Society, the club of presidential ghosts, I see—in my mind's eye—great phrases hung around the necks of the members.

See, in the corner, there is Richard Goodwin, identified with Lyndon Johnson's *Great Society.* Nobody can find the Reaganaut with the sign for *truly needy,* but there is Tony Dolan, the unadmitted author of Ronald Reagan's most memorable phrase, *evil empire;* that speechwriter's now-rejected Reaganism was the most resounding use of alliteration since Warren Harding's *not nostrums but normalcy.* (Did Welliver, the first White House "literary clerk," write the *normalcy* speech for Harding? Could be. For some reason—perhaps the choice of the less obvious word than *normality*—the string of *n*'s clicked, while its companion phrases, *not surgery but serenity* and *not experiment but equipoise,* never got off the ground.)

Other modern alliterators are here at the Nixon table. The sign across my chest is *nattering nabobs of negativism,* a blast at pessimists coined for Spiro Agnew to parallel Adlai Stevenson's *prophets of gloom and doom.* Pat Buchanan sits nearby, lumbered with *pusillanimous pussyfooters* but wearing more proudly the nonalliterative *New Federalism* and *instant analysis* (which is not alliterative, but is catchily consonant, with its repetition of *n* and *s* sounds). And there is Ray Price, with his soaring but dimly remembered *lift of a driving dream.*

I am slightly embarrassed by another of my badges. When a Nixon campaign aide came to me in late 1971 to pick a name for the reelection effort, I suggested Committee to Re-Elect the President. That was pretty shrewd, I thought, using the title of the office rather than the candidate's name, and downplaying the running mate. Then along came Watergate and Bob Dole's reference to the committee by its pseudo-acronym, CREEP.

That isn't much to show for a lifetime in the phrasemaking arena, and my habit of adding a *-gate* to every political transgression is strictly derivative. (*Koreagate* and *Billygate* were duds, but I thought *doublebillingsgate,* about a minor expense-account flap, had a nice ring. Don't blame me for today's *Pentagate.*) However, a neologism I threw in the pot back in 1969—which then did not catch on—seems finally to be making it.

We were looking for a name for welfare reform. Counselors Pat Moynihan and Arthur Burns had locked horns on a program, and George Shultz, then Secretary of Labor, had come up with a synthesis: The result embodied Moynihan's family-sustaining dream and Burns's stern work requirement.

"Family Security" was the suggested name; I shot that term down—too much like Social Security. The "Family Assistance Plan" was put forward, and despite my protestation that the acronym sounded like an expletive used by Major Hoople, FAP was adopted.

As the sore loser—these nomenclature fights get fierce—I threw a line in the covering speech, and repeated it in the President's message to Congress a few days later: "What America needs now is not more welfare, but more 'workfare.' "

Everybody winced—too cornball!—but President Nixon liked it. Ed Morgan, the unsung attorney who worked out the details of the proposal, was worried that the gimmicky word trivialized a great idea. I became stubborn and, after everybody reviewing the speech had crossed it out, I slipped it back into the reading copy.

Workfare, the word, came and went as welfare reform, the program (called later by rueful liberals "Nixon's Good Deed"), was rejected by a Democratic Congress. But in the intervening years, with no push from me or anybody taking up its sponsorship, the rejected word puffed determinedly uphill like the Little Engine That Could.

In 1977: "Gov. Michael S. Dukakis of Massachusetts predicted success," wrote the Associated Press, "for a 'workfare' program he unveiled . . . aimed at putting welfare fathers on the public payroll." In 1980, under a headline reading MAKING 'WORKFARE' WORK, *The New York Times* hailed a Connecticut plan for "a tough 'workfare' bill." The little-engine word was scorned by the big dictionaries, but it kept puffing up the linguistic hill.

Today, with the passage of Senator Moynihan's long-overdue bill giving a work theme to the new welfare, *workfare,* the word, is rolling merrily along. The unexpectedly sturdy new noun has even been used in a compound adjective in Britain: "Lord Young, the Employment Secretary," wrote *The Financial Times,* "last night issued a statement saying he had no plans to introduce a workfare-type program in the United Kingdom."

As I write, the Nexis computerized library system reports that *workfare*— this ugly duckling of a neologism, derided at launch, neglected by word mavens—has passed the two-thousand-citations mark, and it is in just about every new dictionary I own.

When it was included in the final volume of the *Supplement to the Oxford English Dictionary,* I learned that the coiner was someone else. The July 1968 issue of *Harper's Magazine* had a piece about Charles Evers, a Mississippi congressional candidate, that included this line: "One of Evers's programs is what he calls workfare; he has said that everybody ought to work for what he gets."

That's all right; I may not have been the first to use the word, but I had a hand in its nationwide launch and feel a stepfather's pride. There goes *workfare* chugging down the hill, puffing "I-filled-a-void, I-filled-a-void," and as much a part of today's language as the ancient word it was bottomed on.

Dear Bill:
Re: Workfare.
Nice. And honor to you for remembering Ed Morgan.
If you ever, in the manner of the Order of the Eastern Star and suchlike lesser denominations of distinction, decide to establish a Welliver Auxiliary for Presidential Memorandum Writers, I would like to apply on behalf of "benign neglect." At the time I used the term in my memorandum to Richard Nixon of January 16th, 1970, I thought *I was citing (without reference, but in quotation marks) a phrase by John George Lambton, first Earl of Durham, a Whig peer who was dispatched to Canada as Governor General and Lord High Commissioner to learn what had caused the civil uprisings of 1837 and what might be done to confer a greater measure of self-rule on this remaining North American possession. Lest matters regress as they had done further south in the 1770s. Durham returned to Britain and wrote a much celebrated report in which he stated that* nothing *need be done. Canada had by then endured two generations of non-involvement by the Mother Country and, perforce, had had to learn to govern itself, which it was doing quite nicely and in consequence ought to be left*

alone. Nice Whiggish stuff. (Although it caused Durham much grief at the time.) Anyway, that is how I remembered the text. Poor Billy Kristol came to work for me in the White House a few months later. I made him read the whole thing. Problem. No benign neglect. And so I am forced to suppose I may have thought it up myself, as a kind of summation of the Durham report.

The phrase is now in wide circulation and, properly understood, means leaving an improving situation undisturbed in the understanding that whatever is working well had best not be interfered with. My concern, at the time, was to direct attention to the increasing salience of <u>class</u>, as did William Julius Wilson in <u>The Declining Significance of Race</u> eight years later. About half the time I encounter the phrase, this is the meaning intended. The other half, it implies malicious disengagement of which the President (and I) were charged.

Best,

Daniel P. Moynihan
Senator, New York
United States Senate
Washington, D.C.

You express puzzlement that <u>normalcy</u> caught on and some other neologisms didn't. One reason that the use of <u>normalcy</u> in Harding's address was so catchy is that with that form of the word the alliteration is between two syllables that bear the primary stress (no'strums, no'rmalcy), whereas if Harding had said norma'lity instead, the alliteration would have been on a syllable of that word that had only secondary stress.

Jim [James D. McCawley]
Department of Linguistics
University of Chicago
Chicago, Illinois

I thought I had settled once and for all the origin of the word "egghead" when I wrote you from Le Rouret, France, maybe ten years ago.

But you have repeated the error of crediting Stewart Alsop with coining the word.

In my letter I referred you to the Toledo Public Library, which possesses a letter from Carl Sandburg to my grandfather Negley Dakin Cochran, for whom the poet worked on the <u>Chicago Day Book</u> back in the days preceding the First World War.

In your follow-up column, in which you corrected your mistake, you wrote that you had sent for and received a copy of the Sandburg letter, from which you quoted: " 'Eggheads' is the slang here for editorial writers here [<u>sic</u>]."

You also quoted what I consider to be a great tribute to my grandfather. Mr. Sandburg wrote, "And since we got into the war I notice more writing like people talk. They are copying your style, which is no style and yet all style."

Katharine Opper
Westport, Connecticut

In President Nixon's speech on the Family Assistance Plan, "workfare" aimed to make a liberal idea—a guaranteed annual income, in fact—look conservative. (Or so Pat Moynihan used to tell me.) Today, of course, "workfare" really does refer to a conservative idea—putting welfare recipients to work, rather than giving them money—and even liberal advocates, like Governor Dukakis, rarely use the word to describe their own programs.

To confuse matters further, some mavericks (like Peter DuPont and Mickey Kaus) believe that what most of us now call "workfare" won't succeed and will wind up being just another form of welfare. They call for giving welfare recipients jobs instead of money on the theory that "only work works" (as Kaus put it in The New Republic in July 1986).

Perhaps the lesson of all this is that we are in danger of overworking "work."

Leslie Lenkowsky
Washington, D.C.

You gave me a vicarious thrill when you mentioned Pop's "Cold War" contribution and particularly when you mentioned the Lippmann involvement. If you don't already know, you'll be interested that Professor Seabury of Stanford told me he had become curious about Lippmann's claiming the phrase had been used by the French press in the '30s. He said they had referred to what Hitler was doing behind his borders as "La Guerre Blanche" or "La Guerre Froide." However, Seabury did great research on this, both personally and in studying the French press of those days, and no one in or out of journalism had ever heard any such usage. Seabury was convinced. I suspect Lippmann may have been trying to justify his 1947 columns headed "Cold War" by shunting it off on the French.

Your column set in motion a number of political phrases coursing through my mind. Does anyone other than you recall "Economic Royalists" which he followed—and I was in the Garden (Madison Square)—with: "They have met their match; now they shall meet their master!" a statement more forceful than modest. But FDR could handle it with ease!

Herbert Swope, Jr.
West Palm Beach, Florida

Dear Bill:

Your puzzlement about the origins of The New Frontier *leads me to set down the following extremely minor footnote to history, as I remember it.*

Early in the Kennedy administration David Wise wrote a piece for the New York Herald-Tribune *asserting that I had provided JFK with "Let's get this country moving again" and "The New Frontier." I knew Wise as the nephew of Professor M. M. Postan, a distinguished economic historian at Cambridge and a friend.*

I called and told Wise I had, indeed, given JFK the first of those phrases but not "The New Frontier." After I had gone on for some time in this vein, he asked: "Are you finished?" He then said: "First, the President of the United States said the phrase came from you; second, he showed me a speech draft of yours containing the phrase; third, he told me it came from your book The Stages of Economic Growth.*" I subsided and, indeed, found three references to the new frontier theme in* The Stages, *which I had forgotten.*

Then Max Freedman sent a letter to the Tribune *saying that Ted Sorensen had used the phrase in a draft of his for Kennedy.*

When the question has been raised with me occasionally, I have responded that it is wholly possible Freedman was correct; the phrase may well have been in the air at the time; and the issue is trivial because the working politician alone deserves whatever credit there may be in such phrases because he alone takes the responsibility and risk of using them.

Thus, I leave the matter as still undecided, with ample scope for further revisionism.

> *Walt [W. W. Rostow]*
> *Austin, Texas*

You discussed the origins of the phrase "the cold war." In this reference, you noted Lippmann's use of the phrase but went on to indicate that he had taken it from Bernard Baruch, who had picked it up from Herbert Swope.

You might be interested in reading what Ronald Steel makes of the Baruch-Swope claim on page 445 of Walter Lippmann and the American Century.

> *The first of Lippmann's articles appeared on September 2, 1947, and by the time the final one was printed a month later, they were a topic of discussion wherever people gathered to talk about international politics. A few months afterward they were published in book form, and the title he gave the book,* The Cold War, *became part of the world's political vocabulary. Lippmann is usually given credit for the phrase, although he said he merely picked it up from one used in Europe during the late 1930s to characterize Hitler's war of nerves against the French, sometimes described as* la guerre blanche *or* la guerre froide. *Herbert Bayard Swope, still doing public relations for Bernard Baruch, claimed that his client was the first to use the phrase.*

Given Baruch's propensity to take claim for everything in sight, I am inclined to share Mr. Steel's skepticism.

You will also note that Lippmann claimed to have first heard the phrase in the late 1930s used by the French to describe Hitler's War of Nerves (La Guerre Blanche and La Guerre Froide).

I have checked with a colleague who is a specialist on French history for that period, and he has never seen a reference to either French phrase.

You might also be interested in taking a look at an article by Adda Bozeman, "War and the Clash of Ideas," Orbis (Spring 1976). On page 67 of this article she refers to the "uneasy coexistence of Christian and Muslim in the lands of the Mediterranean, for which contemporary Spaniards coined the term Guerra Fría."

The precedent that Bozeman cites is obviously the more interesting and relevant of the two. However, given the difference in the phenomena involved, I see no apparent reason why the French would have thought to use the Spanish term (even if they had been aware of it).

> *Warner R. Schilling*
> *James T. Shotwell Professor*
> *of International Relations*
> *Columbia University*
> *New York, New York*

For future revelation you may be interested in these:

In 1949, I was asked to join the first (I think) "think-tank" in the U.S.: the RAND Corporation, then a part of Douglas Aircraft, nominally (to be eligible for federal funding: RAND, meaning Research and New Developments, was funded by a grant from the Air Force, to Douglas, and subsequently received contracts from the State Department, etc.).

I was the first RAND member who was not a mathematician, aerodynamicist, economist. In fact, I recruited the entire Social Science Division, hiring such luminaries as Hans Speier, Bernard Brodie, Herbert Goldhamer, Joseph Goldsen, etc.

At a staff conference, the word "elite" came up several times. The usage was from Roberto Michel's famous "circulation of the elite." I said that "elite" was a poor word for American political/sociological research: "I think we are talking about the 'decision-makers.' Consider the vast number of people in power, in the government, in industry, who are where they are not because of their heritage or wealth, but because of their success in having made superior decisions. In Washington, some of the most important problems are being handled not by the White House, or the Secretary of War, or the heads of U.S. Steel or Standard Oil—but by relatively unknown decision-makers, who are working for or under them."

The term was so affective that it gained wide usage inside RAND and was often shortened, in written communications, as "the D-M's" (Nathan Leites, especially).

Soon I began to emphasize how little was known about "the decision-making process."·(Only the Webbs had written up a study of committee size and efficiency, as I recall—a simplified but interesting foray.)

Another phrase/neologism I introduced was "peacefare." By this I meant the systematic study and practice of creating/sustaining the peace. "There are studies galore of warfare, but where are the analyses of peacefare?" This word, "peacefare," never achieved the success of its antonym.

> Leo Rosten
> East Quogue, New York

In connection with President Reagan's designation of the Soviet Union as an "evil empire," I thought it was an original statement. However, on reading Ben Gurion and the Palestinian Arabs by Shabtai Tevelth, on page 111 I came across a statement by Ben Gurion castigating England in connection with the Passfield White Paper in which he states, among other things, "If the creative force within us is capable of stopping this evil empire etc. etc."

I thought you might be interested.

> Emanuel Weidberg
> New York, New York

Contrariwise

"A rap against Baker is that his reputation rests mainly on his skill with the press," wrote the *National Journal* early this year, referring to Secretary of State James Baker. "That was the thrust of a splashily contrary . . . *New Republic* cover story that branded him 'Washington's most overrated man.'"

Seated in his office on the seventh floor of Foggy Bottom, Secretary Baker must have read that, thinking: Why *contrary*? Why not *contrarian*?

The same thoughts occurred to Burt Solomon, the writer of the piece, who asked his editor why *contrarian* had been changed. He was told that *contrarian* was not in Merriam-Webster's *Third New International Unabridged* (the noun does appear in that dictionary's 1986 supplement, *12,000 Words*); moreover, says Mr. Solomon, the editor "considers *contrarian* a word that doesn't add any meaning to *contrary;* he likens it to the way the newfangled *adversarial* means precisely the same, as an adjective, as *adversary.*"

The reporter argued otherwise: "I think of *contrarian* as a Wall Street term describing an investor who purposely goes against the market's thinking as a strategic means of turning a profit. I regard *contrarian* as connoting an obsessive quality that distinguishes it from *contrary*—a being contrary for the sake of being contrary. You can tell from my story who won the argument (that being the way with editors)."

Virginia, your little editor-friends are wrong. Both words are both adjective and noun: A *contrary* (adj.) view is one that is on the *contrary* (n.); a *contrarian* (adj.) view is the persnickety position taken by one of those ultra-independent, different-drummer *contrarians* (n.).

Contrary means "opposite, against, opposing," while *contrarian* as a noun, and lately as an adjective, refers to more than "one who is contrary"; the word as noun means "one who sees a value or an advantage in taking an opposing view" and, in adjectival form, "deliberately opposing for the strategic reason of being against the trend."

The father of contrarianism was Humphrey Neill, the author of the 1954 *Art of Contrary Thinking.* His former aide, James Fraser of Burlington, Vermont, recalls that the financial adviser began a newsletter in the 1940's called *The Neill Letter of Contrary Opinion.* In the 1960's, he began changing the key word to fit his philosophy of deliberately going against the grain of current investor sentiment.

Elizabeth M. Fowler wrote in *The New York Times* on June 11, 1966: "Mr. Neill, who calls himself a contrarian, which means he tends to act just the opposite of the crowd or general public, now advises caution."

In 1980, David Dreman titled a book along these lines *Contrarian Investment Strategy,* defining the term as "principles that normally result in going against the popular opinion of the day."

The word, with its unique sense of purposeful opposition, soon spread beyond Wall Street to politics, where the adjective has positioned itself between *iconoclastic* and *ornery,* and the noun has become synonymous with "young curmudgeon."

Now, *contrarian* is also part of the general language. When other New York builders cut back on construction in Battery Park City after the 1987 stock-market crash, Frank E. Linde plunged ahead: "We took a contrarian view," he told *The New York Times.* "We decided to go full steam ahead." (So far, that means merely a *contrary* view.) "We figured that if the other developers were holding back, there would be less competition." (With that clear purpose of taking advantage of the different action of others, his view becomes *contrarian.*)

Conventional Wisdom

"The term 'the conventional wisdom' has become so much a part of the language," wrote *New York Times* columnist Leonard Silk, "that people forget that the phrase was coined by John Kenneth Galbraith just 30 years ago in 'The Affluent Society.' "

This triggered a query from Richard A. Rettig at the National Academy of Sciences: "I find that assertion astounding. Is it correct? What took so long for such a conventional phrase to appear?"

Mr. Silk, himself the coiner of "double-digit," as in inflation, is a careful coinage attributor. In 1958, the economist John Kenneth Galbraith titled a chapter "The Concept of the Conventional Wisdom," explaining that "the hallmark of the conventional wisdom is acceptability. It has the approval of those to whom it is addressed."

The phrase was intended by the coiner to be pejorative, because, he wrote, "Ideas need to be tested by their ability, in combination with events, to overcome inertia and resistance. This inertia and resistance the conventional wisdom provides."

For a time, the noun phrase seemed to me to have adopted a neutral tone, as "consensus," "popular belief" and "generally accepted view," and even, as defined in *Random House II Unabridged,* "prudence"; recently, however, it has regained its original overtone of stodginess and ultimate wrongheadedness. The phrase "popular belief" is almost always used in "contrary to popular belief," and *conventional wisdom* goes one step further.

Placing the phrase firmly where Mr. Galbraith intended it, *Newsweek* magazine began a "Conventional-Wisdom Watch"; each week, presidential candidates were shown to be up or down according to the prevailing breezes of punditry. Implicit in the "watch" was the message: Stick around, because conventional wisdom will change soon.

Phrasemakers used to envy the lanky Mr. Galbraith his coinage of "Affluent Society"; now that is all but forgotten, and his *conventional wisdom* has taken hold as if it has always been with us. (*Founding Fathers* is another such phrase; for more than a century they were called the "framers," and it took the phrasemaker Warren G. Harding, with his not-nostrums-but-normalcy aptitude for alliteration, to come up with *Founding Fathers.*)

With the coming of the political conventions this summer, the phrase will undoubtedly suffer some confusion, but after the conventioneers go home, the too-easily accepted wisdom of the wise guys will again be with us.

Isn't this phrase just an inferior version of the wonderful oxymoron "received wisdom," which also has a long and honorable history in French (including

Flaubert's dictionary of the same name and of precisely the same meaning: the *Dictionnaire des Idées Reçues)?*

> *Joseph Asch*
> *Paris, France*

You say: "his conventional wisdom has taken hold as if it has always been with us." Surely it should be "as if it had always been with us."

> *Lillian Kent*
> *New York, New York*

You write, "his conventional wisdom has taken hold as if it has always been with us." "As if" here should be followed by the past form of the conditional and not by the present indicative (cf. Fowler).

> *Ed Cashin*
> *Bronx, New York*

Country Matters

The whole country has gone *country.* Dolly Parton and Ralph Lauren have won.

Consider the support you reach for when climbing a flight of stairs. In Standard English, or citispeak, that is called the *banister,* a corruption of *baluster,* from the Italian word meaning "the calyx of the pomegranate flower," because that is the way the supports for the railing were originally shaped.

City folks usually think of the *banister* as the whole contraption: the railing, the *balusters* or *balustrade* and the *posts* at top and bottom. ("If you slide down the *banister,* dear, you may hurt yourself on the *post.*")

When you are talkin' country, however, the terminology changes: The *handrail* is supported by the *spindles* and end—top and bottom of the staircase—at the *newels.* According to Eben Conner, of Master's Woodshop in Hagerstown, Maryland, *baluster* is a word he seldom hears; "the turned piece from the handrail to the step is almost always called the *spindle.*" ("If you

slide down the *handrail,* li'l feller, playin' a tune on the *spindles,* you'll tangle your tail in the *newel* and scuff up my stenciled floor.")

Country antiques are the hottest *collectibles.* (That word is country for "junk," derided in citispeak as *dust collectors.* Speakers of country rarely include furniture in the *collectible* category, limiting that word to a description of small items like cowbells.) If the object is beat-up enough, or *weathered,* it is a *primitive,* a word borrowed from painting. If the chair or table is old, original and in good shape, it becomes *folk art* and is avidly sought.

"The main term that we use in describing country antiques," says Thomas G. Kreuz of Bobbie's Antiques in Kensington, Maryland, "is *handcrafted.* A handcrafted item is uniquely decorative, the product of the one person who crafted it—more primitive, down-to-earth, utilitarian, durable."

Artist is citispeak; *artisan,* less presumptuous, is country. City folks see a *stream* or a *brook;* country people see a *creek* or *crick,* a *run* or a *kill.* "In real-estate advertising," reports Nancy McBride, a realtor in Harper's Ferry, West Virginia, "the preferred term for a creek is *stream.*"

Country people who are liberals, as some are, may be horrified to learn that *country* is derived from *contra,* the word recently applied to Nicaragua's rebels. Where's the connection? *Contra,* Latin for "against," was the basis of the Vulgar Latin *contrata,* used for "region lying opposite" or "land spread out before one."

The first use of *country* as an attributive noun (a noun acting like an adjective, as in *killer rabbit*) was in the latter part of the fourteenth century: "To make songes and ditee in the contre longage," or songs and ditties in the country language. Then came *country house,* in the late 1500's, followed in

1632 by *country gentleman* as opposed to city dweller. *Country life* appeared in 1669.

In the United States, *country store* and *country cousin* of pre-Revolutionary times were followed by *country club* and *country road,* launched in the mid-nineteenth century (and the latter immortalized in a 1971 song by John Denver after a happy day in West Virginia). In the 1950's, along came *country music* and *country singer,* a Southern and Western cultural explosion that changed *rustic* from faintly pejorative to assertively proud.

The nonmusician who has done as much as anyone to extend the popularization of *country* in American culture is John Mack Carter, the Hearst magazine editor who conceived of *Country Living* in 1978. He spotted the trend and pushed it hard; I asked him to select a dozen words that exemplify country language. Here is his list, with his reasons in parentheses:

· Whole- (as in whole-wheat, whole-earth, wholesome)
· Split- (split-pea, split-rail)
· Fallow (sounds so peaceful and restful, far from the madding crowd)
· Furrow (as close as one need get to farming talk)
· Sweetwater (from the well or cistern, no minerals and no fluorine)
· Post-and-beam (whatever it means, the only way to construct barns, stables, country houses)
· Hominy (country-most form of corn)
· Deep-dish (bountiful and generous, as opposed to unleavened bread)
· Daisy (the honest flower, the easy pattern)
· Sassafras (the root of genuine natural flavor)
· Muslin (fabric doesn't get more country than this)
· Dappled (nature's own design, suitable for fawns and lawns)

Doesn't the very listing of such words evoke the *down-home* thoughts of a babbling brook at eventide, *handcut* nails in a *batten* door? O.K.—a *batten* door has its tongue-in-groove planks backed by a horizontal or diagonal length of wood for strength, like most barn doors.

Down-home, like the German-Yiddish *haimish,* is a compound adjective meaning "with a homelike, nostalgic quality"; although the use of *down home* as a prepositional phrase for "at one's home" or "in one's native region" has been traced back to the early nineteenth century in Britain, the hyphenated *down-home* is an Americanism that appeared in the 1930's. It should not be confused with the Southern English *down hearth,* an open fireplace in which the fire is directly on the floor next to the *inglenook,* which is a recess for a seat beside the fireplace.

To Carter's wholesome dozen, I would add *quilt*—that handcrafted folk art you will find draped over half the antique wheelbarrows in America, its patterns now available on your country credit cards. According to Patricia

Smith, a leading quilt historian and dealer in Washington, quilts are identified as *legitimate*—that is, unaltered—or *not of a piece,* without integrity and presumably dog-eared.

Quilt patterns have names ranging from the familiar *Log Cabin* and *Schoolhouse* to the esoteric *Double Wedding Ring, Triple Irish Chain, Burgoyne Surrounded* and *Rocky Road to Kansas.* The word Ms. Smith uses to refer to badly damaged quilts is *cutters,* and a poorly made item is a *toenail-catcher.*

Tired of country? Want a synonym? Both *rural* and *rustic* come from the Latin *rus,* "open land," related to *room.* Although of similar origin, these fifteenth-century adjectives conjure different senses of country: *Rural* calls up the pleasures of country living, while *rustic* often suggests a lack of city refinement in country life.

Pastoral, a Wordsworth favorite, suggests the simple, idyllic life of shepherds; it comes from *pastor,* used in English in the 1300's for "herdsman," by extension, a shepherd of souls, the spiritual *pastor* of a flock or congregation. *Bucolic* is pejorative, a 1613 adjective from the Latin *bous,* "head of cattle." A synonym for *pastoral* in poetry, *bucolic* has otherwise grown to describe loutish people or behavior.

Pass me that deep-dish pie, to be washed down with sassafras tea while one rusticates, contemplating the dappled down-home daisies. If I get the hang of the lingo, maybe I can fit in these designer country jeans.

Perhaps you said, "tongue-in-groove" with "tongue and cheek."

If not, remember the old sage who said, "It's not what we don't know that does us in; it's what we know for damn sure—that happens to be dead wrong."

> Roscoe H. Canadey
> Rochester, New York

Harper's Ferry, indeed!
Governor's Island and St. Elizabeth's Hospital next?

> Larry Pellettier
> Ellicott City, Maryland

We, who build stairs, use terms in a relatively consistent manner throughout the English-speaking world.
The terms _newel_, _post_ and _newel post_ are used interchangeably within all the

references. We always refer to a baluster by its proper name, but have noticed that some iron stair builders use the term spindle.

> P. B. Withstandley
> Mount Laurel, New Jersey

Primitive, *in the antiques trade, has more to do with the manufacture of an item than whether it is beat up or not. A Garden Way yard cart will never become a primitive, no matter how much it is weathered or worn; the wheelbarrow great-grandpa fashioned for his own use from the scraps in back of the barn was a primitive right from the start.*

John Mack Carter suggests that one can't get more country than muslin. *I think* homespun *(or, to take it even further,* homespun linsey-woolsey*) tops it.*

You call the kind of boards used in batten doors "tongue in groove." The correct term is "tongue and groove," as any carpenter (even a country carpenter) could tell you. (Always assuming, of course, that he wrote it out—he would tell *you it was "tongue 'n' groove"). You may be interested to know that the groove is* ploughed *into the edge of the board with a* plough plane *(or, nowadays, routed into it with a spindle shaper, but we were discussing country matters). The tongue (now formed with a spindle shaper) was formerly formed by planing two* rabbets *into the edge, one on each face, leaving a protruding tongue. (You may be interested to know that the English usage is* rebate, *and according to the O.* O.E.D. *[Old* O.E.D.; *can't swing the price of the new one] is a later version of* rabbet. *Probably the result of a Lesser Vowel Shift.) But I digress.*

A batten door, by the way, must *have at least two horizontal planks backing it: these braces are what holds the vertical planks together and keeps them parallel. A diagonal brace is used on all but the lightest of doors to keep the door from sagging out of square.*

I regret to inform you that only *a city-slicker would wear designer jeans. Some country folk wear plain old* jeans; real *country folk wear* overalls.

> Edward J. Lefkowicz
> Fairhaven, Massachusetts

Nigh on Cincinnati is Kaintuckee, where "Country Matters" are very important. Rillastate has made rich men out of poor boys and some folks even buy country sausage at a store. I dint see nuthin in your article about no pickup trucks. Hit don't matter none.

Ever good wish,

> Morton L. Spitz
> Cincinnati, Ohio

Day Care, Child Care, Word Care

"Child care," writes Lisbeth B. Schorr in *Within Our Reach: Breaking the Cycle of Disadvantage,* a new book being lapped up by politicians eager to show an interest in families without actually having to kiss babies, ". . . must go beyond custodial care to provide intellectual stimulation" and then on to "nurturance, hugs, approval, and responsiveness."

Nurturance I can figure out. This cuddly new vogue term was created by the nounification of the verb *nurture* (originally a noun itself, from the Latin for "suckle, nourish") and was coined in 1938 on the structural analogy of *governance* for "the process of governing." But when did the old baby-sitting *day care* become the hot domestic issue now called *child care*?

Child care came first. In 1915, the novelist Jean Webster wrote about the need for "modern, humane views on the subject of child-care," with the general meaning of "oversight or supervision of a young child." Not until the Depression of the early 1930's did *day-care center* come on the linguistic scene as congressional bureaucratese for *nursery*.

During World War II, the Lanham Act put money into what were called *day-care centers* and *day nurseries* to free mothers to work in defense plants (then called *war plants;* after that war, the word *defense* was substituted for *war* in Washington).

At that time, many parents who had the money put their children in *nursery school,* which was called by professionals *preschool.* Those parents who preferred that their children be supervised at home employed *baby sitters* (a coinage first cited in 1937, used most often by lower-middle-class parents), *housekeepers* (upper-middle-class use of a word that dates back to the 1400's) or *governesses* (upper-class usage since the 1700's, with its 1795 baby-talk alternative, *nanny*).

"For the mother to be able to work," Li Schorr tells me, "the child had to be taken care of all day, hence *day care.*" But whence the switch back to the original *child care?* "When Senator Fritz Mondale and Representative John Brademas put together their bill in 1971, they called it a *child-development* bill, and a subsequent version, the *child and family services* bill. That changed the emphasis from *day* to *child.* You probably remember that from your White House days."

(Mrs. Schorr is gently referring to the veto message of that bill by President Nixon, which denounced committing "the vast moral authority of the national Government to the side of communal approaches to child rearing"; one of my colleagues wrote that message, and I salute him for knowing the difference between *raising* and *rearing.* You *raise* cattle, issues and hell; you *rear* children.)

I think that *child care* was meant to encompass both the out-of-home supervision in nursery schools and the in-home nannying, while the narrower *day care* came to mean only the care in "centers." Because the political issue was drawn by some conservatives as encouraging the career woman at the expense of the stay-at-home mother, savvy liberals adopted the broader term, placing their concern for children both at home and in the workplace. (Besides, the child was being cared for, not the day; strictly speaking, I think it should have been *daytime care,* but the language likes to shorten phrases, which is why we never had *nighttime baseball.*)

The ripening of the issue has brought some other words to fruition. "Longer school days and years," suggests Secretary of Labor Ann McLaughlin, who is taking the lead in developing the Reagan Administration policy on what she embraces as *child care,* "could certainly help to address the *latchkey-children* issue."

That phrase has been in use since 1944 to denote, in Merriam-Webster's *Ninth New Collegiate Dictionary* definition, "a young child of working parents who must spend part of the day at home unsupervised." A *latchkey* is the British word for a key to an outside door, usually the front door; a *latchkey child* is one who uses that key when no adult is at home. Sometimes the latchkey is proudly worn around the neck, as a badge of honor, or symbol of defiance, or because the kid keeps losing the damn key otherwise. George Bernard Shaw used the word to signal self-reliance in *Major Barbara,* a 1905 play: "Your independence is achieved: you have won your latchkey."

Americans have adopted the British usage for this phrase, primarily because it is colorful, perhaps also because *doorkey*—the American word for a key to the front door—has a slang homophone in *dorky,* meaning "klutzy"—clumsy—or in a second sense, "acting like a nerd."

Word care is significant in child care. *Day care* is now applied to the elderly or the ailing as well as the young and means simply "attention during the day." And *day-care worker* is being replaced by *caregiver,* apparently coined on the analogy of *caretaker;* it was spotted in *U.S. News & World Report* in 1976 as "postfuneral counseling by the funeral director as a caregiver is on the increase." This term has the advantage of not being stereotyped as feminine the way *nurse* is—*male nurse* is specified when a man is meant, like *male secretary*—and *caregiver* does not have the passive connotation of *caretaker.*

The hot new gerund *parenting* is similarly nonsexist. *Fathering* has a second sense of "originating"; *mothering* can also mean "protecting." *Parent* was first used as a verb in 1663, meaning "produce, beget"; it produced the gerund in the late 1950's, a noun with the sense of taking care of children, not just producing them. (*Gerunding* is a word not yet coined; it means "giving birth to a noun formed from a verb.")

The biggest mistake that can be made in writing about the child-care issue is to use a phrase that derogates mothers who do not choose to pursue careers outside the home. (*Derogate* means "belittle, demean," on a level with *disparage,* meaning "diminish, put down"; *denigrate* is much stronger, meaning "abuse, blacken, defame, calumniate." That's the latest from Accuracy in Maligning. I misused *derogate* recently, but that was not half as bad as calling mothers who do not have outside jobs *nonworking mothers.*)

"As one who is the exemplar of correct use of language," wrote Phyllis Schlafly of Alton, Illinois, my longtime buddy and often but not always ideological soul mate, "you should know how offensive is the expression 'nonworking mothers.' If you know any nonworking mothers, I would like to meet them. I've never met any."

The proudly "pro-family" Mrs. Schlafly (never "Ms."—if in doubt about her marital status on a second reference, call her Phyllis) raises an interesting side issue: What do we call women who work at home raising a family? (And why do we *raise* families if we *rear* children?) We cannot call them *unemployed,* because that suggests "unable to find work," and mothers find plenty of work rearing children and raising families or hell at home; *self-employed* connotes other than child-rearing activities; *home-working* suggests doing lessons; perhaps *nonemployed* or *noncareer* answers the need, but those locutions are negative. This department is open for suggestions.

Tread carefully among the words of this caregiving world. *Maternity leave* spawned the question—"Should Papa have no responsibility?"—that led to the androgynous *infant-care leave.* (Why not *paternity leave?* Says linguistically sensitive Li Schorr: "That sounds too much like the man is dumping the wife and kids.")

You mentioned that you were interested in the earliest use of the term "Caregiver" in literature. May I suggest that I (and I suspect also Dr. T. Berry Brazelton at Harvard) may well have coined this term and are surely two of the earliest users of this term in articles and books.

I am enclosing the copyright front page of the first edition of Infant Caregiving: A Design for Training, which was published in 1972 by myself and Dr. Lally. The second edition of this book is available from Syracuse University Press.

I believe we were the earliest users of the word "caregiver" to denote the person who provides care for infants and very young children. During the writing of this book, the word "caretaker" was deliberately rejected as too cold and as an unappetizing reminder of caretakers of animals in zoos rather than nurturers of young children.

> *Alice S. Honig, Ph.D.*
> *Professor*
> *College for Human*
> *   Development*
> *Syracuse University*
> *Syracuse, New York*

Much more numerous than day care centers are "family day care homes." The latest figures I have seen on out-of-home care for young children indicate that about 80 percent are in family day care and 20 percent are in center day care. The family day care home is often in the same neighborhood as the child's own home, and the family day care mother is an acquaintance of the child's own mother. This day care mother may have only two or three children in her care, or she may have several more.

> *Alberta E. Siegel*
> *Professor of Psychology*
> *Stanford University Medical*
> *   Center*
> *Division of Child Psychiatry &*
> *   Child Development*
> *Palo Alto, California*

Dear Buddy,
Glad you read your mail.
*   Best,*

> *Phyllis [Schlafly]*
> *Alton, Illinois*

Debatemanship

The Latin root for the word *debate* is the same as that for *battle: battuere,* "to beat," as in whacking your opponent over the head.

In introducing the first confrontation between the Democratic and Republican candidates for President, CBS's Dan Rather wondered aloud whether *debate* was the proper word to describe what could otherwise be called *orchestrated press conference* or *joint appearance.* He seemed to want to limit the meaning of *debate* to a formal contest between orators, or an organized discussion among legislators.

Debate has a stormier history. It was first a noun for "quarrel," and its "do battle" sense was figurative by Shakespeare's day: "Where wasteful Time debateth with Decay" is in Sonnet 15. The formal sense of the noun-turned-verb was most ringingly used by John Adams, in a letter to his wife, Abigail, dated July 3, 1776: "Yesterday, the greatest question was decided which ever was debated in America, and a greater perhaps never was nor will be decided among men. A resolution was passed without one dissenting colony, 'that these United Colonies are, and of right ought to be, free and independent States.' "

So here we are, a couple of centuries later, with potential leaders of the free and independent states jousting on television. The confrontation, despite the intercession of reporters and the lack of resemblance to the Lincoln-Douglas format, can properly be called a *debate*.

Now to the language chosen by the debaters.

The most vivid metaphor was used by George Bush, answering a question about the homeless. "I see an involvement by one thousand points of light" was part of his answer, an allusion—obscure to most viewers—to his acceptance speech a month before in which he spoke of "a brilliant diversity spread like stars, like a thousand points of light in a bright and peaceful sky."

He did not give that context of diversity and voluntarism to his first use of the phrase in the debate, and when he returned to it—"do not erode out of the system the thousand points of light"—Governor Michael S. Dukakis picked up on the obscurity of the reference: "Being haunted, a thousand points of light, I don't know what that means." At his next chance to speak, the Vice President slipped in a context: "When I talk of the voluntary sector and a thousand points of light . . ."

Trigger words? Each man was primed to repeat his central code word as often as possible. Mr. Dukakis said *tough* eight times, which is a defense against the charge of weakness that has been hurled at him; Mr. Bush said *liberal* ten times, which used to be a well-liked word but now has a big-spending connotation. He also explained his use of the compound adjective *card-carrying,* which was exhaustively treated in this space in time for both debaters to study it.

When it came to arms-control lingo, some snickering took place about the Vice President's momentary confusion over the names of missiles, but more important was a phrase he got right in which he agreed with a Dukakis position: "I want to see asymmetrical reductions in conventional forces." This communicated nothing to most of the audience.

I vividly remember *asymmetry.* Trying to shorten a Nixon speech, I cut the words "and balanced" out of "mutual and balanced force reductions"; after the speech, an anguished Secretary of State, William P. Rogers, called to say, "That saving of two words could cost us six divisions." (It is only fair to expect the Russians, who have more forces in Europe than we do and have them much closer to what might be a front line, to pull back more forces; I hastily put the two words back in the printed text and the Soviet negotiators never knew.)

The word *asymmetry,* which comes to us via mathematics and chemistry, means "disproportion." The prefix *a-* is not from Middle English meaning "in, on," as in *abed, afire,* but is the Greek prefix meaning "not, without," as in *atypical, amoral.* Therefore, with *symmetry* meaning "the beauty of being in balance," *asymmetry* means "disproportionate, unbalanced," or the more colloquial "out of whack." When I asked Peggy Noonan, the Bush speechwriter, for a synonymous phrase, she instantly said, "Uneven cuts"; we can look for that phrase in future answers.

After the debate, a speechwriting friend called me to say, "Bush used both *apophasis* and *paraleipsis,* but Dukakis slammed back pretty good with *anaphora* at the end."

Of course, I knew what that meant. When Mr. Bush began a rebuttal with "There's so many things there I don't quite know where to begin," that disarming pretense of being at a loss for words is called by some, but not all, rhetoricians *apophasis.* In the mine-commission hearing involving the Pennsylvania coal-mine strikes of 1903, Clarence Darrow started his classic summation with "I scarcely know what to say." He knew what to say, and George knew where to begin.

Paraleipsis may refer to the denial of what you are saying or are about to say. I won't call George Bush a congenital paraleiptic, but—you see, I just did. "I hope people don't think I'm questioning his patriotism" was Mr. Bush's way of doing just that, and Mr. Dukakis scored his most emotional point in resenting it.

In his summation, the Massachusetts Governor reprised an *anaphoric* technique he first used in his victory statement after the New Hampshire primary. According to Bill Woodward, his principal speechwriter, the idea for "the best America" came out of a theme proposed by Marcia Hale, a staff member, just before the candidate was to head southward, and was refined by the speechwriter Martin Kaplan and Governor Dukakis on the stump.

Anaphora, from *ana-,* "back," and *pherein,* "to carry," uses the repetition of a word or clause at the beginning of successive sentences. It can be found in Lincoln's Gettysburg Address: "We cannot dedicate—we cannot consecrate—we cannot hallow this ground." In more extended form, it was used by the speechwriter Samuel I. Rosenman in F.D.R.'s much-imitated "I see an America where . . ." speech and in Martin Luther King's "I have a dream" address at the Lincoln Memorial.

"The best America doesn't hide, we compete," said Mr. Dukakis, in what had been a reference to the protectionism of a primary rival, Richard A. Gephardt. "The best America doesn't waste, we invest. The best America doesn't leave some of its citizens behind, we bring everybody along. And the best America is not behind us; the best America is yet to come."

That passage could use some more work; the second antithesis ("doesn't waste, we invest") makes no pertinent point. If Mr. Dukakis should go all the way, it's likely that will be replaced by a more relevant and less banal sentence, and we would be well advised to keep our eye on that phraseology in the inaugural address. He likes the way it sounds, he likes the way it plays, he likes it because it's easy to remember, and it could be he likes it because that's what he believes.

I shall not mention that few, if any, rhetoricians would concur with your definition of "apophasis," nor can I begin (in the space available) to enumerate the inaccuracies in your discussion of "paraleipsis."

> Maggie Keane
> Cambridge, Massachusetts

Don't Stare

After observing a crowd I estimated at 292,354 marching in Washington to preserve the status quo on abortion law, I wrote: "They marched up Constitution Avenue in dignity and order to stare decisively at the Supreme Court and to ask that institution not to change its mind by overturning the Roe v. Wade decision. . . ."

That drew a few letters objecting to the use of inside lingo, or private professional wordplay, in prose aimed at a general audience. "Elitist," complained one populist complainant; "snobbish," said another; "arch, too coy by half," wrote a third, using the British *by half* construction in what strikes me as an affectation.

The fuss was about "stare decisively." These words were based on the legal principle *stare decisis et non quieta movere,* Latin for "to adhere to precedents in decisions, and not to unsettle things that are established." In its short form, *stare decisis,* usually pronounced "STAIR-ee de-SIE-sis," means "to stand by things decided" or, more generally, "to respect precedent." *Stare* in Latin and *stereo* in Greek denote rigidity; the English infinitive *to stare* means "to gaze fixedly," and *stark* is an adjective meaning "stiff, harsh, unsoftened."

Here's a horrible admission: As a student at the Bronx High School of Science, I was too busy trying to keep up with the technological overachievers to take Latin or Greek. Frankly, I don't know *mutatis* from *mutandis.* When you see classical root canals drilled learnedly in this space, it's not because your local pop grammarian is a classical scholar whistling *ipse dixit;* on the contrary, it's the result of looking up derivations in dictionaries or rooting etymologists out of bed.

When I pop off with *obiter dicta* such as *post hoc, ergo propter hoc,* it's because I've been hanging around lawyers who know how to jack up a fee with a show of arcane argot, which brings us to *stare decisis* and "stare decisively."

When a writer slips in a foreign phrase to show off erudition at the expense of readers and the discomfort of the audience, that writer communicates contempt rather than meaning; such a writer, speaker or poet is rudely, blatantly elitist (which is being too snobbish by half).

When, however, a writer can slip in a message to a few readers that does not discombobulate or annoy the rest of the readership—if a signal can be flashed to be caught by a few and be safely missed or ignored by the rest—that writer shares a private joke without insulting anybody not in on it.

Instead of being challenged to pout, "Why am I being left out?" most readers are unconcerned with the wordplay and get out of the passage what they bring to it; at the same time, a few specialized readers catch the unobtrusive allusion and get an inexpensive little thrill out of squeezing more juice from the same lemon.

Now I'll look up *mutatis mutandis.* It means "with all due adjustments." Yeah. We have to make allowances for writers who like to fool around.

Down by the Old Mainstream

"Kennedy and Johnson were both mainstream Democrats," wrote Richard Nixon in a recent memo to George Bush, explaining why he thought liberal pundits were misreading the parallels to the 1960 campaign. "They had no significant differences on issues such as strengthening the economy, defending the United States, or fighting the spread of Communism."

Then the man narrowly defeated by the Kennedy-Johnson ticket drew his distinction for students of the 1988 campaign, identifying vice presidential candidate Lloyd Bentsen as "a mainstream Democrat. But Dukakis definitely is not." Rather, the presidential nominee was called a member of "the McGovern-Mondale wing of the Democratic party."

In this leaked analysis (not to me, I only know what I read in the papers—or, to be pedantic rather than idiomatic, I know only what I read in the papers), the former President focused on the word *mainstream.*

Jesse Jackson did, too. When accused of being out of the mainstream, he said his critics were correct. "The mainstream is too narrow, too elitist," he said. "What we need is a broad river. You get your yachts on the mainstream. We need a river wide enough for a big boat with a lot of people."

That daringly turned the metaphor of the majority upside down. In John Milton's 1667 *Paradise Lost,* the poet first used the collocation (found together, but not yet joined) to mean "principal, most": "The neather Flood . . . now divided into four main Streames." The first figurative sense of the phrase was used by Thomas Carlyle in 1831, writing of "the Didactic Tendency . . . admitting that it still forms the main stream . . . is no longer so pre-eminent."

The word came to mean "centrist, or reflecting the prevailing culture or attitudes of the majority," and was used in politics as a synonym for the tired "middle of the road." In June of 1963, President John F. Kennedy told the Irish Parliament in Dublin: "Ireland is moving in the mainstream of current world events."

A month later, New York Governor Nelson Rockefeller, competing with Barry Goldwater for leadership of the Republican party, charged that "well-drilled extremist elements boring within the party" were "wholly alien to the broad middle course that accommodates the mainstream of Republican principle."

At the 1964 Republican National Convention in San Francisco, I recall helping to carry across the floor a thirty-foot banner urging the party to "Stay in the Mainstream." That was when Senator Goldwater moved it sharply rightward with his memorable "extremism in the defense of liberty is no vice." (While the convention roared its approval at this rejection of mainstreamism, Richard Nixon sat in his front-row box and refused to rise or applaud.)

The word has moved beyond politics. The gerund *mainstreaming* is applied to the education of gifted, handicapped or retarded children with others closer to the norm, and the training of handicapped workers alongside the more fortunate. Paul Goldberger, architecture critic at *The New York Times,* wrote of the architect Frank Gehry that he "has been neatly positioned in the last few years at the edge of the mainstream, neither too commercial nor too much the eccentric."

The noun was used adjectivally in the early 1970's in the phrase *mainstream smoke,* meaning "the smoke passing through the length of a cigarette or cigar," as against *sidestream smoke,* which just drifts off the tip.

Now it is applied to politics to mean "the dominant course." Although we now see it can be attacked for not being wide enough, it modifies the place where elections are won.

Drop That Card

Creepy-looking guy sidles up to you and whispers, "Wanna buy a pornographic record?"

You reply cheerfully, "I'd love to, sir, but I don't have a pornograph."

That joke doesn't work with young audiences because the pun plays on a word—*phonograph*—that is rapidly disappearing, and soon will exist only in the minds of people who used to read Big Little Books and listen to Victrolas while chewing Beeman's Pepsin Gum or nibbling India nuts. (Whatever

happened to India nuts? Readers with fond memories of disappeared products are invited to send the memories to this department for an article on the vocabulary of nostalgia.)

Although *phonography* never made it the way *photography* did, a related term—*pornography,* from the Greek *porne,* "harlot"—is doing fine as a noun, with its adjective *pornographic.* A clipped form, *porno,* is used as an adjective (*porno* flick) and, when clipped further, to *porn,* is the shortened form of the noun *pornography.* That word, in all its forms, is used only in a pejorative sense. If you are condemning *smut,* you call what you see *pornographic;* if you are defending *sexually explicit material,* you call it *adult fare* for audiences so *mature* as to be jaded.

This came to mind in reviewing a file on a hyphenated term that has been thrust into the 1988 presidential campaign.

Robert Scheer of the *Los Angeles Times* was interviewing Michael Dukakis on the subject of pornography. When the Democratic candidate took a somewhat restrictive position, associating himself with Supreme Court Justice Potter Stewart's "I know it when I see it" subjective decision, the reporter asked sharply: "Are you endorsing the work of the Meese Commission?"

"No, no, no, no," said the candidate, who apparently did not want to be identified with the intensely antipornographic views of the commission headed by then Attorney General Edwin L. Meese 3d. "Look, I'm a card-carrying member of the American Civil Liberties Union and I think you have to be very restrained," he said about the prospect of censorship, "but I'm not somebody who takes the position that under no circumstances can society impose restrictions on material that, by any standard, is clearly porno-graphic."

His statement, in context, shows Governor Dukakis trying to be a reason-able or moderate civil libertarian, aware of the need to protect freedom of speech, but drawing the line when it comes to outright smut, which we all know when we see it.

But Governor Dukakis made an error that came back to haunt him. As he very carefully avoided the appearance of being "soft" on smut-peddling, he thoughtlessly used *card-carrying* in a way that dealt a hot card into the hands of his opponents.

That noun-participle compound was born in the 40's to describe a specific card: the one carried by members of the Communist party. Its first citation appeared in 1948, according to Merriam-Webster, when the reporter Bert Andrews used it in his book *Washington Witch Hunt:* "The most dangerous Communists in the nation today are not the open, avowed, card-carrying party members."

In that early usage, the modifier meant "overt" in contrast to "secret" or "covert"; it came to mean "unequivocal" to the point of "defiant," and ultimately "authentic, genuine," but always conveying the additional mean-ing of "unabashed, unapologetic" when used admiringly, or "shameless, arrant" when used critically. To Senator Joseph R. McCarthy in the early 1950's, *card-carrying Communist* was an alliteratively emphatic way of dif-ferentiating a "real" Communist—a dues-paying member of the political party—from a *fellow traveler,* or one who generally agrees with the party's aims. (That comes from a Leon Trotsky remark in the 1920's derogating some foot-dragging Russian authors: "They are not the artists of the proletarian revolution, but only its artistic fellow travelers [*poputchiki*].")

In *card-carrying,* then, we had a modifier willing and able to make its way into the general language but carrying political baggage labeled "explosive." When modifying a nonpolitical noun—*card-carrying redneck, card-carrying genius, card-carrying member of the baby-boom generation*—it meant "au-thentic, unmistakable," almost "rootin'-tootin' "; but when used in any ideo-logical setting, it had old leftist overtones that resonated.

That meant, to avoid offense or smear, the modifier could be used only with a rightist noun. "The socialist left and the card-carrying capitalists will find it equally objectionable," wrote *The Economist* in 1975; that magazine also liked to identify William Simon as "a card-carrying capitalist," which the then-Secretary of the Treasury could only find flattering. In 1983, Senator Jake Garn, Republican of Utah, proudly proclaimed himself "a card-carrying conservative."

When used that way, with a right-leaning noun, the modifier could not be considered objectionable; it meant only "authentic," and its baggage was nullified or reflected a nicely oxymoronic irony.

But people in politics remembered the Communist history of the word and were careful not to apply it to a left-leaning noun. A *card-carrying hawk* offended nobody, but a *card-carrying dove* was an insult. A *card-carrying capitalist* was a salute, but a *card-carrying liberal* was a slur.

Nobody could call the at-least-slightly-left-of-center Michael Dukakis a card-carrying anything, in light of this unspoken rule; anybody who did would have been engaging in a McCarthyite smear, which invites opprobrium. Nobody, that is, except Governor Dukakis himself.

In that *Los Angeles Times* interview, when he used the term to mean "authentic," he opened the way for George Bush to respond with glee: "He says, 'I am a card-carrying member of the A.C.L.U.' Well, I am not and I never will be." The American Civil Liberties Union, which defends the most unpopular causes on constitutional grounds, had been savaged by Ed Meese as "the criminals' lobby" and is perceived by many as leftist, although some card-carrying hard-liners and right-wingers identify themselves proudly as civil libertarians, resistant to governmental intrusion on individual rights. That leftist perception, though shallow, is widespread.

The cat was out of the bag: Mr. Dukakis had described himself as *card-carrying,* and now others could belabor him with that as well. It sanitized what would otherwise be widely condemned as an unfair and objectionable imputation of Communist associations. (Note: the A.C.L.U. happily issues membership cards, which are giving a certain cachet. If you dare to join, write to the A.C.L.U., 132 West 43d Street, New York, NY 10036.)

Pass the Indian Nuts

Yesterlingo is the fondly remembered language of the recent past. Nostalgia may not be what it used to be, as Simone Signoret suggested in the title of her autobiography, but the ghost words of our youth haunt us still.

In a recent piece, I wondered whatever became of *India nuts,* those tiny nuts we bit open to get at a kernel that wasn't worth the work. I can hear it

now: the relentless cracking sounds around me in the cheap back-balcony seats at the Loews 83d Street movie house.

"They were known as *Indian nuts*," reports Joe Pollack of St. Louis, "or, by their correct name of *piñon nuts*," or *pine nuts*, from the Southwestern *pinyon* tree. Other correspondents, misty-eyed at the recollection, suggest that the term came from Native Americans, or Indians, who gathered and sold the nuts in the Southwestern United States. That may have influenced the spelling of the term, but I think that *Indian* in this phrase is a corruption of *pinyon*. At any rate, it's not "India" nuts; I had broken the phrase by ear, mistakenly losing an *n*, much as I once did with Guy Lombardo, thinking the band leader's first name was Guylom.

The names of vanished products, or at least products that are no longer advertised the way they used to be, make up a part of the lexicon of yester-lingo. "All my age cohorts [*sic*—should be "all members of my age cohort"] fondly recall the fat cylinders of ice cream called *Mello-Rolls*," writes Ruth B. Roufberg of Kendall Park, New Jersey. "They were wrapped in two overlapping strips of paper, which, when pulled from opposite directions, exposed the cylinder and neatly deposited it into the ice-cream cone."

Funny how so many people miss Mello-Rolls. "When you licked the ice cream," explains Patricia Maloney Bernstein of Great Neck, Long Island, "the roll shape caused it to turn round in its cone, so as the ice cream melted it did not run down the outside of the cone, but rather melted within the cone, running down into the hollow in the handle."

Gone. Gone not only with the wind, but with *wax lips* and *wax buck teeth* and *charlotte russe* and *barley candy* and *button candy* on a long strip of white paper and *licorice whips,* and *Beeman's Pepsin Gum, Walnettos* and *Sen-Sen.* Where have all the *Jujubes* gone? Lean your head back on the antimacassar and dream of *jawbreakers.* To cool your thirst, *Moxie* is still around.

I'm tired of all the brans and fibers; bring back *Force* and *Pep.* Austin Hamel of Pound Ridge, New York, wants his *Wings, Spuds* and *Twenty Grand* cigarettes, but will settle for *Continental Balsa Wood Model Airplane* kits because he got a kick out of sniffing that glue. I washed the "dope" off my fingers with *Kirkman's* soap and *Swan* soap, rarely *Fairy* soap. (It had the slogan "Have you a little Fairy in your home?" They're not writing slogans like that anymore.)

Frank Ford of Jacksonville, Florida, still goes into a drugstore hoping to find *Seidlitz powders, Antiphlogistine Plasters, spirits of niter* (for his stomach), *Freezon* (for his corns) and a tube of *Ipana.* And while you're there, pick up *BC Headache powders* for the *grippe,* some *Argyrol* and a *Venida* hairnet.

Go try to find *flypaper.* (And while we're at it, "Quick, Henry, the *Flit!*" What happened to *Flit*? Where's Henry?) You can't even find a decent *pen-wiper.* These useful items are as hard to come by as *bookstraps* and *skate keys.* My colleague Philip Shabecoff at *The Times* heard I was on this kick and sent in a list of needs: "milk in glass bottles, pickles in open barrels, penny gliders, cap pistols, sneakers and Big Little Books." The other day we stood in front of the White House and watched the President take off in his modernized *autogyro.*

Kids these days are deprived of *Lincoln Logs* and think *Ringolevio* is a Beatle's full first name. They don't know from *stickball, stoopball, curbball, punchball* or *Johnny-on-the-Pony.* You cannot find a peer-groupie who wears *bobby socks, bobby pins, Cuban heels* or *open-shank shoes* and smiles fetchingly at a boy in *knickers* and *storm shoes.* Nobody gives anybody a *hotfoot.*

What all of this shows is the reflection of life's changes in the language. To stay with-it, we ordinarily report in this space the latest slang and most egregious circumlocution; a look backward makes the same point. Trade names vanish with old clichés; as locomotives pull out of our lives, so do expressions like *all fired up, get up a head of steam, let off steam;* a friendly *put 'er there* changes to *gimme five,* and *mazuma* becomes *bread.*

What happened to *nostalgia* itself? Used to be, the word reflected its Greek roots, *nostos,* "return home," and *algos,* "pain," to mean "severe homesickness." It first appeared in a ship's journal in 1770, which reported that the ship's company was "far gone with the longing for home which the Physicians have gone so far as to esteem a disease under the name of Nostalgia."

That meaning is buried now, sad to say. Thanks to the novelist D. H. Lawrence's use in 1920, in "The Lost Girl"—"the nostalgia of the heathen past was a constant torture to her mediumistic soul"—the word began to mean "wistful memory, melancholy recall of earlier times." No meaning is permanent (sigh).

Here's further amplification of Indian(n) nuts.

Most of the confusion arises from the fact that "pinon" is a misspelling. In the Spanish alphabet the letter "n" (e-ne) is one letter followed by an "n" with a tilde above it, called "enya," which is a different letter. The last syllable of "pinon" [sic] must carry an accent mark over the vowel, as it is an exception to the rule for placing the accent in Spanish pronunciation. As most newspaper fonts make no provision for printing the "enya" or the written accent, "pinyon" better approximates the correct spelling but gives no indication that the accent falls on the last syllable, so some people pronounce it like "pinion."

As there is no way "pi-nyon" can be confused with the word "Indian," I agree with Joe Pollack of St. Louis that they were called Indian nuts because they were gathered by Indians, as they were and still are. The best way to collect them is to locate a pack-rat's hoard—time-saving, but a rather unfair way to treat pack-rats.

By the way, the plural for the nuts (sorry, my typewriter can't spell it correctly, either) is "pi-nyon-es," written accent no longer necessary as the accent in this case falls on the next-to-last syllable, in agreement with the rule.

> Nadine Robinson
> San Diego, California

The President did not take off "in his modernized autogyro (sic)," as you state. Rather, the autogiro, an invention of Juan de la Cierva of Spain (first flight January 9, 1923) was a conventionally powered airplane with stubby wings and a normal propeller in the front. The helicopter-type rotors were not powered but rather windmilled by virtue of the prop's action and the plane's forward momentum.

The modern helicopter with powered rotors was a German invention of the 1930s (Focke-Achgelis FW-61),* but the breakthrough with such a design came with Sikorsky's first flight of the U.S. 300 in September 1939, which eventually led to the President's helicopter of the 1980s.

> Lothar Zeidler
> Rutgers University
> New Brunswick, New Jersey

*The Germans called it "HUBSCHRAUBER," literally "lift-screwer."

Your column was the second reference I'd seen in as many weeks to an autogyro as some kind of helicopter precursor, to helicopters as fancy autogyros. (No, I can't remember who made the first reference.)

Actually, the helicopter came first by far. And the autogyro is basically a relatively conventional airplane with a revolving rather than fixed wing, intended for short (not vertical) takeoffs and landings, since its unpowered but freely revolving "wing" can briefly store, or create, lift thanks to its flywheel effect. The autogyro was an airplane that tried to act like a helicopter—a helicopter without a helicopter's mechanical complications, but also without its capabilities. (How useful is it, after all, to perhaps be able to land at the 60th Street Heliport if you certainly have to be trucked to LaGuardia to take off again?)

Helicopters and autogyros are different approaches to the same concept: that an aircraft's "wing" can create lift by being pulled through the air either by the forward progress of that very airplane, thus speeding the airflow over the wing and creating lift, or by somehow revolving the "wing"—then it becomes a helicopter's or an autogyro's rotor blade—to create lift even if the aircraft is stationary.

*(There's a nice distinction there, by the way. There are air**planes** and air**craft**. Airplanes are all aircraft, but only certain aircraft are airplanes. To be considered an airplane, the device must have a fixed lift-producing "plane"—a wing. Everything else that levitates with the help of some kind of lift rather than pure acceleration—balloons, helicopters, autogyros, blimps, zeppelins, but not golf balls, rockets, bullets or darts—is an air**craft**. But I'll bet you already know that.)*

*Anyway, the helicopter dates back to da Vinci, who intuited that with a screwlike rotor somehow powered from within the craft, he could auger his vehicle into the air, a huge Renaissance Black & Decker. It remained for Igor Sikorsky, already a noted designer of Russian air**planes** big enough to be the jumbos of their day, to realize that da Vinci's screwing force would have to be counteracted by an opposing tail rotor. If it wasn't, the screw might stand still when it met the air's resistance while da Vinci and his fellow passengers spun into dizziness in the craft's cabin. Igor invented the practical helicopter, although it took him until the late 1930s to prove it.*

*The Spaniard Juan de la Cierva took a different tack when he postulated the autogyro in the early 1920s. An autogyro is an air**plane** with its planes— wings—mounted as a free-spinning pinwheel on a mast above the fuselage. Once the normal propeller and engine in the nose (normal for the era when Cierva was dreaming and inventing) dragged the autogyro's quite conventional but wingless fuselage along the runway a sufficient distance, the pinwheel set to spinning vigorously from the force of the airstream and consequently lifted the machine. (Trust me. It wasn't quite that simple, but it worked.)*

The real difference between Cierva's autogyro and both a true airplane and a helicopter was simply that the autogyro's wing rotated, flinging itself through the air to achieve lift, solely as a consequence of the airplane's forward motion. No forward motion, no lift. Or at least rapidly diminishing lift as the rotor spun down, since nothing powered it but the pinwheel effect. A helicopter has an engine-driven rotor and thus can hover in one spot; its forward motion has little to do with the rotor's lift.

So it's less of a leap, technically speaking, to watch the President take off from Andrews in Air Force One—think of it as an autogyro with wings—than it is to imagine that Igor's Sikorsky flailing off the White House lawn is a "modernized autogyro." If you put a pair of conventional wings on an autogyro and sawed off the rotors, it would fly quite normally. Put wings on a rotorless helicopter and all you'd have would be a large, noisy, stationary power plant.

I fly a wide variety of airplanes but no other aircraft. There's something reassuring about large, fixed, solid, stable wings, and it's no coincidence that the final fastener holding everything together atop a helicopter's enormously complex rotor mast is called the Jesus Nut.

> Stephan Wilkinson
> Cornwall-on-Hudson,
> New York

You write that "Nobody gives anybody a hotfoot."

Wrong!

When not pitching for the New York Mets, Roger McDowell keeps his unappreciative teammates on their toes throughout the season by delivering one of the most blazing hotfoots on record.

> Robert H. Spero
> Great Neck, New York

Did you really play "curbball" once upon a time, long long ago when coffee sold for a nickel a pound and Nelson Rockefeller was poor? I have my doubts. On 100th Street and West End Avenue in those ancient days, we played "curve ball." Who knew from curbs?

Another question: Why were you permitted to sit in the back balcony at the Loews 83d? My friends and I were imprisoned in the Children's Section, closely watched over by the Matron and her dreaded flashlight. (Hm, now that I think of it, what ever happened to the Children's Section?)

> Aben Rudy
> Randolph, New Jersey

Drug-War Lingo

In the *crackdown* on *crack* and other drugs, there may be no *magic bullet,* but *drug kingpins, narco-terrorists* and even *casual users*—not to mention *carpers* on the sidelines—can expect *zero tolerance.*

This is the lingo of drug warfare. The nation is hooked on it (we are all linguistic junkies), and because there is no getting this particular monkey off our backs, let's at least dig up the derivations of the phrases being pushed in the discourse of drug dudgeon.

In the early days, about three generations back, we had *hopheads* ("hop" for *opium*) and *dope fiends* ("dope" from the Dutch *doop* for "sauce" or "dip," referring to the sticky opiate). The Standard English covering these slang terms is *user,* in contrast to *pusher.*

"To the so-called '*casual user*' " was the beginning of a warning by President Bush in March of 1989 to *recreational users,* a phrase chosen by some drug users to differentiate themselves from addictive users. *Casual user* is not rooted exclusively in the drug culture; the phrase can be found in a 1976 *Business Week* story about a computer system "not geared for the *casual user*"; other early citations also point to popularization by computer whizzes derogating those of us in the nonserious software crowd. Crossover use was natural: Mary Jane Hatcher, the widow of a murdered law officer, said, "We middle-class suburban Americans, we *casual users* . . . must accept blame. . . ."

(Curiously, *casual*—rooted in the Latin for "chance"—has a military sense, first as a clipped form of *casualty,* later as a soldier in temporary status on the way to another station. The use of *casual* in the 1593 term *casual poor,* for those who drift in and out of poverty, has been carried over into *casual labor,* used for transient or migratory workers since 1852.)

"American cocaine users need to understand that our nation has *zero tolerance* for casual drug use," said the President in his September 5 speech outlining what he labeled his "drug strategy."

Zero is from the Arabic *sifr;* the first citation for *zero tolerance* in the Barnhart Books files is from a 1958 *Science Newsletter:* "A good example of the care taken to protect against pesticide poisoning is the minimum tolerance set for milk: zero. . . . Recently, *zero tolerance* was set for methoxychlor and malathion." In the Nixon White House, H. R. (Bob) Haldeman was known for demanding *zero mistakes,* and the *zero tolerance* phrase was popularized in the drug world by William von Raab, then United States Customs chief, when he sought last year to impound yachts that had even a single marijuana cigarette aboard. Lately, *zero* has become an emphatic way to say "no": Margarine makers promise "zero cholesterol," and economists warn of "zero growth." The word has been bombing ever since the atomic age's "ground zero," and one of these days I will zero in on it.

A *narc* was long the slang name for a narcotics law enforcement officer, rooted in the Greek *narke,* "numbness, stiffness, stupor," but now the first two syllables of *narcotics* are frequently found in longer terms. Like *klepto-* and *crypto-, pseudo-* and *porno-, narco-* is a combining form, which can now be applied to anything in the illicit drug trade. Nestor K. Ikeda, reporting from Lima for the Associated Press in 1982, attributed the coinage of *narco-terrorism* to Fernando Belaúnde Terry, at that time Peru's President, who was describing a union of drug dealers and political terrorists. In his Democratic response to President Bush's message, Senator Joseph R. Biden Jr. lashed out at *narco-terrorism,* which had been used on the cover of *Newsweek* that week.

Kingpin seems to be the only acceptable term for drug bigshots, just as *vice overlord* was once the only title journalists permitted for a leader of the prostitution racket. Disagreement rages among etymologists about the metaphoric origin.

One school holds that *kingpin* comes from the sport of bowling. In the game of kayles, played with a set of ninepins, the tallest pin was called the *kingpin.* In modern bowling, the kingpin is the pin numbered 5 and is surrounded by the other pins.

Some dictionaries, even some bowling aficionados, have been using *headpin* as a synonym, but this is confusing; the headpin is the pin numbered 1, placed at the head of the triangle of pins.

If you are right-handed and hook your ball (thereby causing it to curve slightly to the left), the best place to aim is between the headpin (the number 1 pin) and the pin to its right facing you (the number 3 pin); this will allow the bowling ball to crash into the kingpin, directly behind the headpin, perhaps leading to a strike and waking the pin boy if the alley is not automated. (There will be mail on this paragraph from irate expert bowlers, who should be reminded that *bowler* was the name for an opium smoker, taken from the bowl of the smoker's pipe. I am not without defenses.)

Other lexicographers argue that *kingpin* is akin to *kingbolt,* which was in use as early as 1825 for the main bolt in a machine. The *Oxford English Dictionary* holds that this is the sense that led to meanings of "that which holds together any complex system or arrangement" and "the most important or outstanding person in a party, organization, etc.," as first used in *Harper's Weekly* in 1867: "His best position was as a batter. He was a 'King-pin' there."

Crack (originally, the word referred to a noise) is recent. The term for pellet-sized pieces of cocaine prepared for smoking was just becoming popular when the 1986 *Slang and Jargon of Drugs and Drink* was being printed, and was not included. The author, Richard A. Spears, professor of linguistics at Northwestern University, suggests a clue to the etymology in the entry for *crystal.*

"What is now called *crack* was known as *crystallized cocaine* in the early medical days, and that hard form is still known as *rock.* There's no definitive evidence," says Professor Spears, "but it makes sense that *crack* comes from the physical cracking of those rocks and crystals—literally, the crackling sound of those rocks as they are broken up."

Crackdown, the sudden introduction of severe discipline, is not all that old, either. The noun made its first appearance in a May 18, 1935, *Washington Post* story about punishment planned for liberals who wanted to abolish public-utility holding companies.

When pledging a crackdown on crack kingpins and narco-terrorists, zero-tolerant drug strategists are careful to refrain from promising a cure-all. "There is no *magic bullet,*" said William J. Bennett, director of national drug-control policy. (He is called a *czar,* and claims he calls his wife the *czarina* and his children *czardines.*) This was a reference to the German bacteriologist Paul Ehrlich, who was seeking a treatment for the scourge of syphilis and discovered the drug *arsphenamine,* better known by its trademark name *Salvarsan,* or by the number *606,* which was its numerical order in a series of experiments.

Dr. Ehrlich, who shared the Nobel Prize in 1908 for his work in immunology, is credited with having first used the term *magic bullet* (in German, *Zauberkugel*) to mean that ideal therapeutic agent that destroys unhealthy cells while sparing healthy tissues. The phrase was popularized in the United States in the title of the 1940 movie about his life, starring Edward G. Robinson. (A related phrase, *silver bullet,* was a talisman thought to ward off werewolves and vampires, and was modified as a kind of trademark by the radio cowboy "The Lone Ranger.")

Today, a *magic bullet* is a cure without side effects, and can be applied to any headaches, from air pollution to the economy. However, the phrase is almost always used in the negative, in cautioning against over-optimism, as in "This is no *magic bullet,* but . . ."

President Bush characterized critics of his program as partisan *carpers* who are intent on hiking taxes. That is an old noun now heard infrequently. Robert Browning used it in his 1868 *The Ring and the Book:* "Carpers abound in this misjudging world."

We are more familiar with the verb *carp,* which means "find fault, complain without reason"; this is from the Old Norse *karpa,* "to boast, brag," influenced by the Latin *carpere,* "to pluck, gather," which led to the sense of "to slander" as one snatches the reputation of another. The have-tux, will-cavil verb is not connected with the freshwater fish of the same name, first reported in the West by the sixth-century Roman statesman Cassiodorus as swimming in the Danube, and best known today for its use in the making of gefilte fish.

As a recovering cocaine addict and former expert in the art of freebase from the time before crack, I can probably indicate to you more accurately from whence this term derives than could your linguistics professor.

As anyone who has ever cooked base can tell you, the sound made by the cocaine when the oil ball hardens (in the baking soda version of the cooking process, which contrary to popular belief was used long before crack was sold as such) is more aptly described as a "crack" than any other sound I know. It is the sound that indicates that the stuff is ready to be smoked, and the capitalists who decided to sell readymade freebase thus probably thought it to be the perfect name. Just thinking about it makes me taste cocaine—so it's off to a meeting for me and perhaps a correction for you of your etymology of this word. When rocks of base are broken up, there is little or no sound.

[Name Withheld]

I was surprised to see you accept the folk-etymology derivation of "nark" from "narcotics officer." The word "nark" existed in mid-nineteenth-century criminal slang at a time when there were no laws regulating the possession or use of drugs. The OED offers several citations from the 1860's, with a meaning of "police informer" or "detective." There seems to be no reason to doubt the derivation from Romany "nak," "nose."

Jonathan Towle
New York, New York

You quote this passage from a 1958 Science Newsletter:

> *A good example of the care taken to protect against pesticide poisoning is the minimum tolerance set for milk: zero.*

While you zero in on the phrase "zero tolerance," you leave unscathed the very curious notion of "minimum tolerance" to denote the largest amount that can be tolerated. This use is so common now that no one, not even you, gives it a second thought, but it does need scathing. When tolerances are set—so many pbb (parts per billion) of pesticide, or one mouse excrement per bread stick—the intention clearly is that this is the maximum amount that will be allowed. A maximum tolerance sets the upper limit of a contaminant; a "minimum tolerance" can only mean that there must be at least one mouse excrement per bread stick to make the product legally marketable.

This is not the only case where mathematical and scientific illiteracy has stood the meaning of a word on its head. "Quantum leap" is now widely used to mean a large and dramatic change. Apart from its traditional (and now archaic) use for "sum" or "quantity" (cf. OED for uses since 1619), the term "quantum" was added to the language by the German physicist Max Planck (1858–1947) to denote a minimum, indivisible quantity of energy. In the special case of radiant energy, that smallest possible packet is called a photon. The analogy is to the pre-Rutherford atom as the smallest (and then supposedly indivisible) amount of matter. The quantum is the tiniest imaginable (albeit discontinuous) change. There is no excuse to let it stand for the exact opposite.

Curt W. Beck
Professor of Chemistry
Vassar College
Poughkeepsie, New York

I assume that Dr. Ehrlich's zauberkugel is the same operatic reference I had assumed everybody else is making in the modern citations. In Carl Maria von

Weber's 1821 romantic opera <u>Der Freischütz</u> ("The Free Shooter") the bullets are referred to in the libretto as <u>freikugeln</u> (free shooting bullets), but seemingly everybody who speaks, or more importantly <u>writes</u> about the opera refers to them as "magic bullets." Their magical quality is that no matter how you aim the gun they will hit and kill the specific prey you had in mind. Since (I am told) in Germany productions of <u>Der Freischütz</u> are as ubiquitous as <u>Carmen</u>, <u>La Bohème</u>, or <u>Madama Butterfly</u> are here, I believe that my assumption about Dr. Ehrlich's reference is well founded.

Dov Treiman
Johnson City, New York

Dry's New High

"Kazuyoshi Takei, barkeep at a watering hole in the Ginza," went the bright lead on a story from Tokyo by Fred Hiatt of *The Washington Post*, "admitted that the word *dry* used to conjure nothing but dry cleaning in his mind. That was before the 'dry boom' hit Japan, before 'the dry wars' began. . . ."

The Japanese bartender's problem was that he could not get enough "dry beer" from the Asahi Brewery to satisfy his customers. That is not what Americans call a "light beer," which is reduced not only in calories but also in alcohol content; on the contrary, the adjective *dry* is used to mean a sharper taste with a slightly higher alcohol content.

Americans—New Yorkers, especially—have associated the word *dry* with beer ever since the singing commercial (to the tune of a German drinking song) that went "My beer is Rheingold, the dry beer." (As a press agent, in my youth, it was my idiot's delight to accompany a group of models called the Rheingold Girls to the Oktoberfest in Munich; Who knew, then, that a fortune could be made with dry beer in Japan?)

The use of *dry* to describe a liquid is curious, because the essential meaning of *dry* is the absence of liquid. A synonym, *arid,* was taken up in the naming of an antiperspirant. *Dry milk* is dehydrated; *dry cereal* has no milk on it, not even dehydrated; *dry gas,* the etymologist Sol Steinmetz informs me, is natural gas without liquid hydrocarbon.

The figurative sense is also "with vital juices missing": a *dry run* is only a trial, or a practice firing without live ammunition, and a *dry lease* is the rental of an aircraft without crew or maintenance team. A *dry hole* is a well drilled for naught, and its figurative sense can be found in old Watergate transcripts, which I keep next to my copy of the Dead Sea Scrolls: "JOHN DEAN: I don't think they ever got anything. THE PRESIDENT: A *dry hole*? DEAN: That's right."

Where, then, did we get *dry* to describe a liquid? Probably from the French *sec,* used in English since the 1800's to describe a wine that is not sweet; in English, the contrast is most apparent in the designation of vermouth as sweet (used in a cocktail called the manhattan, if anybody remembers it) or dry (as used in the martini). Thus, *sweet* obtained a new antonym: not *bitter,* or *sour,* but *dry.*

Dry had a good run in American politics to describe those favoring the prohibition of the sale of alcoholic beverages, with Al Smith running in 1928 as an outspoken "wet." Today, only *wet* survives, as a British description of a politician favoring a relaxation of the sort of monetary discipline espoused by Prime Minister Thatcher. A *wringing wet* is a softie in other matters as well.

Some liquids are "wet," i.e., they contain relatively high amounts of water, evaporate slowly; and, should you, say, spill some on your hands, they feel "wet."

On the other hand, some liquids, among them acetone, methyl-ethyl-keytone, and good British gin, are by nature "dry." They evaporate freely; contain no water; are aromatic; and, theoretically, feel "dry" in comparison to water. A cloth soaked with acetone, for instance, does not get "wet" in the same manner that water "wets" it. The wrinkles don't come out, and in a matter of seconds the acetones will have totally evaporated, leaving the scrap basically cleaner but otherwise untouched. Acetone and other "dry" liquids are noted for their grease-cutting properties. I personally call gin "Phlem-Cutter." Think "DRY CLEANING."

Ian C. Short
Edinboro, Pennsylvania

Dry cereal, also known as cold cereal, requires no water to be made ready to eat. (Corn Flakes, Cheerios, Shredded Wheat, etc.) Hot cereal has to be prepared by mixing with water and bringing to a boil. (Oatmeal, Wheatena, Cream of Wheat, etc.) The water makes it "wet" although the term is not used. Either kind of cereal may be eaten with milk, or not, but that has nothing to do with the distinction or the meaning of dry in this context. Maybe you don't eat cereal for breakfast. Obviously you don't prepare breakfasts.

James Tobin
New Haven, Connecticut

I wonder what made you think that "My beer is Rheingold, the dry beer," that famous singing commercial of yesteryear, was sung "to the tune of a German drinking song." That tune is actually the main theme of Emil Waldteufel's 1883 waltz "Estudiantina" (according to Andrew Lamb's liner notes for a recent recording, itself based on a Spanish duet of that title by Paul Lacombe). I suppose the advertising slogan's rhythm called for a Hispanic tune—or perhaps the well-known propensity of the rain in Spain to stay mainly on the plain was deemed to be a fitting tribute to that beer's dryness.

Harry Zohn
Professor of German
Brandeis University
Waltham, Massachusetts

Gotcha! In today's column you note parenthetically, "As a press agent, in my youth, it was my . . ."
    As I am sure you are aware, this says that "it" was a press agent! The

sentence should have been recast or should have said, "As a press agent, in my youth, I . . ."

Peter Singer
Riverdale, New York

You wrote, "As a press agent, in my youth, it was my idiot's delight to accompany a group of models . . ." That opening prepositional phrase has nothing logical to modify. I suspect that the dangler resulted from your desire to use "idiot's delight" and the inefficient expletive construction that you devised to accommodate the phrase. A perfectly simple and straightforward "I accompanied a group of models" would have avoided the error.

Carl Ladensack
Lancaster, Pennsylvania

Eat Your Peas

"I hate my mother-in-law," muttered the cannibal.
  The cook sternly pointed to the plate and said: "At least eat your peas."

This hoary joke, a mean-spirited slur at both mothers-in-law and canni-bals, is evidence of a longtime derogation of a vegetable as something unpal-atable to young people: good for you, but requiring some persuasion to eat—wholesome, nourishing. BOR-ing.

E. B. White's caption for a 1928 *New Yorker* cartoon drawn by Carl Rose expressed the same idea:

"It's broccoli, dear."

"I say it's spinach, and I say the hell with it."

The *pea* is a back-formation from the Middle English *pease,* which was mistakenly thought to be a plural. It wasn't a plural—*pease* was like *porridge,* an edible mess in a dish—but enough speakers of the language thought of it as the plural form of *pea* that the back-formation took place and what we now call *peas* is thought of as the plural.

The same change is now taking place with the Greek word *kudos,* which means "praise." Many people who do not speak Greek mistakenly assume *kudos,* a singular noun pronounced "KU-dose," to be a plural pronounced "KU-doze." Acting on that misconception, they back-form a singular *kudo.* One "kudo" is like the sound of one hand clapping, and upsets purists, but the bastard back-formation is coming into the language same as the pea.

Kids who enjoy eating peas are named Rollo; most red-blooded kids hate peas, or pretend to, because they know the vegetable is good for them. This has led to the linguistic use of peas-eating as a requirement: "Remember that carrots make your hair curly," the food writer Sarah Fritschner ironically advised in *The Washington Post* in 1982, "and if you don't eat your peas, you get no dessert."

The direction to eat peas is resented not only as imperious, but boring. In the *Los Angeles Times* last year, Judith Michaelson quoted Lynne V. Cheney, chairman of the National Endowment for the Humanities, criticizing the prosaic quality of elementary readers used in today's schools: "They string sentences together about how to find a job, how to read the telephone books, how to eat your peas."

The reader now has eyes narrowed: What is all this seemingly disconnected background preparing us for?

Only for an appreciation of the best coinage of a compound adjective in the 1988 election campaign. Paul Taylor of *The Washington Post* quoted "a Democratic strategist with ties to the Dukakis campaign" as warning fellow Democrats of a problem their candidate may face: "He can come across as a stern, *eat-your-peas* figure."

That, to my mind, is a glorious use of language. The imperative clause, "Eat your peas," undergoes a functional shift, from verb phrase to hyphen-ated adjective, in the manner of "a *take-charge* guy" or "a *drop-dead* look." The resulting "*eat-your-peas* figure" immediately calls up a picture of un-wanted parental authority, with connotations of "or else" to follow.

Whoever is the coiner is now in a bind: Should he or she indulge his or her passion for semi-anonymity, thereby avoiding the wrath of the Dukakisarians, or should the coiner step forward to receive hosannas from language mavens?

Whoever you are, you have come up with a beaut, which should last long after the heat of this campaign has cooled. But as long as you remain in the shadows, you can have only one kudo.

Your mention of the substance "pease" finally illuminates for me an ancient mystery. During that same childhood period already evoked, we used to play a cross-clapping game, the words of which went, "Pease porridge hot, pease porridge cold, pease porridge in the pot, nine days old." I always thought I was yelling "Peas porridge hot . . . etc.," which, manifestly, would be nonsense. I shall now go make my peace, stir my pease and eat my peas and stop bothering you.

> *Robert O. Vaughn*
> *West New York, New Jersey*

Everyone has a sensitive point, and I take exception to your article on "eat-your-peas politics." Peas are an important member of the pulse family and pulses can be delicious if cooked well. Although they have a high protein content, they do not have harmful side effects such as coronary diseases normally associated with meat and meat products.

You can read about pulses in the Bible (Book of Genesis, Esau selling his rights of first-born against a plate of lentil broth) or in some versions of Cinderella (her stepmother feeding her with green lentils). So, do not underestimate them.

> *Ahmet İlyas Özgüneş*
> *Ankara, Turkey*

Your pronunciation of kudos is open to question. The o is the short Greek o (omicron), not the long o (omega). A purist would pronounce the word koodoss (see Webster's Second International Dictionary), not kyoodose.

> *Jean Holzworth*
> *New Preston, Connecticut*

I was stunned to read your phrase as to whether someone should ". . . step forward to receive hosannas from language mavens."

Quite apart from the improper plural ending, you are evidently using "hosan-

nas" (sic) as a synonym for "kudos" (the improper use of which was your subject to begin with). Hosanna is, of course, a transcription of the Hebrew "Hosha'na" meaning (more or less) "Oh, save our souls." It is thus a desperate cry for help addressed to the Almighty and never a shout of joy or admiration. To employ the term as some sort of cheers is therefore quite wrong, although I must admit that you appear to be in very distinguished company: In fact, most if not all composers of Christian religious works have set Hosanna to rousing, exultant music (see, e.g., the last part of Bach's B Minor Mass or of Mozart's K.427 in C Minor). The only exception known to me is the Choral Mass by Liszt, where the words are sung in appropriately anguished and beseeching tones.

> *Meir Leker*
> *Paris, France*

How come "a mean-spirited slur at mothers-in-law and cannibals"? On or upon, surely? Not even ½ a kudo for that.

> *Heyward Cutting*
> *Concord, Massachusetts*

Your recent piece on "Eat Your Peas" reminded me of my favorite misplaced plural.

You are, I am sure, familiar with the Arthur Kober stories about the Jewish family in the Bronx that were a staple of The New Yorker and subsequently appeared in book form (Thunder Over the Bronx). I recall in one story the mother asked her daughter Bella for a "Kleeneck." Bella said "Ma, it's Kleenex." To which Ma replied, "Yeah, I know, but I only want one."

> *John M. Wilkoff*
> *Pleasantville, New York*

The Elision Fields

"*Gunna* (sometimes *gonna*) is epidemic in spoken English," reads a postcard from John Jakes, the novelist. "I hear it in everyday conversation (my own included, alas). I hear it from esteemed TV commentators. It will be in the dictionary soon."

Ommina do something about such elision right now. The English words are *going to,* but people have been running those words together for a long time. In Scotland, citations of *ganna* and *gaunna* date back to 1806, and in the United States we have the novelist Clarence Edward Mulford's use in a 1913 Hopalong Cassidy story: "Yo're gonna get a good lickin'."

Readers other than Mr. Jakes have asked, "Whaddya think about this?" I say, "Gimme a break." I dunno; it's sorta rough, but language mavens gotta take a stand, even though alotadatime we don't wanna. Shoulda stood in bed. Coulda been a contenduh.

Today's epidemic of elision was helped along by those of us who write fiction. In *North and South,* Mr. Jakes is careful to keep his elisions within quotation marks: "I'm sure, Cap'n," says a farmer in his novel, and a stevedore calls a young soldier a "sojer boy." That's because novelists writing dialogue like to convey the actual sounds made by their characters.

Stephen Crane, in his *Maggie, a Girl of the Streets,* in 1896 pioneered *wanna* in literature with "I didn' wanna give 'im no stuff." The spelling is designed to recreate the way the spoken word pounds, shapes and knocks about the original words.

Every novelist has to work out the problem of dialect in dialogue. Does the author show disrespect for the characters, or racial or religious or social bias, by portraying their speech as it really is? Does the author insult readers by forcing them to read the transcribed dialect, rather than hint at it at first and then let readers do their own transpositions as they go along?

I ought to point this out: If you, dear reader, mentally pronounce what you read, then you probably pronounced the words *ought to* at the start of this sentence as "oughta"; most of us do, except when the two words end the sentence, at which point we do what we ought to. (You probably pronounced that concluding *to* as a clear "to" and not as an elided schwa.)

That means that novelists need not always specify exactly the way their characters sound; authors often depend on readers to supply the elisions, as well as the dropped *g*'s, in their own heads.

We come now to the first issue of elision: Do writers contribute to everybody's sloppiness in speech by recording the sounds of speech, thereby legitimizing the elided words by giving them a spelling? I think not; the Yankee dialect *yep* is one word, the New York *yop* is another, and the Standard English word *yes* does not flavorfully represent either.

The second issue is this: Outside of quoted dialogue, should we make an effort to resist the trend toward elision, accelerated by the spelling-out of the melded words? I think so; to some degree in speech, and to a much greater degree in the written word, we ought to, not *oughta,* give crisp clarity a shot.

Why? Not because *Ommina,* or the New York variant *Onganna,* is less clear in meaning than the Standard English "I'm going to," but because Standard English is worth preserving. It's important to have something solid to deviate from.

Henceforth, I will eschew such observations as *I dunno* in my prose; it not only contributes to the legitimization of elision, but also it's cutesy. I have a highly literate, articulate readership and can depend on them, when they see "I don't know," to internally mumble *I dunno.*

Let's not get hung up over this. In some instances, elision creates a useful word. Take the burgeoning *wannabe,* a new noun and adjective, which is the would-be replacement for *would-be.*

Donald Trump was described by the magazine *7 Days* as "the *wannabe* airline mogul." In *The New York Times,* Michael Gross wrote of money spent on clothing "by people surfers call '*wannabes.*' They don't surf but they want to, so they dress the part. . . ." A frequent usage for imitative singers is "Madonna *wannabes.*" And *The Christian Science Monitor* asked: "Do some 'black nationalists' have their own bigotry against what they call 'wannabes'—light-skinned blacks who allegedly '*wanna be*' like whites?"

The new word implies more insistent yearning than *would-be,* and usually has a connotation less dishonest than *imitation, bogus, sham;* it is never to be confused with *unreal,* which has a dialect sense of "terrific." In the synonymy of those hopefuls waiting in the wings, *wannabe* is eager to force its way in. In a *Times* review of *When Harry Met Sally . . . ,* Caryn James put down the film as "a perfectly pleasant Woody Allen *wannabe,* full of canned romance."

I tried out the plural of *wannabe* myself not long ago, describing the Washington Establishment as "an amalgam of officeholders, power brokers, *wannabies,* ustabies, think-tankers and a legion of world-weary thumbsuckers." In this foray, I amended the spelling to *wannabies,* to get the *ee* sound of the plural, which may be doubtful in *wannabes.*

This change met with no success; the only person who noticed wrote that we did not need "neologistic wannabes." (I still say that looks like *wan nabes,* or pale neighborhood theaters, but I withdraw my suggestion: The plural is *wannabes,* and on that analogy, the latest word for has-beens is *ustabes.*)

Vacation cumminup. Wannado one more item, then I gotta go.

Farewell, Supply

The Veterans Administration, which is soon to be upgraded to a Cabinet department as part of Ronald Reagan's pledge to trim the size of the federal bureaucracy, has already begun to go high-hat.

A memorandum dated September 7, 1988, from William H. Manley to "All Service Chiefs" on the subject of "Organizational Name Change" reads in its entirety:

"In accordance with a Central Office directive the title 'Supply Service' has been changed to 'Office of Acquisition & Materiel Management Service.' All future correspondence should be addressed Office of Acquisition & Materiel Management Service (90)."

I don't know what the "(90)" stands for; perhaps the average age of the people in the "Central Office," a place or disembodied committee with Soviet-sounding connotations that could use a little perestroika. And the repeated use of the ampersand in the memo from Manley suggests that any bureaucrat who uses the simple English *and* in the title, when sending in a requisition slip for paper clips, will be shipped to Novosibirsk.

In the Army, when we turned in our government-issue uniforms and gear before being discharged (explaining the damages with an innocent "but this is the way it was issued, Sarge"), the man who glowered back at us was known as the supply sergeant. As bureaucratic pomposity continues to triumph, he will become known as the Acquisition & Matériel Management Sergeant.

Economists are already bracing for an updating of the theory developed from the discussion of *supply* and *demand* by Adam Smith in his 1776 "An Inquiry into the Nature and Causes of the Wealth of Nations," a theory that will soon be known as the Theory of Acquisition & Matériel Management & Demand. (The old *demand* can be replaced by "Necessitation & Requirement Management.") Arthur Laffer, Jack Kemp and others who believe in growth through tax cuts will be called Acquisition & Matériel Management-Siders.

The name of the upgraded agency with the upgraded titles is Department of Veterans Affairs. It is the only department with an error in punctuation built into its name. Maybe its Central Office can cause its Office of Acquisition & Matériel Management to buy or otherwise acquire or accession what is evidently considered immatériel: an apostrophe to put after the "Veterans."

Afterthought: As the misspelling of *immatériel* above indicates, I have always had a problem with *material* and *matériel*. The former means anything made of matter and having substance. *Matériel,* with its acute accent, comes from French and refers to work equipment or tools, specifically the weapons and supplies of armed forces.

You want to know about the "(90)" after an office title. It is just a mail drop. These are standardized in this agency, so that any department of surgery in any VA is "112," etc. Of course, the VA makes the convenience obscure for the outsider by not identifying such drops as such. Instead, they put the above noted "in reply refer to," which is supposed to be followed by the appropriate number. They must have determined in the distant past that there is money to be saved by avoiding typing "department."

There are other stylistic peculiarities within the old US Govt. For example, it is policy that no agency place its telephone number on the letterhead. Given the cost of toll-call information services, you would think that it would be a convenience to all to have this information, but I think that it is designed to prevent government bureaucrats from being bothered. In fact, as you know, not even the White House letterhead has the phone number.

Another interesting format at this agency is the numbered paragraph. It seems that VA and other US Govt. employees need to have exact accounting of ideas in each memorandum. As such, paragraphs are kept short, typically one or two sentences, and each paragraph is numbered. Note also in the rules enclosed that the US Govt. has omitted the need for a salutation, which to me is a bit of a discourtesy.

J. Kaufman, M.D.
Albany, New York

I don't know who or why the decision was made. Likely it is the same person who decided that VA hospitals should be called VA Medical Centers; that Hospital Administrators should be called Medical Center Directors; and that the College of Home Economics at Cornell University should be called the College of Human Ecology.

Please let my friend Bill Manley off the hook. When I read your piece to him he laughed and remarked that he told the Chief of Supply (90) that he didn't think that anyone would call his operation anything other than Supply Service.

*He will remain the Supply Officer in the hearts of old-time VA employees
everywhere.*

> *Philip Lenowitz*
> *Medford, New Jersey*

*May I submit, sir, that the omission of the apostrophe is an error in spelling
rather than an error in punctuation.*

> *Irving Landau*
> *Woodside, New York*

The Feeling Is Mutual

Charles Dickens fuzzed up the meaning of a good word when, in 1865, he
titled a novel *Our Mutual Friend.*

Strictly speaking, *mutual*—rooted in the Latin for "exchange"—implies reciprocity, as when two people feel the same way about each other. But when the intended meaning involves no reciprocity, and instead refers only to a feeling or relationship shared about a third party, purists insist on *common,* rooted in the Latin *communis,* in its sense of "shared." (*Communism* is "enforced sharing," which leads to a need for perestroika.) You and I, Mrs. Thatcher, can be *mutual friends* (just *friends* would be better), but that smiling fellow in the Kremlin is our *common friend.*

"*Our mutual friend Jones* (meaning Jones who is your friend as well as mine)," wrote Henry Fowler in his *Modern English Usage,* "and all similar phrases, are misuses of *mutual.*" That usagist was fairly severe about this; he grumbled at the many examples of looseness cited in the *Oxford English Dictionary* and added that the Dickensian use of *mutual* "betrays ignorance of its meaning."

The misusers include some big names. In his "Essay Towards Facilitating Instruction in the Anglo-Saxon and Modern Dialects of the English Language," Thomas Jefferson correctly denounced "mutual vituperations" but incorrectly urged Britain and the United States to "yoke ourselves jointly to the same car of mutual happiness." He meant "common happiness," just as he went on to write of "common efforts."

Mutual admiration society was an 1851 coinage by Henry David Thoreau and uses the word correctly: The admiration goes back and forth. But what about the phrase *mutual interest,* meaning "shared concern" or, less compassionately, "partnership"? Should we permit that?

Let's not. Because the sharing involves no back-and-forth, no tit-for-tat, call it a *common interest.* To preserve a clear distinction in meaning, let's stick with the purists, for a change. Give clarity a shot.

Don't use *mutual,* meaning "reciprocal," when you mean *common,* meaning "shared." And *mutual* always requires two; if you're alone, you can take reciprocal action, but not mutual action.

Some have come to the defense of Dickens. Wilson Follett's *Modern American Usage,* for example, points out that it was "not Dickens's fault—he was quoting a semiliterate one-legged man," while conceding that "Dickens's title has clamped down the error of one of his low-life characters upon the English-speaking world and it will probably not be shaken off."

Do you suppose Dickens felt guilty about his assault on *mutual*? More than one of his admirers assumes he must have: "In the event that you should ever treat the use and misuse of that difficult word *mutual,*" writes the novelist Louis Auchincloss, "I have just happened upon the Mea Culpa of the great novelist whose title has done so much to perpetuate the confusion."

In his unfortunately titled novel, *Our Mutual Friend,* Dickens used the right word for a shared feeling: "He thanks Veneering for the feeling manner in which he referred to their common friend Fledgeby."

Remember Fledgeby, Dickens fans; writers and readers should have mutual respect, trusting each other to know that Fledgeby's our common friend.

Charles Dickens has not "fuzzed up the meaning of a good word" because he used mutual *in what may be one of the most misunderstood titles in English literature. Henry Fowler, Wilson Follett, and Louis Auchincloss have, I think, missed the point of* Our Mutual Friend. *Fowler claims that Dickens's use of* mutual *"betrays ignorance of its meaning"; Follett erroneously attributes the origin of the title to a "semiliterate one-legged man"; and Auchincloss seems to think that the title refers to Fledgeby! None of these learned men has read the novel carefully enough. Silas Wegg, the one-legged man in the story, never uses the expression; Nicodemus (Noddy) Boffin uses it several times. Dickens's title was a deliberate reference to a pivotal character in the novel. The character is John "Rokesmith," who is really John Harmon, believed to have been murdered. "Rokesmith" is Mrs. Reginald Wilfer's lodger* and *Noddy Boffin's secretary. Thus Boffin describes him to Mrs. Wilfer as "our mutual friend," naively thinking this phrase is an elegant locution. Dickens knew what he was doing and used the phrase* and *the title purposely, both to illuminate the personality of the lovable Boffin, and to emphasize the importance of the mysterious "Rokesmith" by making* him *the title character. As for Fledgeby, he may have been the common friend of Mr. Lammle and Mr. Veneering, but he is definitely* not *the "mutual friend" of the title.*

> Wendy Dellett
> Alexandria, Virginia

You failed to mention perhaps the most glaring misuse in Wall Street and by newspapers everywhere, including the N.Y. Times: Mutual funds.

> William C. Lazo
> Chapel Hill, North Carolina

Find Your Comfort Level

"It's a mutual growth process," said presidential candidate Jesse Jackson of his appeal to white voters, "what I call 'raising the *comfort level.*'"

It is one of Mr. Jackson's favorite locutions. "The more access I have to people," he told a few of us at lunch recently, "the more I'm able to raise their *comfort level.*"

He is not alone in the use of this soothing phrase. *Business Week,* reporting on the supersonic Concorde aircraft in 1975, wrote: "Its *comfort level* is roughly similar to some of the smaller and older jets, although it is much

quieter." That sense of physical well-being is still widely used in travel writing, but the meaning has been extended in voguish prose to a relaxation of mental tension.

Stockbrokers took to using the phrase in lieu of "sense of security," which securities dealers might have found confusing. "Customers can be systematically advised as to the status of their trust investments," a worry-conscious executive was quoted as saying in *The American Banker* in 1979, "according to the nature of their program and the *comfort level* they require." A broker told United Press International in 1986: "If you got a 25 percent return in a year's time but . . . you got an ulcer . . . the *comfort level* was not there."

Madison Avenue picked it up: "The *comfort level* is very high between ourselves and that agency," said Donald E. Holman, a partner in a Toronto advertising agency, referring to Backer & Spielvogel. Retailers bought it: "The issue of the female shopper and their [*sic*] *comfort level*," said a 7-Eleven ad manager to *Advertising Age,* "is probably as high a priority of a segment that we have."

With investors and media executives embracing the phrase, its leap into politics could be predicted. David Dreyer, in the office of Representative Tony Coelho, Democrat of California, looking sharply at White House lobbying on the Nicaragua issue, told the Associated Press: "We have to raise their *comfort level* with life after contra aid." With the phrase thus bruited about, it was a natural for a candidate such as Jesse Jackson, sensitive to sensitivity, to seize upon.

Where's it from? My first guess was psychiatric jargon. Dr. Jerry M.

Wiener, chairman of the department of psychiatry at George Washington University, says it is not in the standard vocabulary of psychiatric terms, "but might be used in the assessment of acute depression or in monitoring the effects of medication. It would be used most often in the negative sense, involving discomfort, to describe how uncomfortable the patient is."

If not rooted in shrinkage, what's the *comfort level* etymon? Fred Mish, editorial director of Merriam-Webster, flipped through his extensive citation files and came up with a 1938 book, *Labor's Progress and Some Basic Labor Problems* by H. A. Millis and R. E. Montgomery, which says: "At the *comfort level,* a family is able to live in a decent house or apartment, modestly equipped and decorated. . . ." That seems to be comparing levels and is not the origin of the current sense. But here's a clue: In John E. Haines's 1953 book, *Automatic Control of Heating and Air Conditioning,* he discusses maintaining "temperature levels as near as possible to the *comfort level.*"

My guess is that "climate control" was the field in which *comfort level* was first popularized, the key word influenced by its earlier use as a euphemism in *comfort station.* I remember Joe Frederick, president of Long Island's Sheet Metal Workers Local Union No. 55, using the phrase frequently in the 1950's: "You can't get a consistent *comfort level* without warm air heating."

The word, in its negative form but its current political sense, made the front page of *The New York Times* recently. AT WHITE HOUSE, SOME "DISCOMFORT" was the headline, based on this statement by an unnamed senior White House aide: "There is discomfort over what the contras are apparently agreeing to."

That brings us, finally, to *discomfort* vs. *discomfit.* The *fort* in *comfort* is from the Latin for "strong," and to be comfortable was originally "to be made strong or secure"; later it became "at ease, unafflicted by pain, consoled." To be *discomforted,* it follows, is to be "uneasy, annoyed, irritated," perhaps in minor physical or mental pain.

Discomfit is not the same: It is from the Old French *desconfire,* "to destroy, defeat," and it first meant "to defeat in battle, overwhelm"; *discomfited* came to mean "frustrated, thwarted," and has evolved into "perplexed, embarrassed," with an overtone of "disconcerted"; Harpo Marx wrote that when playwright George S. Kaufman "was acutely discomfited, he would try to wind his right arm twice around his head and reach back to his right ear." That's the effect of true *discomfiture.*

I was surprised you did not refer to the very common term, in the security law field, of "comfort" letters, since I suspect that usage considerably predated and quite possibly led to the "comfort level" usage.

In connection with significant corporate transactions, for example, an underwriting of a new stock issue, or the sale of a company, the underwriters (or buyers) seek as many "comfort letters" from relevant experts familiar with the affairs of the company as they can get. The company's outside general counsel and outside accountants are always required to furnish these. Typically, these opinions do not furnish firm guarantees against exposures, but instead are much hedged, the experts merely stating "we are not aware of" any claims, etc. These letters are not intended to flatly rule out areas of exposure, but merely to give "comfort" to the underwriters (buyers), etc.

By reason of the (intended) loopholes in such letters, in recent years they have sometimes been referred to sardonically as "cold comfort" letters, a play on the lack of comfort the hedges may well produce in the recipient of the letters.

Neil E. Falconer
San Francisco, California

As an elderly man was being prepared for transport after a car accident, the ambulance attendant inquired, "Sir, are you comfortable?" The victim replied, "I make a nice living."

Edward Simpson
Kew Gardens, New York

Finlandia

"The talk is of the decay of the Soviet Union's western empire," reported *The New York Times*'s James M. Markham from Bonn, "that could, in optimistic scenarios, lead to the 'Finlandization' of Eastern Europe."

If you're escorting Rosy Scenario to the Think-Tank Ball, you'd better be ready with a deliciously nuanced version of the *Finlandization* gavotte. The word, in its new and different context, is the hottest term in diplolingo. (A related term, *Ottomanization,* which likens the Soviet Union to the weakening Ottoman Empire in Turkey a century ago, is also being bruited about; I doubt it will fly. One *-ization* at a time.)

The word was first cited in the *Manchester Guardian Weekly* of May 22, 1969: "There is a foreign policy called Finlandisation, which allows more independence than Rumania has." Its first appearance as a verb came in a column about the NATO countries of Europe by C. L. Sulzberger in *The New York Times* in 1972: "The voters want comfort more than protection; their governments worry about letting this area gradually become 'Finlandized.' "

Hard-liners like me have always defined *Finlandize* (always capitalized, and with the American *z*) as "Soviet action to intimidate a neighboring noncommunist nation into adopting a foreign and defense policy of accommodation and acquiescence." The case in point is Finland, which for two generations has been permitted by the Soviet Union to maintain its independence so long as its external relations are considered by the Kremlin to be supportive of its superpower neighbor. Soft-liners, in deference to Finnish national pride, use kinder words in their definition of *Finlandize:* "to cause a neighbor to adopt a policy of neutrality," but the geopolitical fact underlying the term's use in most cases has been superpower domination.

Most Finns, especially those who dared to fight against Stalin, have long resented this use of their nation's name to describe a policy of subservience. "It takes the good name of our country," says Seppo Harkonen, the spokesman for the Embassy of Finland in the United States, "and uses it for purposes that we do not ourselves recognize."

Up to now, that use has been negative, connoting domination; lately, however, the word has been given a new and positive twist to fit a possible outcome of the turmoil in the Moscow-controlled Communist nations behind the Iron Curtain. Editorialist Stephen S. Rosenfeld, in his *Washington Post* column, described a diplomat's suggestion of "promoting the desired 'Finlandization'—internal choice in a setting of respect for legitimate Soviet security interests—in Eastern Europe."

Here is why the word augurs controversy. If the West's policy goal is a *Finlandized* Eastern Europe—that is, with Poland's future foreign policy still dominated as Finland's now is—then hard-liners will holler, "Another Yalta! Sellout!" and will hoot at accommodationists in grand-designer jeans. On the other hand, if the Western allies refuse to settle for the relaxation toward a state of *Finlandization,* with its concessions of more economic and perhaps political freedom, perhaps a Western hard line would cause a new wave of repression.

Thus, lexical relativity reigns. A negative word is being used positively; an insult can now be taken as a kind of compliment, if your policy is to achieve, or accept, a Finland-like Eastern Europe.

Big fight brewing over this, with the Conceptual Frameworkers Union picketing the think tanks. Choose your interpretation of the word, and meet me at the ticket counter of Leningrad's Finland Station.

You state that the term "Finlandization" was "first cited in the Manchester Guardian Weekly of May 22, 1969."

The Finns, however, have been bothered by the term longer than that. They point out that it is a West German creation that first made its appearance at the beginning of the nineteen-sixties.

Keijo Korhonen, the former Finnish delegate to the United Nations and currently foreign policy adviser to Prime Minister Harri Holkeri, quotes a West Berlin professor as having said he used the term during the Berlin crisis of 1961. Those Germans speaking of "Finlandization" in 1961 were describing what they thought would happen to West Berlin if the Western allies were to pull their forces out.

Korhonen says the term was forgotten for a time after the Berlin crisis but then was given renewed currency in West Germany toward the end of the nineteen-sixties as a weapon against Willy Brandt's "Östpolitik." Conservative critics of Brandt warned that he was taking West Germany down a path that would eventually lead to the withdrawal of American troops and the country's "Finlandization."

To the chagrin of the Finns, the term now spread to—and remained rooted in—newspapers and lexicons of other countries. "Finlandize," as you no doubt are aware, has made Webster's New World Dictionary, second college edition. Noting that the term is an "allusion to an allegedly similar relationship between Finland and the U.S.S.R. after World War II," the dictionary says to "Finlandize" means:

"To cause (a country) to accommodate its foreign policy to that of the U.S.S.R. as in order to maintain its autonomy."

Werner Wiskari
Charlestown, Rhode Island

A footnote to your column in which you mention, inter alia, Finlandization of Eastern Europe.

I used this term in a confidential discussion with US Ambassadors and State Department officials at a chiefs-of-mission meeting in London in December 1975. The topic was the future of Eastern Europe and US policy with respect thereto. In the course of the discussion, I referred to the endemic pressures in the region for greater independence from the Soviet Union and the need for the US to develop long-term policies to encourage these trends. When I suggested that Finlandization would be a good goal for us to pursue in Eastern Europe, the then US Ambassador to Finland protested about my use of that term since it caused him constant trouble with the Finnish government. Someone in the room pointed out that when applied to Western Europe, the term did indeed have pejorative connotations whereas using it in regard to Eastern Europe could not possibly offend the Finns, though it might strike them as being too provocative toward the Soviets. It was in the context of the notion of working toward Finlandization in Eastern Europe that I used the word "organic" to describe the sort of relationship between the countries of the area and the USSR that would spell the removal of the straight-jacket that Stalin had imposed on them. In that

*context, I used the word "organic" to mean natural, as between living orga-
nisms, as opposed to the unnatural use of repression and force to impose
conditions on people against their will.*

*When the State Department's telegraphic summary of the discussion was
leaked many weeks after it took place, "organic relationship," as used in the
above way, was transmuted by certain unscrupulous columnists into "permanent organic union" of Eastern Europe and the USSR. A political furor resulted
in the midst of the 1976 primary season and led eventually to the Polish "gaffe"
in the second presidential debate that year. The State Department telegram had
omitted my use of the term "Finlandization," apparently because of the protest
of our Ambassador in Helsinki. Not appearing in the telegram, it was not leaked
and therefore could not serve to put my use of the word "organic" into its actual
context. To this day, there are people who like to claim that I was conveying
some secret Ford (Kissinger) Administration scheme to sell Eastern Europe
into permanent Soviet slavery. In fact, to have called for Finlandizing Eastern
Europe as long ago as 1975 was to advocate the liquidation of the Stalinist
empire, the beginnings of which we may perhaps now be witnessing.*

*Helmut Sonnenfeldt
The Brookings Institution
Washington, D.C.*

Fish Story

"In a piranha-like feeding frenzy," wrote Don Kowet in the *Washington Times*, "yesterday television news tossed away any pretense of fairness. . . ." This was the first shot in the counterattack against questioners
of J. Danforth Quayle 3d at the Republican National Convention in New
Orleans, from the newspaper that had been first to suggest the Indiana
Senator was being seriously discussed by the Bush staff.

Feeding frenzy, not yet in the dictionaries (welcome to the cutting edge of
lexicography), is now the attack phrase of choice to describe an explosion of
media interest. The earliest citation in this sense that comes to hand is an
Associated Press story on March 9, 1977, reporting a speech by Gerald L.
Warren, a former Nixon press secretary who was editor of the *San Diego
Union.* He called for an end to the "jugular journalism" that caused some
writers to act like "sharks in a feeding frenzy."

Felix G. Rohatyn, the farseeing financier (alliteration is mother's milk to
old Nixon hands), picked up that image in 1979 to warn "there's a feeding
frenzy of sharks and the philosophy that tomorrow will take care of itself."

When this metaphor was seized upon in Wall Street, the venture capitalist Thomas P. Murphy wrote in *Forbes* in 1983: "A feeding frenzy, in case you are not a fisherman, occurs when bait is thrown to a school of hungry fish. They go wild, slashing at the bait, each other and anything else with the temerity to move."

In case you are a fisherman, you would know from Theo W. Brown's 1973 book about sharks that these blood-lusty creatures "switch off their sense of smell in a feeding frenzy." That term was used in a July 1962 article in *Scientific American* magazine, page 68, by Professor Perry W. Gilbert of Cornell: "As the blood and body juices of the marlin flow from the wound, the other sharks in the pack become more and more agitated and move in rapidly for their share of the meal. Frequently three or four sharks will attack the marlin simultaneously. A wild scene sometimes called a 'feeding frenzy' now ensues."

Shades of Hemingway's *The Old Man and the Sea.* Reached for his source at his home in Ithaca, New York (some would call this hunt for the earliest citation "coinage frenzy"), Professor Gilbert passed me along to Richard Ellis, the shark expert, who promptly cited page 47 of a 1958 book, *Shark Attack,* by V. M. Coppleson. That Australian author discusses "slow feeding" as "distinct from 'collective behavior' or 'frenzied feeding,' seen under somewhat rare conditions. In this case, sharks compete with others for possession of the prey and attack everything within range."

For current usage in swift currents, you would turn to Todd Woodward, an editor at *Field & Stream,* who says the term is no longer limited to shark fishermen and *Jaws* audiences: "It's when open-water predator fish, like striped bass, chase a group of bait fish into shallow water and start devouring them. It's pretty exciting to watch."

And so it is, and not just for anglers. In the terminology of suddenly seen scandal, a *firestorm* is a neutral term for an explosion of coverage and concern; a *flap,* from Royal Air Force World War I usage meaning "air raid," is a dismissal of the excitement; a *brouhaha,* perhaps from the Hebrew *barukh habba,* "blessed is he who enters," is much noisy ado often about nothing, and a *feeding frenzy* is a derogation of those who treat the newly entered as less than blessed.

As a confirmed pyromaniac I must insist on equal time for the great fire metaphors. Your listing of "firestorm" was titillating. But how could you resist such related favorites as "conflagration," "maelstrom," "inferno," and "prairie fire"? Surely the blazing confrontation between nature and man in Yellowstone National Park will "reignite" interest in these vivid terms. (And what could be better than the scent of natural disaster and religious damnation evoked by a word like "inferno"?)

I have a "burning" question for the Squad Squad: Is it permissible to precede these "fire" words with the terms "raging" or "blazing"?

Scott H. Nichols
Carbondale, Illinois

NOTE FROM W.S.: Blaze away.

Fodder, Forgive Them

When George Bush was asked whether the "sleaze factor" was a political liability in his campaign, he came back aggressively with "I think the Democrats are trying to make it that, but we will have some fun too. . . . You know, we've got some cannon fodder, if you want to get into that."

The Vice President could not have meant *cannon fodder.* His unfortunate choice of that phrase reveals the same tin ear for colloquialism that he showed when responding to an offer of more coffee in a meeting with truck drivers. ("Just a splash," he said cordially, extending his cup; what most native speakers would say is *fill it up* or *heat this up for me.* The locution *just a splash* is far more often used to request a little water in a whisky on the rocks.)

Cannon fodder has its roots in "food for powder" in Shakespeare's *Henry IV, Part One;* to Prince Hal's taunt that his recruits are pitiful rascals, Falstaff replies, "Tut, tut; good enough to toss; food for powder, food for powder; they'll fill a pit as well as better. . . ."

In 1891, the *Oxford English Dictionary* first used *cannon fodder,* defining it in its first supplement as "men regarded merely as material to be consumed in war," as if food for the cannon. George Bernard Shaw castigated Peter the Great in 1898 for "regarding children as future cannon fodder. . . ."

In World War I (which was not then called "World War I," of course), the bitter phrase referred to young, inexperienced infantrymen sent into battle likely to suffer many casualties with little hope of winning.

From the context of his remark, it appears that Mr. Bush meant to say *grist for the mill* or *ammunition* in its metaphoric extension; he was misled by the remote relationship of *ammunition,* the inanimate material used against an enemy, to *cannon fodder,* the human material wasted against an enemy.

The Vice President was not alone in his metaphor-mangling that week. Susan Estrich, the campaign manager for Mr. Dukakis, was quoted in the *Los Angeles Times* as saying, "I'm not casting a line in the sand." Either she meant she was not casting a line in the *water* (fishing, thus "being speculative"), or she was not *drawing* a line in the sand (daring an opponent to come nearer, thus "being confrontational"). It is possible that she was misquoted; I'm not drawing a line in the sand, lest I provide, in this scrupulously nonpartisan column, fodder for political attack.

Gaffe Me Your Tired . . .

Senator Lloyd Bentsen "was not likely to make any big national news," said his press secretary, Michael McCurry, "because he's not prone to error. He registers very low on the gaffe meter."

This was an obscure play on *laugh meter,* a device to register audience merriment on a radio show named *Can You Top This?* starring the comedians Harry Hershfield and Joe Laurie Jr. Those of us who have been tracking the progress of *gaffe* to its present preeminence in the vocabulary of blooperdom caught it instantly.

"Language gaffes and misspoken phrases," writes the columnist Suzanne Fields in the *Washington Times*, ". . . call on associations that automatically sweeten or offend our emotions, if not our intellects." When Vice President George Bush erred egregiously on the date of Pearl Harbor, ". . . the network-meisters of the Gaffe Patrol packaged the uncorrected version for the evening news, and led with it."

Asked by a reporter whether he was "prone to gaffes," Mr. Bush replied ruefully, "That's true, that's true." He also benefited from one: When the Chinese leader Deng Xiaoping said of Bush, "I hope he will be victorious in the elections," Reuters wrote, "Diplomats say Deng made a protocol gaffe, but his views probably reflect the views of China's leadership."

As a result of what William F. Gavin, a Republican congressional aide, derides as the "Great Gaffe Flappe," it behooves us to research the word describing an action on which an election could turn.

It's a French synonym for *faux pas*, or "false step," but its roots may be found in the Old English *gaf-spraec*, "coarse, ribald speech," remarks that must have shot skyward the eyebrows of Spenser's Fairie Queen.

Gaffer, which began as a term of respect for an old man, is apparently unrelated. It originally appeared as a contraction of *godfather*, or perhaps *grandfather*, when it was first used in the 1570's. By the 1800's, *gaffer* meant "foreman, overseer," and the term has been applied in glassmaking to the master glassblower. Now, *gaffer* also refers to the chief electrician for a film production, but the most widely used meaning is as an affectionate synonym for *codger*, without the power overtones of *geezer*.

Gaff—without the *e*—has many meanings in slang, from a fisherman's tool to a county fair, but the meaning that ties the current use to the past is "rude speech, vociferation, harsh criticism." That underlies the slang expression, *to stand the gaff*, or "to put up with the abuse that comes with the territory." Thus, *gaff*—or in French, *une gaffe*—is speech that shocks or embarrasses, which in politics is a mistake.

To the synonymy: *Error* and *mistake* are simple English words seldom used in political reporting, and we can ignore them. *Fluff*, more often used as a verb than a noun, means a mild slip of the lip, a mispronunciation or misreading. *Flub*, again both noun and verb, has a stupider connotation; *boner*, from "bonehead," has fallen into disuse; a *boo-boo* has a jocular baby-talk overtone; a *goof* is a mere slip-up quickly forgiven. A *blooper* is a stunning mistake, getting serious, usually resulting in a flap, currently being exceeded in attention-getting coverage by a *gaffe*, our word of the day.

Beyond a *gaffe* lies a *blunder*—a strategic error that goes beyond "misspeaking." To fail to exercise damage control on a gaffe—using self-deprecating humor or promptly apologizing or issuing a correction called a "clarification"—is a blunder, committed by campaign managers who cannot stand the gaff.

"Faire une gaffe" indeed means to make a shocking or embarrassing mistake of language or behavior.

"Faire gaffe," on the other hand, means to be wary or careful so as to avoid error. The expression comes from the early nineteenth-century usage "porter gaffe," which means to stand guard. It is possible that this expression in turn comes from the fisherman's usage of "gaffe"—a pointed, hooked or dashed rod for landing large fish such as salmon or pike. It is not too fanciful to imagine the "porter de la gaffe" first keeping a keen eye open for the fish in the waters, then taking care to avoid its sharp teeth as he lands it.

Francis Baron
Paris, France

Can't stand the gaff *is in fact a cockfighting term. A "gaff" in that sport is a needle-like steel artificial spur that is attached to the cock's heels over, or in lieu of, his natural spurs. A cock who* can't stand the gaff *is a coward—he's* chicken.

Ever realize how many phrases come from cockfighting? I can think of the following at least:

> *can't stand the gaff*
> *chicken*
> *cockpit*
> *to pit against*
> *a set-to*
> *to show the white feather*
> *game, in the sense of courageous; also "dead*
> *game," i.e., game to the death*
> *battle royal*
> *to raise one's hackles*
> *to crow over (a victory).*

Thaddeus Holt
Carlisle, Pennsylvania

Noted your reference to Can You Top This? *You mentioned Harry Hershfield and Joe Laurie Jr., but what have you got against Senator Ford? I'm old enough to have been in the audience during one of their shows, and the good "Senator" was as funny as the rest of them, beginning with his comic-somber walk onto the stage. Ah well, I'll attribute the omission to dimness of memory (your part, not mine).*

Do you remember the announcer? It was Peter Donald.

George H. Spencer
Washington, D.C.

You mentioned Can You Top This? It brought back fond memories to me. I must have been about twelve years old when I heard the following joke, and have remembered it all this time:

A young man was in love with two girls and he could not decide which of them to marry. He was so confused that he finally went to a marriage counselor. When asked to describe the two girls, he said that one was a great poet and the other made great pancakes. The counselor said: "Oh, I see what the problem is. You can't decide whether to marry for batter or verse."

Karan F. Minick
Stockton, California

Getting Serious

When the firestorm broke at the New Orleans Republican National Convention about Senator Dan Quayle's military service, James Baker, the Bush campaign chairman, smoothly turned aside the question about whether the running mate was in danger of being dumped. Mr. Baker said that such an option "was never seriously discussed or considered."

Here is an interesting use of the adverbial form of the adjective *serious,* which ordinarily means "sober, grave, momentous, solemn, earnest," with each of those synonyms carrying a different sense.

In Mr. Baker's delivery of the phrase, emphasis was placed on "never" and "discussed"; the "seriously" was tossed in, as if frivolously. The impression deliberately given was that the option to dump was not discussed, but of course it was—at great length, until three o'clock in the morning, when the Bush aides adjourned to go to sleep or make notes for their memoirs.

Mr. Baker's problem was to seem to deny the truth without telling a lie. The solution: The slippery *seriously,* which says, "Yes, that choice was discussed, as all the memoirs will show in great detail, and we were all certainly serious (somber, nobody smiling) at the time, but it never reached the point in my mind of a likely recommendation for action." Since what went on in Mr. Baker's mind is known only to him, his subjective assessment of "never seriously discussed" cannot be seriously challenged.

Another sense of *serious* has been spotted in bakeries. At a Bridgehampton, Long Island, bakery called "Simple Pleasures" (an allusion to Oscar Wilde's observation that "simple pleasures are the last refuge of the complex"), *serious brownies* are on sale. These are very expensive squares of cake, aimed to taste rich and be purchased by the wealthy, and named for those people who do not lightly stuff their faces with the chocolate pastry but who take their brownie-eating seriously—thinking about each bite, chewing over the idea behind the recipe as well as the substance in their mouths.

The word *serious* is rooted in the Latin and Middle English words for heaviness, and the weighty moistness of these pastries makes the appellation *serious brownies* accurate.

At the risk of immodesty, I cite my coinage of the phrase "very serious cookie" for Peek Freans (for what is a copywriter but a coiner for coin?) in 1978. This campaign (including the jingle I wrote and sang) has run steadily in New York for more than ten years now. Perhaps "serious" has now entered common usage as a modifier for baked goods of all types.

Spencer Michlin
Dallas, Texas

Gifts of Gab for 1989

An Italian, when bidding farewell formally, says *arrivederci* (literally, "to see each other again"). When more relaxed, the person waving goodbye says *ciao.* (I pause for the reader to ask: Where does that come from?)

Ciao is a dialectical alteration of *schiavo,* meaning "slave"; the original phrase that was used in saying "bye-bye, bambino" was *sono vostro schiavo,* "I am your slave."

That strikes me as a pretty sexy way of saying "so long." Italians are not the only Continentals to use that servile idea in salutations: the German *Servus*—from the identical Latin word—means "servant, slave," and also gets across a now-ironic grovel. (In English, the idea used to appear at the end of letters—"Your obedient servant"—but nowadays that has been replaced by the more democratic "Ta-ta, good buddy, I'm history.")

This background on *ciao* is the sort of delicious information you cannot find in most general dictionaries. It comes popping right out at you, roots and all, from the *Barnhart Dictionary of Etymology,* published by H. W. Wilson, $59, Robert K. Barnhart, editor, Sol Steinmetz, managing editor.

How about *graham crackers*? No, it's not an allusion to Southerners who work for *The Washington Post;* rather, it is rooted in the product of Sylvester Graham, 1794–1851, who pushed bakery products made from unsifted whole-wheat flour as part of what he believed was "dietary reform." (No listing in the *B.D.E.,* as lexicologists and lexicographers will call the great new work, for *bibb lettuce,* the green thumbchild of Major John Bibb, the eminent horticulturist. But that's show-off reviewing; no dictionary covers everything.)

The above is a *puff*—a plug, boost, plaudit, rave, or other form of acclaim—set forth to encourage a purchase. (First use in 1602: "Blowne up with the flattering puffes / Of spungy sycophants.") Today's article is a *puff piece* for books on the English language that are worthy of holiday giving. This continues a tradition started here some years ago that has become useful to sycophants, *spungy* and otherwise.

There's been only one major new general college-sized dictionary published this year (you can't use the adjective *collegiate* in modifying dictionaries, because the word in that sense is trademarked by Merriam-Webster, an old-line outfit way ahead of everyone with computer software including an electronic dictionary and thesaurus). The new book is *Webster's New World Dictionary of American English, Third College Edition;* Victoria Neufeldt, editor in chief; list price $17.95, but available at Crown Books for under ten bucks (and yes, you can find in it the definition of *loss leader*).

Oh, the brave new words that have made it in *W.N.W.D.: contrarian,* for those smart apples who were selling before the market crash; *ROM* (read-only memory) for the inalterable Mr. Computer Chips, and *RAM* (random-access memory) for the other kind that you can call up directly; *low-ball,* a verb meaning "to give an understated price . . . especially without intending to honor it," which is not identified as an Americanism. Those takeover terms—from *cash cow* to *junk bond* to *greenmail* to *poison pill*—dominate the list of new inclusions, but you can also get jolted by a *speed bump,* then *pig out* on a *profiterole.* Missing: *sound bite,* but that only made it big this summer.

Candy-ass made it, too; the slang term, defined as "a weak, hesitant, or ineffectual person; wimp; sissy," was first printed in *The New York Times* as part of the Watergate tapes, when Richard Nixon used it to derogate a recalcitrant colleague. *The Times* printed the term reluctantly then because it is the newspaper of record; if it prints it again here today, maybe it's because the shock has worn off. I would not use the hyphen in the word as a noun, as *Webster's New World* does, but would hyphenate in the adjectival form, which the dictionary does not yet recognize.

Word lovers enjoy a good quotation book. Here's a ring-a-ding (*W.N.W.D.*: "wildly exciting") entry that belongs between your Bartlett's and your Mencken's: *Simpson's Contemporary Quotations,* by James B. Simpson, Houghton Mifflin, $19.95, which compiles "the most notable quotes since 1950."

The famous words are here: from the astronaut Neil Armstrong's "One small step for man, one giant leap for mankind" to Eisenhower's "I shall go to Korea" to Senator Joe McCarthy's "I have here in my hand a list . . ." to Betty Friedan's "Their comfortable, empty, purposeless days are indeed cause for a nameless terror."

The anthologist, Simpson, includes Henry Kissinger's "Next week there can't be any crisis. My schedule is already full." (But leaves out "Peace is at hand.") Bob Considine: "I believe in opening mail once a month, whether it needs it or not." And George Bush, speaking in 1987 about his vice presidential running mate for the next year: "I haven't chosen her yet." (He was kidding, presumably.)

If your giftee is a word specialist, and you can afford the product of small press, try this: *Loanwords Dictionary,* Laurence Urdang and Frank R. Abate, editors, $80, a lexicon of foreign phrases used in English that retain their exotic flavor—*roman à clef* and *lingua franca* and *ad astra per aspera.* (No! It turns out to be *per aspera ad astra,* "through hardship to the stars." Remember that, aspiring Bush appointees.) Mr. Urdang is becoming America's own Samuel Johnson, tirelessly turning out dictionaries of allusions, of mottoes, of idioms and you name it. Gale Research, at Book Tower, Detroit, MI 48226, can send you a list of his books.

Gale has also published *Similes Dictionary,* $68, Elyse Sommer and Mike Sommer, editors, the only place you can readily find alternatives to President-elect Bush's *like ugly on an ape:* Ms. Sommer suggests *like ducks to popcorn* or the more specific *fall on me like pigeons on breadcrumbs.*

Something less expensive? A stocking stuffer that is also a mind stuffer can be found in these paperbacks:

There Is No Zoo in Zoology and Other Beastly Mispronunciations: An Opinionated Guide for the Well-Spoken, by Charles Harrington Elster, Collier, $6.95: "ek-STROR-di-ner-ee," not "EKS-truh-OR-di-ner-ee."

Family Words: The Dictionary for People Who Don't Know a Frone from a Brinkle, by Paul Dickson, Addison-Wesley, $6.95. This appears to be just kidding around with malapropisms and goofy coinages, but such terms as *googol, humongous* and *nerd* started that way. If you're a *wordo,* you'll like *jet leg*—"a foot that has fallen asleep on a long flight."

How to Write, by Herbert E. Meyer and Jill M. Meyer (Why don't married authors use a single last name anymore?), published by Storm King, $4.95, was plugged here a couple of years ago and is perking right along, still the most helpful book for the beginning writer.

And *The Elements of English,* by Stan Malless and my language researcher Jeffrey McQuain (Madison Books, $5.95) is a most useful glossary of basic terms of grammar, literature and composition, now in its second edition, which is more than I can say for some of my own books.

Idiom's Delight is an inexpensive little hardback by Suzanne Brock (Times Books, $13.95) that shows how imagery travels through different languages: Here it rains cats and dogs, in Italy it rains water basins, in Spain it rains jugs, and in France it's coming down in ropes.

The best new quick glossary of Yiddishisms can be found in the back of Howard Simons's *Jewish Times* (Houghton Mifflin, $22.95), and the best lift for English teachers can be found in William Zinsser's *Writing to Learn* (Harper & Row, $15.95).

Finally, the best compliment you can give to somebody who appreciates the gentle art of essay-writing is a gift of *America Observed* by Alistair Cooke (Alfred A. Knopf, $19.95).

My responsibility discharged, I will now take a brief vacation, so—*Ciao.* (No, I am not your slave.)

In re ciao: In the Bible the humble "your servant" is used many times instead of "I."

> *Rabbi Samuel M. Silver*
> *Temple Sinai of Palm Beach*
>   *County*
> *Delray Beach, Florida*

Forgive my asperity, but have you never heard of the motto of the Royal Air Force—"per ardua ad astra," the origin of which is well documented; and how could you have surrendered the high word play in ardua, while allowing aspera to clunk its low way along the wounded earth?

> *W. D. McHardy*
> *Königstein, West Germany*

I wouldn't give a bean
To be a candy-ass Marine,
I'd rather be a dog-faced soldier like I am.

I wouldn't trade my old OD's
For all the Navy's dungarees
'Cause I'm the walkin' pride of Uncle Sam.

Army Song—late 40's or early 50's—was featured in movies in which the
phrase was changed to "fancy pants."

George Winship
Montclair, New Jersey

For sheer groveling, nobody could hold a candle to the Spanish grandees, who
used to close their letters (to friends, lovers, employers, etc.) with:
S.S.S.Q.B.S.M. That stands for Su seguro servidor que besa su mano, *and* that
translates into "Your obedient servant who kisses your hand."

Norman Gold
Rio Rancho, New Mexico

Gladly, the Cross-Eyed Bear

Never try to steal a man's down-home, cracker-barrel, man-of-the-people
metaphor.

Trying to explain to reporters hot for bold initiatives why a cautious
approach to Mikhail Gorbachev's proposals was necessary, Secretary of
State James A. Baker 3d, a Texan, said that the Soviet leader was "singing
out of our hymnbook."

This was not a suggestion that the Soviet leader had abandoned godless
Communism; rather, the figure of speech was drawn, with evident care, from
an expression the folks at the *Dictionary of American Regional English* suggest may be of Texas origin. The only *DARE* examples of usage indicate a
sense of cohesion: *Singing out of the same hymnbook* (or *hymnal* or *choir
book*) means "acting in unison."

The Baker usage, however, adds to the religious trope a proprietary sense:
"following the words and music as sung by one sect." Mr. Baker was trying
to put in familiar terms his point that the Soviet leader had been induced by

internal contradictions and Western resolve to operate in our context of freedom and market forces.

In a question period after the Secretary's statement, a filmmaker complained that we were not taking the initiative: "It just seems that we're singing out of their hymnbook."

Secretary Baker responded with firmness if not acerbity: "They're singing out of our hymnbook." After a few minutes, the very thought that his figure of speech could be turned around caused him to return to it: "It is the policies we've pursued the last forty years that have kept the peace," he said, adding resolutely, "and brought the Soviets to the point where they are in fact singing out of our hymnbook."

The Glasnost Dangle

Edward Jay Epstein is my kind of spywriter. Not only does he believe that the Central Intelligence Agency's late James Angleton was right about Soviet penetration and manipulation of Western intelligence services, but also my coconspiracy theorist uses the words of espionage strategy and defines them as he goes.

In *Deception: The Invisible War Between the K.G.B. and the C.I.A.,* he cites a Soviet agent who was a *dangle:* "someone who, while loyally taking orders from his own intelligence service, feigns disloyalty to his country to attract the attention of the other side, like the bait on a fish hook."

He reminds us, too, of the origin of *disinformation,* first used by the predecessor to the K.G.B. to mean "the manipulation of a nation's intelligence system through the injection of credible but misleading data." In recent years, the term "came to mean the manipulation of newspapers and television through propaganda."

Even *glasnost,* now taken to mean "openness" and seemingly the most innocent of terms, has its sinister roots. Drawing on the work of Mikhail Heller in *The Formation of Soviet Man,* Epstein notes that *glasnost*—"public airing"—has been an instrument of Soviet policy since long before the Gorbachev era.

Lenin used the term at least forty-six times in his writings. His object was to make local officials vulnerable to periodic purges, and he forced them to confess to mistakes and to point to errors of others. In so doing, he strengthened the dictatorial hold of the men at the top while appealing to the West with the appearance of free speech. Lenin's nicely turned description of this: "*Glasnost* is a sword which itself heals the wound it inflicts."

You used a formulation that is epidemic. It makes for a redundancy, then a re-redundancy (a tridundancy?). Of Edward J. Epstein you wrote (emphasis added):

> *Not only does he believe that the Central Intelligence Agency's late James Angleton was right about Soviet penetration and manipulation of western intelligence services, but also my coconspiracy theorist uses the words of espionage strategy and defines them as he goes.*

By using not only, you automatically set up the following clause. So but becomes redundant; also becomes redundant. (At times, you even see this pattern freighted with in addition for a quadridundancy or something.)

Proof of the garbage verbiage is elementary: Remove the but and the also from your sentence (change the preceding comma to a semicolon if run-on sentences bother you), and viola!

Emerson Stone
Greenwich, Connecticut

The Great Beyond

"Now it is time to move beyond containment," President Bush told the Texas A & M graduating class on May 12, 1989, "to a new policy for the 1990's—one that recognizes the full scope of change taking place around the world and in the Soviet Union itself."

In subsequently defining his foreign policy, the President has quoted himself saying those words—"I call it 'beyond containment' "—evidence that he considers the phrase the one that he wants to be used in any labeling of his foreign policy. White House staffers tell me, in passionate anonymity, that (contrary to the claims from Foggy Bottom) the persons who put the idea on paper before the President are Robert Blackwill, the European and Soviet Affairs man at the National Security Council, and Condoleezza Rice, the resident Sovietologist.

The useful phrase is bottomed on a sentence in a February 1946 memo from George F. Kennan, a scholar of Russian history who was counselor of the United States Embassy in Moscow: "Soviet pressure against the free institutions of the Western world is something that can be contained by the adroit and vigilant application of counterforce at a series of constantly shifting geographical and political points, corresponding to the shifts and maneuvers of Soviet policy. . . ." That became known as the policy of *containment.*

Here we are beyond it. The same phrasedicks who tracked Winston Churchill's *Iron Curtain* to everyone from Joseph Goebbels to the stage managers of early English theaters are sure to be after "first uses" of Mr. Bush's favorite label, so let me start the hunt.

In the spring of 1984, Robert C. McFarlane, then Mr. Reagan's national security adviser, told a graduating class at Annapolis that because the Russians had become "militarily strong and adventurous enough to leapfrog the buffer states and jump anywhere in the world that suits their own strategies," it was necessary to go "beyond containment." New York's Democratic Senator Daniel Patrick Moynihan called attention to this phrase, and its justification of the mining of Nicaraguan harbors, in a *New York Times* Op-Ed piece two years later.

A book of essays, edited by Aaron Wildavsky, was published in late 1983 with the title *Beyond Containment: Alternative American Policies Toward the Soviet Union.*

The earliest use of the phrase I can find in a political context (setting aside reports of fires spreading "beyond containment doors") is by Charles Wolf Jr. The veteran Rand Corporation economist presented a paper to the California Seminar on International Security and Arms Control in November 1981 that was soon printed in the *Washington Quarterly,* a publication of Georgetown University's Center for Strategic and International Studies. The title was "Beyond Containment: Redesigning American Policies."

Recalls Charley Wolf today: "I was thinking of 'containment plus' or 'Where do we go from containment?' But 'beyond containment' had a better ring to it."

Beyond that, what figure of speech lies beyond containment? According to Mr. Bush, it is a "new path," a phrase that was floated out in the same speech. That trope of pioneering has been tried out by speechwriters for at least a generation, along with *new beginning* and *new dawn,* but you just can't get buyers for a *new* anything anymore. That sends us out back of *beyond,* where no new path is found. Beyond the blue horizon, we know, lies the rising sun, but that image would be rejected as a threat of a newly imperial Japan.

The Center for Strategic and International Studies became formally independent of Georgetown University on July 1, 1987.

Candace Crandall
Director, Public Affairs
Center for Strategic and
International Studies
Washington, D.C.

Beyond and Above

The "beyond containment" coinage hunt is happily under way.

President Bush had been searching for a label for his foreign policy. The *Bush Doctrine* would not do, because we are pushing Mikhail Gorbachev to repeal the intrusive *Brezhnev Doctrine,* and *doctrine* is out this year in the phrase-coinage dodge. The White House choice, *Beyond Containment,* was enunciated in a speech and repeated in press conferences; its provenance in a 1981 article, boosting on a word made famous in diplomacy by George F. Kennan, was set forth in this space.

Comes now Gloria C. Phares of New York City to report that Robert W. Tucker and William Watts edited a book with that title in 1973. She was about to claim that her husband and fellow lawyer, Richard Dannay, had written his Harvard senior thesis in 1961 using that title, but was compelled to pass on that its bibliography contained a book by William Henry Chamberlin, published in 1953 by Regnery in Chicago, entitled *Beyond Containment.*

This is not to derogate the choice of Mr. Bush and his speechwriters, or to cast aspersions on their originality; on the contrary, my point is that just about every good combination of words has a history in the language. Who can forget Theodore Parker's "of the people, by the people, for the people"? Good phrases have resonances and roots, and tracking them back illuminates the trail on which all orators walk. We await a pre-1953 citation.

In an unrelated linguistic development involving President Bush, we have this curious usage: Looking forward to a trip abroad, he began by telling a group of visitors, "I hope you will find the next couple of hours exciting." He then helped make them so with the sort of unconscious slip in speaking that occurs more often than most of us realize: "And as I look back and sit at the world . . ."

The word for the affliction of seeing printed words backward is *dyslexia;* the tendency to reverse familiar phrases is by no means as serious, but the word for such a tendency awaits coinage (dyspeaksia, flop-flipism). Think and stop about it; we'll have to see and wait.

The Greenroom Effect

"Before the Brinkley program began," I wrote at the start of a political harangue, "in the 'green room' (so named for the guest-relaxing color on its walls) . . ."

Watch those parenthetical etymologies. In the column that followed, I banged my spoon on the highchair while furiously cultivating the garden of controversy, but nothing I wrote on the hot topic of conflicting power drew mail like that offhand reference to *greenroom* (one word, as I discovered).

"Regarding your recent statement that the *greenroom* is so named for the guest-relaxing color on the walls," writes Vincent T. Bugliosi, coauthor of *Lullaby and Good Night,* "I am not sure about it. I've noticed that the TV waiting room is called the greenroom even when the color on the wall is not green. When I asked one television station employee years ago about this, he said the greenroom was the name of the waiting room at Shakespeare's Globe Theater."

"Back even before the time of Shakespeare and the Globe Theater," writes Bernard Ryan Jr. of Wilton, Connecticut, "a room backstage, just off the wings, was called 'the actors' *attiring room.*' Gradually it became the *tiring room,* long before the term *dressing room* was used."

That checks out. In *A Midsummer Night's Dream,* the carpenter Quince chooses the location of the stage in the wood: "This green plot shall be our stage, this hawthorn brake our tiring-house. . . ." This sense of *tiring* would have been an aphetic form of *attiring,* perhaps influenced by *retiring.*

"Eventually, someone decided to bring small trees and shrubbery into the theater as set dressings," continues Mr. Ryan. "These were parked in the *tiring room* until moved onstage, and the actors were squeezed out. The room then gradually became known as the *greens room,* until the *s* was dropped."

That's one theory. Michael C. Hardy of Detroit offers another: "It was one of many occurrences of the color green in the English Restoration period. The groundcloth on the stage was green, the stagehands were called 'the greencoat men,' the seats were covered in a green baize, and the front curtain (when it came into fashion) was green. All this dated from the medieval practice of presenting outdoor performances on a 'greensward.' "

Robert P. Fitzgerald, a professor of English at Penn State University, looked up the term in his *Oxford English Dictionary* and directed me to a 1700 play by Colley Cibber. In *Love Makes a Man,* this line appears: "I do know London pretty well, and the Side-box, Sir, and behind the Scenes; ay, and the Green-Room, and all the Girls and Women-Actresses there."

There is a leering quality to that first citation of *greenroom* that persists in the theater-lingo term *greenroom gossip,* where our word is a more specific place than *backstage.* But where was the first *greenroom?*

Charles Earle Funk and son in *Horsefeathers* speculate that the word may have been coined when the Dorset Garden and Drury Lane theater companies merged in 1682, and place the first *greenroom* at the Drury Lane. The timing seems right, given the Cibber citation, but no proof is offered. In the *Facts on File Encyclopedia of Word and Phrase Origins,* Robert Hendrickson also speculates that the word takes its name "from such a room in London's Drury Lane Theater, which just happened to be painted green sometime in the late 17th century." But that's just educated guessing.

What about the notion, repeated by me, that the room is painted green to soothe the performers' eyes? Unlikely; the spectators, rather than the players, suffered more from the candles in the chandeliers. The diarist and theatergoer Samuel Pepys recorded in 1669 that "the trouble of my eyes with the light of the candles did almost kill me."

We can thus state, with certitude but not certainty, that the term that is now used to mean "a holding room for guests before being interviewed on television" is rooted in the name for a small attiring room, perhaps in the Drury Lane Theater, probably around the end of the seventeenth century, and that more hanky-panky went on in the original *Green-Rooms* than takes place in today's stress-ridden *greenrooms.*

The reason for the name remains obscure. It could have been one of the explanations presented above, or it could have been a theater manager named Sam Green. A final theory is presented with a straight face by Douglas Kiker, a veteran correspondent of NBC News who was present at the creation of television as we know it.

"Back in the olden days," Mr. Kiker writes, "when *Today* was the only morning network news show, guests waiting to go on the air were assembled in a small room just outside the studio in New York City. The room was furnished with castoff office furniture, including an old discarded wooden desk.

"Every morning a food cart with coffee and sweet rolls was placed here. Nothing fancy.

"For some reason, one morning a crew member rummaged through the drawers of the old desk and found a danish left there a long, long time ago. So long ago that the sweet roll had turned green.

"So, the *greenroom*. At least that's the story I was told by an old-timer at NBC."

The first known instance (not in O.E.D.) of "green room" is in a play by Thomas Shadwell, A True Widow, printed in 1679. The action in the second half of the fourth act occurs on the stage of a theater (the stage represents a stage), and one character says, "Selfish, this Evening, in a green Room, behind the Scenes, was beforehand with me."

Evert Sprinchorn
Professor of Drama
Vassar College
Poughkeepsie, New York

In medieval time, pageant wagons toured the countryside. When they set up, a green cloth covered the perimeter of the lower half of the wagon. It was within the privacy of this green cloth that the actors changed into costume and awaited their entrance onto the scene. Today, in this world of specialization, there is a tiring or dressing room and a greenroom set aside as a place to await their own entrances or rest after a scene. Although I have been involved with over one hundred productions, it has never been my experience to see one either painted or decorated in the color green.

Gigi Cascio
Forest Hills, New York

Gun That Rumor Down

For language mavens, the dispute that culminated in the nonconfirmation of John Tower was memorable for the blossoming of *gun down* as a synonym for *squelch*.

President Bush drew first. After perusing a report by the Federal Bureau of Investigation about his nominee, he announced that the allegations against Mr. Tower "have been gunned down in terms of fact." Reporters enjoyed using the unfamiliar extension of the metaphor; in a news conference, a

question began, "You have said that the F.B.I. report guns down the accusations against Senator Tower, and yet . . ." Mr. Bush used the colorful figure of speech again weeks later, explaining that his own delay in sending the nomination up to Capitol Hill was caused by his concern for "gunning down groundless rumors."

A computer search for the earliest use of this verb phrase in its extended sense turns up a 1977 story about a *Face the Nation* appearance by—you guessed it—George Bush, chief of the Central Intelligence Agency. He said he was appearing on the program to "gun down" speculation that a Team B, which had been appointed by him to challenge his agency's assessment of Soviet power, had leaked its conclusions in order to dissuade President-elect Jimmy Carter from cutting the defense budget.

In its original sense, *gun down* means "shoot and cause to fall." One of the senses of the verb *gun* in Merriam-Webster's *Ninth New Collegiate* (it's their ninth edition, but only the eighth that could be called a *new* collegiate, and the fourth with *new* in its title) is "shoot," with the example given of "gunned down by a hit man."

Naturally, with all the publicity deservedly coming to the *Oxford English Dictionary*'s glorious second edition, I looked there for the definition. The phrase is not there. (Gee. How long till the third edition?) It can be found, instead, in the *Oxford Dictionary of Current Idiomatic English,* identified as a transitive verb ("gun") followed by a particle (adverb or preposition "down"); labeled "informal," it is defined as "shoot unmercifully, often with the implication that the victims are defenseless."

For a rundown on *gun down,* I turned to Stuart Berg Flexner at Random House, who told me: "Mafia hit men were said to *gun* somebody, without the *down.* The *down* wasn't added until after World War II, then mainly in newspaper use about mobsters who had *gunned down* someone. Probably influenced by *run down,* which dates back to the sixteenth century, and a hunting term, *hunt down.* There are also *ride down* and *track down.*"

For a time, *gun up* was preferred, synonymous with "shoot up a town," but the power of the image of a fall—as in *bringing down* an animal or a human target—prevailed in the language.

It remained only for that former Navy pilot, who may have heard the phrase in World War II, to extend the metaphor. The target became a rumor, not a person or an animal, and the phrase in this usage loses its mercilessness, since a rumor is not innocent.

Rumor-denial needs linguistic help, which is why we welcome this new and heroic sense of what had hitherto been a coolly cruel verb. *Gun down* is now the fashionable synonym for such terms as *squelch,* an onomatopoeic term from the sound of stepping on a soft object; *quell,* which originally meant "kill" but later came to mean "crush" or "suppress," and *put the kibosh on,* its origin a mystery that begs for solution. (Some suggest the *kibosh* is related to *bosh,* meaning "nonsense," but I would *shush up, tie the can to* and *clamp the lid on* that speculation, not to say *gun it down.*)

KIBOSH: *Corrupt rendering from the Gaelic for* <u>Death Cap</u>* *placed by the hangman over the head of his unfortunate charge; ritualistically, and to conceal the grotesque metamorphosis of a bulging face that, imminently, shall have stared into the abyss. Put the kibosh on: To condemn to death, or to render one dead.*

Thomas O'Malley
Garden City, New York

*<u>Caipín bás</u> (<u>kye</u>-peen <u>boss</u>; hence: Kye-bosh)

I am a casual researcher into and an admirer of the richness of Yiddish: <u>Kibosh</u> *had a tantalizingly Semitic flavor. My authority in this area is Leo Rosten, whose* <u>The Joys of Yiddish</u> *is always on my working-library shelf. Rosten dedicates two full pages to the possible etymology of* <u>kibosh</u> *because it is deeply embedded in Yiddish usage: Alas, after running the gamut of several Oxfords, two Websters, Partridge, Holt, Mencken (H. L.), William and Mary Morris, and Berrey and Van den Bark, Leo came up almost as dry as most of the rest.*

Two promising clues (which he doesn't speculate on further) lie in the works of the Irish poet, Padraic Colum, and A Dictionary of Rhyming Slang by Julian Franklyn. The former suggests it is from the Gaelic "cie bais", meaning "cap of death." The latter is inclined toward the heraldic "caboshed" or "caboched."

"Caboche" is Middle English for "to behead (a deer)," and the heraldic form ("caboshed") shows the head of a deer facing forward (no neck). The sources are the 1966 Random House, unabridged, and the 1955 Oxford Universal (Onions). The latter dates the usage back to 1572 while at the same time indicating that "kibosh" dates back to 1836 and may be of Yiddish origin.

So, the bottom line is: Ya takes yer money and takes yer choice (or "cherse" in the Brooklyn demesne). Though both the Gaelic and the ME seem to reasonably satisfy the current meaning/usage, I lean toward the ME—however, the Mystery lingers on!

> *Hank Dutton*
> *Sherman, Connecticut*

I seem to remember the expression "put the kibosh on" has its origin in a Gaelic word for a cap or cover that was placed on a corpse prior to burial. The source may have been an article in The Times about twenty-five years ago on the so-called Brooklyn dialect (doity-toit for thirty-third) which also was traced to Gaelic pronunciations which arrived with Irish immigrants in the 19th century.

> *Howard I. Heitner*
> *Stamford, Connecticut*

Handlers

"John Sasso, his principal *handler* . . ." There is a word getting a ride in the 1988 campaign.

"I do not believe in the genius of the *handlers*," wrote A. M. Rosenthal. "They are all brilliant during the campaigns. How come 50 percent of them turn out to be so wrong on election night, when their man loses?"

After Senator Dan Quayle was criticized as being a robot in the tight control of his *handlers,* he announced (some said at the behest of his shrewd advisers) that he would no longer be "programmed" by his traveling chaperones. As he put it: "Now it's my turn. I'm my own *handler.*"

The term was originally applied in the fourteenth century to money changers, who were handlers of silver. It gained a figurative sense more than a century later, when a preacher was criticized as being "an unreverent handler of God's word," and in the 1800's entered the bloody world of animal fighting. A man who held or set a gamecock or fighting dog (see *pit bull*, a new word for feisty political competitor, explained on page 27) was called a *handler*.

In this century, the term referred mainly to the proud people who showed the best points of a dog to the judges in dog shows, which led to the word's application to police officers in charge of trained dogs. Not until a generation ago was the word applied to boxing seconds: "His handlers threw in the towel," wrote Jack Dempsey in 1950.

Dogs are not insulted by the presence of men who "handle" them—controlling, directing and managing their actions—even when it causes them to jump through hoops. And fighters accept without question the value of an aide massaging their backs between rounds, whispering instructions and exhortations and popping mouthpieces over their gums.

However, in politics, although we have opened a new era of candor in the acceptance of manipulation as an art form, the appearance of being too tightly managed is considered a negative. For that reason, handlers recommend that their handlees fire them on occasion, with appropriate fanfare.

In the world of intelligence and espionage, an "agent handler" is the spy master who runs the spies who get the information; it's the person to whom the spy in the field turns over his or her intelligence. The implication is that the handler actually runs the show, while the field agent is just an employee carrying out assignments. For obvious reasons, the association is also clandestine. The parallel to a candidate's handlers is obvious.

It is interesting that "agent handlers" are what we call our own spy runners. If they work for the other side, they are called "control agents" or, simply, "controls." I never asked the reason for this difference; I always assumed that the connotation of "control," with its suggestion that the field operative has no options or, indeed, individual will, was too derogatory to be applied to our side. After all, anyone working for us did so by free choice because we were the good guys. No one ever confirmed this interpretation of the different terms.

Richard E. Kramer
New York, New York

Handmade Flatware

"Handmade silver flatware" is advertised by James Robinson of New York City, a firm that uses these comparatives: "More than hand forged. Superior to hand crafted. Better than hand finished."

Yeah. What does *hand-forged* mean, anyway? "It could mean a process called 'cold forging,' " says M. Kim Harwood, the manager, "which involves cutting a utensil from a sheet of silver, then hammering it to shape it."

Hand-finished? "Sounds good," sniffs Mr. Harwood, "but it may mean only that someone holds the almost-completed piece in hand while the wheel turns and polishes it. *Handcrafted* is even more unclear—it tells you that somebody's done something by hand, but not what or how much."

Ah, but *handmade* is the real thing: "Hammering from the start makes the piece stronger and tougher. You have to be sure to control the balance and mold the metal properly in working a silver bar out. That gives the quality to handmade silver."

Edward Munves, president of James Robinson, adds, "The surface of machine-made silver can become scratched. Handmade work hardens the metal and makes it tougher and stronger, harder to scratch or mar its surface."

Hammering the words gives quality to advertising copy, too. Both *handmade* and *handcrafted* have been around so long they are single words; the newer *hand-finished* and *hand-forged* should be hyphenated until in wider use. But watch 'em: They're weasel words.

Watch *flatware,* too. Here's an ad by the Royal Viking Line in a recent *Connoisseur* magazine: "In a glass and flatware world, there is still a place for crystal and silver." Doesn't scan. *Glass* is to *crystal* as *base metal* or *silver plate* is to *silver.*

Flatware is neither cheap nor classy; it just lies there, flat, not rolling around. Applied to cutlery, the word means knives, forks, spoons or the little gizmos you use to get the meat out of lobster claws, or the grabby devices that hold escargot shells (and must never be confused with eyelash curlers); these utensils can be made of plastic or stainless steel and still be classified as *flatware,* though the word is used more often in regard to silver or silver plate.

"The contrast to *flatware* is *holloware,*" writes Burton D. Hunter of Memphis. He's right. Applied to dishes, *flatware* means plates, as distinct from *holloware,* which covers cups, soup bowls and pitchers. Like today's column, they, too, can be *hand-finished.*

The Hard Truth About Soft Money

Moneta was the cult title of the Roman goddess Juno, in whose temple coins were stamped out; that's where the word *money* comes from. The root of much evil, however, is in the modifiers of *money*—the adjectives that sow such confusion that you have to flip a coin to decide their meanings.

Funny money is clear: counterfeit. *Tight money* is equally specific: money that is costly to borrow, coming from a policy aimed at stifling inflation; the opposite is *easy money* or *cheap money,* when the money supply is increased by the central bank to commercial banks, and loans are available at low interest rates.

After *easy,* it gets hard: *Hard money* was originally specie, coin made out of durable metal, distinguished from paper currency. *Hard money* today, however, is the opposite of *soft money* or *soft dollars,* and now we are into an area of confusion between the worlds of politics and finance.

To political reformers, ethical straight arrows and other goo-goos (a century-old term based on "good government"), *soft money* is sinister. Before Robert A. Mosbacher, Mr. Bush's chief fund-raiser, was confirmed as Secretary of Commerce, a *New York Times* editorial called on him to help in "clearing the air about the millions he raised in so-called 'soft-money' campaign contributions."

Soft money, in politics, is free of the restrictions imposed by the Federal Election Commission on national campaigns. Unions and corporations may still give as much as they want to assist voter-turnout drives and to publicize local and state candidates; individual fat cats are also free to contribute with no limit in these areas without embarrassing public identification, same as in days of pre-Watergate yore. Politicians, especially those running against entrenched incumbents, hail this system as free speech in action; groups such as Common Cause claim that it allows fat cats (a 1928 term based on *fat-frying,* an 1888 description of fund-raising) and faceless corporate entities undue influence.

" 'Soft money' abuses in the funding of Presidential campaigns," wrote Robert Walters in the *Washington Times,* "have attained the proportions of a major national scandal." This is because national parties have been able to circumvent the limits on federally financed presidential campaigns by coordinating and targeting the soft money raised ostensibly for local usage.

A *New York Times* editorial treated the phrase with severity in 1988: "Soft Money? No—Sewer Money." Many liberals have failed to join the movement to restrict this outside-the-limit fund-raising because, as *National Journal* headlined during the Bush and Dukakis campaigns, " 'Soft' Money Is Closing the Gap for Democrats."

To financiers and stockbrokers, *soft money*—usually expressed as *soft dollars*—means something else. First, set aside *soft currency:* A nation's currency was once said to be soft when it was not pegged to a reserve currency or some official rate, but in an age of floating rates, that is no longer the way the world works. For our purposes, we can dispense with phrases like "the dollar is softening": That means demand for it is lessening or weakening, and the dollar's price in other currencies is becoming cheaper—in simple terms, it buys less.

The *soft dollar* that is the center of attention these days cannot be held lovingly in the hand or run happily through the fingers. It is the unprinted, unminted currency of third-party barter, creatively and sometimes illegally assigning a value to a service not received and arranging for that value to be spent elsewhere. Soft dollars are the currency of the cushion-shot.

"I realize there is a fixed [commission] price here," says a fictional customer in a 1979 *Fortune* article by Carol J. Loomis, "and that therefore I have to pay the full spread. But since I think I am overpaying for this particular merchandise—after all, is it not pretty cheap to process my big order?—I wish to assign the excess dollars to other firms, for services they are rendering me." The customer knows the securities dealer is making a big profit on his transaction, and wants a part of that profit returned. He seeks a partial rebate—the euphemism is *recapture*—payable to somebody else in lieu of real, or "hard," dollars.

The Securities and Exchange Commission finds some forms of soft-dollar discount bartering acceptable, but draws the line at payments unrelated to investment decisions. "Soft-dollar arrangements are one way of capturing more commission business," writes McGraw-Hill's *Securities Week,* rejecting quotation marks in favor of hyphenating the phrase used adjectivally, "but in the end the business can end up causing problems if it is not handled correctly at the back-office level." ("In the end . . . can end up"? "Back-office level"? That's soft editing.)

In academia, "hard money" is the term for salaries that appear in the regular budget based on annuities or grants. "Soft money" comes from one-time sources or is based on renewable grants. It makes a difference to the recipient, who usually must apply for the grants.

> John R. Knott
> Iowa City, Iowa

Soft Academics

In a recent piece about the new meanings of *soft money*—to pols, "unrestricted political contributions," and to stockbrokers, "the currency of third-party barter"—I neglected another meaning that touches a sensitive spot with a great many academics.

One of my ivy-covered correspondents is James D. McCawley, a professor of linguistics at the University of Chicago, whose new book, *Syntactic Phenomena of English,* has sparked great controversy between syntacticians and syntacticists.

It has, by the way, a good index. When next I review a book, I will give close attention to the useful or inadequate index, which tends to be overlooked by reviewers who work from unindexed galley proofs.

Here's an example. In Bergen Evans's *Dictionary of Quotations,* under "alliteration," you can find the usual references to quotations containing that word. But follow the subentry that says "illustrations of dangers of" and you are directed to the 1884 quotation that contains the alliterative phrase, *rum, Romanism and rebellion,* a slur that backfired on the Republicans of that era. That's creative indexing, which is an aid to scholars and too often dismissed as drudgery; publishers try to get authors to pay for the indexing, resulting in quick-and-dirty jobs.

Book critics: Finger those indexes. Now back to the subject at hand.

"*Soft money* in an academic context," writes Professor McCawley, "is money (especially from an outside source) that is available only for a limited period of time and carries no commitment of expenditures after that period is over; negotiations to lure a faculty member from one university to another occasionally include questions such as 'Would you be willing to come on soft money for a year, while we try to talk the administration into putting up hard money for a position for you?' "

Haven Maven

A pundit careless with his usage wrote this about the astrophysicist Fang Lizhi, the Beijing dissident who is now a house guest of the United States: "You can send him and his family a welcome note care of the U.S. Embassy in Peking [Box 50, FPO, San Francisco, CA 96655], where they are holed up under our protection. The asylum granted him has infuriated the Deng regime. . . ."

As soon as I saw this in print, I barked, "Gotcha!" despite the fact that the offending pundit was me (not *I*). This is a manifestation of Writer's Self-Flagellation Syndrome. One's own words always seem different in print; a writer reads himself with a touch of disbelief because the words stand proudly out there on their own, more respectable and permanently independent than the author. That's why some of us get a perverse kick out of finding mistakes in our own work; it makes the creator feel smarter than his smugly frozen creation.

Asylum was not quite the right word. Nor were Fang Lizhi and his family granted *sanctuary,* strictly speaking; better to say they were granted *refuge.*

Splitting hairs? Hardly; in the synonymy of *haven,* we are stepping into a sensitive field of international law. A call to the Office of Legal Counsel in the Department of State meets with a stiff rebuff; in this case, the normally instructive Judge Abraham D. Sofaer won't say a word about choosing the right word. With legal eagles seeking maven-haven, let us approach the subject linguistically.

Haven is the oldest and broadest term. The noun is related to the Middle High German *habene,* "harbor," and its early English use about a millennium ago referred to an inlet for safe anchorage. Now the word's figurative extension carries it beyond a safe port in a storm to any safe place for people in trouble. *Harbor,* on the other hand, has taken a sinister turn in its verb form: You can *offer haven* to the hunted, thereby winning sympathy as a protector of the persecuted, but you *harbor* a criminal or a suspect on the run, thereby abetting a crime.

Asylum is rooted in the Greek *asylos,* "inviolable," from *a-,* meaning "not, without," and *sylon,* meaning "right of seizure." The right of *asylum* in a *sanctuary* is ancient, going back to Egypt's Temple of Osiris and Greece's Temple of Apollo at Delphi. But frequent abuse of this right, and the decline of the secular power of organized religion, led to its curtailment in modern penal codes.

To provide for the extradition of fugitive criminals, nations sign treaties voluntarily limiting asylum—making it clear that the "right of asylum" belongs to the state to offer, and is not an entitlement for the individual to claim. (Another sense of the word, as a place where care is given to an unfortunate—as in *orphan asylum* or *insane asylum*—is no longer used.)

Refuge today has a more temporary and less legal connotation. Rooted in the Latin *fugere,* "to flee," it first appeared in *The Canterbury Tales,* as a captured knight tells the ruler Theseus: "Yif us neither mercy ne refuge, / But sle me first." ("Give us neither mercy nor refuge, / But slay me first.")

Refugee, which was used in America as a word for marauders in the Revolutionary War who claimed British protection, in 1914 gained the meaning of "someone displaced by war or driven from home by fear of death or persecution."

For the difference between *asylum* and *refuge,* let us turn to Duke Austin, a press officer of the United States Immigration and Naturalization Service: "It depends on the process and place of applying, and the formal status received. To get asylum in the United States, you must be within our territory when you apply. Also, you must be able to prove a well-founded fear of persecution based on your race, religion, nationality or membership in a social or political group."

How is a *refugee* different? "Refugees must also establish that they will be persecuted," says the immigration official, "but a refugee applies outside the United States and is examined by an I.N.S. examiner—no judicial review, no appeal, though you can ask for a reconsideration based on new information."

Sanctuary? "We recognize no such concept; no one is above or beyond the laws of the United States, whether in a church or hospital or whatever."

Presumably, then, Fang Lizhi sought *refuge* in the United States Embassy, and may now be seeking *asylum,* since he is under our protection and is obviously in danger because of his political beliefs. However, the Beijing "authorities" (a more neutral term than "blood-spattered regime") have ordered his arrest on criminal charges, and remind us that we do not harbor criminals. That's why State clams up on definitions.

Associated terms are *safe conduct* and *safe convoy,* by which a person in legal limbo in an embassy is permitted to leave the country. This began in the Middle Ages, according to Robert of Gloucester's 1297 chronicle of a nobleman let out of England. Sanctuary was short-term; fugitives could stay in sanctuary but not leave without being arrested.

To get around this, a process of *abjuration* was designed—from *abjure,* "to swear away, to renounce under oath"—requiring a renunciation of citizenship and a promise to leave the realm. This was the way the impasse of the state, the sanctuary and the persecuted was resolved. As part of an agreement of abjuration worked out among the United States, the Vatican and the Hungarian government, Jozsef Cardinal Mindszenty was allowed to depart Hungary after leaving the protection of the United States Embassy in Budapest in 1971.

That may or may not be the route taken in the case of Fang Lizhi and his family. In any event, the vocabulary of *haven* will be in the news, along with the name that Americans will not find easy to pronounce. Is it "fong lee-DZUH," as I have advised readers, or "fong lee-JER," as we hear on television? That final syllable gets the emphasis, and some of us pronounce it like the French *je,* while others add an *r.* Chinese officials in Washington don't use the *r,* to my ear. According to Norman C. C. Fu, chief of the Washington Bureau for the Taiwan-based *China Times,* "There's a sort of *r* sound at the end, but it isn't completely sounded."

This is disputed. "Pinyin spelling looks funny," writes John S. Major, a senior editor of Book-of-the-Month Club, "but its rules are reasonably consistent. The initial consonant cluster *zh* is pronounced exactly the same as an English hard *j;* thus, for example, *Zhou* (as in *Zhou Enlai*) is a homophone of *Joe.*

"I as a final vowel following *c, s* or *z* is pronounced 'uh,' as in *huh;* as a final vowel following *ch, sh* or *zh,* it is pronounced 'ur,' as in *urgent.* Therefore, *zhi* in *Fang Lizhi* is pronounced 'jur'—approximately a homophone for the start of *journalist,* spoken with a New York accent."

That makes the pronunciation of *Beijing* "bay-JING"—with the *j* as in *Joe* or *jingle*—rather than "bay-SHING."

The particular situation in which astrophysicist Fang Lizhi finds himself is more than mere "asylum," or seeking refuge. When individuals guilty of political offenses, or qualifying as political persecutees, choose or are compelled to remain in their own countries, some may seek asylum in foreign embassies or legations. When this occurs, under international law the situation is properly known as diplomatic asylum.

The stated policy of the United States is to refuse to grant requests for diplomatic asylum on grounds that unlimited stay in an embassy can constitute unwarranted intervention into the affairs of the host state. When such situations do occur, the U.S. State Department labels them grants of "temporary refuge," not "diplomatic asylum," since that would contravene U.S. stated policy.

> *Christopher C. Joyner*
> *Visiting Professor*
> *Department of Political*
>   *Science*
> *George Washington University*
> *Washington, D.C.*

High Jinks and Low Bogeys

"Bogeys," cried a United States fighter pilot facing fast-closing Libyan jets, "have jinked back at me again for the fifth time. . . . Fox One!"

These words, taped by the Defense Department and released after the incident, were played on every network and boxed on front pages of newspapers. The unfamiliar words used by the four Americans in the pair of F-14's are rooted deeply in armed-forces lingo, and can be tracked even more deeply into general slang.

Bogey, according to Eric Partridge's slang dictionary, is Royal Air Force

usage from early in World War II meaning "an aircraft suspected to be hostile." American aviators picked it up from the R.A.F. veterans; in 1945, *Newsweek* used the term to mean "in radar code, an unidentified enemy aircraft." The essence of the term is suspicion but not positive identification; after a bogey has been proved hostile, it becomes a *bandit*.

Apparently the *bogey* is the same as the one in *bogeyman*, rooted in the circa-1820 term *Old Bogey*, meaning "the devil." (Some slanguists guess that the word comes from *bog-house*, or toilet.)

A golfer in 1890 named Major Wellman imagined "par" for each hole to be the score of an imaginary player, and named that player "The Bogey Man," which was the title of a British song of the day about a scary demon. A *bogey* has since meant "par" in British usage, one stroke over par in American golf.

Jink? This verb is identified as "chiefly British" in *Webster's New World Dictionary* and defined as "to move swiftly or with sudden turns, as in dodging a pursuer." As a noun, it refers to "an eluding, as by a quick, sudden turn"; according to the usage by the American pilot facing the Libyan MIG-23's, it also refers to sudden movements in an attack.

The intransitive verb *jink* is originally Scottish, and the *Oxford English Dictionary* speculates that it may be of onomatopoeic origin, "expressing the idea of nimble motion." Maybe it's also connected to *jig*, which has a meaning of "to move quickly," as "in jig time." Since 1914, *jink* has been applied to a tricky or unexpected turn in rugby, akin to a "dodge" in American football. It is also related to the last part of *high jinks*, or horseplay—and a warm hello to Jinx (short for Eugenia) Falkenburg McCrary, whose husband-and-wife radio interview program in the 1950's began with "Hi, Jinx."

Fox is part of the old military phonetic alphabet, with its initial capitalizations, just after *Easy* and before *George.* (In 1955, we crumbled to North Atlantic Treaty Organization demands that we change these easy-to-understand words to *Echo, Foxtrot* and *Golf.*) The use of *Fox* remained in armed-forces lingo, however, to mean "Fire," for reasons I have yet to hear explained rationally; if it's code, it's not fooling anybody. *Fox One* was used by the pilot to mean "I have fired One," with the "One" identifying a Sparrow missile; *Fox Two* refers to a Sidewinder missile.

Thus, in one brief burst of slang, centuries of informal usage are brought to bear. Yet many thought that *Bogey* was only an affectionate reference to Humphrey Bogart.

You say "some slanguists" trace bogey back to old bogey (devil) or to boghouse (toilet). Others, me included, think bogey is a cleaned-up version of bugger.

In the South to this day you hear children afraid (or so threatened by adults) of the buggerman. And bugger, as you have pointed out in other places, goes back to bulgar (for Bulgarian), labeled by some as a pederast—unjust as this stereotype may have been.

Isn't it likely that bugger man was euphemized to bogey man—thus giving us bogey?

Roy Alexander
New York, New York

Here is a possibility for the origin of the word bogey. Bogey is the name of a tribe in Sulawesi Selatan. The Bogey tribe is noted for their untidy habits and menacing ways. Many think they kidnap small children, giving rise to the expression used to intimidate small children: "The bogeyman (orang bogey) will get you if you don't watch out."

It could be coincidental, but the word bogey surfaced in the English language shortly after the British quit Indonesia in 1816. Could it be that Sir Stamford Raffles is responsible for bringing the word to the English language?

David Strickland
Jakarta Selatan, Indonesia

Webster's New Collegiate Dictionary, Merriam, Springfield, Conn., 1976, asserts an older root for *bogey* than you do. Although like you it derives *bogeyman* from *bogey,* it then relates *bogeyman* to *bogle, boggle,* both in northern English dialect meaning "terrifying apparition, object of fear or loathing" (hence perhaps "boggles the mind"). Both are said to be akin to *bug,* the obsolete meaning of which is "bogey, bugbear." *Bug* is related to Middle English *bugge,* meaning "scarecrow," which is akin to Norwegian dialect *bugge,* meaning "important man," akin to the English and Middle English *big* and to the Old English word for a "boil," the Latin word for "bubble" and to the Sanskrit word for "abundant" (and, I suggest, possibly to the Russian root *pookh,* meaning "[to] swell").

In addition, the cited Webster gives the alternative form *boogeyman* as derived from *booger man,* from *man* plus English dialect *buggard, boggard* (meaning "bogeyman"), which also are from the first meaning of *bug.*

Now, though aware of the perils of armchair etymologizing, I venture to suggest two additional cognates.

One possible cognate of *bogey* is *Puck,* archaically meaning "an evil spirit or demon," derived from Middle English *puke* (of course pronounced with two syllables), from Old English *puca* with a long *u,* akin to the Old Norse *puki,* meaning "devil." This may be related to the classic Greek *psyche,* soul or spirit, especially as (1) *pooka* is a Slavic word for English *fart* (which itself is probably related to Russian *veter* meaning "wind," as well as to French *petard,* said by Partridge (in *Origins,* which I just thought to consult) to be from Sanskrit *pard* meaning "fart"); (2) wind was anciently identified with spirit, for example being thought able to inseminate mares; (3) the Pythagoreans would not eat beans, because beans caused farts, which Pythagoreans thought the spirits of their ancestors, whom they felt should not be subject to the indignity of anal venting, and (4) the possibly related Greek word *pneuma* meant "gas, vapor, air." I now see that Partridge (p. 52) explicitly relates *bogey* to *Puck,* but without any reference to the "psyche/wind" possibility.

The other possible cognate of *bogey* is the Old Slavonic and Russian word *Bog,* meaning "God." This might be related to the source of the Norwegian *bugge,* inasmuch as important men were sometimes deified in ancient times, and in view of the fearful meaning of all the "bogey" words.

With regard to the slanguists' guess that "Old Bogey" comes from *boghouse,* "toilet," I venture two further guesses: (1) *bog-house* could have meant "god-house," applied irreverently to an outhouse the way a toilet-seat-and-bowl is jokingly called a throne, or (2) the *bog* here is Gaelic and means "mire," meaning "swamp."

Theodore Melnechuk
San Diego, California

A bogey is a pay increment for hourly paid workers in the steel industry.

We start with base pay rate. One step up (say time-and-a-half for overtime) is a bogey. An additional increment bringing pay up to double time (say, for holiday work) would be two bogeys.

Why, I do not know.

> Sheldon Wesson
> American Iron and Steel
> Institute
> Washington, D.C.

"Fox" is used to mean "I have fired" because, not only is it shorter, it won't be confused with an announcement of a fire, meaning conflagration, on board the aircraft. The same logic exists in the RTO use of "Say again" when asking for a repeat of part of a transmission. The reason is simple: In the Artillery, "Repeat" means to remount the last barrage using the same coordinates. If an artillery forward observer, speaking to the fire control officer, shouts "Repeat" over the radio when he wants a reiteration of the last transmission, he could get a load of artillery on his head—or on the friendly infantry up ahead.

> Richard E. Kramer
> New York, New York

Logic in lieu of knowledge might provide a rational explanation for the use of "Fox" to mean "Fire."

Rifles, shotguns, and pistols were marked "Fire" or "F" and "Safe" or "S" to indicate readiness of a weapon long before the advent of fighter pilots and missiles. The use of "Fox" for "F" under combat conditions would appear logical and using the cumbersome "Foxtrot" under such conditions illogical.

Interestingly, German weapons also use "F" and "S" for the same purpose but different words. Perhaps the French also but I'm not sure.

> John C. Davis
> Dallas, Texas

When I was in the U.S. Navy, 1961–64, a distinction was made between "fire" for burning and "shoot" a gun. In battle you didn't want the ambiguity of two meanings of "fire."

> Neil Grant
> Rockaway, New Jersey

Hit My Hot Button

"What's a *hot button*?" *Newsweek* asked itself in the homestretch of the 1988 campaign. "It's something a candidate says to instantly show that his values are the voters' values." The newsmagazine, in the forefront of popularizers of this phrase, listed Republican *hot buttons* as the American Civil Liberties Union, abortion and guns, and those of the Democrats as Social Security and Panamanian leader General Manuel Antonio Noriega.

Although *Newsweek* makes a point of separating the meaning of *hot button* from an "issue" or anything a candidate will have to deal with if elected, the magazine sometimes uses the noun phrase adjectivally to modify *social issue,* a term coined by Ben J. Wattenberg and Richard M. Scammon in 1970. It reported after the first debate that Mr. Bush had held his own on "the *hot-button* social issues of crime, abortion and the death penalty," but later added that "the *hot-button* attacks that had tarred Dukakis as unpatriotic and soft on crime were beginning to backfire."

The Wall Street Journal also treated *social issue* as subsumed by the broader category of *hot-button issues:* "Take the social issues . . ." wrote the *Journal* editorialist. "Outside of places such as Cambridge and Georgetown, these are *hot-button issues.*"

The adjectival button was born in this campaign, but the noun form predates it. An aide to Senator Bob Dole was quoted last year describing Ambassador Jeane J. Kirkpatrick as a speaker who "hits a hot button with conservatives on foreign policy," picking up a usage of the Senator's in regard to Social Security. As early as 1981, John L. Stevens, then director of the Republican Governors Association, was quoted in *The Washington Post* as saying, "There are a whole lot of hot buttons waiting to be pushed; we're still trying to find out what those buttons are."

The phrase was created in the hard-sell field of consumer marketing, which offers a silent commentary on the central thrust of this year's political campaign. "The marketers are searching," wrote Walter Kiechel 3d in *Fortune* on September 11, 1978, "for what they call 'consumer hot buttons'—needs to be satisfied, desires to be slaked—and the means to push those buttons." *Forbes* magazine was on top of the neologism a month later in a piece about direct-mail solicitation of companies for sale: "The hot buttons are money and leisure."

The computer world, which operates on keys and buttons as well as mouses, picked up the term in 1983: hot-button windowing uses a single keystroke to split screens, allowing users to view different sets of data at the same time. Another consumer use of the phrase is in home sales, with real-estate brokers pointing to bathroom details—sunken tubs, saunas, gold-plated faucets—as hot buttons that lure buyers into closing a deal. (A gold-plated knob that causes cold water to flow from the faucet can be called a hot button, but may confuse the user.)

The columnist Ann Landers was bombarded with mail in 1984 after wondering in print whether women preferred cuddling and tender stroking to the sex act. "Apparently I had touched a hot button," she said, and *Time* magazine in 1985 agreed: "The Landers survey appeared to have touched a hot button among sex therapists. . . ."

Today, the term is used more frequently as a modifier than as a noun, and has its most frequent play in politics, but the noun is still used to mean "exposed nerve" generally; in the magazine *Manhattan Inc.,* a subhead in a story about the MacNeil-Lehrer report on public television read, "Comparisons with *Nightline* are a hot button among the staff."

A *hot-button issue* (the compound, used adjectivally, requires the hyphen) is one that causes anger, fear, passionate support or active loathing in potential voters. It is usually, though not always, an issue concerning the values held or the way one's personal life is to be lived, rather than an issue idealized by political scientists as "substantive."

It is replacing, perhaps temporarily, *gut issue;* like that predecessor phrase, its meaning can include *bread-and-butter issue* and *unspoken issue.* A *hot-button issue* is more specific than *switcher issue,* which is a position that, taken alone, can cause some voters to change candidates. *Paramount issue* is obsolete. *The issues,* a phrase usually pronounced in a censorious or whining tone, means "serious policy matters that should be debated rather than the sensationalist subjects that the candidates, pollsters and media editors have decided interest most voters."

I think the term hot button comes from psychotherapy, not marketing. In What Do You Say After You Say Hello?, published in 1972, Eric Berne, the originator of transactional analysis, defines button as "an internal or external stimulus which turns on scripty or gamy behavior." Berne's Games People Play was a best-seller in the mid-1960s.

Computer users do not refer to hot buttons. The keystroke combination that activates certain programs is called a hot key or a trigger key. A button is a mechanical switch on a mouse. On the Macintosh, button can also mean an outlined area on the screen that the user selects to choose, confirm, or cancel a command.

The usual plural of mouse is mice, although mouses is known.

> Alan Wachtel
> Mountain View, California

The term "hot button" appeared in the private pilot's magazine Aviation Consumer back in 1979. (I was an editor there at the time.) We published an article critical of Piper Aircraft Corp., and the company responded by cutting off all communication with us. In a follow-up article describing the blackballing, we quoted Piper's former public relations chief, who described how company president J. Lynn Helms had issued the blackball edict personally, over the P.R. department's objections. The ex-P.R. man told us, "Everybody has their hot button, and I guess that's Helms's."

> Dave Noland
> Mountainville, New York

While a student representative at the University of Vermont Admissions Office in 1981, I conducted evaluative interviews of prospective freshmen. The evaluation form contained a section titled "Hot Buttons." They were explained to me by the Admissions director to be those intangibles that set a student apart from his contemporaries. Those with buttons hot enough usually were admitted.

> Steven A. Weissman
> West Lafayette, Indiana

Holier Than Who?

In zapping a self-righteous politician, I wrote that he was filled with the spirit of Isaiah, and quoted that prophet as saying, "Stand not next to me, for I am holier than thou."

"You have turned Isaiah inside out," protests Michael Sanders of Monsey, New York. "*Holier than thou* (Isaiah 65:5) is not the spirit of Isaiah, but of those whom he excoriates as 'a rebellious people' in the verses preceding."

Watchman, what of the preceding verses? Sure enough, I owe Isaiah an apology. The prophet was lambasting the unruly people hanging around graveyards, eating swine's flesh and stirring caldrons filled with a tainted brew—presumably a near-primordial moonshine—and he quoted them as saying to him, "Stand by thyself, come not near to me; for I am holier than thou."

It was a quote-within-a-quote, but the clarifying punctuation was not in use at the time of the 1611 King James translation, and so I have been attributing to Isaiah the hypocritical words he was attributing to the targets of his wrath. But the words, which we would now characterize in a hyphenated compound adjective as *holier-than-thou,* had been spoken by Isaiah to describe others, not himself.

Call off the postcard barrage, Isaiah fans. As Lyndon Johnson used to say, "Come now, let us reason together."

You quote Lyndon Johnson as saying, "Come, let us reason together." No less eminent a theologian than the late Dr. Reinhold Niebuhr chided Johnson for quoting Isaiah out of context. From the verses preceding and following 1:18, it is obvious that God is not inviting the rulers of Sodom and the people of Gomorrah to reason with Him. He is saying, "Come, let us reach an understanding." He's commanding them to cease from evil and do good, or else!

Louise Sklaroff
Philadelphia, Pennsylvania

Hopeless

The minute you get elected, you get the idea you can rewrite Lincoln.

In his Second Annual Message to Congress, President Lincoln wrote:

"We shall nobly save, or meanly lose, the last best, hope of earth." This was not some ad-lib taken down by a reporter, subject to error in transmission; this was a written message between branches of government, set in type, immutable, the way Lincoln wanted it. (Controversy exists about the comma after *best*. The comma belongs between the two adjectives *last* and *best,* and not after the *best;* however, it is not for us, the living, to switch the commas.)

One of Jimmy Carter's speechwriters, who knew the accurate wording, changed *of* to *on* because he believed that *of earth* jarred, and that most listeners would think the correct Lincoln version a misquotation. And so the Carter version of the Lincoln quotation was "the last best hope *on* earth."

Ronald Reagan evidently did not like the idea of the Earth doing the hoping. On innumerable occasions, he edited Lincoln's line to read "the last best hope *of man* on earth." (A side issue: *Earth,* the planet, should be capitalized; Lincoln made a mistake there, but let's not nitpick. Imagine quoting him this way: "the last [*sic*] best hope of [*sic*] earth [*sic*]." That would be disrespectful.)

Along comes George Bush. On his election eve telecast, he called up the ghost of Lincoln and referred to America as "the last *great* hope of man on earth." Lincoln's *best* was not good enough; now the hope, with Mr. Reagan's *of man* added, has been elevated to *great.*

What next? I can hear it now: "America, the *first* great aspiration of humankind on this wonderful planet."

You indicate speechwriters' problems with President Lincoln's reference to freedom as the "last best hope of earth."

It might have helped if the speechwriters had known that the original line was taken from William Hazlitt's essay on Byron (written in 1824), ending: "Lord Byron is dead: he also died a martyr to his zeal in the cause of freedom, for the last, best hopes of man. Let that be his excuse and his epitaph" (emphasis added; note the single comma). Lincoln changed "hopes" to "hope" and "man" to "earth." Carter's speechwriter changed "of [earth]" to "on [earth]." The Reagan version, "of man on earth," blends the original Hazlitt with the Lincoln version. The result is either a pompous superfluity or a religious reference to man's existence elsewhere.

There is a hidden irony: Byron's zeal was to the cause of Greek "freedom" from Turkish rule; Lincoln's was certainly not for the self-determination of the Confederate States, but for a human "freedom" on a different level. The shift from politically organized "man" to politically neutral "earth" seems to have a subtle connection with that change, broadening the nationalism implicit in the Hazlitt to a universal. But unless the original words and political context are pondered the switch seems arbitrary. I wonder if the Reagan speechwriters had something else in mind.

> Alfred P. Rubin
> Professor of International Law
> Tufts University
> Medford, Massachusetts

In fairness it should be noted that President Lincoln's "last best, hope on earth" was in itself an emendation of a predecessor's felicitous phrase; Thomas Jefferson, in his first inaugural address, referred to our government as "the world's best hope."

By the way, Mr. Bush could profit from reading that speech, which was given following a campaign even nastier and more divisive than 1988's. Jefferson, whose patriotism, morals, and character had been viciously attacked, called for reconciliation and urged that "every difference of opinion is not a difference of principle."

> Charles Stephen Ralston
> New York, New York

How *Managing* Is Managing

A *manager* is not as big a deal as an *executive.* If you do not understand this, you will never get ahead in business or in the media.

The difference is plain in the roots of words themselves. *Manage* is from the Latin *manus,* "hand," and the original meaning of the verb *handle* was "to direct by hand." Even today, we speak of *hands-on managers,* accepting the redundancy as emphasizing direct control; the picture is of a boss grabbing his assistant by the lapels.

On the other *manus,* the verb *execute* is from the Latin *ex-,* "out of," and *sequi,* "follow"—literally, "following out" or, as executives and golfers would put it, "following through." No labor in which the hands are involved is suggested. While a *manager* organizes and supervises the work of others, an *executive* follows through on the mission itself.

At the New York *Tribune* during the Civil War, the journalist-politician Horace Greeley was not about to share the title of *editor* with Charles Dana, who happened to be running the day-to-day business of putting out the paper. Greeley's solution: He became *editor in chief,* and Dana was the first

man to be dubbed *managing editor*—first, that is, until somebody sends in written proof to the contrary. The word *managing* meant "in charge of operations but not policy."

Today, newspaper reporters still try not to run afoul of the managing editor, but the one to really worry about is the editor in chief. Nope; hold the presses; that title, with its ring of tradition, is on the way out. The top gun is now *executive* editor, presumably because editors would rather be executives than chiefs. In journalism, the adjective *executive* sounds more important than the modifying participle *managing;* in business, executive vice presidents lord it over mere vice presidents.

But here comes a strange linguistic twist: In business, *executive vice president* is on the way out and *managing director* is in. Suddenly, *managing* has overtaken *executive* as the desirable adjective in executive (soon to become managing) suites.

Managing director is British usage, recorded first by John Stuart Mill in 1861: "Even a joint-stock company has always in practice, if not in theory, a managing director." In the City, London's financial district, when the *chairman* is the policy-setting chief executive (and is sometimes called the *executive chairman*), the *managing director* is number 2, running operations. The managing director fills the job Americans have called *president* or *executive vice president,* when the person in that slot was not chief executive officer. When the managing director is the boss, *"and chief executive"* is often added to the title. The British *chairman* is chairman of the company, while the American *chairman* is chairman of the board of directors, more markedly removed from active management. Because too much power in one individual is considered worrisome, the trend in Britain is toward the combination of a chairman and a chief executive who is the managing director.

Nowadays in the United States, the top person adds the *C.E.O.* designation to avoid confusion; when Americans work abroad, they often recognize the confusion inherent in the different ideas about *managing director.* In London, John G. Heimann, the top man of Merrill Lynch Europe Ltd., eschews all other labels and carries the unambiguous title *chief executive.*

To give cachet to their inferior positions, American executives who are not chief executive officers—especially investment bankers—have lustily embraced *managing director.* "It's starting to take hold in the U.S.," says Robert Newton of the American Management Association. "It wouldn't be exactly on a par with executive vice president, but that's the sense of the job's importance."

At Shearson Lehman in New York City, about 120 managing directors manage, direct and otherwise busy themselves, compared to about 100 executive vice presidents. The pecking order there is chairman, vice chairmen, senior executive vice presidents, senior managing directors, managing directors, executive vice presidents, followed by all the Little People.

Thus we have taken the power of management out of the participle *managing;* when a dozen managers exist, an *executive* becomes necessary. In years to come, we can look to a furious battle for dominance between the senior executive managing director and the managing vice chairman. I'll keep you informed unless the managing editor comes after me.

In Nine Little Words

According to Rich Jaroslovsky of *The Wall Street Journal,* George Bush described a photo session at which he makes remarks but refuses to answer reporters' questions as "a modified limited photo op cum statement sans questions."

How richly those nine little words resonate, with their deep-rooted, vividly remembered allusions setting up sympathetic vibrations in four distinct areas.

Modified limited, especially without the comma that ordinarily separates adjectives in series, harks back to Watergate's *modified limited hangout,* from a statement made by John D. Ehrlichman about taking "the modified limited hangout route."

Note the deliberate absence of a comma between what seem to be adjectives in series; one possible reason is that *modified* seems to modify the adjective *limited,* not the noun *hangout,* and therefore serves the emphasizing function of an adverb; a different reason, if you treat *modified* as an adjective joining *limited* in modifying the noun *hangout,* is that the comma's absence fuses the adjectives in recollection of the phrase's history. Were a comma inserted, young readers, who tend to think of Watergate as a Washington altercation in the aftermath of the Spanish-American War, might miss the distinctly Nixonian allusion.

(The omitted comma should always be examined. In the name of Wall Street's Merrill Lynch, Pierce, Fenner & Smith Inc., a comma would ordinarily appear between the *Merrill*—Charles Merrill—and the *Lynch*—Edmund Lynch. Why doesn't it? Because in 1941, when the firm that was once Merrill, Lynch & Company joined with Fenner & Beane, together with Edward A. Pierce, the top man, Charles Merrill, wanted the name of his original firm separated from the rest of the "thundering herd." Without the comma, *Merrill Lynch* remains pristine—the name the firm is known by, followed by the rest of the guys, with Alpheus C. Beane's name later replaced by that of Winthrop Smith. How do I know this? Charlie Merrill told me in 1949, in my first interview for the New York *Herald Tribune* syndicate. He also advised me not to ask silly questions about commas in a serious interview, because "nit-picking never gets you anywhere in life." Little did he know.)

A *photo op,* short for *photo opportunity,* was also a Nixon Administration coinage. In those days of Jill Wine and roses, Mr. Nixon's press secretary, Ron Ziegler (now the president of the National Association of Chain Drug

Stores, a group that treats *drugstore* as two words), turned to his aide, Bruce Whelihan (now a stockbroker with Alex Brown, which has no comma because Alex was the founder's first name), and said, "Get 'em in for a picture." Mr. Whelihan dutifully announced to the White House press room, "There will be a photo opportunity in the Oval Office."

In a trice, all previous descriptions of picture-taking became *inoperative,* a word first used in the White House by President Lincoln. *Op,* a clip that used to be taken to mean *operative,* as in Dashiell Hammett's *Continental Op,* has come to mean *opportunity.*

The next of Mr. Bush's classic nine-word burst to study is the Latin preposition *cum,* pronounced halfway between "come" and "koom," meaning "with" and often used in hyphenated compounds to mean "combined with" or "plus," as in "speechwriter-*cum*-flack."

The use of *cum* was a Yuppie-ism in the 1970's, and is now in declining usage; Mr. Bush's steadfast use of the term is an example of his unwavering loyalty to causes and terms considered passé by avant-gardists.

No decline in voguishness, however, can be reported about *sans,* the French word for "without," which was borrowed frequently by Shakespeare ("sans taste, sans every thing") and has been used for centuries by speakers of English who have some knowledge of French. For those upscaling the power heights in Washington, the flash of old-line elitism in speech remains the way to go, especially if you're in a milieu of Cabinet-cum–White House staff (sans John Tower).

"Merrill Lynch" is certainly a fine example of the fused function of a comma-less construction, a grammatical expression of Charlie Merrill's desire for a strong continued bond to his longtime friend and partner, Eddie Lynch. But some of your details are based on misleading information.

By the time of the Fenner & Beane merger in August 1941, the comma was already gone three years. It was on August 1, 1938, that Merrill, Lynch & Co., a partnership then carrying on a rather limited investment banking business, incorporated as Merrill Lynch & Co., Inc., with the comma banished from then on. When Merrill was persuaded to re-enter the brokerage business, launching the firm that would bring "Wall Street to Main Street" on April 1, 1940, the commaless name was brought into the new partnership of Merrill Lynch, E. A. Pierce & Cassatt. The other big merger 16 months later created Merrill Lynch, Pierce, Fenner & Beane.

You may recall that you ran an earlier item on our comma (or lack thereof) in the mid-70s, or perhaps early 80s. Your staff contacted me at the time and you were nice enough to give me credit for supplying information, though you voiced doubt about some of it.

Since that time we've gathered considerable additional data (the editorial "we" particularly refers to the extensive work done by my research associate, Rosemarie Wenick) as part of the research for the centennial history I wrote in 1985.

As the enclosed excerpt from that history indicates, there have been numerous "explanations," most of them derived from revelations by Charlie Merrill himself. It would seem that while Mr. Merrill was one of the earliest and strongest advocates of full disclosure of investment information, when it came to what he considered "non-material" or, as he put it to you, "nit-picking" matters, he preferred to give rein to his impish sense of humor. He must be having a grand time now, watching from above (I trust) the continued competition of hypotheses he launched.

The most prevalent belief was that the comma disappeared much earlier, when a printer (or perhaps a sign painter) shortchanged the fledgling firm around 1915. In fact, when our history appeared, it elicited a "Gotcha" from Don Regan (for whom I wrote speeches in his pre-Washington days) when he came across our references to "Merrill, Lynch" in the 20s. He, too, had heard an Authorized Version from the man himself, and I suspect that, despite all the documented proof we pointed out to him, deep within he still harbors some nagging doubts.

Incidentally, while Ms. Wenick was able to interview one of Mr. Merrill's lawyers from that period, we never could pin down the precise reason for the 1938 comma shift, nor whether they had planned to drop the comma even before Mr. Lynch's death that May.

However, a story that went around the firm in the 40s is that the lack of comma came in handy two years later when the Merrill Lynch, E. A. Pierce & Cassatt partnership was formed in 1940. It was said that New York partnership law at the time permitted only names of actual (i.e., living) partners to go into the name of a new firm, but that Charlie Merrill was able to qualify "Merrill Lynch" as the name of an existing company rather than the names of two persons. Whether there is any validity to this story I do not know.

> Henry R. Hecht
> Merrill Lynch
> New York, New York

I refer to the name "Alex. Brown." You point out quite correctly that the name requires no separating comma, as "Merrill Lynch" would have required without that firm's express desire for onomastic distinction. "Alex. Brown" requires no separating comma, rather a period to reflect the shortened form of the founder's full name, "Alexander Brown."

Judging by the firm's longevity (established in 1800), Alex. Brown & Sons Incorporated appears to have succeeded in distinguishing itself from "the thundering herd" while retaining a period and eschewing a comma.

> Albert Nekimken
> Crofton, Maryland

On the use of "op" for opportunity: You quote Dashiell Hammett's reference to his character "the continental op" as an "operative."

I don't think so. He was an "operator," the noun that signifies his profession. When a word signifies that something is working it is "operative." The man or woman that does the job is an "operator."

> Edward Greeman
> Bay Harbor Islands, Florida

Weren't they "those days of Jill Wine and Rosemary Woods"?
Groans and cheers,

> Bruce Lambert
> The New York Times
> New York, New York

Inside Baseball

"It is one of those underappreciated, 'inside baseball' moments that ratify politics as the Ultimate Game. . . ." So begins a Michael Kramer column in *U.S. News & World Report.*

"Jack Germond produces a self-described 'inside baseball' syndicated political column," writes William Prochnau in *The Washington Post,* "with his partner, Jules Witcover." A couple of years ago, Tom Oliphant of the *Boston Globe* said that the columnists Rowland Evans and Robert Novak had been "marvelous on the *inside baseball* of the Democratic Party."

"The people in my state," said Richard Weiner, chairman of the Michigan Democratic party, "are interested in jobs, the economy and education. The rest is *inside baseball.*"

The phrase has been used outside baseball for at least a decade. Senator

Edward M. Kennedy, wrote Myra MacPherson in *The Washington Post* in 1978, "chairs endlessly boring hearings . . . then cuts through testimony with *inside baseball* jokes that no visitors understand but laugh at anyway."

The meaning of the phrase can best be ascertained from a brief study of its origin. In *Fungoes, Floaters and Fork Balls,* a 1987 baseball dictionary, Patrick Ercolano defines the term as "The style of play in which the offensive team tries to score one run at a time through such tactics as the bunt, the steal, the hit-and-run, the well-placed hit and the squeeze."

The Baltimore Orioles of the 1890's perfected this type of play; the baseball was then "dead," in contrast to the livelier ball of today, and usually traveled short distances even when a batter connected squarely. Wee Willie ("hit 'em where they ain't") Keeler of Baltimore was an exemplar of inside baseball, now frequently called *scientific baseball;* by the 1920's, along came Babe Ruth, then the livelier ball and a more wide-open, aim-for-the-fences game.

But the earlier style of play is still with us. Whitey Herzog, manager of the Kansas City Royals, who liked to put on the double steal or hit-and-run, was quoted in 1978 as saying, "If you understand 'inside' baseball, you gotta love us."

According to Red Barber, the former voice of the Brooklyn Dodgers, the phrase was a familiar one to baseball fans: "I've heard *inside baseball* ever since I've been in baseball. The idea of an inner circle, or *sanctum sanctorum,* goes back all the way to the days of tribal government."

From its sports context comes its political or professional denotation: minutiae savored by the cognoscenti, delicious details, nuances discussed and dissected by aficionados.

In politics, candidates who say they want to discuss larger issues look down their noses at the journalists and think-tankers who bedevil them with questions about campaign techniques, fund-raising plans and poll results. To them, *inside baseball* has a pejorative connotation that the phrase never gained in the baseball world. There, out-of-season reminiscences by avid fans, accompanied by rumors about next year's activities, are called the "Hot Stove League."

Coming up fast on the outside is a synonym for *inside baseball* from those more familiar with the sport of kings. A *horse race* has long had a sense of "hard-fought competition," but when the word *stories* is added, a new sense is born: emphasis on the who's-ahead aspect of a campaign to the exclusion of the substance presumably being discussed.

In 1984, Gerald Warren, editor of the *San Diego Union,* told a journalism audience that "some say the *horse race* is the story." In 1988, the *New York Times* reporter Irvin Molotsky wrote that defeated presidential hopeful Bob Dole complained that "reporters repeated gossip, wrote 'horse race stories' that concentrated on who was ahead and put 'titillation above education.' " In this criticism, the Republican Senate minority leader repeated the charge of President Jimmy Carter late in the 1980 campaign: that *horse race stories* contributed to voter apathy.

"Few stories are easier," wrote David Shaw in the *Los Angeles Times* in 1986, "to write—or read—than the *horse race* story: who's ahead and why." He was referring not to politics, but to the newspaper coverage of television news competition: "There is now a horse race almost every week in the evening news ratings."

Several of us here several weeks ago were a bit perplexed by your column on the term "inside baseball." Among American Leaguers in the 1920s and 1930s, inside baseball was associated with the National League and John McGraw, manager of the Giants. McGraw and most NL managers stubbornly refused to change tactics even after the advent of free-swingers like Ruth changed the game. Relying on the sacrifice, hit-and-run and stolen base, McGraw kept playing for one run. AL teams went for the three-run homer. And the AL became the dominant league for a generation. Junior Circuiters meant the term "inside baseball" to be disparaging. Studies by the sabermatician Bill James have recently confirmed this judgment. The three-run homer is the better tactic.

As you rightly noted, the phrase is misused by various Washington types. I wasn't sure, however, if you had the negative connotation clear.

James L. Baughman
University of
*   Wisconsin—Madison*
Madison, Wisconsin

Invent Me Again

"Reinventing the C.E.O." is the name of a survey of 1,500 executives from around the world conducted by Korn/Ferry International, the executive search firm, and the Columbia University Graduate School of Business.

There's an old word that fought off the drag of a denigrating cliché to come into its own in our time. *Reinvent,* based on the Latin *invenire,* "to come upon," was coined in 1686 when Robert Plot wrote in his natural history of Staffordshire about "This not being the first time, that the same thing has been reinvented."

From the context of the coinage, such reinvention was apparently suspect; the word's meaning had a slightly phony or larcenous ring. Then somebody—we don't know who, because it's not in the cliché dictionaries—lumbered (British colloquial usage) or saddled (American colloquial usage) or burdened (Standard English) the verb with the dramatically foolish notion of *reinventing the wheel.* As defined in Robert L. Chapman's *New Dictionary of American Slang,* the familiar verb phrase means "to go laboriously and unnecessarily through elementary stages in some process or enterprise; waste time on tediously obvious fundamentals."

In the 1985 book on management by John Naisbitt and Patricia Aburdene, the word threw off its pejorative connotation (a phrase for which we need a new word—*lowvertone?*). "Re-Inventing the Corporation" (which unnecessarily added a hyphen in *reinventing*) treated the verb as meaning "to take a fresh look at methods that have hardened into conventions; to thoroughly reorganize."

Merriam-Webster's *Ninth New Collegiate* treats the original meaning in the earliest sense listed, "to make as if for the first time something already invented," and offers two more recent senses: "2: to remake or redo completely (radicals who want to reinvent America) 3: to bring into use again: reestablish." (On that last word, with the double *e,* I would insert a hyphen: re-establish.)

That's how meanings change; soon we will forget the sneer in the first meaning of *reinvent* (maybe the wheel needed reinventing after all) and use the verb as a synonym for super-perestroika. Punctuation styles change, too: Look at that modern, punctuating slash between *Korn* and *Ferry.* (I call the search firm "Korn virgule Ferry," but I also call the department store "Lord ampersand Taylor.")

Fiddling with the voguish virgule reminds me: What do we call the symbol on our word processors that is a virgule that tilts the other way, the sloping line that warns the monster within the hard disk that a directory is being sought? No, it's not a *promiscule,* on the analogy of *virgule;* it is a *backslash,* a compound based on *slash.*

But where can this term, used for the past few years in increasing frequency by writers, be found in our dictionaries? In vain, you search amid *backside, backslap, backslide* and *backspin*—nope, no *backslash.* Every year we have to reinvent the dictionary.

Just the Fax, Ma'am

"You got a *fax*?"
"Uh-huh."
"What's your *fax* number?"
You mumble a telephone number.
"O.K., I'll *fax* it to you."
In this brief modern conversation, you have heard the word *fax* used as noun, adjective and verb.

Thomas Fuller, the seventeenth-century theologian, would have been thrilled. It was he who first used *facsimile,* in *The History of the Worthies of England,* applying the Latin phrase to the sort of writer we all know: "He, though a quick Scribe, is but a dull one, who is good only at *fac simile,* to transcribe out of an original."

The Latin meant "make similar," and since 1815, the compressed phrase has meant "exact copy from transmission." *Scientific American* in 1935 wrote that "The home radio set will produce a copy of the printed material that was fed into the broadcasting machine, with picture and text reproduced in *facsimile." The New Yorker* in 1948 defined *facsimile newspaper* as one that "travels through the air."

Although the news carrier who flips your newspaper irretrievably into the boxwood has not yet been replaced by an electronic signal, today *fax* is surely on the make. *Telefacsimile,* which appeared in 1952, is the system of sending and reproducing written material via telephone lines and, on the analogy of *telex,* was shortened to *telefax* and then to the simple *fax. The Economist* in 1976 defined *facsimile transmission (fax)* as "a hybrid between telex and photocopying."

Maybe we've simplified too much. "There can be confusion," says Dan Minchen of Xerox, "when people say, 'Where's the fax?' That could refer either to the document or to the location of the fax machine."

The language did the right thing in changing the end of the first syllable of *facsimile* from *c* or *cs* to *x.* The plural of *fax* is *faxes,* not "facs" or "facses," which leads to the inexorable conclusion that in work conducted at home or at the office, the only certainties are death and faxes.

Most feature articles on this hot new device will play on the nearly homophonic "facts," as in the quotation of television's Sergeant Joe Friday that entitles this item. Get used to it.

A new worry: *junk fax,* on the analogy of *junk mail,* which is on the analogy of *junk jewelry.* "We got our first junk fax recently, and it gave me a horrible chill," *The New York Times* recently quoted an irate fax owner as saying. "It uses up our paper and ties up our machine." The unwanted fax came from a company that sells facsimile supplies, including the paper the fax was printed on.

The topic conjures up my radio days in the 40's where listeners were offered a secret code ring or some such adventuresome goody in return for boxtops or wrappers of the sponsor's product or a "reasonable facsimile thereof."

As a child, I didn't understand what that phrase meant. I just nagged my mother until she bought the product and sent in the boxtops or wrappers.

As I enjoyed my code ring I would feel sorry for the kids who were unlucky enough to send in an unreasonable facsimile.

> Frank Roberts
> Spring Valley, New York

I wonder why you believe that the correct plural of fax is faxes, when the correct plural of fex is feces.

> Frank Kofsky
> Sacramento, California

Kind 'n' Gentle

Somewhere in this land there is a marketing specialist working on a hand lotion or a drainpipe cleaner to be called "Kind 'n' Gentle"; it seems the most natural product name to adopt in the Bush era. (Lipstick manufacturers are surely competing for the rights to "Read My Lips"; if not, get on it today, fellas.)

Ever since his use of the phrase "a kinder, gentler nation" in his acceptance speech and reiteration of the modifiers in his inaugural address, those two adjectives have been identified with George Bush. The question arises: Have they ever been used together before?

"It didn't sound right to my ear," writes Bruno Stein, director of the Institute of Labor Relations at New York University. "It began to occur to me that I had seen the phrase before. . . . After some research, I have found the answer. The first adjective, as I had remembered it, is *kindlier*. That word sounds warmer and cuddlier than *kinder*, but perhaps you can explain the difference in meaning to your readers."

I'll noodle that around. Meanwhile, here's what Mr. Stein found. The great American defense attorney Clarence Darrow once made this comment about Eugene V. Debs, the labor leader and Socialist who drew more than 919,000 votes for President while serving a jail term stemming from his pacifist convictions: "There may have lived somewhere a kindlier, gentler, more generous man than Eugene Debs, but I have not known him."

With regard to your discussion of the President's "kinder, gentler nation," I thought you'd be interested in the following from F. A. Hayek's The Fatal Conceit. *(Although just published, it was actually written about a decade ago.)*

In a chapter entitled "Our Poisoned Language"—which I believe you'd thoroughly enjoy—Hayek writes: "To Marx especially we also owe the substitution of the term 'society' for the state or compulsory organization about which he is really talking, a circumlocution that suggests that we can deliberately regulate the actions of individuals by some gentler and kinder method of direction than coercion."

Another great insight by Hayek, regrettably germane to the speech in question.

> *Edward H. Crane*
> *Cato Institute*
> *Washington, D.C.*

"Kind and Gentle" Department:

Your researchers didn't have to noodle around to find the previous use of the two adjectives. Just turn to our old friend Bill Shakespeare. The last three lines of Chorus' "O, for a Muse of Fire" speech in Henry V, *go:*

> *Admit me, Chorus, to this history*
> *Who prologue-like your humble patience pray,*
> *Gently to hear, kindly to judge, our play.*

OK. So they're adverbs! Still . . .

> *Arnold Moss*
> *New York, New York*

A search on the Nexis data base of periodical articles reveals, not surprisingly, that a Democratic politician was talking of compassion years before Mr. Bush discovered it. New York Governor Mario Cuomo, in a commencement address at Barnard College quoted in The Christian Science Monitor, *June 21, 1983, expressed hope to the graduates "that you will be wiser than we are, kinder, gentler, more caring."*

> *Fred R. Shapiro*
> *New Haven, Connecticut*

Although I have only Webster's Seventh New Collegiate Dictionary *to consult, I think it did pretty well with the following:* Kind *and* kindly *both imply sympathy and humaneness and interest in another's welfare;* kind *stressing a disposition to be helpful (a* kind *heart) and* kindly *stressing more the expression of a sympathetic nature or impulse (take a* kindly *interest)."*

George should probably, to emphasize his extreme good will, have used the word kindlier. *How we can become a "kinder, gentler nation" is beyond me, as we are not kind or gentle to begin with.*

> *Mildred Cameron*
> *Lake Elsinore, California*

Recently I read Anne Tyler's book Searching for Caleb *and on page 282 I read: "Now everything came clear to him. He saw kinder, gentler meanings in Daniel's words; the other meanings were no longer there.*

Is it possible that Searching for Caleb *is the source of the phrase that President Bush used in his memorable remarks?*

> *Dorothy G. Rosenglatt*
> *Asbury Park, New Jersey*

Kissing and Telling About Kiss-and-Tell

Because I once wrote a White House memoir of the Nixon era, and because I often issue diatribes or hosannas about books written by more recent White House aides, I am often asked: "Where do you stand on *kiss and tell?*"

My position is unequivocal, unwavering and on the record: When used adjectivally, the phrase must be hyphenated, as in " 'I have no affection for

these *kiss-and-tell* books,' said President Reagan." But when the phrase is part of a predicate, and does not modify a noun, the hyphens are not used: "A gentleman," wrote George Bernard Shaw to the actress Mrs. Patrick Campbell in 1921, "does not kiss and tell." (Mrs. Campbell created the Eliza Doolittle role in Shaw's *Pygmalion;* they maintained only a friendship, which probably did not include the kissing that would be the prerequisite for kissing and telling. Shaw, whom she addressed in one letter as "Dear Liar," did not want her to publish his letters.)

Here comes the difficult part: The former White House spokesman Larry Speakes and the ex-domestic adviser Martin Anderson, like the former budget chief David Stockman, have been attacked as "being involved in kiss-and-tell." No noun is present, but "activity" is understood; the phrase modifies the understood noun and should therefore be hyphenated.

But the phrase itself is undergoing what grammarians call functional shift—a pair of verbs being used adjectively before becoming a hyphenated noun, the way *show-and-tell time* became *show-and-tell,* defined in Merriam-Webster's *Ninth New Collegiate Dictionary* as "a classroom exercise in which children display an item and talk about it." Similarly, *the hit-and-run game,* an 1899 description of baseball, led to *hit-and-run driving*—a 1924 expression that identifies a felonious act—with the hyphens intact in the adjectival phrase; the line between adjective and noun is blurred when there is an implied noun being modified, as in "a case of *hit-and-run.*"

The *kiss-and-tell* phrase is always used pejoratively or in denial. The biographer Merle Miller quoted Harry Truman as saying that Dwight Eisenhower had once considered divorcing Mamie to marry "this Englishwoman," a reference to his wartime driver, Kay Summersby, who steadfastly commented: "I am admitting nothing except that I have never been one to kiss and tell." (Correct, no hyphen.)

"It won't be a 'kiss and tell' book," said Robert Gottlieb of the William Morris Agency, announcing the contract-signing of Donald T. Regan, the former White House chief of staff, in early 1987. (The choice to go with quotation marks rather than hyphens was *The Washington Post*'s, I think in error, but that's arguable; the inaccurate prediction was Mr. Gottlieb's.) "The new book by Donald Regan," said the White House spokesman Marlin Fitzwater in 1988, launching a counterattack at the memoir that revealed the First Lady's dependency on an astrologer, "is a kiss-and-tell story in the mold of all books that seek to exploit the Presidency or the First Family for personal self-interest." (Correct punctuation, modifying *story;* Mr. Regan took issue with the assault on his motives.)

The book by the former presidential aide Michael K. Deaver is "a bunch of sleaze," said Edward T. Chase, a senior editor of Charles Scribner's Sons, publisher of the Speakes book, but "Regan's book, there's a lot of valuable information in it. These books are not all just kiss and tell." The *Washington Times* chose not to hyphenate or place the term in quotes, and is not incorrect, but I say hyphenate the noun phrase. That way, the only time the phrase is not hyphenated is when it is used as a verb. That should clear everything up.

The original meaning of the infinitive phrase *to kiss and tell* was "to boast of one's sexual exploits." It was coined, or first used in print, by the playwright William Congreve in his 1695 comedy, *Love for Love:* "O fie, Miss," said a swain worried about his love's indiscretion (she was in the process of blabbing all to her stepmother), "you must not kiss and tell."

That sense has given way to a figurative use in recent years, meaning in its most neutral sense "behind the scenes" or "revealing," and in its most frequent sense "with warts and pimples" or "containing embarrassments." Inherent in the phrase is a report by a participant or an insider; a journalist or pundit cannot write a kiss-and-tell book, unless it is about his own organization.

On the contrary, Shaw was all for kiss-and-tell, so long as it was accurate <u>and</u> did not needlessly hurt someone. Anent Mrs. Pat, see his letters to her (11 August '37 and 18 March '38), where he is making it possible for her to publish them (or at the least, sell them) so that she may benefit.

As I read the letters, delay in publishing would be only to avoid hurting his wife. Shaw was both a gentleman and generous.

Gabriel Austin
New York, New York

You noted that the first recorded use of "kiss and tell" is Congreve's in 1695. But Henry Purcell used the expression in 1693 in some incidental music to accompany a play of Congreve's; i.e., The Old Batchelour.

Michael Guemple
Lawrence, Kansas

Le Tout

"*Le tout* New York has been talking about Nancy Reagan's star-gazing," wrote Howard Kurtz in *The Washington Post.*

He'll get a letter on that, and not just about hyphenating *stargazing.* The week before, in an effort to appear breathlessly gossipy, I wrote, "Le tout New York was agog," about some misspelling by a major advertiser. In came a letter from Thomas E. Reid of Oakville, Ontario: "That spinning sound you hear are [*sic*] French eyeballs. It should have been *toute la New York.*"

His rationale: "*Tout* is an adjective and takes no article, i.e. never *le tout;* always *tout le* monde, for example. But New York is a *ville,* therefore feminine. Therefore, *toute* (feminine form of *tout*) *la New York.*"

Tout au contraire, my friend. We are dealing with an idiom here, and in every living language, the greatest edifices of grammar collapse before the innocent power of idiom.

Toward the turn of the last century, the phrase *tout Paris* was in use—among the English, at least—without the preceding article *le,* and was defined in the *Oxford English Dictionary* as "all Paris, i.e. Parisian society. . . ." By 1921, Gertrude Bell, the English author and political adviser to Middle Eastern potentates, was writing, "Le tout Bagdad was there—the Arab world." In 1982, *The Times* of London reported: "It is the talk of le tout Paris in the French business world. Who will be getting the plum jobs?"

Is this an example of the abuse of the French language by the English and their ilk? "Absolutely not," says Bernard Garniez, a professor of French at New York University. " 'Le tout' is the accepted usage with a city. You can use the feminine *toute la* before a country, such as France or Amérique, but not before a city. The established idiom with the name of a city is the article *le* preceding *tout* and the city's name."

As George Bush said, snatching a flier from the supporter of an opponent, *"Fini!"* (I wish George would lay off the French. Both he and Michael Dukakis could have a good debate in Spanish, which both men speak; that's where the votes are in Texas, California and Florida. But French still carries a connotation of preppiness, and the wise candidate avoids such expressions as *déjà vu,* unless it is used as a pseudo-Yogi Berraism, "It's *déjà vu* all over again." The first one to say "It's the talk of *le tout* Washington" would lose, although that construction is idiomatically unassailable.)

You may be taken to task by some guardian of the French language who may very well carry the battle for purism into the United States and insist that you hyphenate and capitalize le Tout-Washington as the French do.

> *Bernard Garniez*
> *New York University*
> *New York, New York*

Like Ugly on an Ape

"I knew the minute I said 'card-carrying member of the A.C.L.U.,' " George Bush told Maureen Dowd of *The New York Times,* "a couple of your best columnists would jump all over me like ugly on an ape."

Now there's a simile to be your umbrella on a rainy, rainy day: *like ugly on an ape.* As one of the columnists so calumniated, I have undertaken research on this locution.

The only other use of this expression in the computerized files is dated August 10, 1981, from a United Press International story datelined Meridian, Mississippi. The speaker was George Bush: "The Vice President said Russia pounced on the neutron-bomb decision 'like ugly on ape,' but the Soviet Union's reaction was 'thoroughly expected.' " (No *an* was quoted before the *ape;* this was probably an error in transcription of a most unfamiliar phrase.)

Evidently this is an expression George Bush, and perhaps only George Bush, has been using for many years; it is not a with-it expression adopted for a presidential campaign, such as the musical "Send a Message to Michael" or "Don't Worry, Be Happy."

Where does it come from? Etymologists will await the answer at the first

post-election news conference. None of the slang or simile dictionaries have it; the nearest is *ugly as a hairless monkey,* used by Margaret Mitchell in *Gone with the Wind.*

Primates have long been equated with ugliness. In his 1699 *Voyages and Descriptions,* William Dampier reported: "The Monkies that are in these Parts are the ugliest I ever saw." Like toads and deceptive ducklings, these animals—attractive to their peers—are associated by humans with frightening or repulsive appearances. An objection to this was registered as far back as 1643 by the English physician Sir Thomas Browne: "I cannot tell by what Logick we call a Toad, a Beare, or an Elephant ugly." Curiously, one of the most famous and fearsome apes in captivity was Bushman ("dweller in the bush"), in Chicago's Lincoln Park Zoo.

The meaning of the Bush phrase is "total, unmitigated, all-encompassing," with an overtone of fierceness; a synonymous Southern simile, much better known, was often used by President Jimmy Carter: *like a duck on a June bug.*

Purists will wonder: Why is *ugly,* an adjective, used instead of *ugliness,* the noun? Shouldn't the expression be *like ugliness on an ape*? Not necessarily; *ugly* has a history of use as a noun in colloquial Americanisms. The American humorist Augustus Longstreet wrote in his *Georgia Scenes* in 1835: "I want to get in the breed of them sort o' men to drive ugly out of my kin folks."

Moreover, we are in the midst of a vogue for what grammarians call *absolutes,* the use of an adjective with no noun to modify. You want explanatory? I'll give you explanatory: in the Emma Lazarus phrase, "Give me your tired, your poor," *tired* and *poor*—both adjectives—are used absolutely, while in the next phrase "your huddled masses," the adjective *huddled* is not an absolute, because it modifies the noun *masses.*

When Michael Dukakis was criticized as being insufficiently passionate, he donned a yellow satin jacket and kissed the two cheerleaders from North Dakota State University who presented it, then worked the crowd with gusto, eagerly grasping for extended hands. Wrote Bernard Weinraub of *The New York Times:* "John Sasso, his principal handler, smiled on the sidelines. 'Hey, you want warm?' he said to a reporter."

He did not say "you want warmth?" using the noun; in the vogue absolute, "you want warm?" is the preferred form. The locution, spread by television comics and talk-show hosts, is all over the language these days like white on rice.

"Like ugly on an ape" is one of several zoological similes I remember from 25 or more years ago in high school in San Antonio. Usually they were a friendly threat, as when discussing the prospects of an opposing quarterback: "I'm going to be all over you like wet on a whale."

I recall they were supposed to be spontaneous in the down-home mode, so of course once any one of them fell into common use, it was discarded as a cliché and its user scorned as a poseur. "Ugly on an ape" is definitely a cliché around the barnyards of Texas. This would explain why there was only one earlier archival reference to "ugly on an ape" and it was by George Bush.

Some others were "like mean on a snake," "like stubborn on a mule," "like stink on [poop]."

Charles Stough
Dayton, Ohio

I believe that you were wide of the mark on "like ugly on an ape." The way that I have heard that expression used connotes a relationship between two persons or things that is so close as to be inextricable. No relationship could be closer than a thing and a salient quality of that thing. In the "like ugly on an ape" example, the expression implies that the ugliness cannot be removed from an ape.

Variations on this theme (common in this part of the country) include "like white on rice" and (pardon my language) "like stink on shit." Of course, this type of structure lends itself to creative interventions. My own favorite is "like polyester on a salesman."

Please be careful in your interpretation of Southern similes.

Robert Craycroft
Jackson, Mississippi

You really should have spent more time watching television than consulting computerized files. Festus Haggen of Gunsmoke used that expression many times. I don't know if Festus (or the script writer) invented "ugly on an ape," but Gunsmoke, which ran for 20 years, went off the air before 1981.

Robert J. Marquette
Nokomis, Florida

The term "like ugly on an ape" is one I have used for many years. I picked it up as a child in the 60's. It was used regularly by the character "Festus Haggen" on the original Gunsmoke series. To be more precise, however, the saying goes, "like ugly on a ape." The "a" being pronounced "uh."

Perhaps you will recall Festus. He was the scruffy, but golden-hearted, deputy of Marshal Matt Dillon. He preferred to ride a mule instead of a horse. I hope you can have some fun with this.

Tedi M. Bell
Monroe, New York

This afternoon, while reading The Times Magazine and watching a Gunsmoke rerun, "Like Ugly on an Ape" leaped from the page. Coincidentally, I first heard this locution used many years ago by a Dodge City denizen named Festus Haggen, deputy to Marshal Dillon. He used it at various times when referring to those who would get on his case, or he on theirs.

Festus was an illiterate, transplanted Texas hillybilly whose colorful speech certainly enhanced the popularity of that television series. I would suggest that the Vice President may also have been a Gunsmoke fan who fancies using a phrase or two of Festus Haggen.

Mary Anne Velz
Amsterdam, New York

Confident you were not expressing an anticlerical view, I conclude that your assertion, "Primates have long been equated with ugliness," refers to biological, not holy orders. If you did indeed intend what is generally the second dictionary definition of "primate," many vertebrates and perhaps most mammals would agree. And the tailless creature that walks upright probably looks a little silly, even to his fellow primates.

Much as I dislike to monkey with your prose, I believe the word you wanted was "simians."

G.J.A. O'Toole
Mount Vernon, New York

There's a difference between "ugly" used to mean "ugliness," and "tired" and "poor" used to mean "tired [people]" and "poor [people]." One uses the adjective to refer to the noun ("absolute," in your terminology), and the other simply leaves out an understood noun that the adjective modifies.

Esther Dyson
New York, New York

Perhaps Mr. Bush, sometime in his nomadic life, has spent time in rural south central Ohio, although I doubt it. I have heard this expression, sometimes as "ugly on the ape," all my life, or as we occasionally say, "since Rex was a pup."

If this expression is as unusual as you say, then my neighbors, kin and I must be as "queer as Dick's hat band." For this, see And Ladies of the Club.

Roberta Barnett
Springfield, Ohio

As an addition to your computerized files of "ugly" as a noun let me nominate "Man, you got so much ugly you could open a branch face!" heard in a black ghetto. Incidentally, "ugly" is more than onomatopoetic. It not only sounds ugly, the word looks ugly too.

John R. Scotford, Jr.
East Thetford, Vermont

". . . like white on rice," or, if you want healthy, like brown.

Arthur J. Morgan
New York, New York

Ugly on Ape

George Bush was spotted here using an unusual simile during his presidential campaign: *like ugly on an ape,* or, seven years earlier, *like ugly on ape.* The question was raised about the origin of a simile that has escaped all dialect and slang dictionaries.

"I first heard it spoken on the western classic series *Gunsmoke,*" reports Bill Becker of Woodland Hills, California. "It was regularly delivered by a curmudgeonly character named Festus Haggen, played by the actor Ken Curtis. The phrase was *ugly on ape,* definitely not 'ugly on *an* ape.' " A dozen pioneer couch potatoes agree.

But was George Bush's source that mid-60's television character? David Frost, a Lexicographic Irregular from London, put the question squarely to Mr. Bush in the following television colloquy:

FROST: [Mr. Dukakis] embraced the label, *liberal.*

BUSH: In that debate, he got all over me like ugly on an ape for even bringing it up.

FROST: You must put Bill Safire's mind at rest on that phrase. He wrote a whole column about it last weekend.

BUSH: I didn't see it.

(Shocked readers will wonder: How can that be? It should be interpolated here that candidates for the presidency, in the final weeks of the campaign, sometimes lose touch with vital sources of information. They return to their normal reading habits after the election, sometimes.)

FROST: Where did you get *like ugly on an ape?*

BUSH: That's all over the oil fields. I got it in Odessa in 1948—that's when it started, I guess.

Rarely do dialect etymologists or linguistic mapmakers get such high-level help with specific citations, and we are all grateful to Mr. Frost.

The newspaper-deprived candidate was referring to his oil-drilling business in Odessa, Texas, and not to the city in the Soviet Union. Also note that—contrary to the television character's subsequent use—Mr. Bush now uses an article before the word *ape.* Because his recollected and present usage antedates Festus's, and because he is now President-elect, dialect historians are likely to accept *like ugly on an ape.*

I found the phrase quite annoying when you first discussed it. It is forced, clumsy, inept, and unclear. Furthermore it reflects an anthropocentric attitude toward animals that we humans would do well to reconsider. Who says that apes are ugly? I know an ape who certainly does not think her mate is ugly. And I know many people who would agree with her.

Albert E. Robert
New York, New York

Litterbugs in Greenhouses

The United States Environmental Protection Agency's European program manager, David H. Strother, writes that he has been "assigned action on a letter . . . from a Belgian looking for the origins of the word *litterbug*" and has turned to me.

I like action assignments, which are presumably less subtle and more satisfying than passive assignments.

The headline 47,000 SUBWAY "LITTERBUGS" PAY $107,000 IN FINES IN 1946 DRIVE appeared in the New York *Herald Tribune* on February 16, 1947. That was the first recorded citation of the term, probably coined by a neologistic publicist or adman in the New York City Department of Sanitation. It was one of flackdom's finest hours.

The coinage was based on *jitterbug,* a 1934 coinage in the title of a Cab Calloway song, "Jitter Bug," describing those who enjoy the frenetic movements of a dance such as the Lindy. *Jitterbug* was coined in turn on the analogy of *firebug,* which was based on the 1841 *tariff bug,* a derogation of believers in trade barriers. As we can see, the slang noun *bug* has long meant "enthusiast"; that sense has passed as the word has been used as a verb, meaning to eavesdrop upon or to annoy.

In return for this service to the E.P.A., I would like to get from that agency the origin of *greenhouse effect,* the warming of the earth's temperature caused by the increase in carbon dioxide produced by the burning of what are always called "fossil fuels."

Ever since learning that bibb lettuce was named after Major John Bibb, the noted horticulturist, I have been attuned to eponymy in coinage. However, it appears that nobody named Greenhouse was involved; the earliest sightings of the word were in a 1937 textbook by G. T. Trewartha, who wrote of the "so-called greenhouse effect."

That means he picked it up from what people were saying. But who said it first, and where? A mystery; if the E.P.A. can find out, that would be helpful to those of us, here and in Belgium, who care about these things.

If the world starts cooling off rapidly in the next few decades, that will be called the "room heater that keeps blowing the fuses effect," its first use in this newspaper on this day.

You talk of the "warming of the <u>earth's temperature</u>." Is this usage correct? Should not temperature increase or decrease, or become higher or lower, while the earth, or atmosphere, or weather, or climate becomes warmer or colder? Actually, isn't temperature a measure of the amount of heat?

> *Melvin Jacobson*
> *Brooklyn, New York*

Look to It

Like a linguistic Loch Ness monster, some locutions poke their heads above water, then submerge for centuries, then surface again, causing word mavens to wonder what is "correct."

"Looking to reaffirm their party's traditional values and sharpen its public image," wrote Susan F. Rasky in *The New York Times*, "the Senate's 55 Democrats today selected George J. Mitchell of Maine as majority leader."

This was what journalism classes call a *punchy lead*, far more interesting and informative than "Senator George J. Mitchell of Maine was chosen today, etc." Several *Times* editors, however, wondered whether this use of *looking to* was Standard English. (The paper frowns on dialect leads.) They put forward *seeking to*, which is undeniably Standard, as the alternative.

The question is: Does *looking* followed by an infinitive—as in "looking to reaffirm"—have standing to sue for a place in the current formal language?

You won't find the answer under *look to* in the *Oxford English Dictionary*, because that *to* is a preposition, needing a noun or pronoun as its object, as in "Look to it." Instead, since we are seeking *to* as the beginning of a verb in its infinitive form, turn to that dictionary's figurative use of *look* in the sense of "expect." You will find: "To expect. Construction *to* with *infinitive*. . . . Also, to expect, await the time *when* something shall happen; to be curious to see *how, whether,* etc."

Aha! We were seeking a precedent for *look* preceding a verb in the infinitive form, and have found it. Examples include this use in Sir Thomas More's 1513 work on Richard III: "In these last wordes that euer I looke to speake with you." Shakespeare's Juliet says, "I'll look to like, if looking liking move. . . ." In his 1651 *Leviathan*, Thomas Hobbes wrote, "By whom we look to be protected." And in 1830, the poet Robert Southey wrote, "I too had been looking to hear from you."

Freeze that Southey frame. Along the way, *looking to* was beefed up with a *forward*. The expression *looking forward to*, however, uses *to* as a preposition preceding a noun or pronoun, not an infinitive. As *I look forward to* elbowed aside *I look to,* the latter took on the appearance of an archaic term, perhaps non-Standard or dialect.

But *look to,* as we have seen after this painstaking search, has an impeccable pedigree. It's not dialect; it's Standard English, now come back to claim its place in the dictionaries. You can hear it in western films (as in "that hombre is looking to cause trouble") and in a recent television drama: "He was selling [Christmas trees], and I was looking to buy." You can even read it on the front page of *The New York Times.*

Welcome home, Nessie of expectation. We can look to many more uses of *look to,* and look to find it followed by a verb as well.

Make 'n' Shake

I suppose it all began with *fish 'n' chips,* or *ham 'n' eggs.* But the conjunction of two nouns or two verbs with the shortened form of the linkage "and"—*'n'* —has been adopted with a vengeance by product manufacturers and has been getting out of hand.

A stroll down a supermarket aisle is like an extended visit to a world of conjoined words. Among the imperative-mood verbs living in wedded bliss are *Spray 'n' Wash, Mop 'n' Glo, Shake 'n' Bake, Brown 'n' Serve, Crunch 'n' Munch, Rinse 'n' Vac, Come 'n' Get It, Klean 'n' Shine.* Nouns that have set up housekeeping together are *Kibbles 'n' Bits, Wings 'n' Things, Nut 'n' Honey, Fruit 'n' Fibre* (with the British spelling of our *fiber,* used presumably for trademark purposes).

Connubial adjectives include *Sweet 'n' Low, Neat 'n' Tidy* (kitty litter, material to absorb feline waste), *Moist 'n' Beefy* (dog food), *Dark 'n' Lovely* (hair coloring, not to be confused with *Nice 'n' Easy,* which uses *haircolor* as a single word), *Light 'n' Lively, Good 'n' Plenty, Spic 'n' Span.* (The last, an aid to floor-mopping, picks up a phrase first used in Pepys's *Diary* with a deep etymology: The *spic* is related to *spike,* a bright new nail, and the *span* is from the Old Icelandic *span-nyr,* combining *spann,* "spoon, chip," and *nyr,* "new." To be *spic 'n' span* was thus to be "as new.")

Alert label-readers will note that I have treated all the conjunctions the same—apostrophe, *n,* apostrophe—using the apostrophe as substitute for the unpronounced and missing letters. This is correct, but not the way it is in real supermarket life. Sometimes -*'n'-* products spell out the *and;* in other cases the packagers use an ampersand (&), or prefer to omit the two apostrophes: in each case, the user is expected to provide the elision in pronunciation. Thus, *Nut & Honey* cereal is advertised to sound like "nuttin', honey," which can be construed for commercial amusement purposes as "nothing, honey."

The use of the ampersand is fine with me, as is the double apostrophe or the simple *and*. What is incorrect is the treatment of *and* as if it were *an*—that is, the inconsistent use of the apostrophe. The *n* sound requires two apostrophes, front and back, replacing the *a* and the *d*. I would go back to the supermarket to check out which brands offend good grammar, but the lines at the checkout counter are too long.

The conjoined product name may be a fad, or may be with us in the future (*Compute 'n' Confuse* software, *Launch 'n' Zap* antisatellite missiles). Either way, the product-naming conjunctivitis has left its mark on users of other familiar two-noun phrases using *and*.

In an advertisement announcing the naming of former Defense Secretary Caspar W. Weinberger as publisher and columnist for *Forbes* magazine, Malcolm S. Forbes said that Cap "will give readers his unvarnished comments and opinions—which were reserved heretofore for the President alone or for the topmost makers and shakers of D.C. and other world capitals."

Makers and shakers? No. Nor is it *makers & shakers* or *makers 'n' shakers*. The correct phrase involves *movers* and shakers.

That often-used combination in Washington and Wall Street, *movers and shakers,* was not coined by a chronicler of tycoons, influencer of activists, or ghost of powerful pols. Although it is used today to refer, sometimes ironically, to opinion leaders and power brokers, the phrase was coined in an 1874 ode by the poet Arthur O'Shaughnessy to make a quite different point: that the true influentials are not the big shots, but the world's poets and novelists, so often derided as "dreamers" by the pragmatic powerful.

> We are the music-makers,
> And we are the dreamers of dreams . . .
> Yet we are the movers and shakers
> Of the world for ever, it seems.

The phrase has never been commercialized by moving 'n' storage companies because the shaking, though accurate, is not sufficiently promissory and indeed would put off some customers. Chairman Malcolm, always conscious of good grammar, should be the last to reduce that ringing poetic phrase to a product called *Make 'n' Shake*. To the budget-cutter known as Cap the Knife, that must have been the most unkindest cut of all.

If I remember correctly, the shortened form of the linkage "and"—'n'—began during World War II, when the shortage of meats led to a product called Spam, and advertisements showed a happy youngster saying "Mm-m-m-m! Spam 'n' eggs!" Now shops are named after their main stock (say, shoes), followed by " 'n' Things"—except, as you noted, when either or both of the apostrophes may be omitted. And the n may or may not be capitalized.

How to pronounce the result? <u>Shoes 'n Things</u>, or <u>Shoes 'N Things</u>: "shooz unn thingz"? <u>Shoes n' Things</u>, or <u>Shoes N' Things</u>: "shooz nuh thingz"? I've even seen the <u>n</u> with quotation marks instead of apostrophes: hence <u>Shoes "N" Things</u>. The silliest I've seen, however, was the abbreviation of "and" not to <u>'n'</u> but to <u>'a'</u>. <u>Shoes 'a' Things</u>?

I could continue, but I must return to a book I'm reading, Tolstoy's <u>War 'n' Peace</u>.

Willis Conover
Arlington, Virginia

<u>Spick and span</u> was used by Sir Thomas North (1579), Thomas Nashe (1590), Anthony Munday (1595), John Withals (1616), John Ford (1629), Ben Jonson (1640), John Clarke (1639) and James Howell (1659), all of them before it was "first used in Pepys's <u>Diary</u>."

Mac E. Barrick
Shippensburg University
Shippensburg, Pennsylvania

A musical titled <u>Harrigan 'n Hart</u> opened on Broadway not too long ago. Because of a book I'd written about Harrigan and Hart many years earlier, I owned a small piece of the show. Or, rather, owned it until, in a moment of unusual generosity, I gave it to my sons. Even a small piece of a big musical can, of course, come to a lot.

Unfortunately for the young men, the show closed almost as fast as it opened. It has long been my hunch that it didn't so much succumb to the harsh things the critics had to say about it as to the ridiculousness of its name.

E. J. Kahn, Jr.
The New Yorker
New York, New York

You assumed the name of the artificial sweetener in the pink packet was "Sweet and Low" (shortened to Sweet 'n' Low). Actually, the name is Sweeten Low (shortened to Sweet'n Low). If you look at the packet I have enclosed, you will see only <u>one</u> apostrophe (between the "t" and the "n") and a space before the "Low."

Barbara Novack
Laurelton, New York

The Man with the Pictures

When the actress Lucille Ball died, a CBS reporter went to one of her longtime friends, the comedian George Burns, for his comment.

Mr. Burns, then ninety-three and giving new force to the meaning of the adjective *spry,* offered this sound bite as food for thought: "When the Man shows up at the door to return the pictures, you've got to go."

That sense of brave resignation, at odds with Dylan Thomas's defiant "Rage, rage against the dying of the light," was expressed in an equally poetic figure of speech. Then I wondered: What was the allusion?

A search of the dialect dictionaries offered no help on *the Man* returning the pictures, nor did my vast library of quotation books. Aside from the capitalized *Death,* the most frequently used personification of death is the *Grim Reaper,* from the ancient iconographic depiction of Death swinging a scythe. But I cannot find a first use of the phrase, or of the midlands Americanism *Old Man Mose* that may be its synonym; that figure is often confused with *Father Time,* who also wields a scythe and appears with a baby on New Year's Eve.

The *Pale Horse* offers another literary reference to Death, this time from the Bible. Revelation 6:8 contains "Behold a pale horse: and his name that sat on him was Death. . . ." The writer Katherine Anne Porter entitled a short novel about love during an influenza epidemic *Pale Horse, Pale Rider.* The *Iceman* in the title of Eugene O'Neill's *The Iceman Cometh* is Death, among other things. In his final memoir, *Stay of Execution,* the columnist Stewart Alsop referred to the ominous presence as *Uncle Thanatos,* from the Greek word for death.

Movies have frequently cast actors in Death's role, with a variety of names. In the 1939 film *On Borrowed Time,* Cedric Hardwicke played Death trapped in a tree by an old man who didn't want to go; an associated word was chosen for the personification's name, *Mr. Brink.* In the 1941 film *Here Comes Mr. Jordan,* Claude Rains was the *Angel of Death* whose name may have been taken from the river in the Holy Land. (That slightly flip "Mr." had also been used by e. e. cummings in his poem about Buffalo Bill: "how do you like your blueeyed boy Mister Death?")

The allusion cited by George Burns—*the Man* with the pictures—is an example of reference to a missing specific that troubles lexicographers, quotation anthologists and regional dialecticians. A century from now, someone will see or read that mysterious trope and have no way of getting to the figurative roots.

I queried the source by mail: "The 'Man' in your philosophical comment is Death; but what does the rest of the saying mean?"

"I got your letter," George Burns replied promptly, "and I'm glad you asked about my comment on Lucille Ball after she left us.

"Let me try to explain it," he wrote; apparently he had been asked about his cryptic statement by others. "You see, I'm an old vaudeville actor—I'm going back 65 or 70 years—and in those days your contract had a cancellation clause in it. If the manager didn't like your act, he was able to cancel you after your first show.

"All the actors carried their own pictures," continued Mr. Burns, "so after the first show if the manager knocked on your door and gave you back your pictures, you started packing."

Transforming that almost-forgotten metaphor into a philosophical comment on mortality is a good contribution to American show-biz folklore. His remark, unlike most sound bites, is an observation worthy of slow mastication.

George Burns, snapping out of this uncharacteristically lugubrious mood, added this postscript: "When the Guy knocks on my door with the pictures, I'm not going to answer."

Fred Allen told me that when the theater manager came around to fire an act after the first show (usually Monday matinee), he'd say, "Don't send out your laundry."

Fred was a juggler in his early days. One of his bits was to catch a turnip on a fork held in his mouth. One Monday he bought enough turnips for the week (14) and used one on Monday matinee. The others were on the high sill of the little window in his dressing room at the theater on 181st and Broadway. He got canned, packed up his clothes and left. He told me that he often wondered what the act that took his place thought about the thirteen turnips on the sill.

Henry Morgan
New York, New York

More on the man with the pictures.

When, in a Today show interview years ago, Gene Shalit asked George Burns whether he ever thought of death, George told the picture story but used an alternate second-punch line: ". . . I'm also gonna take my music. I don't know where I'm going but I want it in my key."

Ray Lockhart
New York, New York

Your files should include the following citation:

Burns, George. 1988. Gracie: A Love Story.
Putnam, N.Y.

Page 26: In vaudeville, every performer was required to give the theater manager a black and white glossy photograph when he or she arrived for a booking. The manager would post the picture out front. Normally, at the end of the booking, they would give you back your pictures. But if the act turned out to be terrible, the manager would take down the picture right away and give it back to the performer. Nobody in vaudeville "got fired," instead they got their pictures back.

G. Sharman
Hollywood, California

Marking Bush's Inaugural

And now the big news, strictly from the point of view of grammarians, about the inaugural address of President George Bush: He has legitimized and popularized the use of the conjunction *and* to start a sentence.

He used this dubious construction sixteen times, ten planned and six ad-libbed. Think of it—11.1 percent of a speech's sentences (mostly short) beginning with *and.* Unheard-of. Eisenhower used four in his first inaugural; Kennedy, two—but sixteen times? Mr. Bush suggested that "this is the age of the offered hand," which may come to pass, but it is already the age of the offered *and.*

And that's not all. (Advertising copywriters do not use that phrase anymore, not out of any compunction about starting with a conjunction, but because it can be replaced by *plus,* saving costly split seconds.) The new President made clear he was unafraid of conjunctionitis only weeks after he was elected; in an opening statement announcing his choice for the new Defense Secretary, four out of the first six sentences began with the little word that originally meant "thereupon" and now means "also." This was followed by another quick burst about John Tower: "And he's a true expert on defense policy. And he understands the challenges ahead. And he's established great credibility. . . ."

And is this incorrect? Look no further than the second verse of Genesis for precedent: "And the earth was without form, and void. . . ." And in some cases, as in Mr. Bush's "And vigilance," even a sentence fragment begun with *and* has force and is suitable. But enough is enough; when overused, the form produces too choppy an effect (the voids are widout form). And the speaker loses the punch that an isolated sentence starting with a conjunction offers.

I liked most of the metaphors. "We meet on democracy's front porch" was doubly apt: Not only did this refer to the newly rebuilt west front landing of the Capitol, but it also had the easy familiarity of an image of neighborliness in a community of single-family houses. William McKinley in 1896 refused to travel to solicit votes, preferring to meet voters on his own front porch; that became known as "the front-porch campaign," and is remembered by some today as more neighborly than lazy.

The *new breeze* was the central metaphor of the speech. The new President could not very well speak of a *new broom* because that would reflect badly on his predecessor, but the waft of fresh air was intended to put some distance between administrations. The thrice-repeated phrase was also extended to totalitarian ideas that have "blown away like leaves from an ancient lifeless tree," as well as to "freedom is like a beautiful kite that can go higher and higher with the breeze . . ." (Those three dots appeared at the end of the sentence in the text issued by the White House—not as an ellipsis noting material left out, but as a device intended to give a dreamy, dribbling-off quality to the thought. Ellipsis-abuse is rampant among radio and television writers; the inaugural speechwriter, Peggy Noonan, once worked for Dan Rather.)

The extended metaphor of a refreshing breeze—although not as invigorating as Harold Macmillan's "wind of change"—was emphasized by the hair of the speaker blowing in the brisk Washington breeze; had it been a calm day, Ms. Noonan would surely have been standing off camera holding aloft an electric fan.

New breeze doesn't grab you? Don't go away—this was only one of what Chinese speechwriters would call the *Four News*—a quartet of *new* constructions to suit headline writers. *New engagement* might fly; it was spawned in Gary Hart's *enlightened engagement,* which was repeated recently by George Shultz. *Engagement,* which has a military sense of "battle," has another sense of "joining," as in the period before a marriage; this double meaning gives the word a nice ambiguity attractive to diplomats.

Another Bush phrase, *new activism,* may backfire because it offers critics a clean \shot for derision whenever this Administration shows less-than-masterly inactivity. Finally, Mr. Bush referred to the *new closeness,* a surefire title in foreign-affairs publications for learned dissections of summitry; some pseudosociologists may even stretch it into a denunciation of dirty dancing.

Although the "through the door" sequence was labored, the Bush metaphor of "the offered hand" shows careful selection of verb: Note that he chose not to use the more familiar "helping hand" or even "extended hand," which calls to mind handouts. A hand "offered," on the other hand, is one extended to be shaken. He closed out the thought and the image with "The 'offered hand' is a reluctant fist"—not an original figure of speech, but one that pleased hard-liners suspicious of glad-handing evil empiricists.

A single dependent clause—"though we bless them for choosing life"—lightly touched an antiabortion base.

Another line that was obviously worked over carefully, but not carefully enough, was "America is never wholly herself unless she is engaged in high moral purpose." That was in the distributed text, but in delivery Mr. Bush changed the last word to "principle." The thought was taken from Charles de Gaulle's "France is not France without greatness," a phrase frequently quoted by Richard Nixon. In Mr. Bush's line, something is missing: You do not "engage" in a principle or a purpose; you engage in action that adheres to principle or advances purpose. Leaving out words for the listener to supply can be poetic, but in this case, the jump was awkward and showed a need for more work; perhaps he will take another crack at this line in his second inaugural.

Alliteration? Here's a memorable sentence: "We have more will than wallet; but will is what we need." That's six *w* sounds in twelve words, nearly matching Warren G. Harding's oratorical record. (Mr. Bush used the word *normalcy,* too, an archaism until popularized by President Harding in the alliterative "not nostrums but normalcy.") He likes the technique: "A President is neither prince nor pope" suggests we will be hearing more in the coming years.

In translation of quotation, we have a daring President. He quoted an unnamed saint as having said: "In crucial things, unity—in important things, diversity—in all things, generosity." This was a creative translation of Saint Augustine's *In necessariis, unitas; in dubiis, libertas; in omnibus, caritas,* rendered into English by a nonconformist clergyman in the 1600's as "In necessary things, unity; in doubtful things, liberty; in all things, charity." (*Dubiis* is more faithfully translated in terms of "doubtful" than "important," but the old "charity"—which is now often burdened with a demeaning connotation—is better translated by Mr. Bush's "generosity.")

Enough of this deconstructive buildup; in its totality, how did this well-delivered, deliberately low-key speech rate in the farrago of inaugural addresses?

Not in the inspiring class of Lincoln, F.D.R. and Woodrow Wilson, but better suited to the occasion than the offerings of George Washington and Andrew Jackson. Turning to recent times, I believe George Bush was not as eloquent as John Kennedy ("Ask not . . .") or fitting as Lyndon Johnson ("Let us continue . . .") or surprising as Richard Nixon ("the lift of a driving dream"), but far more uplifting than Jimmy Carter and on a par with, or more authentic and quietly moving than, Dwight Eisenhower or Ronald Reagan.

The 1989 inaugural address was a good speech, suitably solemn and unifying, coherent and appropriately brief. It did not soar and cause listeners to tingle, but that is not the Bush style. A good speech is not a collection of crisp one-liners, workable metaphors and effective rhetorical devices; a good speech truly reflects the thoughts and emotions of the speaker, which is what this speech did. And as George Bush would say, "And that's that."

After your strangely un-Safireish complaint about Peggy Noonan's—or Peggy Noonan Bush's—habit of starting sentences with "And" (I couldn't write my talks if I didn't start about every fifth sentence with an "And"—in talk, it's a kind of friendly caesura) I think you must get hold of a formidable work of scholarship recently presented as a lecture in Wellington at New Zealand's centennial commemoration of Katherine Mansfield's birth. The distinguished (I guess) Japanese academic, Ginsaku Ohsawa, delivered a paper on—wait for it!—"Katherine Mansfield's Stylistic Use of 'And' "!!!!

Alistair [Cooke]
New York, New York

The supposed rule against using <u>and</u> to start a sentence is a schoolmarmish idea that never had currency off the blackboard. <u>But</u> as a starter was prohibited too—and regularly used. What is more, these conjunctions have begun paragraphs by thousands of good authors.

The rationale is easy to see: In a compound sentence of which the parts are tied by <u>and</u>, with a comma preceding the second part, that comma is not grammatical but rhetorical. In other words, the second part is a complete sentence that begins with <u>and</u>. Therefore replacing the comma with a period changes nothing but the length of the interval, mentally speaking.

As for your adding "popularizing" to "legitimizing," how can someone make popular something that is already done by nearly every writer? Certainly by every professional. If you doubt this last statement, consult the professional who wrote the inaugural. But the president deserves full credit for reading it with the right rhetoric—slightly longer pauses before the <u>And</u>'s than if they had not been capitalized.

Jacques [Barzun]
New York, New York

President Bush's speechwriting office called us a few days before he delivered his Inaugural Address, to verify a quotation (in necessary things, unity; in uncertain things, diversity; in all things, charity) to be used. Bruce Miller, of our Theology-Philosophy library, corroborated what our principal Augustine scholar thought, namely, that the statement cannot definitely be attributed to

Augustine (reference the enclosed copies of pertinent documents from Vatican II and an earlier encyclical from John XXIII), but is of uncertain attribution—which is what was related to President Bush's speechwriter; and that, no doubt, is why it turned up in the speech as "the hope of a saint."

Susan Needham
The Catholic University of
America
Washington, D.C.

You cite Genesis 1:2 ("And the earth was without form, and void . . .") as a venerable precedent for [President Bush's] *frequent use of the conjunction "and" at the beginning of sentences ("sixteen times, ten planned and six ad-libbed . . . 11.1 percent of the speech's sentences").*

While acknowledging that the 1611 Anglican translation of the Bible (the "Authorized" or "King James" version) has had a profound influence on the English language, it is often forgotten that, although inspired and inspiring, it is, alas, a translation. Its frequent use of the conjunction "and" at the beginning of sentences is based on the Hebrew, not English, construction and syntax, and therefore ought not to serve as a model for proper English usage. While, to our ears, such usage sounds very "Biblical," it is based on a misunderstanding of the original. It is doubtful that all those conjunctions belong in any translation, and the King James Version ought not to serve as a proof-text for Mr. Bush's dubious construction.

In Biblical narratives, the letter vav is often used to begin sentences, and was seen as having the strange effect of converting the verbs in the sentence which follows, from past to future and vice versa, hence this vav is often referred to as the vav ha-ipuch, or the "vav conversive." Example (Genesis 1:3): "And (the vav ha-ipuch) the Lord said (future tense, literally "will say"), 'let there be light!' (future form is used), and there was (literally, "will be") light." More recent scholarship has traced this usage, not found in post-Biblical Hebrew, to earlier Semitic languages.

The older Biblical translations beautifully preserve the word order and flavor of the Hebrew original—while modern translations are more literal.

I do not know if Mr. Bush (or his speech writer) was inspired by the nuances of the King James version—but English is not an ancient Semitic language, and it is forced and artificial to make it sound like one. Perhaps this is just another Presidential quirk, like Reagan's "Well . . . ," Nixon's "Let me make it perfectly clear . . . ," or Kennedy's "Let me say this about that . . ."

(Rabbi) Kenneth L. Cohen
Beth Shalom
Columbia, Maryland

Your reference to William McKinley's 1896 front porch campaign, i.e., he "refused to travel to solicit votes, preferring to meet voters on his front porch," is inaccurate and misleading. The "front porch" campaign occurred in 1900, when he ran for a second term. He had Theodore Roosevelt travel around the country in his stead so that he could stay at home to care for his epileptic wife, Ida (cf. Carol Felsenthal, <u>Alice Roosevelt Longworth</u>, N.Y.: Putnam, 1988, p. 56).

It is not a major point to make, but I think viewed in this light, McKinley's porch campaign may be seen to stem more from the courageous decision of a devoted husband than as an expression of indolence or overconfidence.

Francis J. Bosha
Tokyo, Japan

Primed for his inaugural address, President Bush proclaimed "the age of the offered hand." Why didn't Peggy Noonan prefer "proffered?"

Francis R. Erville
New York, New York

Dear Bill,
Thank you for a more-than-fair review. Q: What's unoriginal about "the offered hand is a reluctant fist" etc.? I thought it was . . . real good.

There's one thing in the speech that I thought only Jackson Bates and William Safire will notice: ". . . our relationship is the triumph of hope and strength over experience." It was from Dr. Johnson's definition of a second marriage: "the triumph of hope over experience." "And strength" got added in the editing process. Anyway . . . you're a very nice man.

Best,
Peggy [Noonan]
Great Falls, Virginia

Marry-o? Mahr-yo?

"I have a sensational exposé for you," writes Mario E. Severino of Colesville, Maryland. "Mario Cuomo isn't really of Italian descent and he was not raised in an Italian family!"

This would indeed be news, clearing the path for Bill Bradley to the next Democratic presidential nomination, provided he never bet on basketball games.

My informant bases his wild charge on what he has heard in commercials broadcast in the Washington area in behalf of the State of New York's tourism. Governors of neighboring areas like to saturate the nation's capital with spots featuring themselves, thereby saving the state money normally spent on announcers and—more to the political point—reminding national politicos and media biggies that the state's governor is alive and working.

"Cuomo's voice," writes Mr. Severino, "says, 'This is *Marry-o* Cuomo.' Any Italian will tell you that the first name is pronounced 'Mahr-ee-oh,' the first syllable to rhyme with 'car' as pronounced outside of New England. In Italy, Mario is really a two-syllable name—Mahr-yo. Never, never Marry-o."

With the writer's permission, I forwarded his letter to Governor Cuomo. The New York Democrat and I had not spoken recently, perhaps because I neglected to point out in this space that President Bush's use of "a kinder, gentler nation" was antedated by five years by Governor Cuomo's hope that the next generation "will be wiser than we are, kinder, gentler, more caring. . . ."

Even so, he called. I immediately said it was kind and gentle of him to do so, and the Governor generously forgave my nonnotice of his previous usage.

"I never mind when the President uses my stuff," Governor Cuomo said. "He lifts quotes, too. You hear him say the other day that 'Most of life, as Woody Allen says, is just a matter of showing up'? I must have used that forty times in the past few years. I think the Republicans have a plant in my office."

(What Mr. Bush said was "It's what Woody Allen said —90 percent of life is just showing up." Presumably, the President's writers took this from *In Search of Excellence,* the 1982 best-seller by Thomas J. Peters and Robert H. Waterman Jr., which quoted Mr. Allen as having said, "Eighty percent of success is showing up." I have written to Mr. Allen about this quotation, which bids fair to immortalize him if we can just get the percentages straight.)

Enough of this sparring; was I talking to *Marry-o* or *Mahr-ee-oh* or *Mahr-yo*?

"Look, I know how to pronounce the name in Italian." He proceeded to do so, opening the *a,* rolling, almost trilling, the *r,* eliding the sounds of *ee* and *oh* into a richly Mediterranean *eeyoh* of about a syllable-and-a-half. He followed it with a lilting *Cuomo* that conjured to the listener all the delight of linguini al dente with white clam sauce.

This man grew up in an Italian-speaking household. Why, then, the Anglicized *Marry-o*?

"*Mahr-yo* is an affectation," he replied. "If you are going to use it, you have to go all the way, rolling the *r,* and using your hands. Gotta use the hands; it's part of the pronunciation. When we choose to sound Continental, we say *Mahr-yo*—you can't see my hands over the phone, but I'm using them—but when we want to be ordinary Americans of Italian descent, it's *Marry-o.*"

Exposé denied, but the conscious reasoning behind the assertion of the American pronunciation provides a quick insight. Sometimes this language work takes relatively little effort—passing on a note, taking a call, retailing wisdom without attribution. Most of life, as Woody Allen says—or 80 percent or 90 percent or whatever—is just a matter of showing up.

I asked my mother why she called me "Marry-oh" when your experts say she should have been calling me "Mahr-yo."

She said that in her humble village they didn't have any "unassailably Italian sources" to correct the problem. Those people had already left for America.

All the best.

Mario [M. Cuomo]
Governor of New York
Albany, New York

Secret of Success

A dispute was begun in this space recently between President Bush and Governor Mario (pronounced "Marry-o") Cuomo about the accurate quotation of the philosopher Woody Allen.

The President quoted him as saying, "Ninety percent of life is just showing up." (His speechwriters later assured me that Mr. Bush has used that reference frequently; it's one of those things that get stuck in a public speaker's head and he never needs prompting to use it.) The Governor, in his equally frequent usage over the years, says, "Most of life is just a matter of showing up," and the expression in a self-help best-seller is "Eighty percent of success is showing up."

Readers were promised that clarification of this seminal thought would be sought from the author; Mr. Allen has responded to my query.

"The quote you refer to," Mr. Allen writes, "is a quote of mine which occurred during an interview while we were discussing advice to young writers, and more specifically young playwrights.

"My observation was that once a person actually completed a play or a novel he was well on his way to getting it produced or published, as opposed to a vast majority of people who tell me their ambition is to write, but who strike out on the very first level and indeed never write the play or book.

"In the midst of the conversation, as I'm now trying to recall it, I did say that 80 percent of success is showing up."

Why that particular percentage? "The figure seems high to me today," Mr. Allen says, "but I know it was more than 60 and the extra syllable in 70 ruins the rhythm of the quote, so I think we should let it stand at 80."

The Most Victimless "Crime"

In a cartoon by Jeff MacNelly, carried in hundreds of newspapers around the world, a figure wearing a western lawman's hat and badge labeled "Sheriff Meese" sits at a desk in front of a "wanted" poster. The man pictured as wanted by the law is the same Sheriff Meese, and the caption lists his crimes as "loitering" (presumably staying too long in office under fire) and "aggravated mopery."

What's *mopery*? You won't find the word in most dictionaries, though some of our best writers have used it. Red Smith, in *The New York Times* in 1981, wrote tongue in cheek about an umpire's view of the baseball manager Billy Martin: "He talked about haling Martin into court on charges of assault, battery, smoking in the subway, spitting on the sidewalk, heresy, violation of the Mann Act and mopery."

Note the trivial implication, at the end of a list of hard-to-prosecute offenses. Russell Baker used the word in his column and gave the definition and origin: "I even found a man who committed mopery. Actually, mopery isn't a crime, but only an old policemen's joke in which it's defined as the act of displaying yourself in the nude to a blind person."

Thus, the most common sense of *mopery* is "trivial violation"; when jocularly juxtaposed with *aggravated,* the phrase used by cartoonist Mac-Nelly has a nice sense of "trumped-up charge." (In legal terminology, *aggravated* means "made worse"; *aggravated assault* is more serious than *common assault* because it is usually combined with an intent to commit another crime, such as armed robbery. In general English, the verb *aggravate* is often used as a synonym for "irritate, annoy," which is not new or incorrect, but I like to reserve it for the sense of "worsen, exacerbate," because *aggravate* comes from the Latin *aggravare,* "to make heavier," from *gravis,* same root as *grieve* and *gravity,* as well as *gravitas,* which all presidential candidates are supposed to have.)

A second sense exists to *mopery,* quite different from the meaning in the joke that some people will consider a slur on the disabled. That comes from the verb *to mope,* meaning "to hang about in a state of dejection, to sulk, to behave like a listless teen-ager rejected by the opposite sex." This is perhaps akin to the Danish *moppen,* "to grimace, to make a wry face," and the noun is *mopery:* The *Time* magazine reviewer Richard Corliss referred to direction "sympathetic to the awkward pauses in teen talk, to the mopery of first love." *Fortune* magazine's Daniel Seligman wrote, "Young adults are a problem because . . . they won't lay off the pot, and they incline to mopery."

This second, nonslang sense is the source of *mope rock.* An article in *The New York Times* in 1987 titled "Glum Rock: Mope Around the Clock" elicited a letter from Lawrence Haddad of Washington, protesting the assertion that "Mope bands don't lighten up," and arguing that members of "the Mopery" have consciences that can be expressed in lyrics set to melodies that can be danced to.

Be very careful with *mopery.* You may offend a disabled person, a rock group or an Attorney General.

I agree with you that aggravated *means "made worse" because aggravate comes from the Latin* aggravare. *But you also write that "*aggravated assault *is more serious than* common assault *because it is usually combined with an intent to commit another crime, such as armed robbery." This meaning is false. Although some armed robbery may be accompanied by aggravated assault, most aggravated assault stands alone as a specific offense without a connotation of intent to commit an additional offense. Your reference to "intent to commit another crime" as part of the meaning of* aggravated assault *is simply wrong. The* Uniform Crime Reports *of the Federal Bureau of Investigation, pub-*

lished annually, as well as the statutes of most state criminal codes, defines aggravated assault as follows: "Aggravated assault is an unlawful attack by one person upon another for the purpose of inflicting severe or aggravated bodily injury."

Marvin E. Wolfgang
Professor of Criminology,
Legal Studies and of Law
The Wharton School of the
University of Pennsylvania
Philadelphia, Pennsylvania

From 1934 until 1942 I was a mounted state trooper in the Pennsylvania State Constabulary. In that period the State Police Force was not exactly crowded with scholars and I knew troopers who could not read or write above a bare minimum. Yet, perhaps because we were mounted policemen, many of these men exhibited a lot of what one might term "Horse Sense." They frequently used terms which aptly fit the occasion.

Law enforcement was still pretty basic in the rural areas of the state but we had learned one thing in arrest procedures. If an arrest was made and subsequently it was found that it was invalid as there was no specific statute to cover the action, one could not simply tell the culprit he was free to go. He had to be formally arraigned so he could be discharged to prevent legal recourse against the officer. The old cover-all "Disorderly Conduct" usually sufficed.

However, I recall one proposed charge termed, "Mopery and Gapery with Intent to Gawk." I can't swear that it was ever used but before some of those backwoods justices of the peace it would not have been beyond belief!

James H. Griffith
Port Richey, Florida

I'm a police patrol sergeant in Montgomery, a 33-square-mile township just north of Princeton. I remember being a naive trainee in the police academy during a section of instruction on the laws of arrest. One of my classmates was bombarding the older, streetwise instructor with "what if" situations. At one point the instructor jokingly gave us the following great piece of advice.

"If push comes to shove, you can arrest him for mopery and dopery with intent to gawk and sort it out later."

It's a phrase I've heard hundreds of times since that afternoon.

Chuck Person
Belle Mead, New Jersey

Mother's Work

What do we call a woman who manages the household finances, bears the babies and educates the preschool children, does the shopping and cooks the meals, organizes family social functions and serves as confidante, lover and constructive critic to her husband?

One thing we do not call her is *nonworking mother,* as I mistakenly did in this space (see pages 50–53), thereby earning me opprobrium as a nonthinking writer. Indeed, motherhood begins with *labor,* and the work does not end when the little job product is brought home.

The subject at hand was child care, a political topic of more than passing interest to those who used to be called *working mothers,* meaning "women who pursue careers outside the home." The opposite of that phrase is neither *nonworking mothers* nor *working nonmothers.* The meaning of *working mothers,* as long understood, implicitly derogates women who work hard at home. "If you know any nonworking mothers," observed Phyllis Schlafly acerbically, "I would like to meet them. I've never met any."

O.K., put that down as a slur; in modern, nonsexist, uncondescending lingo, a *nonworking mother,* like a *nonworking father,* is to be considered a loafer and a no-goodnik. In the sense of doing a job, almost all mothers "work."

But how do we label the mother whose work is done only at home, and thereby differentiate her from the mother who works at home and out there among what used to be called "the gainfully employed"? That outside-the-home worker was dubbed *career girl* in 1937 by *Collier's* magazine, and is now a *woman worker* or *female executive.* What shall we call her counterpart at home?

That question was put to the Lexicographic Irregulars, and answers are now available.

Housewife? Forget it; although many women take a fierce pride in that word, the time-honored term has been used as in "I'm only a housewife" too often to have the bezazz and connotation sought by many of the productive beings described in the first paragraph of this piece. The word derived from the Middle English *huswif* was shortened to *hussy* in 1647, and that form has now been fused to the adjective *brazen*. (Contrariwise, *hubby,* formed from *husband* in a 1688 farce *The London Cuckolds* by the playwright Edward Ravenscroft, remains an affectionate sentimentalism.)

Homemaker was born a gerund in 1876 when the English novelist Charlotte M. Yonge wrote, "Home-making is . . . her paramount earthly duty." The word became a euphemism for *housewife* for those who thought that word inadequate or demeaning; the *Oxford English Dictionary* supplement contrasted it with *housekeeper* in this way: "A housewife, especially one in charge of the domestic arrangements (as opposed to a paid housekeeper)." Tiba Thompson of Brooklyn likes *homemaker* because it busies itself on the analogy of *automaker* and suggests it parallels *kingmaker.*

Full-time mother was suggested by 20 percent of the public likely to vote. (Look, I got thirty letters on this, and six chose *full-time mother;* on smaller samples, we estimate the status of presidential candidates.) However, this locution contains a hidden slam at career women (*career girls* is a phrase that heaven did not protect). It suggests they are *part-time mothers* and thereby unloads the whole nine yards of guilt on them. (Can one unload nine yards? Yes; *the whole nine yards* refers to the contents of one fully loaded cement truck, or concrete truck to the strict-constructionists, and as such can be unloaded. Where was I?)

At-home mother, sometimes expressed as *at-home parent, home-working mom* or *home-employed mother,* is the term preferred by a significant portion of the sample. All three feel that *at-home* is short, unambiguous and self-explanatory. That prepositional phrase has been a hyphenated adjective since 1951, meaning "occurring at or suitable for one's home," though it is sometimes confused with a term in cribbage or a Britishism for doubting identity: Both Kipling and Joyce asked variations of "Who's he when he's at home?"

"On my income-tax return—for many years—I have listed my spouse's occupation as *home manager,*" writes Thomas M. Burton of Wheaton, Illinois, whose wife evidently is too busy coordinating "such diverse experts as plumbers and TV repairmen, interior decorators and domestic help, landscapers and painters" to participate fully in the filling out of the couple's joint return. "My hope is that more and more American girls will catch a vision of the rewards and demands of the Home Manager career."

Other entries included the creative *factotum,* from New Latin with the literal meaning of "do everything," submitted by Marianne Roberts of Farmington, Connecticut, who describes herself as "wife, mother, cook, housekeeper, volunteer, etc." but resists *housewife* when confronted with the "occupation" question. Dr. Henry D. Isenberg, chief of microbiology at Long Island Jewish Medical Center, describes his wife's occupation on the forms he faces with *architect of human character.*

Nobody suggested *home economist* or *domestic engineer,* though one Lex-Irreg—Madeline Scheiman of Brooklyn—put forward *domestic executive,* which is a good alternative to *business executive* but ignores the world's nonexecutives. Roseanne Barr, the television comic, refers to herself as *domestic goddess.*

One reader holds that no word is needed. "In a world hungry for 30-second sound-bytes," writes Louisa P. Young of New York City (preferring her spelling to *sound-bites*), "we all need career sound-bytes for social purposes. This is a particular problem for the *at-homes,* but they are not alone. . . . I think we might just have to grin and bear the fact that our language can't always be succinct and meaningful at the same time."

That is where we now stand. At the Department of Labor, the term for women who are not employed in outside careers was, for a brief moment, "women who work at home," but that was confusing—it seemed to refer to those who did *home-based work,* which was once called *piecework.* Now the at-home mothers are called "women who work as homemakers" or "women who are their own child-care givers."

The language is groping for a word. Sorry, I cannot give it to you, because that would undermine linguistic free will. Try these submitted by the Irregulars today, and add your own. Thrash around. Make fun of the mouth-filling euphemisms and avoid the phrases with the built-in propaganda. You can fill the vocabulary void. Work on it at home.

You ask "What do we call women who choose to work at home raising their families?" Now, the Danes have an answer to that question, in Danish, of course. They call her a "hjemmegående husmor" (pronounced hyemmegawende hoosmore), which in literal translation would be "at home working house mother."

I realize that in English "house mother" has a different meaning and "at-

home-working" is not working in English. But we could perhaps simply call her a "mother-at-home."

Incidentally, the Danes also have a male counterpart in the "hjemmegående husfar," the father who prefers to work at home and raise children and lets the woman pursue her career.

Moshe Leshem
Tuckahoe, New York

You indicated that you were open to suggestions about what to call women who work at home raising a family.

I believe that it would be useful to adapt the adjective "full-time" as a verb, so that it becomes common for persons (men or women) without outside-the-home jobs to discuss their careers by saying, for example, "I full-time as a parent and homemaker."If there are objections to this use of "full-time," one could more conventionally state, "I'm a full-time parent and homemaker."

Shirley Petchel Damrosch
Baltimore, Maryland

To fill the "vocabulary void," I suggest <u>homecare.</u> It may be used to answer the question about "Occupation" and expanded to <u>homecare worker</u> or <u>homecare provider.</u>

"Healthcare" may not be in a dictionary, but it is a widely used idiom and had no difficulty in gaining acceptance.

Albert B. Honig
Chevy Chase, Maryland

Upon finishing the column I turned to my domestic goddess, Claudia Dosch Newton, and asked her for a term describing all the work she does. The response was instantaneous: hometender.

I like it! The "tender" evokes both the child-care/spouse-care gentleness required and the overseeing needed in tending to the home. "Hometender" is neither sexist nor materialist like "housewife." "Hometender" is also more inclusive than the nest-building title of "homemaker."

John E. Newton
East Aurora, New York

How about "Home anchor"? Although I have six children and ten grandchildren, my husband often laughingly teases me, saying, "You're just along for the ride, aren't you?" And so it seems most of the time. But once in a while a ship really <u>needs</u> its anchor.

> *Irene Eelkema*
> *St. Paul, Minnesota*

I, myself, am a "housewife, domestic engineer, homemaker, domestic goddess and/or factotum." (Factotum is my personal favorite. I just may put that on my husband's and my joint return this year. By the way, I do have time to "participate fully in the filling out of our forms between the plumbers, repairmen, etc." Where was I?) However, at the risk of sounding opinionated and bigoted, the term "full-time wife and mother" describes my career most accurately. I realize I am unloading "the whole nine yards of guilt" on those women who choose to work outside the home in addition to mothering. Let's face it, though, career women do get eight hours or more daily vacation from the runny noses, sticky fingers, loud music, endless questions and demands, not to mention spilled milk and wet diapers.

I suppose I would most like to call myself a catalyst, a stabilizer, an educator, a student, an encourager, a safe port and a shaper of the future because the fruits of my efforts may not appear as obviously or as soon as the banker's big deal, the lawyer's won case, the architect's new building, or the speculator's latest acquisition, but when my husband travels daily into a world filled with tension and anxiety and my children finally fly from the nest into their uncertain future, they will hopefully be happier, more secure human beings ready to go about the business of peaceful, productive living for me having stayed home full-time with them.

In this culture so filled with substance abuse, stress-related illness, suicide and insecurities, isn't that what it's all about? I'm fiercely proud to call myself a full-time wife and mother, and I wouldn't have it any other way. You must excuse me now for my children are awakening and my day begins.

> *Robin Guerra*
> *Castaic, California*

What to call a mother who stays home to care for her children? "Home Manager" has a nice ring to it, but I don't stay home to manage the house; I stay home to manage the children.

Which is why I call myself a "Professional Mother."

> *Nancy Goodspeed*
> *Plainsboro, New Jersey*

After reading your column on the problem of what to call those mothers who do not work outside the home, I have an idea. Why not call those mothers motherworkers and the mothers who work outside the home working mothers? I know. It sounds too much like that other word beginning with mother. Other than that none-too-small problem, I really like the way simply switching the nouns to modifiers and vice-versa works.

Wendy Beck
Kew Gardens, New York

I personally detest the term housewife, and I shudder at the thought of my son checking with the domestic engineer before going to a friend's house to play. I go with mother—not at-home mother, not full-time mother—just plain mother.

By definition, a mother is one who "exercises control and responsibility." Yes, she educates, plays, shops, cooks, cleans, plans and manages. She lectures, checks homework, disciplines, laughs, hugs and kisses. She may or may not have a job outside the home. Above all, she is there when you need her. Why not leave this overloaded word adjective-free? The kids fill in the best modifiers on their Mother's Day cards, where "sweetest," "greatest" and "loving" top the list.

Karen M. Sloan
Plainview, New York

Domestic Director. That coinage is actually from my wife, Mary Jo, and since she is one, I cast my vote with hers. Domestic Director seems preferable to Madeline Scheiman's "Domestic Executive" (too highfalutin') or Roseanne Barr's "Domestic Goddess" (too arch). If our household is typical, it also has the advantage of being accurate.

F. C. Marston
Milwaukee, Wisconsin

I'm writing to offer a possible solution to the problem of what to call a mother who is not employed outside the home: She is a career mother. The career mother has decided to spend a number of years actively mothering her children, not for lack of opportunity elsewhere, but because mothering—the intellectual, emotional, spiritual, and physical nourishment of her children—is her vocation.

Janet Podell
Englewood, New Jersey

There's a perfectly good and distinguished-sounding word for a woman who runs a household rather than a business: chatelaine. It's also kind of romantic.

Betsy Frankel
Alexandria, Virginia

The Mulvihill Perplexity

"When I was taught to write a business letter," wrote Jane Mulvihill of Sag Harbor, New York, "the proper salutation, unless one knew the name of an individual to be addressed, was *Gentlemen*. What do we do now? *Ladies and/or Gentlemen*? . . . I need some advice."

After the Mulvihill Perplexity was published in this column, seven hundred dear readers (How does *Dear Reader* grab you?) contributed their advice. Never has a mail pull of mine tugged so hard on the sleeve of language; evidently this problem of salutations, precipitated not so much by a fear of sexism as by a recognition of outdatedness, is roiling correspondents around the world.

Ten percent of the respondents in this survey, which is based on the scientific polling principles that enabled *Literary Digest* magazine to predict an Alf Landon victory in 1936, reject not only *Gentlemen* but any salutation at all.

"No salutation whatsoever is particularly helpful," writes Carl H. Burkhart of Greenville, South Carolina, "when you have no idea to which of the sexes you are writing. Further, if writing to a known individual, such as you, I now eliminate the quasi-affectionate *Dear*. You are not, for example, dear to me in any way. . . ."

Nine out of ten people, however, are pro-salutation. I'm in that majority; a letter without something between the address and the body seems unfinished, or looks like a transcript of voice mail. Worst of all is the inclusion of a name in the first sentence, as in "I'm writing, Mr. Safire, because I'm so excited about salutations. . . ." That looks like a computer trying to do direct-mail tricks.

In business correspondence, *Gentlemen* is out. You can't even find that word on a lavatory door anymore; the sign reads *Men*, or seeks to leap language limitations with a stylized picture of somebody in pants, which must be confusing and ultimately embarrassing to women in slacks. Today the only place for the phrase *ladies and gentlemen* is in the mouths of old-time emcees. (That's a phoneticism for the abbreviation of "masters of ceremonies." Research is needed on phoneticisms such as *emcee, deejay, Seabee,* but I digress.)

As the British say after the toast to the Queen, *Gentlemen* may now go up in smoke. We have entries for *Gentlepeople, Gentlefolk* and *Gentle persons,* even *Gentle/wo/men,* each of which solves the sexism problem, but not one has that cool crispness associated with commerce. The sense of *Gentlemen* in salutations was not that of gentlepersons, or even of men of honor, but was more in the nature of "You guys!"

Adam Yarmolinsky (who is neither Adam Walinsky nor Daniel Yankelovich, but is provost of the University of Maryland) finds an answer in Shakespeare's *A Midsummer Night's Dream,* when Puck concludes with "Gentles, do not reprehend. / If you pardon, we will mend. . . ." Echoes J. Quinn Brisben of Chicago: "*Gentles* has the warrant of Shakespeare, the feminist imprimatur of Virginia Woolf and—unlike those adjustments to feminist consciousness which end in *person*—subtracts rather than adds a syllable, thus beginning business correspondence with a vigorous trochee rather than an ambling dactyl."

Dear has the strong support of a third of all respondents. The problem is, dear what or who? The ludicrous *Dear Sir or Madam* has been nicely mocked by the addition of *as the case may be;* it is not salvaged by modern virgulization into *Sir/Madam.* (If you must use it, avoid spelling *Madam* as *Madame,* which is good French but in English is often taken to mean "brothel-keeper.")

We have a heavy run on *Dear Colleague* among academicians, perhaps because *Dear Professional* seems a bit self-consciously elitist, limited to such professions as medicine, the law, journalism and brothel-keeping. *Dear Compatriot* is submitted by Mark P. Yolles of Albany, *Dear Folks* by John H. Vestal of Jenkintown, Pennsylvania, *Dear Gentlepersons* by Fearn Cutler of New York City, *Dear Executive* by Lee B. Rosen of West Palm Beach, Florida, and *Dear Friends* by a host of people who have been on the receiving end of sermons.

The most popular salutation to a company from a customer is *Dear [Company Name]*. (The brackets mean "insert the name of the company"; I had a lot of trouble with that concept when computer guides said *Enter [filename]*. Too many of my files are named *filename*.) The humorist Robert Benchley, afflicted with checkbook-balancing woes, wrote *Dear Bank;* that makes good sense, especially when the specific name of the bank is added.

Dear Kellogg's or *Dear Lands' End* says clearly, "I am addressing you as a corporation"; for those who want some personalization, there's *Dear Ford Branch Manager* or *Dear Bronx Zoo Complaint Division Chief* or *Dear Filename*. "After all, I'm writing to people in their official capacities rather than as individuals," writes Dan Birdsall from our Coast Guard station in Iceland. "I therefore write *Dear Customer Relations Department*."

Single-word salutations, dropping the *Dear,* were well represented. "I have for many years used the opening greeting of *Salutations!*" writes Sophia S. Hsieh of New York City, adding parenthetically, "(the exclamation point is for esthetics)." A clip of that, *Salu,* is the crusade of Tam W. Deachman of Vancouver, British Columbia, while *Hail* is the Caesaresque preference of Phil Ruder of Madison, Wisconsin.

Leo H. Cohen of Holliston, Massachusetts, has an attention-grabber: *PLEASE*. Marjorie E. Jones of Yarmouthport, Massachusetts, knocks *Occupant* but likes *Recipient,* and Steven De Groote of Fort Worth chooses *People*. Others prefer memo style (*To: You-know-who*), and we have a category of multiword salutations from *Good Morning* to *Howdy, Friend* to *Your Attention, Please*. *Lectori Benevolo* was suggested by Steven W. Alpert of Tucson, Arizona, who translates the Latin as "To the kind and gentle reader."

My preference is to get the addressee's name and use it in full: *Dear Mikhail Sergeyevich Gorbachev*. I'm not overly formal or obsequious, as in *Dear Mr. Gorbachev,* or overly familiar, as in *Dear Mikhail Sergeyevich*. Here's a letter to me from Agnes Franz of Prescott, Arizona: "*Dear William Safire:* There—did that offend? Irritate? Depersonalize or seem unprofessional?" Not a bit, Agnes Franz. A full name is best when you want to address someone you do not know, or when you are uncertain about being on a first-name basis with the recipient.

What about an all-purpose, cheerful, one-word salutation with deep roots in the language and never considered offensive or pushy? My longtime favorite, in speech and writing, is preferred by more than 5 percent of the sample: *Greetings*.

In the 1611 translation of the New Testament, an epistle begins: "James . . . to the twelve tribes which are scattered abroad, greeting." In Shakespeare's *Richard II*, Bolingbroke tells his uncle to speak with the Queen: "Tell her I send to her my kind commends; / Take special care my greetings be delivered."

The Old English verb *gretan* means "to approach, to call upon, to accost," and can be found in *Beowulf*, written in 725 or so. It is probably akin to the Scottish *greet*, "to weep" (which is why a Scottish wake is called a "greetin' meeting," and the sad *gretan* may persist in the last syllable of *regret*).

You will have no regrets in adopting the plural *Greetings*. *Greetings* is to *Greeting* as *Regards* is to *Regard.* Why reserve it for Yuletide use alone? The word *Greetings* smiles a welcome. Try it at the start of your next letter, or in leaving your next message on somebody's answering device. In a business letter, follow *Greetings* with a colon, never a semicolon or a comma; if informality is your thing, follow it with a dash or, if you're feeling exuberant, with an exclamation mark.

Greetings is a salutary salutation. The only one to compete is the older and healthier *Salutations!*

Kudos for your effort to disentangle the Mulvihill Perplexity. You give but a passing nod, however, to the Russian variant. Your preference to use all three names is commendable but slightly excessive. Thus, "Dear (or 'the honorable') Mikhail Sergeyevich"—the first name and patronymic—is enough. This usage is standard throughout Russia and it has hoary antecedents dating back to the Viking invasions. The tie can be easily seen by leafing through a Minneapolis telephone book for the Johnsons, Andersons, et al.

True, it takes a little effort to memorize patronymics, but their use simplifies the problem of address overall. Further, it avoids the pre-Revolutionary "gospodin" (roughly, Mr.), which puts up barriers with the West. Finally, there is the simple title "comrade," which, while not recommended outside Russia, serves the Russians well when memory fails.

William Shinn, Jr.
Princeton, New Jersey

Hey, William Safire!
You're going to have a hard time selling "Greetings" as a salutation to anyone who received a World War II draft notice!
How soon they forget . . .

John R. Barrington
Kingston, New York

Your research about style of address overlooked the practice of members of the Religious Society of Friends (Quakers). The vision of the society's founder, George Fox, that "there is that of God in every one" led him to the practice of not employing titles in salutations, but addressing everyone, king and commoner alike, with given and family name. This practice is observed by members of the society even today. The vision also led to the abandonment of the practice of "hat honor," which led to many difficulties, even prison in his day. But that is another story/article for another day. You may notice his method of dating letters, which was a form of protest of the incursion of pagan names into the Christian life of the day. That practice is little employed today.

The retention of "plain Speech"—thee and thy to an individual—I regret to say is most often used as "inside code" rather than for simplicity today. Thee can still hear it used regularly between Quakers and the Lancaster farm vendors at the Reading Terminal Market in Philadelphia today. I feel certain thee knows that this was in contrast to the plural <u>you</u>, which was used for nobility indicating that they were more than a single person in value.

Philip L. Gilbert
Garden City, New York

P.S. Quakers should not conclude a letter with the routine expression "Sincerely" as that might imply that they were not sincere in some other letters.

Name That Decade

"What are we going to call the decade after the decade of the Nineties?"

That's the sort of question—not urgent, not pressing, just pleasantly problematical—that concerns people in the language dodge. Short-range, non-strategic planners are already finding names for what some of us call the *Nifty Nineties.* If our optimism is misplaced, we have a fallback name: the *Nasty Nineties.* (Sorry, Diamond Jim, you cannot call the coming decade the *Gay Nineties* because the meaning of *gay* is no longer the single sense of "high-spirited.") But after the year 2000, in the first decade of the new millennium, all of us will have to face up to the big problem in nomenclature.

I have been calling the first decade of the third millennium of the Common Era (or Christian Era, if that is what you prefer to call the time since the birth of Jesus) the *Zippy Zeros,* but that is only a working title. When the name-that-decade query was placed in this space a few months ago, Lexicographic Irregulars rose to the challenge of the future.

"*Zero* has too many syllables, especially for something with no content," writes Greg Hill of Concord, California. "*Oh* is no good because it is already

a letter. *Naught* is elegant and functional, but it had its chance and did not stick; besides, it is spelled funny. I propose that we take the best of all worlds and coin a new word: *zot.* 'Twenty *zot* one' flows naturally and pleasantly. The decade, of course, would be the *Zots.*"

Zap the zots; artificial words made up by language mavens rarely fly. But that postcard touches on several possibilities suggested by scores of "three-bies," the nickname for third-millennium freaks.

The *Aughties* was put forward by J. William Doolittle of Washington, who added that he supposed the following decade would be called the *Teens* and wondered whether 2011 and 2012 would be considered the *Pre-Teens,* a subject we shall not deal with again in this space for twenty years.

The *Naughties* was suggested by forty readers, and Byrne Balton of New York City was first to go for the *Double Naughties,* but I am turning this down because of the archness of the double meaning.

For those troubled by the spelling of *aught* and *naught,* which can mean the same nothing, the probable explanation is this: *An aught* was pronounced "a naught" as often as *a napron* was pronounced "an apron," and the letter *n* may have just popped over in what some linguists call misdivision.

The *naught/nought* problem—and that's a legitimate use of the oft-violated virgule—was dealt with in 1983, in a *New York Times* editorial that first raised this subject of the first problem of the third millennium.

"In theory, it's as silly to say 'an ought' as it would be to say 'an ewspaper,' " wrote the editorialist, who is always anonymous, but in this case has a nicely wacky quality that reminds me of Jack Rosenthal. "Then why not correct the term and call the decade the *Noughts*? One reason is the potential for more argument, this time over spelling: *naught* or *nought*? Fowler notes that *nought* is usually reserved for zero, leaving *naught* for poetic and rhetorical uses."

The Times came down on the side of the *Ohs* because "That would be accurate; each year in the decade has at least two *O*'s in its name. And the *Ohs*, with a connotation of wonder, would be fittingly optimistic for the start of a century. The one drawback is that someone seeking to make a point about Federal deficits and debt might be tempted to spell it the *Owes*. He or she ought naught."

Oh, no. A survey on this subject was conducted several months ago by Tim Yohn of *Art & Artists* magazine. (You thought I was the only one worried about this? You probably misspell *millennium*.) The *Ohs* and *Double-O's* received a middling response; other entries were the *Digits* and the *Thousands*. Mr. Yohn's early work in this field deserves note, though he spells *millennium* with one *n*, which may be artistic but is incorrect; the mnemonic is *annual*, also with two *n*'s, from the same root meaning "yearly."

O.K., based on my own survey and that of others, and as a result of extensive thumb-sucking, here is my short-awaited recommendation: use *oh* in the name of the year, as in *Twenty oh six*. (Shorter and easier than *Two thousand and six*, and less negative than using *naught*.) But hold off until 2009, when we're in prosperity or depression, before deciding what to call the whole decade.

That's a cop-out, but I cannot here and now solve this problem for the entire English-speaking world. As the parsimonious Yorkshireman advised his son, "If ever tha does owt for nowt, allus do it for thisen" ("If ever you do anything for nothing, always do it for yourself").

I was not persuaded by your preference for "Twenty oh six" over "Two thousand and six" on the ground of its being "shorter and easier." If you change the latter to "Two thousand six" (why not?), it becomes as short (four syllables in each version) and, I assume for that reason, as "easy" as "Twenty oh six." "Two thousand six" has the advantage of being sequential with the Nineteen hundreds. It seems to me that unless there is a good reason to depart from the sequence, we should stick with it.

Norman Dorsen
New York, New York

By choosing to use "oh" in the names of the years (as in "Twenty oh six" for 2006), you perpetuate the confusion between a letter and a number. The letter "oh" is appropriate for words, but the digit "zero" is correct for use in numbers; their mere similarity in shape should not be allowed to confuse us. After all, the digit "one" and the letter "ell" have similar shapes, but we would never refer to the year 2001 as "two thousand and ell."

My response to your suggestion ("Twenty oh six" for 2006) is to follow the example set in the Arthur Clarke/Stanley Kubrick masterpiece, spoken as "Two Thousand and One." It's clear, it's correct, it avoids the use of the dreaded zero.

Christopher Landee
Associate Professor of Physics
University of Paris—South
Paris, France

The year (or for that matter, the number) 2006 is not read two thousand and six; it is read two thousand, six. The comma may not be necessary; but it is necessary to delete the and. (Columbus sailed the ocean blue in fourteen hundred ninety-two, not in fourteen hundred and ninety-two.) In your article, you implied that whether one inserts the and is a matter of choice, but it never is; the rule is clear. And there is a good reason for the rule. (In mathematics, there usually is.)

In naming numbers, the word and is reserved for use with decimals. Thus, 2.04 is read two and four hundredths. When naming a whole number, then, such as a year, and never correctly appears. (You might wish, at this point, to glance at the last formal invitation you received to see whether the year was written correctly.)

Why is the rule so strict? It has to be, to avoid ambiguity. For illustration purposes, try writing the number .305 in words. (No fair writing point three oh five.) If you wrote three hundred five thousandths, you are correct. But if you inserted a "harmless" and and wrote three hundred and five thousandths, you actually wrote the number 300.005, which is clearly very far off the mark.

It is true, I admit, that when naming a year, decimals are never involved, so no ambiguity will ever result if the and is inserted (erroneously, we'll all now agree). The point is, however, that we are trying to teach our students a system for naming all numbers. Please don't confuse them further; they're already so far behind the Japanese . . .

Peter Devine
Englewood Cliffs, New Jersey

Naught is a perfectly legitimate word meaning "nothing"; its <u>n</u> goes back to the Old English negative particle. <u>Aught</u> originally meant "anything," and it acquired the second meaning "nothing" through misdivision of <u>a naught</u> as <u>an aught</u>. (This is explained in <u>Webster's New World Dictionary of the American Language</u> and elsewhere.)

Louis Jay Herman
New York, New York

Never Happeneth

Feeling sorry for presidential dropouts, I wrote about bad luck and bad timing, adding: "But time and chance happeneth to us all."

Prompt chastisement from Robert G. Lopez of Glen Ellen, California: "What a dreadful sentence!"

I reached for the Gideon Bible, nestled against the *Webster's New World Dictionary* in my room at the Stanford Court Hotel in San Francisco. (No guests steal the Bible; a few swipe the dictionary, proving the sad fact that the word is more coveted than the Word.)

There it was, in the King James Version of 1611, Ecclesiastes 9:11: ". . . the race is not to the swift nor the battle to the strong . . . but time and chance happeneth to them all."

So what did I get wrong? Mr. Lopez's objections: "1. Time does not 'happen to' anyone, let alone to us all. 2. Chance does not 'happen to' anyone, either. 3. 'Happeneth' is a third-person *singular* form."

To every objection there is a season.

The Douay Version of the Old Testament, prepared in 1609 at what is now the French city spelled Douai, contains the passage translated from the Latin Vulgate and earlier texts this way: ". . . but time and chance in all." And the New English Bible, published in 1961, drops the "but" and changes the verb: ". . . time and chance govern all." So Mr. Lopez is not the first to look hard at the use of *happen* and the plural use of *happeneth*.

I'll go along with the King James choice of *happen* to use with time and chance, because these great metaphysical ideas can come to, afflict, affect, devolve upon or happen to us all. But *happeneth* won't do.

No problem with *happeneth* as a verb taking the third-person singular subject, as in "As it happeneth to the fool, so it happeneth even to me" (Ecclesiastes 2:15). The archaic *-eth* ending gives an ancient solemnity to the biblical words, but it is an alternative to the *-s* ending—we moderns would say *happens*. (The *-s* ending largely replaced *-eth* in Middle English, according to the grammarian George O. Curme, adding, "In early Modern English, there was a tendency in the literary language for those who employed the ending -*eth* in the third-person singular to use it also in the plural.")

Proverbs says, "Pride goeth before destruction, and an haughty spirit before a fall." (Some of us shorten that.) The subject, *pride,* is singular, and it *goeth,* or *goes;* but if the subject is plural, the -*eth* or -*s* is out.

Take *time and tide,* a plural subject: We say, "Time and tide *wait* for no man"; if we use a single subject, it would be "Time *waits* for no man" or, in archaic form, "Time *waiteth* for no man." (Only if you consider two things to be a singular unit would you add the -*s* or -*eth; "peanut butter and jelly is—not *are*—my favorite sandwich, and waiteth for no man.")

God did not make this mistake, nor should the solecism be attributed to King Solomon, who usually gets credit for Ecclesiastes. The error of not matching a plural subject to a plural verb was made by the translators and scribes responsible for the King James Version, human beings to whom time and chance happen, not happeneth. I would send Mr. Lopez a prize, but riches do not necessarily come to men of understanding.

The translators of the King James Version of the Bible showed Solomonic wisdom when they translated Ecclesiastes 9:11 "time and chance happeneth to them all."

The original Hebrew uses a singular verb (yikreh not yikru). The two Hebrew nouns which serve as the subject (et va-fega) might be considered to be a singular unit in the sense of "happenstance."

The King James scholars knew their dikduk (grammar).

Mordecai H. Lewittes
New York, New York

I ruefully confess that I did not recognize "Time and chance happeneth . . ." as a quotation from Ecclesiastes. Had I done so, I would not have had the temerity to complain about it. Mind you, I still find it a dreadful sentence. Time passes. Time heals all wounds. Time happens to deal harshly with some and gently with others. But—"Time happened to me on the way to the office this morning"? Metaphysics aside, it makes little sense, and worse, seems to fall unpleasantly on post-Jacobean ears—on some of them, at any rate.

But despite all that, to criticize the King James Version exceeds solecism and verges on lèse-majesté. (Lèse-Dieu? Lèse-Safire is foolhardy enough.) Time has rendered it sacrosanct, and rightly so. Some might say, though I can't imagine why, that time has happened to it.

So, "Whoso diggeth a pit shall fall therein." Therefrom, I send you best wishes.

Robert G. Lopez
Glen Ellen, California

The use of the singular "happeneth" in the King James Bible is actually a literal—and accurate—translation of the original Hebrew, which has the verb in the singular yigre and not in the plural yigru. The solecism, if it is one, was Solomon's, and he was very wise and knew which side of his bread the peanut butter and jelly was on.

Joseph A. Reif
Bar-Ilan University
Ramat Gen, Israel

New Template for the Hundred Days

John H. Sununu, White House chief of staff, once objected to the way some pundits were judging the Bush Administration. Too many of us, he felt, are accustomed to a frenetic first *hundred days.*

We will be seeing that phrase a great deal this weekend, because Mr. Bush's one hundredth day in the Oval Office, counting from noon on January 20, is today, April 30.

The *hundred days* is remembered now as the hectic, creative, controversial time of the special session of Congress summoned by Franklin Delano Roosevelt in 1933 to cope with the Depression.

However, here is how to astound your friends with historical trivia: The *hundred days* was first applied to the period in 1815 that the King of France, Louis XVIII, was driven from Paris after Napoleon's escape from Elba. Following Napoleon's defeat at Waterloo, the King returned to his capital, where the prefect of Paris, Louis de Chabrol de Volvic, told him: "A hundred days, sire, have elapsed since the fatal moment when Your Majesty was forced to quit your capital in the midst of tears."

Ronald Reagan was said to have "hit the ground running" in his first hundred days, but President Bush—the first elected successor of a President in the same party since Herbert Hoover—was accused by newsmongers of "hitting the ground crawling."

Mr. Sununu, former Governor of New Hampshire, disagrees. I visited him in the West Wing of the White House primarily to discuss palindromes, because his last name, in a possessive state, forms one perfectly. The chief of staff reported that his favorite was "A man, a plan, a canal—Panama!" (an appropriate choice for a Republican); my own favorites, from William Irvine's *Madam I'm Adam,* are "Sit on a potato pan, Otis" and the suggestive "Naomi, did I moan?" that also serves as a mnemonic for ruthless spellers of Naomi.

While pursuing this linguistic mission, however, I was moved to ask about the inexorable hundred-days judgment. He explained the widespread failure to understand the Bush approach by using a stunning metaphor: "Ours is a different template."

Suddenly everything came clear; such is the power of a fresh trope.

Until recently, the meaning of *template* was primarily important to metalwork, as in this definition offered by Wes Glebe, an industrial designer in State College, Pennsylvania: "a metal plate with openings formed to be used as a pattern or guide."

The *template,* sometimes spelled *templet* (which is how it was pronounced until recently), is a word with different meanings for "aid to reproduction" in building, photogrammetry and genetics (a pattern-setting strand of DNA). A second sense, "a permanent base on which to bolt a piece of equipment," is used in the oil industry and in plumbing (a marble base for a toilet).

The first sense, "guidance in replication," is the one being extended today. Thanks to David Kanicki, publisher of *Modern Casting* magazine for the American Foundrymen's Society, we now have this first synonymy of punched-out patterning:

"*Template* is an external contour for casting, mainly used to check the dimensions of a metal part. A *stencil* is also a negative design to create an identical thing with each use, but opposite from a positive *pattern* because it creates an internal part. A *fixture* sets proper positions each time you're working, like a *jig,* a mechanical device to hold work in place. A *die,* the heart of the whole casting process, is hollowed out, like a mold, to create the same part over and over."

But the hot new application (as the gushies say, "It is to die") is in computer hardware. To hackers, a *template*—pronounced most often with a full "plate"—is a plastic sheet cut out to fit over parts of a computer keyboard. It serves the purpose of what some of us used to call a *crib sheet* to remind the user about the keystroke commands of a software program.

I am blessed with a XyWrite template as I write this; otherwise, I might be tempted to push "NumLock" instead of "Alt-Home" and send this copy to a Martian who might not understand what is spewing out of his interplanetary fax machine. (My template has no explanation for the dread *NumLock;* it may have something to do with what killed Socrates.)

Webster's New World Dictionary of Computer Terms defines *template* as, first, "a plastic guide used in drawing geometric flowcharting symbols," then as a design aid in computer graphics and finally—going beyond the punched-out crib sheet most of us have in mind—"a set of instructions for relating information within a software development package, usually a spreadsheet." Thus, it can be a preconfigured form stored on a disk for desktop publishers, fitting stories into a preferred layout. How's that for extending a metaphor?

The etymology is mysterious: It may come from the French diminutive of the Latin *templum,* in the sense of a plank or rafter used in building a place of worship. In architecture, it was used in 1677 to describe a horizontal piece of timber that distributed the downward thrust of a girder in a building known as a *temple.*

You may feel burdened with more than you need to know about our punched-out term. But consider the workings of the language: Here is this building term, long in specialized use, suddenly being used generally in the world of personal computers and introduced into the home. Quickly, the image of the template on the keyboard is taken up by a presidential aide, and broadcast by at least one pundit. In the meantime, the hardware sense of a plastic sheet laid on keys for guidance is being overtaken by a software meaning of built-in patterning.

In a vast example of trope-a-dope, the ancient and mysterious word is being belted around the ring, but is bouncing back in new extensions of its metaphor. That's because both the technology of reproduction and the art of explication are booming, and a word such as *template* slips nicely over both. To paraphrase Archimedes: Give me a metaphor strong enough, and I will move the world.

"Guidance in replication" has long been known to people who use sewing machines. Any buttonhole attachment comes with various templates for different sizes of buttonholes. If you are making a number of these, the template always makes the same size. I've known it in that sense for many years, as any set of instructions for buttonhole attachments always used it. So it has been introduced *"into the home"* long, long ago!

Dorothy Acheson
Woods Hole, Massachusetts

This is not a gotcha memo, but rather a wishedya note. Knowing your penchant for prose, politics and palindromes, we wishedya had used our favorite palindrome. What better way to bridge the transition from Napoleon to Sununu than "Able was I ere I saw Elba."

Debra and Barry Kosofsky
Jamaica Plain, Massachusetts

No Problem

The world's most famous Americanism is *O.K.;* the 1839 expression (from the slang *oll korrect*) is understood from Timbuktu to Novosibirsk.

The expression of approval now sweeping the world is *no problem,* which is also used to mean "You're welcome." In the Soviet Union, the term is rendered *nyet problemy.*

However, the Russians are apparently resisting this Americanism. According to the family of Jerrold and Leona Schecter, who collectively have written *Back in the U.S.S.R.: An American Family Returns to Moscow,* another word is taking hold with the same meaning.

Normalno, write the Schecters, is "Moscow's most common slang word," which they say is "verbally equivalent to the American 'no problem.' " Not quite equivalent; the assurance conveyed is not as complete.

The word's primary meaning, of course, is "normal," but the Schecters provide the slang term in context and in its specialized sense: "Again, it was what the Russians, smiling, called *normalno*—'normal procedure' or 'no problem'—but every Russian knows the word has taken on an ironic usage to convey the real confusion and discord that prevails beneath the exterior of order."

The nearest American expressions would be "What do you expect? That's the way it goes. Typical. Such is life."

I can hear it now: "How about a summit in June, Anatoly?"
"*Nyet problemy,* Brent."
"You're sure you can schedule it without a hitch?"
"*Normalno.*"

No Shades of Gray

"An unending, Manichaean East-West death struggle" was not something that Senator Albert Gore Jr. believed in, wrote Hendrik Hertzberg in *The New Republic.*

On the other hand, a "Manichaean view of a world that he sees as divided between the bad Soviet Union and the good United States" was attributed to Richard Nixon by a *New York Times* reviewer of the former President's new book, *1999: Victory Without War.*

What about President Reagan—where does he stand on Manichaeism? The sociologist Robert Nisbet, writing in *Reason* magazine, referred to "Reagan's Manichaean division of the world into the Good and the Evil empires," although the President's visit to Moscow subsequently cast that vivid differentiation in subtler tones.

Whence this voguish evocation of an obscure figure fogbound in the mists of history? "Come on, fellas," urges William F. Gavin of McLean, Virginia. "We all know politicians don't have a clue about the esoteric complexities of Manichaean theology. And we also know that not all moral dualities are Manichaean in nature.

"Accusing a politician of harboring a *Manichaean* view of the world," this street-corner conservative protests, "is a shorthand way of saying this poor chucklehead lacks sophistication, is ignorant of nuances and doesn't know— yokel that he is—that there is no black or white, but only shades of gray."

Manichaeism—that spelling I consider to be Good, and *Manicheism,* without the second *a,* to be Evil, accepted only by permissive orthographical descriptivists—is a religious philosophy, which was developed by a Persian named Mani (short for Manichaeus) in Babylonia during the third century after the birth of Christ, and which held some sway until the Mongol invasions of the thirteenth century.

Mani, if I may use the familiar diminutive, held that the principles of Good (light, God, the spirit) contend with the principles of Evil (darkness, Satan, the body) and that the pure spirit can be released from the sullied body's sensuality through strict asceticism. I am not knocking this philosophy, only describing it as the basis of the word used by the great crowd of critics of simplism today.

In Manichaeism, as Benny Goodman used to sing, it's "Gotta Be This or That." One thing or the other will triumph, in this dualistic view, and the winner is supposed to be determined in an apocalyptic struggle involving a world conflagration. (The zodiac fits into all this somehow, but let us not involve the sensitive East Wing of the White House.)

The social order of the Manichaeists, according to W. L. Reese's *Dictionary of Philosophy and Religion,* offers some instruction to today's pundits and their audiences: An inner circle of the Elect involved the devout keepers of the flame, required to exhibit rigorous discipline and eschew fleshly pleasures, while an outer circle of Hearers included those allowed to own property and marry. Recent centuries have seen these lines blurred, even among right-wingers accused of being "unreconstructed Cold Warriors" and evil-empire Manichaeans.

"Maybe we all ought to agree to a moratorium," suggests Mr. Gavin, "on applying theological labels to political figures, who, poor souls (so to speak), have enough trouble with ordinary language. Otherwise, I can see the headlines now: BUSH CALLS DUKAKIS 'PELAGIAN DUPE'; DUKE CALLS BUSH SOFT ON ALBIGENSIANISM.' "

"Mani" is not "short" for "Manichaeus"; rather "Manichaeus" is "long" for "Mani." You should know that Persians didn't end their names with -us; that's a Greco-Roman habit. His actual name ended with a Persian letter usually

transliterated as "gh," which is thankfully silent in final position (so writing "Manigh" would be unnecessarily pedantic) but pronounced as a guttural between vowels, as in the genitive "Manighi" ("of Mani") used to describe one of his followers (usually written "Manichee" in English). Classical writers confused the genitive with the nominative, hence the Greek "Manichaios" (some Byzantine purists held out for "Manes" but, sadly, lost) and the Latin "Manicheus." Your preferred form "Manichaeus" is simply a Renaissance compromise which, like other ae's of similar pedigree as in "Graecian," "haemoglobin," and "caelestial," should be consigned to the dustbin of orthography. To argue about the spelling of the vowel in "Manichean"/"Manichaean" is particularly petty when that vowel is only there by mistake and can only be justified by treating "Manichean" as derived from "Manichee" rather than directly from "Mani."

Robert Eckert
Grosse Pointe Park, Michigan

Now Hear Dis

To be *on the bubble,* as professional football players know, is to be in danger of being cut from the squad. The central quality of a bubble is its fragility, and those who find themselves on it are waiting for the inevitable burst.

That's an example of the new slang—late-1980's lingo that deserves close examination. A quick check with Stuart Berg Flexner at Random House revealed that jazz musicians are falling down on the job of creating the latest argot, but college students are still doing fine.

Def, a clip of *definitely,* is now the word for *terrif,* and on some campuses has outneatened *neat.* No longer do you *cream* a course—you *wax* it, presumably with no buildup. And to have a good time at a party is *to rage,* which we all do against the dying of the light.

Jonathan E. Lighter, working on a new dictionary of slang citations, is attuned to campus use of *from hell* as an intensifier. "That was a party *from hell*" was a gathering not to miss, whereas "That was an exam *from hell*" was a toughie.

Both slanguists are catching *dis,* a verb meaning "to put down, derogate, humiliate," presumably a clip of the noun *disrespect.* To *dis* someone is to show disrespect for that person.

Lexicographic Irregulars: While *lamping* or *living large,* do not be *undecked.* Shake off the *wireheads* and apply your *wetware* to the new inside skinny.

Gotta be *fresh.*

You refer to the expression "to be on the bubble" connoting a dangerous situation as in waiting for the bubble to burst. I first heard the expression several years ago and believe it to have originated with U.S. Marine Corps aviators flying the AV-8 Harrier (now the AV-8B in its most recent configuration).

You may recall that the British-built Harrier is a VTOL (Vertical Take Off and Landing) jet attack aircraft which can carry out military missions at close to the speed of sound, but which can also hover, take off, and land like a helicopter by rotating its engines downward. This creates a "ground effect"—I would have called it an air effect—or bubble of air pressure which the Harrier rides until it reaches the desired altitude.

To achieve this result, Harrier pilots must "stay on the bubble" or "ride the bubble" as I have heard them describe it. It is truly a dangerous situation since the aircraft tends to slide off the bubble, causing the pilot to "run out of airspace, altitude and ideas simultaneously."

James H. Jeffries, III
(Colonel, USMCR)
Alexandria, Virginia

It's interesting to hear that in football circles "on the bubble" implies an impending cut. We in the pseudo-profession of graduate medical training (interns and residents whose lives and motivations are often probed in magazines such as yours) use a similar expression to describe a different, but equally unsettling condition.

Housestaff in many cities use "riding the bubble" to describe waiting for the next admission during an on-call night. This in itself should not conjure up the same anxiety inherent in tenuous employment, but for those of us who every third or fourth day potentially face thirty-six or more hours without sleep, the news that a new, very sick patient has arrived in the emergency room causes a small bang that startles the intern with the realization that on this night he is now less likely to see his cot.

It's been over five years since I've been on a college campus, but I thought I'd throw a little of the medical (housestaff, anyway) vernacular your way as a substitute for your request for currently hip, cool or otherwise gnarly campus lingo. It may, however, be a bit distressing for the layperson, (especially one prone to late-night admissions in teaching hospitals!). Let me illustrate what happens when the bubble the intern is riding bursts.

You're cruising the wards at 2 A.M., tucking in your players (patients) making sure no one's going to crump (decompensate) minutes after you start R.E.M.ing (sleeping). You see two, possibly three glorious hours of rackage, (also sleep; for sleep, like sex for many others, comes up so often in conversation and fantasy that it commands many terms), when you get tagged (beeped on a pager), and you know it's another ER hit (emergency room admission).

*"Got a real trainwreck here (patient with multiple medical problems),"notes
the lone ER resident when you answer your page.*

*You know this is no LOL in NAD (little old lady in no apparent distress) but
the dreaded midnight Gomer (rumored to be an acronym for Get Out of My
Emergency Room, describing a very old, probably demented and near coma-
tose—gomertose—patient. He always arrives after 1 A.M.).*

*"His beans are fried (kidney failure), he's got no squeeze (heart failure), his
squash is squished (demented) and he's percolating (septic)," describes the ER
doc. "He needs to be unitized, lined and get some stat bug juice or he's in box
city." (He needs to go to the intensive care unit, get intravenous access and
receive antibiotics fast or he's going to die.)*

*The ER resident is either a wall (to be praised) or a sieve (to be jeered),
depending on how many people he admits.*

*"He's already got the 'Q' sign" (mouth open, tongue to one side), notes one
astute medical student.*

*"Definitely at the newsstand" (or ATN: when one cancels long-term home
delivery and buys on a daily basis), parrots the other.*

*You swoop (quickly examine) him, plug him in (catheterize), and perhaps
tube him (intubate and put on a respirator—this is a term of multiple uses,
depending on the subject, object and active or passive voice. One can actively
tube a patient, but when a patient tubes, it usually means he's crumping, as in
"down the tube." A resident usually only performs tubes, but may see his career
tube if he tubes the feeding tube instead of the breathing tube).*

*Dawn is breaking and you've managed to turf (transfer) your last admission.
It's time for GI rounds (breakfast). You've had no sleep and you're facing at
least twelve more hours before you can get some. You have to do this for at least
three more years. Your girlfriend has forgotten what you look like. The money
you owe in school loans would buy a modest home.*

To hell with breakfast, you need liver rounds (cocktails)!

*Drew B. Schembre, M.D.
University of Utah Medical
Center
Salt Lake City, Utah*

*You seem to say that the expression "to be on the bubble" is a football
expression and call it "an example of the new slang—late-1980's lingo. . . ."*

*While the expression—meaning to be in a precarious position, as on a bubble
that could burst—has indeed become popular in football and other sports, as
well as in non-sports applications in recent years, it derives from automobile
racing—specifically, from the qualifying ritual at the Indianapolis 500.*

Strictly speaking, to be "on the bubble" at Indy is to be the slowest of 33 qualified cars while there is still time for others to make an attempt. If one of the remaining cars exceeds the four-lap qualifying average of the car on the bubble, the slower car is "bumped," that is, replaced as the last of the 33 cars allowed to start the 500. Then that car is on the bubble and subject to being bumped, a cycle that continues until the end of the last qualifying day.

The four qualifying days at Indy started to become the popular and dramatic event they are today in the late 1940s, when there were suddenly many more entries for the coveted 33 starting positions—the number allowed since 1933 (an exception was made in 1975, when 35 started).

The expressions "bump" and "on the bubble" date back at least to the mid-1950s according to United States Auto Club historian, Donald Davidson, and were certainly popularized, if not coined, by local sportswriters. One of the better known, Indianapolis Star *sports editor Jep Cadou Jr., wrote on May 25, 1959, of the last day's slowest qualifier, Jim McWithey, ". . . and he suffered for an hour, sitting "on the bubble," as driver after driver took a crack at bumping him—and missed."*

> Tim Considine
> Los Angeles, California

On Tezisy Street

A *thesis,* in logic and rhetoric, is a proposition—a theme to be discussed and perhaps proved by maintaining its good sense in the face of anticipated challenge and argument.

In Russian, the word is substantially the same, transliterated by us as *tezis* to reflect the Russian pronunciation in our different alphabet. The English plural is *theses,* pronounced "THEES-ese," and the Russian plural is *tezisy,* pronounced "TEZ-is-ee."

These days, Muscovites are on Tezisy Street. The hot new word in the vocabulary of *perestroika* is *theses.* Members of the world news media at the recent summit conference were handed pocket-sized maroon booklets titled *Theses of the CPSU Central Committee for the 19th All-Union Party Conference.*

Those who dared wade into the morass of bureaucratese denouncing bureaucracy were struck by the use of the *thesis* technique: ten theses, presented like arguable commandments, to be chewed over at the once-in-a-half-century confabulation.

Whence this word? The Greeks coined it for "the act of laying down," from the verb for "to put, place"; that meaning still exists, like a vestigial tail, in the language of music, in which a *thesis* is a downbeat.

Along came the mathematicians Leonard and Thomas Digges in the 1500's with a translation of Copernicus's theory about the earth circling the sun. Thomas Digges published a work in 1579 that discussed "The vulgare Thesis of the Earthes Stabilitie," a notion that Copernicus had been out to demolish. This sense of *thesis* as a "debatable proposition" is what the Soviets have picked up.

However, most Americans think of the noun as meaning a paper or dissertation written to obtain a doctoral degree (hairsplitting academics say it's a master's thesis but a doctoral dissertation); that meaning was taken centuries ago to describe a paper written to prove a thesis. The academic reverence for such work was spoofed by Robert Hillyer in a poem addressed to Robert Frost: "Make me immortal in thy exegesis—/Or failing that, at least a Doctor's thesis."

Let us not confuse a *thesis* with a *hypothesis*. The latter comes first; that is, the prefix *hypo-* means "under" (not *hyper-*, "above"), and a *hypothesis* is placed under a thesis, laying its foundation. Although the words are used interchangeably by those not steeped in logic, a nice distinction can be made: First comes the *hypothesis,* which can be pretty wild, a tentative explanation unsupported by fact, and then a *thesis,* which is a better-developed argument.

Here comes Georg Wilhelm Friedrich Hegel with his famous dialectic: After the assertion of the *thesis* comes the opposition of the *antithesis—*

apparently contradictory—but followed by a third proposition, reconciling the seeming contradiction on some higher level of truth, known as a *synthesis*. That's sometimes how deals are done at party conventions.

Curious that Mikhail Gorbachev should use *theses* as the verbal framework for his struggle to redirect power in the Soviet Union. The most famous historical use of the word was at the start of a reformation likely to prove more lasting: Martin Luther, on October 31, 1517, affixed his "95 Theses" to the door of the church at Wittenberg's castle, implicitly attacking the sale of papal indulgences and starting a theological argument that persists to this day.

Did the Soviet leader use that word deliberately to recall an earlier reform movement? Will his ten theses wind up on what Leon Trotsky liked to call "the ash heap of history"? Watch this space.

The "Theses" on which every budding Marxist cuts his milk teeth are Marx's famous "Theses on Feuerbach" written in the spring of 1845 as the young Marx was weaning himself from the conflict between the idealism of Hegel and the materialism of Feuerbach. This process resulted in his own philosophical position: dialectical materialism. Whether one considers Gorbachev a Marxist or not, his background is steeped in this literature and in this reference for the word "Theses."

> *Jeremiah M. Gelles*
> *Brooklyn, New York*

On April 16, 1917, on his return to Petrograd from exile in Switzerland, via the famous (or infamous) Sealed Train, V. I. Lenin delivered himself of what every Russian schoolboy (but not your computer) knows as the April Theses. These are indeed a Perestroika. They include the abandonment by the Bolsheviks of the March Provisional Government, opposition to Russian continuation in the war (WWI) and the delegation of "all power to the soviets," or local councils, exactly the proposal enunciated in Gorbachev's theses.

In memory of "an earlier reform movement"? You might say so.

One footnote: The April Theses met with considerable opposition even within the Bolshevik Party. Both the Petrograd and Moscow Bolshevik committees voted against them. But within a few weeks they were adopted by the Bolsheviks and became the basis of the October Revolution.

> *Alexander Kendrick*
> *Philadelphia, Pennsylvania*

On the Level

"Can you direct me to the *level playing field*?" asked Allan E. Gotlieb, Canada's Ambassador to the United States. "It seems to be a place that all you Yankees are searching for." I run into the Ambassador and his wife (Sondra, a novelist and columnist who styles herself "wife of") at antiquarian book fairs searching for Thomas Haliburton items.

Nexis, the electronic library of Mead Data Central, is the first place to look for such a combination of words. The first entry: In 1979, *The American Banker* wrote about a scrap involving the Oregon Bankers Association: "Mr. Brawner said the Oregon B.A. welcomed 'any and all competition, on a *level playing field,*' a metaphor the association has used frequently in arguments for 'competitive equality.'" Seven years later, the same publication explained: "When bankers talk about a 'level playing field,' they usually mean that similar financial services firms should be subject to the same 'game rules.'"

Trade policymakers use the phrase, too. Ronald Reagan, in a 1986 antitariff speech, said, "If the United States can trade with other nations on a *level playing field,* we can outproduce, outcompete and outsell anybody, anywhere in the world."

Later that year, Senator Bob Packwood (who collects old leather-bound books, too, and uses the Library of Congress's recipe for leather preservative: 60 percent pure lanolin, 40 percent neat's-foot oil, heat and combine in a double boiler, use at room temperature. Where am I? Racked up in a long parenthesis. No graceful way out; start a new sentence.) . . . Senator Packwood, a Republican of Oregon, a state in which bankers have long disliked uneven playing fields, blasted the protectionists in 1986: "That's their idea of a *level playing field*—a legislative advantage."

Ah, says the reader, now here it comes, the origin of the phrase, satisfyingly pinned down to the first famous user.

Sorry. I dunno. Neither do my etymological friends. Some think it sounds Churchillian, others Rooseveltian; maybe from the playing fields of Eton?

Palindromes

U Nu, the former leader of Burma, is back in the news. I hope he makes it back into power in Rangoon because he was the Last Palindrome—the only recent head of government whose name is spelled the same backward as forward. (France's quisling Pierre Laval preceded him, but only his last name worked; U Nu goes all the way.)

In *Too Hot to Hoot,* by owlish Marvin Terban, a fresh collection of palindromes is presented to linguistic pushmi-pullyus tired of the old "Madam, I'm Adam" and "A Man, A Plan, A Canal—Panama." (Best palindromic riddle: What is 1,999.5 pounds?) The Manhattan English teacher uses these games to interest pupils in the study of words.

If elected chief executive of New York City to replace Ed Koch, I am prepared to ask the New York County Republican leader: "Roy, am I Mayor?" Or if George Bush's running mate loses his enthusiasm, I am ready to report: "Poor Dan is in a droop."

We palindromaniacs missed you—and U Nu it all along.

You refer to the late leader of Burma as "U Nu" (which is correct) and imply that his name, unlike that of Pierre Laval, is a true palindrome. Evidently you are unaware that Burmese use no family names. The "U" is simply an honorific signifying that such a person is superior to the addresser.

> Wilbur M. Rabinowitz
> Carefree, Arizona

Clearly you are trying to forget the late unpleasantness in Southeast Asia. You can be forgiven, therefore, for your failure to recognize that the current wisdom is that: "Now, Lon Nol Won!" But then, U Nu that all along.

> Fred J. Abrahams
> New York, New York

You may or you may not have come across:

"Doc, note—I dissent. A fast never prevents a fatness. I diet on cod."

Which is, I think, the longest palindrome.

> Jeremy Gerard
> The New York Times
> New York, New York

I wonder if you know the composer of the famous:

DOC, NOTE; I DISSENT. A FAST NEVER PREVENTS A FATNESS. I DIET ON COD.

In the <u>Wall Street Journal</u> article on March 7, 1973, the palindrome is attributed to Penelope Gilliatt, but that attribution may not be correct.

> Francis X. Hogan
> Potomac, Maryland

Here are a few more!
  Short:

> *"Yreka Bakery" (this is how it all got started out here)*
> *"Guru rug"*

Brief, but some make sense:

> *"Name no one man"*
> *"Rise to vote, sir"*
> *"Red rum, sir, is murder"*
> *"tis night, I with gin sit"*
> *"Do geese see God?"*
> *"Sex at noon taxes"*
> *"Draw pupil's lip upward"*

> Larry Symmes
> Mill Valley, California

A "fresh collection of palindromes" is an exciting prospect; perhaps one of the palindromes will supplant "Sit on a potato pan, Otis" as my all-time favorite.

> Jay Kenyon
> Victoria, British Columbia,
> Canada

The answer to your palindromic riddle of 1,999.5 pounds is "no ton" or "not a ton."

> Linda Schildkraut
> Bayside, New York

1999.5 pounds is <u>not a ton.</u>
   Here are a few more:

   Pa's a sap.
   Won't lovers revolt now.
   A dog! A panic in a pagoda!
   Draw putrid dirt upward.
   Zeus was deified, saw Suez. (<u>Deified</u> is one by itself.)
   Draw no dray a yard onward.
   He goddam mad dog, eh?
   Able was I ere I saw Elba.
   Never odd or even.

Irving Landau
Woodside, New York

I submit below the longest palindrome in recorded history, not invented by me, I hasten to add, but conveyed by a person of modest literary pretensions who guessed it was Oxbridge in origin.

   T. Eliot, top bard, notes putrid tang emanating. Is sad. "I'd assign it
   a name: gnat dirt, upset on drab pot toilet."

   Its only serious drawback is that it's not all that easy to remember, unlike Napoleon's alleged "Able was I ere I saw Elba."

Harold Steinberg
East Hampton, New York

Palindromic Damn-All

"U *thought* U Nu," writes Joan Murray of Rochester, in correction of my foolish assertion that Burma's U Nu was the last head of government whose name is spelled the same backward as forward.

She was not the only Lexicographic Irregular to join the Gotcha! Gang, Palindrome Squad, and to point to Lon Nol of Cambodia/Kampuchea as the Last Palindrome. My colleague Jack Rosenthal added, seemingly irrelevantly, that Lon Nol "drives a Toyota" (A-ha! The car, with the article, forms a palindrome), and Jan R. Harrington writes from a cramped post office box in New York City that the word probably went from my typesetter to his assistant: "Set at serif, as Safire states."

An even more egregious error can be found in a political harangue about George Bush that included this line: "A few of the people who knew him in the 70's now marvel at how their gentlemanly friend will do damn-all to win." In that sentence, *damn-all* was intended to mean "anything."

"*Damn-all* means 'nothing,'" writes Lars-Erik Nelson, Washington bureau chief of the New York *Daily News,* who used to be a Reuters correspondent, "—at least in British English, which, until I read your column, is the only place I ever heard it." He goes on to explain how the phrase is a euphemism, and I'm sorry I ever got involved.

The earliest citation given in the *Oxford English Dictionary* supplement comes from James Joyce's 1922 novel, *Ulysses:* "Proud possessor of damn-all." Joyce used it again in his 1934 poem "An Epilogue to Ibsen's 'Ghosts,'" which concludes:

> Nay, more, were I not all I was,
> Weak, wanton, waster out and out,
> There would have been no world's applause
> And damn all to write home about.

Damn-all means "nothing," not "anything." Friends of U Nu and Lon Nol care damn-all for the linguistic delights of Westerners.

Sununu Never Sets

Not since Lon Nol and U Nu have we had a public figure whose name (or name and honorific) is spelled the same backward. But we have a close palindrome in the last name of former New Hampshire Governor John H. Sununu, designated as the next White House chief of staff.

Harvey M. Kabaker, news editor of the *Washington Times,* envisioned a headline that would cover a story if an anonymous note charged that Mr. Sununu had a son whose British college résumé was phony: NOTE WAS: NO SUNUNU SON SAW ETON.

This was topped by a reporter in the newspaper's Life! department. (Maybe, with the trend toward punctuation in titles, I should call this the "On Language?" column.) Jennifer Harper dreamed up a scenario in which President Bush's chief of staff was asked to open a Chinese restaurant: "Not Now: Sununu's Wonton."

Another Lifer, David Mills, came up with the longest palindrome on this subject: "Press aide: Sununu son wants it, opens pool every A.M. so staff of fatsos may revel. Oops. Nepotist? Naw! 'No sun unused,' I asserp." (It worked right up to the last letter. "So it's got a typo," muttered the palindromist.)

David Mills's lengthy palindrome can work without a "typo." Change the p in "asserp" to the t it should be, and the assertion is now attributed to an assistant hairdresser. Thus, "Tress aide: Sununu son wants it, opens pool every A.M. so staff of fatsos may revel. Oops. Nepotist? Naw! 'No sun unused,' I assert."
*   You can't say that makes any less sense than the original.*

William B. McIlvaine
New York, New York

An even longer palindrome may be attributed to a bedding store clerk in conversation with Rev. Jim Bakker's wife: "Mattress aide: Sununu son . . . no sun unused, I assert, Tam."

George R. Pryde
Stamford, Connecticut

An envisioning of a headline after a Bush subordinate informs a reporter of the hiring of a Mr. Ott: "Bush sub went to see Sununu. Sees Ott new Bush sub."

Constantine C. Fedak
Darien, Connecticut

I am preparing a book of my own original palindromes entitled "I'm a lasagna—Bang! a salami." Included therein is the following palindrome: SUNUNU'S TONSIL IS NOT SUNUNU'S.

Allan Miller
New York, New York

Pen Palindromes

We recently dipped into the palindromes offered by the surname of John H. Sununu, the White House chief of staff. (Headline about a supposed order to an unnecessarily weight-conscious chef at the White House mess: "DESSERT!" SUNUNU STRESSED.)

"Surely you haven't already forgotten the palindromic Mr. Staats," writes Michael G. Gartner, the editor and language maven who now runs NBC

News. "I think Elmer Staats was Comptroller General, which might give you a chance to tell us that *comptroller* is pronounced 'controller.' At least, that's how we liberals pronounce it. Maybe you compservatives have a different view."

Let us leap into a passing melodrama and snap, "Follow that tangent!"

The word we spell now as *comptroller* began in the fifteenth century as *conterroller* in English, from a French word now spelled *contrôleur;* it was the title of the official in the royal household who examined and controlled expenditures. How, then, did the *mp* get in there?

Whoever was doing the "On Language" column in a monastery five hundred years ago goofed. Some medieval pedant figured the word should come from Latin, on the mistaken analogy with the verb *computare,* "compute." That's when the notion of counting was introduced, instead of controlling; the same happened to *acont* or *acount,* which became *accompt* for a few centuries, until the bean-counters rejected it for *account.* (That's why the Comptroller General does not run the General Accompting Office.)

When a mistake lasts for five centuries, however, it ceases to be a mistake; the solecism burrows its way into the language and is as correct as any other part. We still use *comptroller,* though there has been modern pressure to return to the original *controller,* since the *mp* is not pronounced.

My position: Resist the reformers and stick with the mistake. I like to think that, in the twenty-fifth century, some of my own errors will be so sanctified. In both *Comptroller General* and *Comptroller of the Currency* (the first reports to Congress, the other to the Treasury Secretary), the emphasis is on the first syllable.

Let the silent *p* be the signal to accent that first syllable; when we mean "one who controls" in a nonfinancial sense, then spell it *controller* and say "con-TROLL-er." For example, when we refer to people exercising mind control or spooks running a foreign agent, we can call them con-TROLL-ers, but how many hypnotists and spymasters do we trip over? Most of the time we send in our expense accounts to, or vote for, or appoint the guy whose title has the accent on the first syllable. He or she is the comptroller, pronounced "CON-troll-er." Never pronounce the *p.*

In language as in life, we can learn to live with, and profit by, our mistakes. As the French say, *Compte rendu:* "Report delivered."

We have drifted from the subject of palindromes, those phrases that are spelled the same forward and backward; time to get the cow back in the barn. The best palindromic news of the new year came in this *New York Times* headline: DAMON AGREES TO NOMAD BID. There's a hostile takeover made in heaven: Nomad Partners L.P., an investment firm, bought the stock of the Damon Corporation, a chemical laboratory company. As Gordon W. Grossman of Chappaqua, New York, writes, "Damon was I ere I saw Nomad."

How do you suppose the deal originated? I can hear it now: The comptroller at Nomad turns to his junk-bond investment banker and asks, "Is there any company we can take over that happens to have our name spelled backward?" The high-yield hostilier chortles, "Fat chance. Wait; there's a listing here for Damon Corp. I wonder what they do. . . ."

The term "comptroller," with the accent on the first syllable, is Fedspeak. In the corporate world the officer with comparable responsibilities is almost invariably called a "controller," with the accent on the second syllable. I suspect that your expense reports are in fact reviewed by a controller, which is the title given for Frank R. Gatti in the 10-K report of The New York Times Company.

I teach a required course called "Control" to our MBA students. The course gets its name from the fact that it encompasses topics that are the responsibility of corporate controllers. According to our textbook, Accounting Principles, by Robert N. Anthony and James S. Reece, "one of the top officers of many businesses is the controller. Within the division of top management's duties, the controller is the person responsible for satisfying other managers' needs for management accounting information and for complying with the requirements of financial reporting." The authors never once use the spelling "comptroller." Another book we assign, Accounting: The Language of Business, by Davidson, Stickney, and Weil, defines "comptroller" as follows: "Same meaning and pronunciation as controller."

Professor Anthony, by the way, served as the Comptroller [sic] of the Department of Defense during the Johnson Administration. While in that office he attempted to get the Federal government to conform its terminology to business practice. He was unsuccessful, of course, but please do not inflict the bureaucrats' false etymology on the private sector.

Charles Christenson
Royal Little Professor of
Business Administration
Harvard University
Boston, Massachusetts

You correctly attribute the silent p in the word comptroller to mistaken derivation from the Latin verb computare, "compute," and then go on to say: "the same happened to acont or acount, which became accompt for a few centuries," before ending up as account. However, these two cases are not "the same," since account really does come from Latin computare and the short-lived p in accompt had a valid etymological basis.

Incidentally, inserting silent consonants for reasons etymological or analogical is an old tradition in English orthography. Thus, receipt, debt and doubt (verb) go back, respectively, to Latin recepta, debitum and dubitare by way of Middle English and Old French, which had nary a trace of a silent consonant; the p and b are the work of some long-forgotten Elizabethan classicist, who meant to pay his respects to the Latin original (but evidently nodded over deceit—from Latin decepta).

A classic case of false etymological spelling is island, which goes back to Middle and Old English iland but picked up an s from unrelated isle (from Latin insula). Could (the past tense of can) acquired its silent l by analogy with would and should (the past tenses of will and shall), whose perfectly legitimate l was once pronounced. Analogy is also the culprit in the case of delight, a Latin-derived word which was spelled delit in Middle English and inserted gh only after it came to rhyme with light, right and sight (whose gh harks back to an old guttural sound).

Louis Jay Herman
New York, New York

Palindromic Alert

Sununu's is good news, thought palindrome fans, but 1989 has brought us more excitement: The new President-elect of Argentina is the Peronist Carlos Saul Menem.

The palindromic ball is rolling.

As Thomas Campion of Bowie, Maryland, asked, even before the possibility of the overturn of *Roe* v. *Wade* was raised: "Won't lovers revolt now?"

People of Color

"That's the most adorable little colored girl playing outside," observes a woman in Berke Breathed's comic strip, "Bloom County."

" 'Colored'? You're saying 'colored people' in 1988?" asks her socially sensitive son. "You know better, Ma." He suggests they agree to use "the new-age term 'people of color.' " Ma accepts that, and says, "People of color. Colored people." The son blows his stack.

The term generates controversy on the Op-Ed pages as well. "A new language formation, 'people of color,' is making its appearance . . ." wrote

Jacob Neusner, professor of Judaic studies at Brown University, a prolific scholar who is unafraid of controversy. " 'People of color' are every hue but white and are non-European in origin. And only 'people of color' are authentically American, so we now are being told."

Jack Neusner's concern about the threat of racial quotas at cultural agencies, and about what he saw to be the coming derogation of American art of European origin, provoked disagreement from Frank Hodsoll, chairman of the National Endowment for the Arts, who wrote, "I know of no one who claims that only *people of color* are authentically American. . . ."

Under the general rubric of "being told," some *Times* editors believe Mr. Hodsoll, and I believe Mr. Neusner, which keeps life lively around the office. But we can all agree that the phrase *people of color* has never been more in vogue.

It is not even nearly new, though it was for a time out of fashion. The Reverend Martin Luther King Jr. gave the phrase new life when he spoke of America's "citizens of color" in his August 1963 speech on the steps of the Lincoln Memorial in Washington. (That speech, by the way, is remembered by most of today's generation only in a snippet of film repeating "I have a dream." Studied in its entirety, the King address—delivered in "this sweltering summer of the Negro's legitimate discontent," a Shakespearean allusion—is as well constructed and stirring an example of speechwriting as can be found in any compilation of modern oratory.)

First to *colored people.* If *black* has become the preferred term, why does the National Association for the Advancement of Colored People hold on to its name? According to James Williams, an N.A.A.C.P. spokesman, who must get asked this often: "Times change and terms change. Racial designations go through phases; at one time *Negro* was accepted, at an earlier time *colored* and so on. This organization has been in existence for eighty years and the initials N.A.A.C.P. are part of the American vocabulary, firmly embedded in the national consciousness, and we feel it would not be to our benefit to change our name."

Colored people (which in South Africa means "people of racially mixed ancestry") has in the United States a connotation different from *people of color.* As the keen-eared cartoonist cited above suggested, *colored* is often taken as a slur, even when not so intended, and so this term—first used with this meaning in 1611 by the historian John Speed as "coloured countenances"—is better replaced by its synonym as noun and adjective, *black.*

People of color, on the other hand, is a phrase encompassing all nonwhites; its inclusionary sense, along with its use of two *l* sounds, gives the meaning a connotative lift.

When did it begin? "I've seen *people of color* used in English as early as a 1793 pamphlet about a yellow-fever epidemic," reports Professor Wilson Moses of the Afro-American studies program at Boston University, but the citation is not at hand. "It was probably used earlier than that, however. It later became an attempt by the free black community to dissociate itself from the Africans, and was replaced during the 1920's, when *Negro* became the militant word to use. You will probably find *people of color* rooted in French."

Gail Anderson, at New York's Schomburg Center for Research in Black Culture, agrees: French-speaking colonies were the first to use *gens de couleur libérés,* which translates as "free people of color." She cites an 1818 pamphlet in English entitled "Report of the Committee, to Whom was Referred the Memorial of the President and Board of Managers of the American Society for Colonizing the Free People of Color of the United States." (Who-Whomniks who object to this use of their favorite word can write to the Committee, all of whose members are safely dead.)

Perhaps the association of *free* with the phrase *people of color* gave the phrase its positive connotation; speculation aside, today *people of color* is well received by most blacks while *colored people* is not.

A Hearst News Service editor, Charles Austin of Teaneck, New Jersey, was curious about the vogue term and held an "electronic conference" about it on one of the computer utilities that are bringing the with-it together.

One of his respondents, E. Allison Dittus of East Hartford, Connecticut, said, "I find the phrase *people of color* both graceful and euphonious. It is an old-time phrase used by both older blacks and whites as a dignified term for nonwhites. I vote to leave *minorities* to the newspeakers and keep *people of color* as a beautiful and descriptive folk idiom."

The Hearst editor observed to his electronically linked panel that "*Afro-American,* in vogue a few years ago, never made it, as the connection of most present-generation American blacks to Africa is virtually nonexistent." When he wondered what the opposite of *people of color* was, Daniel J. Ellsworth of Eaton Rapids, Michigan, replied, "People not of color? Colorless? White? Caucasian?"

The answer is *white.* The division is arbitrary between *white* and *people of color,* and in time may break down into particular colors already representing racial groups—red, yellow, white, black, brown. As we speak, however, the English language seems to lump the colors together and treats white—the noncolor—as a race and a word apart.

At the Democratic National Convention in Atlanta, Jesse Jackson reminded his listeners that most of the world is not white. That was a sitter-upper to many white Americans, who are accustomed to thinking of themselves in the majority, much as the traveler sees the natives in a foreign country as "foreigners."

It strikes me, then, that *people of color* is a phrase often used by nonwhites to put *nonwhite* positively. (Why should anybody want to define himself by what he is not?) Politically, it expresses solidarity with other nonwhites, and subtly reminds whites that they are a minority.

When used by whites, *people of color* usually carries a friendly and respectful connotation, but should not be used as a synonym for *black;* it refers to all racial groups that are not white.

In reading your discussion of "people of color," I recalled such a reference early. This is it from the minutes of the Barnwell Baptist Church of Barnwell, South Carolina, in September 1831: "The members of color shall be dealt with according to their wilful neglect, or want of opportunity at the discretion of the church."

> Wallace Alcorn
> Austin, Minnesota

Apropos your advocacy of the term "people of color" (which I continue to deplore), I recall that Peter Ustinov wrote in his autobiography, a dozen years ago or so, that when presented a U.S. Immigration Service form in the 1950s he found it had a space where the applicant was supposed to fill in "color."
Ustinov wrote "PINK."

> David Binder
> The New York Times
> Washington, D.C.

As a physicist, I found myself reading the article consciously on one level and subconsciously on another.

In physics, black is the absence of color. A completely absorbing surface, i.e., one which does not reflect any wavelength of light, is black. White is the totality of color, that is, it connotes light of all wavelengths in essentially equal amounts. Color is light of a specific wavelength, such as red, or a combination of wavelengths in unequal amounts. Neither white nor black is technically (in physics terms) a color. The opposite of color is the absence of color, namely, black.

These technical definitions contradict the social ones. The opposite of "people of color" would be black, not white, since "without color" means black. On the other hand, "all color" would mean white, the reversal of the social usage.

Of course, white, black, brown and phrases like "people of color" are metaphors used in a social context, and it is not surprising that the definitions conflict with those in physics.

Robert W. Conn
Professor
University of California, Los Angeles
Los Angeles, California

Poetic Allusion Watch

"From here in the Irish Republic," wrote Francis X. Clines in *The New York Times,* "Northern Ireland can sometimes seem a place more of relentless torpor than Yeatsian gyre."

Now, that's a lead. Frankie Clines is considered one of the classiest writers in daily journalism today because he can turn out that sort of subtle, insightful prose. He does not treat the newspaper reader as a jerk who never read Yeats.

In that poetic allusion, the reporter felt it necessary to use the adjective *Yeatsian* to alert the reader to the poet being alluded to. Such a pointed reference would not be necessary if the line concluded with "than a place where the center cannot hold"; we are expected to know that Yeats's 1921 poem, "The Second Coming," includes the famous line "Things fall apart; the center cannot hold." It's quoted whenever political polarization takes place and centrists disappear.

However, with the handy pointer that Frankie provides with *Yeatsian,* we can go to that same poem looking for *gyre* and find, two lines before the famous line, "Turning and turning in the widening gyre / The falcon cannot hear the falconer."

A *gyre* (from the Greek *gyros*, "circle") is a spiral; when contrasted to "relentless torpor" in the lead of a reporter slouching toward Dublin, the seldom-used noun conveys the illusion of turmoil. That one word makes the lead of the story resonate with archaic hatreds and visions of things falling apart—at least to those who pitch and catch poetic allusions.

Yeats's second coming is big this year, according to the latest report of the Poetic Allusion Watch, or P.A.W.

A *Washington Times* headline about violence in Israel's disputed territories reads: SLOUCHING TOWARD BETHLEHEM. This phrase, with its implicit menace of an animal's forward-bent droop, is from the poem's conclusion, "And what rough beast, its hour come round at last, / Slouches towards Bethlehem to be born?"

A *Washington Post* headline writer takes the place beyond Bethlehem to SLOUCHING TOWARD MOZAMBIQUE, in a piece about the delay in winning confirmation of an ambassadorial nomination to that country; in this usage, the sense of menace is changed to slowness, with the word *slouch* meaning "droop listlessly" with the downward bend of a slouch hat. The poetic allusion is still apt, though another headline in the same newspaper seems out of place: SLOUCHING TOWARD A FARM CREDIT BILL.

Robert Frost is doing very well. *The Economist* magazine writes: "Russia's revolution has miles to go before gallant Mr. Gorbachev, his promises kept, can sleep peacefully in his bed." This effusive sentence about the Soviet (more than merely Russian) leader alludes to the 1923 Frost poem, "Stopping by Woods on a Snowy Evening," which concludes:

> The woods are lovely, dark and deep,
> But I have promises to keep,
> And miles to go before I sleep,
> And miles to go before I sleep.

Nor is Frost's "Mending Wall" without its alluders. In an Op-Ed article last year about Mexican fears of our immigration law, the political scientist Jorge G. Castañeda writes: "Strong fences make good neighbors, but realism and humility make friendlier ones." The common mistake here (beyond substituting *strong* for *good*) is assuming the poet meant "good fences make good neighbors" to be his message; in fact, Frost put that statement in the mouth of a narrow-minded neighbor, and questioned the good-fences philosophy with "Before I built a wall I'd ask to know / What I was walling in or walling out."

Even sports newsletters allude to Frost. When a New York Giants tackle was diagnosed as having cancer, *Inside Football* commented, "The rest, since there was no more to build on there, turned to their affairs." That's an allusion to a 1916 Frost poem about a boy's accidental death: "No more to build on there. And they, since they / Were not the one dead, turned to their affairs." (The poem's title is "Out, Out—," itself an allusion by Frost to Shakespeare; after Lady Macbeth dies, Macbeth speaks of life's shortness, "Out, out, brief candle!")

Andrew Marvell has been given a hard time. In what was not an allusion, but a deliberate misquotation of "The Garden," these lines were attributed to him in an advertisement for Sterling, a British automobile:

> Fair quiet have I found thee here
> And comfort, thy companion dear?
> Mistaken long, I sought you then
> In busy companies of men
> Society is all but rude
> To this luxurious solitude.

Apparently the writer practicing the inglorious arts of advertising heard the winged chariot of his client at his back. The real Andrew Marvell, writing in the mid-seventeenth century, put the second stanza's opening lines this way:

"Fair Quiet, have I found thee here, / And Innocence, thy sister dear?" The last line sang of "delicious solitude," but the modern editor had neither world enough nor time for *delicious,* changing it (without full disclosure to unsuspecting readers) to *luxurious solitude.* When unscanning poetry to enhance sales in the busy companies of men, writers could at least warn readers with *"after* Andrew Marvell."

Ralph Waldo Emerson's work offered the punning allusion of the year. We are familiar, in this Bicentennial era, with his hymn sung at the completion of the battle monument in Concord: "Here once the embattled farmers stood, / And fired the shot heard round the world." In his review of Sara L. Rath's "About Cows," Clarence Petersen wrote in the *Chicago Tribune* that the author tongue-in-cheekily reported that the National Aeronautics and Space Administration sent some cows up in a rocket to test their reactions; on return to earth, the cows became known as "the herd shot round the world."

Milton is still with us, thanks largely to Wordsworth. The leader of the British Labor Party, Neil Kinnock, in an impassioned speech last year flaying the supposed hardheartedness of Margaret Thatcher, cried out: "Charles Dickens, thou shouldst be alive at this hour." And Alistair Cooke wrote in *The New Yorker* about the privacy given public figures by the press throughout the eighteenth century, adding parenthetically, "Gary Hart, thou shouldst have been running at that hour!" These allusions are to Wordsworth's "London, 1802," a poem that begins, "Milton! thou shouldst be living at this hour: / England hath need of thee. . . ."

The novelist Saul Bellow alludes to a Milton sonnet in *More Die of Heartbreak:* "At least Rudi Trachtenberg was responding to a talent, and a talent will cause your death if you try to hide it." That's a third-generation allusion, writes Madeline Hamermesh of Minnetonka, Minnesota, "since Milton's line is itself an allusion to Christ's parable of the talents."

Does an allusion to prose by a poet count as a poetic allusion? Why not; it's surely not a prosaic allusion. "Many years ago," writes the columnist Jon Carroll in the *San Francisco Chronicle,* "when the world was young and there were wolves in Pasadena, I was a member of the Boys Choir of the local Presbyterian Church." Dylan Thomas wrote in a story published in 1954, "Years and years and years ago, when I was a boy, when there were wolves in Wales . . . when we rode the daft and happy hills bareback, it snowed and it snowed." (Snowy evenings get to poets.)

Most allusions are subtle, as in Jon Pareles's column "Pop View," in *The New York Times,* about the way critics "want to smash those dark, satanic music mills," from William Blake's preface to "Milton": "And was Jerusalem builded here / Among those dark Satanic mills?"

Others pop you in the teeth with the whole passage. *National Review* was commenting with some glee on a survey of liberal media types that showed the right-wing Heritage Foundation to be considered by media eggheads the most biased of sources, but also the most timely and understandable. "In front the sun climbs slow, how slowly," went the conservative magazine's comment, "but westward, look, the land is bright." That's from Arthur Hugh Clough's "Say Not, the Struggle Nought Availeth," published in 1862; *Bartlett's Quotations* says, "Both Sir Winston Churchill and John F. Kennedy liked to quote this line."

A comment about gyre: 20–30 years ago during my geography teaching career I came across this word to mean those large whirls of rotating (2D) or spiraling (3D) air masses that are the huge cells making up the weather patterns on a worldwide basis. They are of course usually alternating HIGHS and LOWS. As the hurricane season approaches, may I encourage you to communicate with your weather page colleagues to see if they can use this word to good advantage.

Franklin R. Stern
Providence, Rhode Island

I am an old Frost lover who at various points knew many of the poems by heart. I also had the opportunity to hear him read on several different evenings in New York and Boston.

I wondered if you knew that when he read this poem he said, on at least one occasion, looking up from the text, " 'Before I built a wall I'd ask to know/ What I was walling in or walling out,/ And to whom I was like to give offense.' Offense—that's a pun, you know!"

It's a comment that has greatly enriched my knowledge of the poem, so I thought I would share it with you.

Ruth W. Messinger
New York, New York

Possessing Dukakis

We can all agree: The 1988 Democratic National Convention was Michael S. Dukakis's.

But wait—not all do agree. Many will write, instead, "the 1988 Democratic Convention was Michael Dukakis'."

Which is it? When a word ends in *s,* how do you form its possessive? Do you add an apostrophe and another *s,* or do you just add the apostrophe and skip the additional *s?*

Great institutions are locked in titanic disagreement about this. Until we resolve the dispute, coverage of the campaign cannot correctly proceed.

The *Associated Press Stylebook and Libel Manual* says this about forming the possessive of a singular proper name ending in *s:* "Use only an apostrophe: *Achilles' heel, Agnes' book, Ceres' rites . . . Moses' law, Socrates' life, Tennessee Williams' plays, Xerxes' armies.*"

The New York Times says, in effect, to hell with that. "Almost all singular

words ending in *s*," rules *The Times*, "require another *s* as well as the apostrophe to form the possessive: *James's, Charles's, The Times's*." This is supported, I am reminded by Michael J. Healey, a political researcher at CBS News, by no less an authority than William Strunk Jr. in *The Elements of Style*, Rule 1: "Form the possessive singular of nouns by adding *'s*. Follow this rule whatever the final consonant. Thus write, *Charles's friend, Burns's poems*."

However, the clarity of *The Times*'s rule (slyly referred to at the A.P. and most of its subscribing newspapers as "*The Times'* rule") is muddied with exceptions: "But the *s* after the apostrophe is dropped when two or more sibilant sounds precede the apostrophe: *Kansas' Governor, Moses' behalf*."

I don't know the reason for that exception, which is accepted also by Mr. Strunk. If most of us say "Kansas-ziz drought," why not express that in writing as *Kansas's drought*? Form should follow function (though, let's face it, it rarely does, or else we would have simplified spelling). Perhaps the reason for the exception is that careful speakers and writers are to be discouraged from using the sibilant possessive after such sibilant words; that's why you hear the clergy intone *the laws of Moses* and rarely *Moses's laws*, or *the steps of Jesus* rather than *Jesus's steps* (which both the A.P. and *The Times* would agree to express as *Moses' laws* and *Jesus' steps*).

The New York Times's style posts a second exception, regarding the vulnerable spot on the body of Achilles: "By custom . . . the possessive of an ancient classical name is formed with an apostrophe only: *Achilles' heel*."

That brings us to the headline over a column by Cord Meyer in the

Washington Times (no kin to *The New York Times*), "Dukakis' Achilles' heel," by which the columnist adverted to what he considered the candidate's damagingly dovish foreign-policy stands. That headline's style had the virtue of consistency; if it had appeared in *The New York Times,* the copy editor would have had to go both ways: "Dukakis's Achilles' heel."

Not all of Xerxes's armies performing all of Ceres's rites would get me to go for that confusing and most unpossessing possessive. My advice: Follow the sound of the language, as *The Times'*s style does, and ignore *The Times'*s exceptions (though it will be as hard as any of Hercules's labors).

In the spoken language, the possessive has worn off the heel of Achilles. Say the phrase aloud yourself—"When I'm dieting, cream puffs are my Achilles heel," not "Achilles-ziz heel." So I write it without the possessive (the copy editor changes it, but that's not my fault).

On the other hand, we all say *Xerxes's armies,* don't we? So write it that way when next you wipe out the Spartans at Thermopylae.

There's a 50-50 chance that some big campaign contributor will get to say, "I'm President Dukakis's nominee to be Ambassador to the Court of St. James's." That's where the apostrophe followed by the *s* is clarifying; the way the London post should be pronounced is "Saint James-ziz," not "Saint James."

So it was *Dukakis's convention* for me. I am prepared to accept the possible confusion in the possessive, "Kitty and Michael Dukakis's children"; the A.P. would stick with "Kitty and Michael Dukakis' children," which is equally confusing.

I was very much interested in your column concerning the possessive of singular words ending in the letter "s." In judicial writing we frequently encounter this puzzle. When Jones makes a motion, is it Jones's motion or Jones' motion?

I enclose two authorities you did not mention, Fowler's Modern English Usage *and a very recent and fascinating publication,* A Dictionary of Modern Legal Usage. *They both strongly support the rule of* The New York Times. *I have found some judges are amenable to correction in this regard, while others are not.*

I would think that Lexis, *the computerized legal research system, would be very valuable in your work for checking out instances of competing usage or of first or early usage of new words.*

> Danny J. Boggs
> Circuit Judge
> United States Court of
>   Appeals
> Louisville, Kentucky

There should be no confusion on the subject of possessives of words already ending in s. The rule is simply: If the word ending in s is a one-syllable word, add an apostrophe and another s; if the word has more than one syllable, it is permissible to form the possessive by adding the apostrophe without the s. I try to remember this by employing a reference to the works of two of my favorites: William Butler Yeats's poetry and Gerard Manley Hopkins' poetry.

Eileen H. Gorman
Basking Ridge, New Jersey

Consistency is a hobgoblin that will never haunt English spelling—or pronunciation. But a little more order could have been introduced into your discussion of "possessives" of words ending in s by noting that the s may stand for either a voiced or an unvoiced sibilant. We tend in pronunciation not to repeat the voiced sibilant in genitive uses, and therefore not to spell them with another s after the apostrophe. The AP rule is clearly ridiculous.

William J. Griffin
Nashville, Tennessee

I couldn't agree more with your pronouncements on the possessive. So, be the court of last resort: What do we do with Illinois? In the possessive, does it require an apostrophe s or just an apostrophe? The issue, I believe, is whether the silent s is pronounced in the possessive. I can't think of any reason that an apostrophe would cause a silent letter to be voiced (or sibilated). What do you say?

Judith Rowan
Champaign, Illinois

NOTE FROM W.S.: Use apostrophe and another s after the singular Illinois. The s before the apostrophe stays silent, so the possessive Illinois's has a pronunciation ending in "noise," not "noises."

Dear Bill,
There are many cases in which form follows function in language, as when one says My family are out to get me, with the plural form of are following not the singular form of its subject, my family, but the function of the subject, which here is presumably intended to refer distributively to the members of the family

and to say that each of them is out to get me. But what the form of Kansas's follows is not any kind of function but another kind of form: Here orthographic form is following phonological form. Similarly with most proposals for simplified spelling, which call for orthographic form to follow phonological form and thus in many cases not to follow function.

There are numerous respects in which our present system of English spelling follows function in preference to phonological form, as where we distinguish between the functions of the plural ending (-es or -s) and of the genitive ending (-'s), even though they do not differ in phonological form. Actually, there is a great generalization about form and function in English spelling, first proposed by K. H. Albrow in his The English Writing System: Notes Towards a Description (Longman, 1972; I know this book only second-hand, through the summary in Geoffrey Sampson's Writing Systems, Stanford UP, 1985), namely, that "content words" in English have to be at least three letters long, but there is no lower limit for the orthographic length of "function words." This generalization requires a bit of fudging (e.g., you have to class go and do as function words, and you have to make an exception for shortened proper names such as Ed and Al), but it makes remarkable sense out of such differences in spelling as:

eye/I bee/be buy/by; awe/law owe/sow rye/pry tie/try egg/leg

In each case, a 3-letter "content word" includes a letter that is otherwise unnecessary.

I agree with you that the -'s of of St. James's is "clarifying," but in the "the Court————" it clarifies the expression into something that I suspect you don't intend. Is St. James the possessor of the Court of St. James, i.e., the person to whom the bills are sent for taxes on the real estate that comprises the Court? If not, the -'s is as inappropriate as in The Spirit of St. Louis's.

I'm surprised that neither you nor either of the sources that you cite mention a factor that is a strong influence on whether one pronounces genitive -'s after a final sibilant, namely, whether the final syllable of the word is stressed: it is almost always pronounced when added to a stressed syllable, a fact that came home to me when I noticed that in a certain paper that I wrote many years ago I kept referring to "Ross's analysis" of something-or-other, in contrast with "Emonds' analysis" of it.

Jim [James D. McCawley]
Department of Linguistics
University of Chicago
Chicago, Illinois

I note that your column on possessives steers clear of the greatest logical problem of apostrophes. It's the question of three s's.

I met this problem head-on in 1985 during the editing of my book Googie:

Fifties Coffee Shop Architecture (*Chronicle Books, San Francisco, 1986*). *So you won't worry about it, Googie is an architectural term describing the most outlandish and delightful roadside buildings of the 1950s. I am, by default, a leading authority on the subject.*

I hated grammar in grammar school. Taught as if it were a science with rules like math, it had none of math's logic. But the working knowledge I managed to glean included the fact that you use only an apostrophe for a possessive ending in s. Why? Because, I was told, that avoided the logical but ungainly necessity of using three *s's if you had a possessive that ended in* two *s's.*

This may seem a rare condition, but to a person named Hess it loomed as a whammy that would follow me my entire life. Maybe that's why it's the only grammar rule I remember.

I wrote my book manuscript following the rules my grammar school teachers had taught me were eternal law—only to find that my editors believed in a different god with too many s's. Someone changed the rules on me. My childhood misgivings about grammar were confirmed.

Googie was my first book. Not wanting to offend my publisher, lest they were hunting for a reason to cancel a book on such a disreputable era and style anyway, I didn't make an issue of it. So my book contains the strange and wonderful configuration, "Henry Dreyfuss's."

It still looks to me as if some law of nature has been violated.

> *Alan Hess*
> *Architecture Critic*
> *San Jose* Mercury-News
> *Laguna Niguel, California*

The problem of possessives pales before this old copy editor's conundrum (and I speak as an old copy editor): how ought one to write the phrase most often expressed as "do's and dont's"? I believe it looks best the way I've just written it—but, of course, it's inconsistent that way.

"Dos and don'ts"? The first word looks extremely odd (and it might easily be confused, these days, with "DOS," a type of computer program).

"Do's and don't's"? Too damned many dots!

> *T.E.D. Klein*
> *New York, New York*

You state: "Great institutions are locked in titanic disagreement about this. Until we resolve the dispute, coverage of the campaign cannot correctly proceed."

Your phrase "cannot correctly proceed" follows the current style in which the modifier precedes the verb.

In my generation, and those preceding and immediately following it, the modifier was always placed after the verb, unless doing so produced an awkward phrase. Today, however, most writers automatically place the modifier ahead of the verb, regardless of its effect on sentence smoothness. We hear, and read, for example:

> *"They were seriously injured . . ."*
> *"I want the problem quickly corrected."*
> *"The temperature is slowly rising . . ."*

Surely, these phrases would be stronger if worded:

> *"They were injured seriously . . ."*
> *"I want the problem corrected quickly!" (In this example, in oral use, great emphasis could be put on the word "quickly" if it followed the verb.)*
> *"The temperature is rising slowly . . ."*

And surely your phrase "cannot correctly proceed" would be smoother and stronger if changed to "cannot proceed correctly."

> *H. Thursten Clarke*
> *Bloomfield, New Jersey*

Saint James's is pronounced SIN JAMES-ZIZ, not SAINT JAMES-ZIZ, yes?

> *Chlorinda V. Russo*
> *Washington, D.C.*

Post-Modernism Out, Neopuritanism In

The most avidly awaited list of the year is compiled by Nina Hyde of *The Washington Post* to let us know who or what is In and who or what is Out. Wider ties are In (it's been a long wait) and bow ties are Out; purple broccoli is In and ornamental cabbages are Out; Wittgenstein is In and Karl Marx is Out (as ordinary language defeats newspeak).

Others may search The List to see how to look (*zaftig* In, *anorexic* Out) or how to impress (car faxes In, car phones Out) or what to serve (pork rinds In, jelly beans Out). This department is on the lookout for what the In folks say.

Here's the big switch: *Neopuritanism* is In and *post-modernism* is Out.

To those of you wondering where you were while *post-modernism* was In, catch the definition in the *Second Barnhart Dictionary of New English:* "a movement or style . . . characterized by a departure from or rejection of 20th-century modernism (including modern and abstract art, avant-garde writing, functional architecture, etc.) and represented typically by works incorporating a variety of classical or historical styles and techniques."

That sounds good to me, but the adjective can be applied pejoratively: "The tag word *post-modernism* has gone on the building," wrote John Vinocur in *The New York Times* in 1981, describing Munich's new art museum, "and with it accusations of mannerism, cut-rate Romanticism, coquettishness, childishness and incoherence." Critics such as Hilton Kramer, who lived in modernist glass houses, threw stones at the columns and arches considered *post-modern* perversions of the twentieth-century ideal.

The general public, however, took *post-modern* to mean "the latest thing, more modern than modern." When Senator Paul Simon, Democrat of Illinois, rejected the term *neoliberal* and defined himself as "an old-fashioned liberal," I described him as *post-modern neoliberal,* which struck me as an up-to-the-minute synonym. (And bow ties are Out, too.)

Are we ready for *neopuritanism?* In 1979, Catharine A. MacKinnon, a Yale professor, used the adjective form: "Objection to sexual harassment at work is not a neopuritan protest against . . . displays of affection," she held. That seemed to attach a Greek prefix *neo-,* or "new" (in the sense of "influenced by"), to *Puritan,* a word that originally signified reformers of the Church of England and later, as *puritanical,* came to mean "prudish or excessively strict." In 1985, the critic Phoebe Pettingell wrote in *The New Leader:* "Poetry's musical heritage bestows a resonance now often abjured, thanks to a *neopuritanism* that associates sincerity with lack of adornment."

Here is a word with its meaning in formation. In The List, we have "living simply" In and "having it all" Out; "real conversation" In and "small talk" Out; "white hair" In and "dyed hair" Out. Taken together, this indicates a trend away from trendiness and glitziness. As Ms. Hyde says, "We're ready for Barbara Bush. We're ready for her natural hair . . . her no-nonsense ways, her *neopuritanism*—the New England style."

In that use, *puritan* has happy overtones of purity and simplicity, rather than a severe sense of stern, even blue-nosed, rigidity. And what will come after that, in next year's List? *Post-modern neopuritanism,* of course—but it may go under a new name.

Power Power

According to Zagat's restaurant guide, the Four Seasons has just passed Lutèce to become the favorite restaurant of those least likely hungry in New York City. That means the *power lunch,* a phrase coined to describe some of the dining by what used to be known as "influentials" at that establishment, is at its pinnacle.

Proof of the puissance of the phrase is the front-page headline in *USA Today* on the day that Mikhail S. Gorbachev, Ronald Reagan and George Bush sat down to dine on Governors Island after a U.N. session: "Power Lunch Is on Tap Today." That, of course, was the ultimate *power lunch.*

The use of the attributive noun *power,* rather than the adjective *powerful,* gained prominence with the sociologist C. Wright Mills's *power elite,* was picked up by Theodore H. White's *power broker* and was thrust forward by the campus slang use of *power boot,* "especially energetic regurgitation."

We can expect this vogue use of *power* as a modifier to wane one of these years. Keep your eye on *greed.*

Praxis Makes Perfect

Was the demonstration by students in Beijing's Tiananmen Square an example of *revolutionary praxis?* This was the phrase used in arguments among Communists around the world.

Nice to see that old Marxist phrase back in action. Until recently, it had been relegated to stories about religion and politics in Latin America: "Liberation theology," wrote Michael Novak in *The New York Times Magazine* in 1984, "says that truth lies in *revolutionary praxis.*" In 1986, Richard John Neuhaus wrote in *National Review* that a reporter covering the 1985 Roman Catholic Synod of Bishops missed its profound meaning because he "had come to cover hot issues, such as *revolutionary praxis* and women's ordination."

Praxis is a no-nonsense word meaning "action based on will," from the Greek for "doing, acting, deed, practice." It came marching into English in Sir Philip Sidney's 1581 treatise analyzing poetry: "For as Aristotle sayeth, it is not *Gnosis* (knowledge) but *Praxis* (action) must be the fruit." (Aristotle was contrasting theoretical reasoning with practical reasoning, sayeth I.)

Grammarians tried to snatch the word to their bosoms in the eighteenth century, as Bishop Robert Lowth used it to mean "an example of grammatical resolution," and some philologists still compare *praxis* with *lexis,* speech as action versus speech as meaning. But historians and political philosophers, led by Count August von Cieszkowski in 1838 and soon after by Karl Marx, made the term their own way of saying "practical activity."

Sidney Hook, the American philosopher, is my favorite analyst of Marx. In books written in the early 1930's, Professor Hook wrote, "Marx claimed that only in practice (*Praxis*) can problems be solved," and "Practice (*Praxis*) was something much wider than *practicability.* It was selective behavior. . . . Marx's theory of the Praxis could explain what all other philosophers recognized but which they could not begin to account for, without writing fairy-tales, *viz.,* how knowledge could give power."

Some neo-Marxists of the *praxis* "school" hold that the consciousness raised on Mao's long march was false. They argue that the only useful praxis is *revolutionary praxis,* which—according to Roger Scruton's *Dictionary of Political Thought*—"sustains itself without ideology, since it is directed to the essential nature of social reality."

I will wade no farther into these murky waters, other than to suggest that two political senses of the word exist: "practicality," such as is put forward by "capitalist roaders" and free-marketers, and "action," such as that undertaken by hunger-striking, freedom-seeking students.

More than one *praxis*? Praxes.

Surely praxis (in Aristotle and Marx) means "application" or "exercise" of what one knows (i.e., gnosis, which had a post-Aristotelian special religious sense, which may have been in Sidney's mind). As a mass noun, how could it have a plural?

Charles-James N. Bailey
Professor of English and
General Linguistics
Technische Universität Berlin
Berlin, West Germany

Primus Inter Whatever

"He was masterful," enthused David Burke, the ABC News executive vice president, about Ted Koppel's town-hall-meeting program from Israel. "In that kind of situation," he told *USA Today,* "Ted is first among equals."

The newspaper dutifully put *masterful* in the headline, and I suppose the distinction between that word and *masterly* is fading. Atheneum, an imprint of the Macmillan Publishing Company, advertises a book by Reynolds Price as "His masterful new novel *Good Hearts.*"

In olden times, *masterful* meant "domineering, overpowering, imperious," and *masterly* meant "skillful." When the Texan asked for directions with a firm "Say there, pardner, tell me how I get to Carnegie Hall," he was masterful, and the violinist who replied, "Practice, practice," was masterly.

I like the distinction and still use it, but *masterly* is in trouble for good reason: It is an adjective that ends with *-ly* (like *worldly, timely, kindly*) in a world that thinks all words ending that way should be adverbs modifying verbs.

If you have the skill of a master (a shortening of the Latin *magister,* akin to *magnus,* "great"), you may be a *masterly* violinist—with your adjective modifying your noun—but how do you play the violin? Now you need an adverb to modify the verb *play;* masterarily? Masterilly? No such animal. *Masterfully*? But if you're a purist, that means "overpoweringly," not "skillfully."

That's why *masterfully* is slopping over to take the place of the missing adverb, and carries back to the adjective the two senses of "imperious" and "skillful." Sorry about that.

You think that people in the word dodge don't get worked up about these controversies? Look up the usage note in the Merriam-Webster *Ninth New Collegiate Dictionary:* "The distinction is a modern one, excogitated by a 20th-century pundit in disregard of the history of the word. Both words developed in a parallel manner. . . . Sense 2 of *masterful,* which is slightly older than the sense of *masterly* intended to replace it, has continued in reputable use all along; it cannot rationally be called an error."

The "pundit" zapped therein was Henry W. Fowler, whose serene and most masterful judgments in *Modern English Usage* sometimes infuriate lexicographers; in this case, he swept aside the lack of historical evidence to espouse the differentiation. I'm with him on this one. (*Excogitate* means "to think out, devise, contrive," one step beyond *cogitate,* which is merely "to think about"; in this case, the unusual verb is an irate lexicographer's dignified synonym for the slang "cook up.")

As for the news executive's description of Mr. Koppel as "first among equals"—from the Latin *primus inter pares*—I think he meant "tops in his field" but was unwilling to offend the other commentators at the network. That's where Latin comes in handy.

As for my use of *enthused* to characterize his statement at the top of this item, that recent back-formation of a verb from the noun *enthusiasm* drives many people up the wall and stimulates apoplectic mail. That's how this column gets its material.

"He swept aside the lack of historical evidence." Is that like combing absent hair? You mean he *"ignored"*? *"Disregarded"*? You can't get rid of what ain't there.

Hal Davis
White Plains, New York

Pro-anti or Anti-pro?

Consider the word *abortion*. The root is poetic, from the Latin *oriri,* "to rise," as a sun rises. Prefixed by *ab-,* which turns the word into its opposite, *abortion* has the meaning of "to set, or cause to fade away." Two generations ago, this noun, primarily meaning "removal of a fetus," was rarely spoken above a whisper in polite company; one generation ago, it surfaced in debate but was treated as an ugly and offensive term.

Advocates of making abortion legal chose not to call themselves "pro-abortion" for two reasons: (1) the word had a negative connotation, and it was unwise to try to persuade people to assert support of what seemed like a "dirty" word, and (2) the decision was made not to encourage abortion itself, but the right of a woman to choose it without breaking the law. They came up with the term *pro-choice,* an inspired selection because most people are in favor of *choice,* a word associated with *freedom.* People surveyed by pollsters identified themselves as being "in favor of a woman's right to choose" more than "in favor of legal abortion."

Anti-abortion advocates then made a linguistic mistake, in my opinion. In an effort to appear positive, and not only *anti-,* as well as to put themselves on the side of the fetus, they followed the format of their opponents and chose the term *pro-life.*

Thus we had *pro-choice* versus *pro-life,* rather than *pro-abortion* versus *anti-abortion.* The word *abortion* was shunned by the disputants, which better suited the persuasive purpose of the side that was in favor of legal abortions. In their effort to be positive, *pro-* something, the anti-abortion advocates gave away their advantage of the public's aversion to the word *abortion.*

That is apparently now changing. The news media have been writing and saying *anti-abortion activists* and the pro-life forces have not been correcting them, because they are now willing to be labeled *anti-* something widely perceived as wrong or at least distasteful. Contrariwise, whenever a reporter says *pro-abortion forces,* pro-choice advocates must make a defensive point that they are not *pro-abortion,* only *pro-choice.*

In the coming political struggles in state legislatures, watch the anti-abortion forces belatedly try to change the terms of the debate from *pro-choice v. pro-life* to the starker *pro-abortion v. anti-abortion.* Watch the pro-choice forces resist this mightily. Words count.

Pushing the Envelope

"I also want to find the edge," said the comedian Will Durst to Stephen Holden of *The New York Times.* "I keep pushing at the envelope."

Only the day before, a camera technician who was quoted in *The Times* giving his opinion of another comic, the Polish satirist Jan Pietrzak, used the same phrase: "He is always at the cutting edge of what is permissible to say—he pushes the envelope, pushes the limits all the time."

"O.K., what's this *pushing the envelope* business?" writes Robert B. Kaiser of Mammoth Lakes, California. "Metaphors are supposed to help me see things more clearly, or in a new way. All this one does is increase my puzzlement."

The earliest citation I can find was in the July 3, 1978, *Aviation Week & Space Technology,* in a report about an aircraft that had been designed for operation at sea level but was being called upon for higher flight: "The aircraft's altitude envelope must be expanded to permit a ferry flight across the nation. NASA pilots were to push the envelope to 10,000 feet."

The phrase was popularized in 1979 by Tom Wolfe in his book about astronauts, *The Right Stuff.* The phrase-sensitive reporter wrote: "The 'envelope' was a flight-test term referring to the limits of a particular aircraft's performance, how tight a turn it could make at such-and-such a speed, and so on. 'Pushing the outside,' probing the outer limits, of the envelope seemed to be the great challenge and satisfaction of flight test."

I called Tom Wolfe, whose current novel, *The Bonfire of the Vanities,* pushes the envelope of urban high life, to find out where he picked it up. "I first heard it in 1972, among test pilots who later became astronauts. They were speaking of the performance capabilities of an airplane as an envelope, as if there were a boundary. Why they chose *envelope,* I don't know, but if you get outside the envelope, you're in trouble." He estimated that its test-pilot use may have begun at the Patuxent River Naval Air Station in Maryland in the 1940's.

Let's push back further with the help of the *Oxford English Dictionary* supplement. As an aeronautical term, *envelope* was in use as early as 1901, meaning "the gas or air container of a balloon or airship." In August of that year, *Scientific American* wrote: "The balloon is inflated with hydrogen, and in order to maintain at all times a tension on the envelope—that is to say, perfect inflation—a compensating balloon filled with air is placed in the interior."

In 1944, the *Journal of the Royal Aeronautics Society* extended that meaning of "perfect inflation" of a balloon to cover optimum flight performance of any kind of aircraft: "Tests at other heights can then be confined to what are termed 'envelope' conditions; that is, the engine conditions which will give the maximum economy at any given speed."

So there were those right-stuff test pilots, familiar with the phrase *envelope conditions,* talking about ways to extend, change, enlarge or make more demanding those conditions—from the inside of an aircraft, to "push" the envelope beyond known borders into untested conditions. (Why the verb *push*? Slang senses of *pushing it*—as in "You're pushing it, Buster"—are "extending beyond reason" and "pressing past boundaries of discretion.")

The space connection is unbroken; William Broyles Jr. wrote in *U.S. News & World Report* in 1986 of Christa McAuliffe, the teacher who was a member of the *Challenger* crew, "pushing out the envelope of the planet." And the metaphorical *envelope* was also taken up by the military: "The three-dimensional space," goes the definition in the *Dictionary of Military Terms,* "that is within range, altitude and deflection reach of a weapon, particularly an air defense weapon."

However, the phrase is now applicable to any reach beyond the boundaries, including a race driver's ultimate effort (usually called "the ragged edge") or a comic's outrageous material, whether merely raunchy or politically gutsy.

How do you pronounce it? The French verb *envelopper* means "to wrap completely," and the noun *envelope,* meaning "the wrapping of a letter," appeared in English in 1714, probably then pronounced "ON-ve-lope," in imitation of the French. But the centuries have Anglicized the pronunciation, and now more people say EN-ve-lope. I'd like to say that ON-ve-lope is incorrect, but that would be pushing it.

There is a theorem commonly used in engineering and economics problems that is known as the Envelope Theorem. This theorem is used to define the locus of points formed by the maxima of a series of related functions. To put it in English, it describes the outer envelope or boundary within which the maximum points fall. The name envelope refers to this boundary on the maxima. To "push the envelope" would therefore suggest an incrementation of the maxima.

Given that a good many test pilots were trained as aeronautical engineers, it is not at all surprising that they would have coined this popular term, borrowing from the technical language of their field.

Eric Stubbs
Department of Economics
Harvard University
Cambridge, Massachusetts

I have just completed reading your column and am stunned to find out that neither you nor the great Tom Wolfe are aware of the genesis of the term "pushing the envelope." Actually the term, as I remember it from my days as a Marine Radar Intercept Officer flying the back seat of the McDonell Douglas F-4 Phantom, was, with all due respect to Mr. Wolfe, pushing the edge of the envelope.

That phrase comes from the graphic representation of an aircraft's known flying capabilities with regard to speed, turning radius, altitude and other performance factors.

According to the theory, one is getting the maximum from the aircraft by flying it at the edge of the envelope. Again, according to the theory, if the "envelope" is an accurate representation of the actual limits of the plane's capabilities, then flying at the edge gives actual maximum performance. If one were to go outside of the envelope, he or she would go out of control.

Now pushing the edge of the envelope means to expand the known or perceived edge of the envelope from that which is presently known to its actual edge if not there already.

The danger in doing so is obvious; if the known edge is the same as the actual edge, then you go out of control if you exceed the envelope. However, if it is not, then the accomplishment in pushing the edge is, again in theory, unique, since no one else has done it before.

Patrick E. Daly
Tenafly, New Jersey

When an aircraft is designed, the manufacturer has a theoretical idea of what its performance will be. In most cases, this performance range can be graphed, and because it looks somewhat like an envelope, it's referred to as such.

Further, because the manufacturer recommends operating within these specific limitations for safe flight, the term "envelope of safety" or "staying inside the safety envelope" has evolved as part of the jargon.

When the new craft is off the drawing board and in the air, it becomes the test pilot's job to determine the now "actual" limitations against the designer's theoretical expectations—"Will it fly safely to 18,000 feet or can it be operated just as safely at 21,600 feet?"—stuff like that. This process of determining . . . expanding the safety envelope if you will . . . is the genesis for the term "pushing the envelope."

I first heard this intoned by American Airlines' Captain Saint in an impromptu discussion of the safety characteristics of the 747 jumbo jet on-board its 1969 inaugural flight in commercial service—JFK to SFO. I remember it vividly because listening to Captain Saint talk about flying and safety inspired my personal interest in learning to fly.

Jesse Califano
New York, New York

The performance limits of an aircraft are often presented to the aviator in the form of curves. Coincidentally, a curve frequently resembles a cross section of, say, the upper right quadrant of a picture of a balloon. A curve depicts the performance envelope: if you stay inside, you're OK; but if you go outside, you may be in trouble. It is more likely that aviators adopted "envelope" from the mathematicians and engineers who drew the curves than directly from ballooning.

"Pushing the envelope," then, is trying to move the performance curve outward—trying to make the curve a cross section of a bigger balloon. You can do this either by changing design or, as pilots would do, by trying to show that the curve was conservatively drawn and can be extended in practice.

Richard L. Conner
Palo Alto, California

The concept of an "envelope" in aeronautics derives from mathematics.

A family of curves, similar in all respects except for their initial directions may have a common envelope—that is, a curve that is tangent to each one of the curves in the family. The significance of the term is obvious—it "envelopes" the collection. The picture lends itself to an extension of the idea—the envelope is a kind of outer limit; hence the meaning you described.

Being no historian, I have no idea when the concept was first used, but in this context it certainly goes back a long way further than you suggested.

Stanley Shapiro
Teaneck, New Jersey

You did not refer to the very old concept in mathematics of an envelope to a set of curves. I believe that the mathematical usage was translated into engineering as a description of the limiting conditions of a mechanical function described by a family of equations (hence, curves) where there is a systematic varying of one or more constants. From its engineering use, it was picked up and became part of the jargon of aviation, because the mechanical constraints in the form of fuel capacity and weight were more stringent than those affecting land or water vehicles.

The mathematics needed to define the envelope of a set or family of curves became available with the invention of calculus, and therefore dates to Newton and Leibniz in the mid-17th century. The nomenclature is certainly later, since neither of these gentlemen would have embraced (or envelopped) the French word.

To push the envelope, mathematically, is to define the limit of the function. In the terms of aviation engineering, pushing means moving the limit. Going outside the envelope places one in an area forbidden mathematically to the points satisfying the given equations.

My copy of Elements of the Differential and Integral Calculus by Granville, Smith and Langley is dated 1934, and chapter XXIII, Applications of Partial Derivatives, describes the envelope mathematically.

Robert S. Rabinowitz
Norwich, New York

Back about 1956, Dr. Gosta Lindblom of Stockholm, Sweden, lectured to a group of dentists in New York City on the physiology of the Tempero-Mandibular Joint (very popular these days, but somewhat esoteric then). Of particular interest was the description of the outer limits of movement of the head of the condyle as the mandible moves in function. The three-dimensional representa-

tion of these limits was called the "Envelope of Movement of the Condyle." Dentistry flies again.

Robert A. Nathan, D.D.S.
Clifton, New Jersey

In scientific parlance, the boundary enveloping a chosen part of this "variable-space" (which may be in any number of dimensions) is called the envelope (naturally).

When aeronautical experts decided to depict the performance limits of an aircraft graphically, it was natural for them to use the accepted scientific terms. Thus, if you wanted to measure performance in terms of just altitude and speed, you could measure speed on the horizontal axis, and altitude on the vertical axis. If you could measure speed and altitude at every point during a flight, you could represent it by a curve (dotted line) on this graph. The boundary enclosing all such possible dotted lines is the envelope, for obvious reasons. If you flew faster, the dotted line would stretch further to the right, and if you flew higher, it would stretch further upward: In the process of stretching, it would appear to "push" the envelope (solid line) upward and to the right (by stretching the boundary).

It is in this sense that "pushing the envelope" meant stretching the limits of the possible.

Anirvan Banerji
New York, New York

Dear Bill,
The sense "smooth geometrical figure surrounding [something not so smooth]" is quite common in a number of scientific fields, such as acoustics, where one will speak of the envelope of a sound spectrum. For example, people sometimes speak of a synthesized musical sound having a flat envelope if the intensities of the various harmonics are roughly equal in the range of sounds that human ears can perceive.

Jim [James D. McCawley]
Department of Linguistics
University of Chicago
Chicago, Illinois

Pushing the Envelope More

A torrent of classy, high-domed mail has come in from scientific types with contributions to the origin of the test pilot's favorite phrase, *pushing the envelope,* which was traced here to the skin of early lighter-than-air ascensions.

"Usage of the term *envelope* in science and engineering goes back at least to the mid-19th century," advises Alexander H. Flax, home secretary of the National Academy of Engineering. (A home secretary handles membership issues within the academy.) "In mathematics the envelope is the outer boundary of a related family of curves (see Attachment A)."

Let's see Attachment A, a page from Goursat & Hedrick's *A Course in Mathematical Analysis,* Vol. I (published in 1904), p. 426: "If each of the positions of the curve C is tangent to a fixed curve E, the curve E is called the *envelope* of the curves C, and the curves C are said to be *enveloped* by E."

Number-crunchers in the aeronautical field applied this word to the limits of aircraft operations, as in Attachment B, which we will all recognize as a velocity-load factor diagram referred to in a 1967 Federal Air Regulations publication. There, in a discussion of flight loads, we can find *flight envelopes, gust envelopes* and *maneuver envelopes.*

Thems that exceed, push. Thank you, scientists and mathematicians, especially those few of you who refrained from pouting in postscripts about the theft of your precious *parameters* and *quantum jumps* by the lay public.

Since before the turn of the century, dentists, especially prosthodontists, have been studying mandibular motion and attempting to duplicate it on devices called articulators.

For several decades, we have been referring to the "envelope of motion" and the "envelope of function." The former refers to the three-dimensional perimeter of the total volume circumscribed by all motions the jaw is capable of (i.e., within the border movements). The latter refers to the perimeter of the smaller volume outlined by customary chewing movements.

Paul J. Hoffman, D.D.S.
New York, New York

Rack Up That City on a Hill

Five days before New York Governor Mario Cuomo was to deliver his keynote speech at the 1984 Democratic convention, he called broadcaster Larry King and read it to him over the telephone.

"What do you think of this?" asked Mr. Cuomo, as Mr. King recalls the conversation in *Tell It to the King,* his new book. "You like this 'city on the hill' idea?"

The Governor was critical, in his draft speech, of Ronald Reagan's use of "city on a hill" to describe America. The all-night interviewer was noncommittal, as objective reporters should be. But if the keynoter had asked me, a card-carrying member of the Judson Welliver Society of Former White House Speechwriters, I would have said, "Mario, throw that part out. The 'city on a hill' stuff was fine when Saint Matthew used it: 'Ye are the light of the world. A city that is set on an hill cannot be hid.' And it was O.K. for John Winthrop to lift it in a sermon aboard the *Arbella* on his way to the New World in 1630. And then John Kennedy started using 'city on a hill' in his stump speech, and then Ronald Reagan picked it up and made it a standard peroration. That beacon to mankind is untouchable. Nobody can criticize it. Don't mess with it."

But the Governor didn't call me. That turned out to be lucky for him: Mr. Cuomo played off the tried-and-true elevated urban metaphor at the 1984 convention, complete with expressive hand gestures, holding that "the hard truth is that not everyone is sharing in this city's splendor and glory." Speechwriters winced, but everybody else in the audience apparently lapped it up; an adept speaker can actually get away with knocking the city on a hill.

Mr. King writes: "Cuomo reminded me that it is the job of most keynote speakers [in the party out of power] to rack up the incumbent." He reports that the Governor eschewed that role, saying: "But I always call him President Reagan in this speech, I never slam him personally. Do you think that's O.K.?"

To me, the interesting point in that paragraph is not Larry King's response—"sounds fine to me," which it was, because no pol has the guts to take on Ronald Reagan directly—but his use of *rack up*. It is uncertain from the text whether Mr. Cuomo used the slang phrase or it is Mr. King's paraphrase, but *rack up* has several senses and deserves close study.

College students will recognize one sense immediately: *racking* means "intense studying," the modern version of *cramming,* an antisocial activity undertaken by *wonks* and *throats* (from *cutthroats*).

This sense derives from medieval torture. Every well-equipped dungeon had a device for extracting information or confession: the frame on which victims were bound and stretched until their limbs were wrenched from their sockets was called the *rack,* probably from the Middle Dutch *recken,* akin to both *reach* and *stretch.*

The noun became a verb and is familiar to millions in the Oscar Hammerstein 2d lyric, "body all achin' an' racked wid pain" from the song "Ol' Man River." When you *rack your brains,* you torture your mind to remember, which fits the meaning intended by the racking wonks and throats in our institutions of higher learning.

(My conclusion is disputed by Thomas de Forest Bull of Boston, who claims that studious *racking* comes from *bookracks,* but most etymologists are willing to take the pain. Mr. Bull is correct in linking *rack* to *sack,* however; in the Navy, *rack time* is time spent sleeping in the sack.)

Thus, the current usage—"that really racks me up" or, in Mr. King's words, "it is the job of most keynote speakers to rack up the incumbent"—flows from the ancient framework used to inflict pain.

But a quite different sense exists, causing confusion. "As [Jesse] Jackson racks up win after win . . ." writes the Associated Press. "If all goes well for the Vice President," comments *The Christian Science Monitor,* "he could rack up as many as 500 delegates." And *Business Week:* "Bantam has focused on salable authors such as Louis L'Amour to rack up stunning success."

That happy racking means "to achieve" or "to gain," and comes not from the torture frame but the triangular frame that brings together, or accumulates, the balls in a game of pool. The expression "Rack 'em up" is the order to assemble the balls for the start of a new game, and is usually spoken cheerfully by hustlers. The past participle, *racked,* means "mastered," from the racking-up of winning points.

There's more to be straightened out here. The verb *rack,* meaning "stretch" as in *nerve-racked,* should not be confused with the verb *wrack,* meaning "to wreck, ruin, destroy" (*wrack and ruin,* in which *wrack* is a noun, has been misspelled *rack and ruin* for so many centuries that it's no longer incorrect).

The New York Times Manual of Style and Usage has a great idea here: Never use *wrack,* because it confuses people. Instead, when *wrack* means "wreck," just use *wreck.* (But when you mean "inflict damage," spell it *wreak.* You "wreak havoc on"; you never "wreck havoc" because havoc is unwreckable.)

O.K., keynoters, let's *rack 'em up:* It's traditional to *rack up* your opponent with a good tongue-lashing for having led the country to *wrack and ruin,* and after you *rack up* a victory, you can *wreak* patronage vengeance from high atop your city on a hill.

I think you overlooked the usage of "rack up" that broadcaster Larry King had in mind when he said that it's "the job of keynote speakers to rack up the incumbent."

Before the development of videotape, much of what was shown on TV was shot in 35-mm or 16-mm movie film. If it was necessary for many executives to view some footage prior to final editing, they would assemble in a screening room. When they were ready, one of the viewers would call out to the projectionist in his booth, "Rack it up." This is film lingo for mounting a reel in a projector, threading it and being ready to "run it." (Why, I don't know—ask a projectionist.) If a second viewing seemed necessary, someone would then ask the projectionist to "rack it up again."

Among broadcasters, to rack something up meant to hold it up before an assemblage so it could be seen and criticized. And wasn't that what the Democratic keynoter was supposed to do to the Republican incumbent?

Bob Matheo
Ardsley, New York

"Racked up another win" does come from pool-hall parlance, but it is the racking up of the balls rather than the point markers that is referred to. In

straight, call-shot pool, a good player can "run the table"—take all the balls but one. It is then that his victory is heralded by racking up the 14 at the bottom of the chute. The victor then continues shooting, hoping to "rack up another win" by again taking 14 balls—and so on.

> *James Leavenworth*
> *New Britain, Connecticut*

"Rack 'em up" may also have a negative connotation in pool. That is because the pool balls are not just placed in the triangle rack and are not placed therein by the previous victor. He may give the order, but the job is handled by the next challenger, who hopes to so tightly pack the balls that the victor cannot break them up to his advantage.

Also, "to rack up" an opponent is a football slang expression referring to a very hard tackle of a ball carrier, preferably one in which the carrier is met head on, lifted off his feet, and unceremoniously smashed onto the turf (natural or artificial).

> *[Name Withheld]*
> *Washington, D.C.*

Read My Lips

"Congress will push me to raise taxes," George Bush told the whooping Republican delegates at the party's convention in New Orleans (pronounced "N'awlins" by the natives, and not, as David Brinkley assured Peter Jennings, "New Or-le-ans"), "and I'll say no, and they'll push, and I'll say no, and they'll push again, and I'll say to them, 'Read my lips: No new taxes.' "

This dramatic use in a formal acceptance speech sealed the phrasal intensifier *read my lips* into the language. It has reached the level of a similar phrase, *make my day,* a line that was originally delivered by the actor Clint Eastwood playing Dirty Harry and immortalized by President Reagan to emphasize his own opposition to the same congressional urge: "I have only one thing to say to the tax increasers—go ahead and make my day." (Indeed, former Reagan speechwriter Peggy Noonan, who drafted Mr. Bush's acceptance address, deepened the resonance by including a parody of that line: "Go ahead and make my twenty-four-hour time period.")

Read my lips is rooted in rock music. In 1978, the actor-singer Tim Curry

gave that name to an album of songs written by others (though it did not include a song with that title copyrighted in 1957 by Joe Greene).

Reached in Washington, where he is appearing in *Me and My Girl,* Mr. Curry recalled that he got the phrase from an Italian-American recording engineer: "I would say to him, 'We got it that time,' and he would say, 'Read my lips—we didn't.' That phrase arrested me, and I thought it would make an arresting album title. Be a good name for Mick Jagger's autobiography, come to think of it." And what is Mr. Curry's definition of *read my lips*? "Listen and listen very hard, because I want you to hear what I've got to say."

Several songwriters in the 1980's came up with other songs with the same title, the best known of which was a Grammy nominee written by Sam Lorber and Madeline Stone, recorded by Melba Moore.

Sports figures snapped up the stern intensifier. The phrase appeared as a nickname suggesting emphasis in orders by a football coach—Mike (Read My Lips) Ditka of the Chicago Bears—and as the name of a thoroughbred race horse. The heavyweight boxer Michael Spinks, before being knocked out by champion Mike Tyson, predicted he would retire after the fight, whatever the outcome: "I'll say, 'Read my lips. I quit. Bye-bye. Forever. In other words, see ya.' "

Politicians also lunged for the phrase. Early in 1981, a Reagan public-relations aide wanted American Embassy hostages being released by Iran to be brought home in planes dramatically marked "United States of America." *The Washington Post* reporter Elisabeth Bumiller wrote a profile later that year about the White House aide, Joseph Canzeri (a Michael Deaver protégé who survived and is today part of the team educating candidate Dan Quayle in political hardball). The reporter quoted a tense interchange between the hard-driving Mr. Canzeri and a Foggy Bottom bureaucrat who had resisted the use of aircraft so marked.

"They're committed," said a State Department official.

"Well, uncommit them," replied Canzeri.

"We can't do that," said the official.

"Read my lips—these are English words," said Canzeri. "Uncommit them." His orders were followed; the planes were made available.

In 1987, Senator Albert Gore was questioning Under Secretary of Defense Fred C. Iklé about his lukewarm support of the Midgetman missile; the Pentagon official did not oppose study of that particular weapon but gave the impression he preferred a mobile missile instead. "You're saying, 'Read my lips, cut the money' " for the Midgetman, said Senator Gore. "Your message is clear."

That imputed a meaning to the phrase of whispering, or using body English to convey meanings other than what is spoken, as if to say "read my mind"; that is not precisely what the rock lyricists had in their minds. On the contrary, the trope most often conjured is that of a teacher who is speaking to a deaf pupil and mouthing the words so that the person who cannot hear can understand.

In the magazine *Automotive Marketing,* Rosemarie Kitchin suggested in 1987 that the action described by the phrase has a double purpose: "Read my lips! Has anyone ever said that to you? If so, you were the object of an intense attempt at persuasion. Your conversational partner wanted to emphasize a point or belief. And he or she wanted to be sure that you looked and listened both, for a dual sensory impact."

Away back when the Catskills Borscht Belt was in its heyday and small night-clubs flourished in all the New York City boroughs, comics, who were the staples of entertainment programs, were often the butt of would-be comedians in the audiences. Heckling, jibes, banter between performer and the soon-to-be-put-down pest were almost de rigueur. I was on hand when (who was it—Jackie Gleason, Jan Murray, Jackie Whelan, Jackie Miles, I can't recall) permanently squelched a pesky heckler while maintaining an innocent-looking mien, with, "Pardon me, but—can you read lips?" (and without waiting for a reply) "You can? Well, read my lips": and gave vent to a full-bodied Bronx cheer—fondly remembered as the Bronx razzberry—THBBTHRRRRRTHRR!!!

Bob Russell
Sarasota, Florida

I have found an interesting antecedent for George Bush's "Read my Lips."

"Watch my lips move," I said helpfully, and pointed to my mouth with my forefinger. "We . . . will . . . bring . . . women . . . in . . . from . . . outside!" I said it very slowly and carefully, like a deranged speech therapist. He just sat there and stared at me transfixed, a rabbit with a snake.

Rt. Hon. James Hacker, M.P. and Minister for Administrative Affairs, to Sir Humphrey Appleby.
The Complete Yes Minister by Jonathan Lynn and Anthony Jay, published 1981.
Life imitates fiction.

Alan Truscott
Bronx, New York

In my high school days in the late 60's, a negative answer to a question or a request was made emphatic by use of an obscene gerund; and, occasionally, the negative answer was expressed by substituting an obscene phrase for a simple "No."
Because such phrases and expressions were cause for reprimand, we would mouth the obscene answer after calling for the questioner to "read my lips." While I have nothing other than anecdotal evidence, my belief is that "Read my lips" became a substitute for the obscene enhancer itself.

Gregory E. Breen
Hermosa Beach, California

The term "read my lips" also has a current usage of the former "Are you deaf or something." There is the implication of "Hey, stupid, I've told you that several times. Don't you understand?" In common parlance, this term has taken on a derisive tone.

Robert Abrahams
Shaker Heights, Ohio

As a New Orleanian, I beg to dif-fah. There is no arbitrary single way to pronounce New Orleans. It's a multi-accented community whose patois and inflection differ, depending on whether you're Uptown in the "silk stocking" district (*N'Awlins* or *New Awl-yuns*) or in the Irish Channel (*New Awl-uns* or even *New Erl-uns*).

Growing up in the 13th Ward, between the swells (the Boggs constituency) and the Channel (the Eddie Hebert constituency), I myself halved it, as did our neighbors. We pronounced it *New Or-luns*.

All of which is to say that Brinkley wasn't that far off the mark in telling Jennings to pronounce it *New Or-le-ans*. It's close enough, considering the fact that *Or-lin-eans* have had to endure the sound of *New Or-leens* from outlanders, thanks to the song-rhymesters. That's definitely out; though the parish, for some reason lost in the bayou mist, is called *Or-leens*, as in, "I live in *New Awl-uns* in *Or-leens Parish*."

Go figure Y'ats. (A New Orleans local; from the native salutation, "Where y'at?," whose origin is also lost in the mist.)

Oh, one more thing. In all my years I never, never heard any genuine Or-leanian call the town "The Big Easy." That's a latter-day hucksterism no doubt invented by the same people who insist on referring to *po' boys* as *hoagies*.

> Victor Gold
> Falls Church, Virginia

I have some expert testimony here from Mel Leavitt, New Orleans radio and television broadcaster since 1949, from his *Short History of New Orleans* (San Francisco: Lexikos, 1982), page 25:

> The approved local pronunciation of "New Orleans"—how a broad-caster would say it—is *New OR-lee-uns*, but this is by no means widespread. The informal, colloquial, working-man's, or "Ninth Ward accent" renders the name as *N'AW-linz* or *N'OR-linz*, depending on where the speaker might be from originally (South or Midwest, respectively). Down-home talk like this is called Yat, as in "Hey, Tom, where y'at?" The pronunciation that raises local hackles is *New Or-LEENS*, as sung in "Way Down Yonder (in New Orleans)"—composed here!

As you like asides, I will add Mr. Leavitt's two asides:

> "Louisiana" should be pronounced with all its syllables, as most out-landers do, but upstate it's *LOOZY-ana*. First-time visitors to the city are usually surprised that Orleanians don't talk like Southerners; in fact, many sound Brooklyn-born.

This testimony is supplementary, for you were not arguing which pronunciation is "proper," only locally widespread. But I hope you would agree that outlanders (particularly naturally snide commentators like David Brinkley) *should strictly avoid use of local pronunciations lest they be thought rude or sarcastic.*

I vividly recall an incident in a Dublin pub in my learning days when I pointed to a dark drink in a large mug (it was Guinness stout) and asked the bartender, "If I want one of those, what do I ask for?" "A point," he said. Naïvely echoing his pronunciation of pint, I said, "Okay, give me a point, please." Did he glare!

Alan Magary
San Francisco, California

Recuse, J'accuse!

"I have always *recused* myself from anything to do with communications," said Clayland Boyden Gray, President Bush's legal counsel and chief ethics adviser. I had just asked him, with no apparent malice aforethought, for copies of his financial disclosure forms for the past three years, a request that puts some government officials on the defensive.

Turned out he was chairman of the board of a half-billion-dollar communications corporation while he was on the federal payroll. *Recusal*—self-disqualification—was not enough; when *New York Times* reporter Jeff Gerth made known the outside income and responsibilities, Mr. Gray was forced to resign from the corporate board and amend his incomplete ethics forms.

To reassert his standing as Mr. Bush's "ethics czar" (counting the drug czar William J. Bennett, we already have a two-czar Administration), Mr. Gray promptly zapped the new Secretary of State, James A. Baker 3d, for failing to divest himself of stock in a bank holding company.

Mr. Baker, wrote Walter Pincus in *The Washington Post,* had been *"recusing* himself" from matters that might cause the appearance of conflict of interest, but counsel Gray's position cited a Justice Department ruling "that top Administration officials whose personal holdings would inevitably and predictably benefit from policies they help establish cannot simply *recuse* themselves from involvement in those policies."

We have here a verb with a small past and a big future. A few years ago in this space, in a piece entitled "Recuse My Dust," lexicographers were put on Red Lex Alert: *recuse,* not in the dictionaries with its present meaning, was no nonce term.

Although the new *Chambers English Dictionary* fails to include the newer sense of this hot term, *Webster's New World,* in its third edition, promptly came through: "to disqualify or withdraw from a position of judging, as because of prejudice or personal interest." The unabridged 1987 *Random*

House II agreed: "to withdraw from a position of judging so as to avoid any semblance of partiality or bias."

Almost right, fellas, but not quite. The reflexive verb is listed there as both transitive (I recuse myself) and intransitive (I recuse), but an intransitive use in the current sense is hard to find. The *Random House* and *New World* definitions are sharply disputed by Bryan A. Garner, author of *A Dictionary of Modern Legal Usage* and editor in chief of the *Oxford Law Dictionary* project.

"Pishposh!" says the lawyer Garner, at the University of Texas/Oxford Center for Legal Lexicography. (Lexies interject printably; I'm working on the derivation of *pishposh*.) "No judge would say, 'I therefore recuse.' Because *recuse* is virtually always reflexive today, it cannot be used in the passive voice, unlike *disqualify*. To say that a judge is *disqualified* is perfectly idiomatic, but to say that he is *recused* is not."

Then what's the difference between *recuse* and *disqualify*? "*Disqualify* might always be used in place of *recuse*," says Mr. Garner, "but the reverse does not hold true. *Disqualify*, the broader term, may be used of witnesses, for example, as well as of judges, whereas *recuse* is applied only to someone who sits in judgment, usually judges or jurors."

Let's snoop around. "The verb *recuse* is not found in *Black's Law Dictionary*," says Nancy Slonim at the American Bar Association in Chicago. She took what she calls an informal poll of her associates ("Hey, guys, I got this reporter on the phone—any difference between *recuse* and *disqualify*?") and reported, "A judge would recuse him- or herself, but would be disqualified by an outside party." Thus, in some legal minds, *recusal* is done to oneself; *disqualification* is done to one.

"The terms are now virtually interchangeable," says Professor Geoffrey C. Hazard Jr. of Yale Law School, who is one of the pioneers in the study of straight-arrowship in the law. But that distinction can still be made: "*Recuse* has the sense of 'I exit' as distinct from 'I am thrown out.' *Disqualify*, on the other hand, has a more sinister or invidious implication, usually indicating what a party would do to someone else, rather than to oneself."

Because there is less presumption of independence from contamination nowadays, both in judges and other officials, the invidious connotation of *disqualify* is withering, and the word is used as a synonym for *recuse*. "I would say the most commonly used word now is *disqualify*," guesses Hazard, "but another possibility is *withdraw*." Others include *remove* (oneself) and *decline to sit*.

The reflexive form of *recuse* came roaring into the language around 1950. A computer search done by the lexicographer Garner shows only thirty-eight cases in which the word appeared that way before then, and more than three thousand cases since then. (The earliest citation was 1849, in Fourniquet v. Perkins. You still find people named Perkins.)

In previous centuries, the verb *recuse*, which dates back to 1387, meant "to reject or object to a judge as prejudiced." *Recusant* was a noun meaning "dissenter"; *recusancy* was a state assumed by Roman Catholics from the sixteenth century on who refused to go to the Church of England.

But then the meaning changed direction, turning the refusal in on oneself. Carla Wheeler of the University of Texas, a student of both linguistics and the law, speculates that the verb *recuse* as we use it now may be a back-formation from the adjective *recusant,* which meant "refusing to acknowledge authority"; it was a short step from that to "refuse to exercise authority."

You want my decision on whether to chuck out *recuse* as legalese, too often confused with *excuse* or *rescue,* and to use *disqualify* in all cases. Well, I'd like to, but you see, I own stock in *recuse.* . . .

Dear Bill:

A footnote to your <u>J'accuse, récuse</u> discussion. "<u>Je me récuse</u>" is used in ordinary conversation to decline giving advice or stating an opinion. It's educated but not technical speech. Without the reflexive, it is technical and means, at law, refusing to accept the competence of a witness or tribunal.

Warm greetings as always.

> *Jacques [Barzun]*
> *New York, New York*

You mentioned an early case between Fourniquet and Perkins, and said, "You still find people named Perkins." Perhaps this to test how widely read you are based on how many Fourniquets write back to you! I cannot claim to have such an unusual name, but I can inform you of the relative odds that you (or anyone else in America) would find someone named Fourniquet vs. Perkins. Perkins is the 186th most common name in America, with approximately 36,666 households having that surname (most estimates of the number of households in America hover near 70 million). Thus, the odds for any one individual being named Perkins is 1,909 to 1. The most common name in America is Smith, much to no one's surprise. According to one of them (Elsdon Smith, <u>American Surnames</u> [Chilton: Rednor, Penn.], 1969), Smith was also the most common name in the first U.S. census—almost twice as common as the second-place holder, Brown. Things have changed a bit in the past 2 centuries: Brown is now in 4th place, after Johnson and Williams, and all 3 have closed in on Smith's lead. (I forgot to mention that 1% of America belongs to the Smith "family.")

Back to your article. You implied that Fourniquet might be a dead name today. Although it's not easy to find out how many there were during the time of the case you mention, my database, obtained from telephone company listings and division of motor vehicle records, shows that there are presently 6 Fourniquet households. That makes your odds of encountering one of them, on the first try, 11.6 million to 1. Not great odds, but I'm sure you know several people who have names at least as uncommon. In fact, in America there are 500,000 people who have a surname shared with no one else in America. I'd say it's likely there's a writer you know or someone at The New York Times whose surname is at least as uncommon (though you or they may not be aware of it). Most people are astonished to find out how diverse American surnames are— there are about 1.5 million different surnames. ·

Murray Spiegel
Morristown, New Jersey

Pishposh!

Now that a certain barnyard epithet has lost its force through overuse, cussers and vigorous vituperators everywhere are searching the language for ringing terms to express irritation, pique, nettlement or disgust.

In a recent discussion of the rise of the reflexive transitive verb *recuse,* meaning "to disqualify (oneself)," I quoted the lexicographer in charge of the new *Oxford Law Dictionary* as he took issue with several general dictionaries' definitions of that term. "Pishposh!" ejaculated Bryan A. Garner, before rendering a more scholarly rejoinder.

Consider *pishposh.* The first syllable of this satisfying interjection saw print in a satire by Thomas Nashe in 1592: "Pish, pish, what talke you of old age or balde pates?" Although *pish-posh* appeared in 1834 as an Anglo-Indian name for a slop of rice soup and meat, the use of the term as an interjection seems less related to Indian soup than to a reduplicative lengthening of *pish* into *pishposh.*

The powerful quality of the letter *p* lends itself to outbursts of disbelief or contempt: In addition to *pish,* we have *pooh* and *pshaw* (although the *p* is not usually pronounced in *pshaw,* and what became of Major Hoople?).

Moreover, *pishposh* qualifies as a third-order reduplication, the most sophisticated kind. In the redupe dodge, according to Wentworth and Flexner's *Dictionary of American Slang,* the first order is simple repetition (*goo-goo, hush-hush*). The second order changes the initial letter to produce a rhyme (*namby-pamby, mumbo jumbo, higgledy-piggledy*). The third order changes the internal vowel sound, as in *fiddle-faddle* or *mishmash.* (Controversy swirls around *mishmash,* meaning "jumble," which some say is a redupe of the cereal *mash;* others consider that theory to be sheer balderdash, and insist the old word is derived from the Yiddish *mischmasch,* a redupe of the German *mischen,* "to mix.")

O.K., *balderdash:* Like the weakened barnyard epithet, this begins with the explosive *b,* as in *baloney!* similar to the powerful *p* (*pishposh! piffle! poppycock!*).

The first user in print was, once again, the satirist Nashe, who wrote in 1596 of "Two blunderkins, hauing their braines stuft with nought but balderdash." The word then suggested "jumble of liquors" and came to mean "nonsense, spoken or written trash" when taken up a century later by the poet Andrew Marvell.

Worth pursuing? You may say *tommyrot!* To which the only response is *codswallop!*

Dear Bill:
It strikes me that Shakespeare (the comedies especially) is/are peppered with Pishposh synonyms, most of them now grotesquely out of date. Retrieve 'em on your data base. In the meantime, I offer you, as one of the more exotic coinings (maybe it was no coining but a regular bit of slang), Sir Toby Belch's "Till-vally, lady!"

Alistair [Cooke]
New York, New York

All I can say is "Pishtosh to Pishposh"!
A quick run through The Oxford Dictionary *convinces me that my sister is totally wrong (I suspected it all along). "Tush" and "tushery" should not be entering into this ejaculatory discussion. "Posh" (another o.o.o.) remains "elegant" or "fashionable." Pre-fixing "pish" makes it less, not more, so.*

The sloppy Anglo-Indian rice and meat soup is pishp̲ash. You may lengthen the pronunciation of the "a" if you so desire, but you may not change the spelling.

Use of "pish" with "tosh" may indicate a connection between nannies and amahs, the former picking up "pish" for use with "tosh" and throwing away the "pash." From the recipe for the soup, that is an action to be recommended and commended.

All that remains is to decide whether to put these words in quotes, or to underline them, and whether to hyphenate or not. Do let me know when you decide about the hyphens.

Margaret M. Jones
Falls Church, Virginia

Regarding the phrase "The powerful quality of the letter p lends itself . . ."

I assume that you are either a linguist, or else that you are at least reasonably familiar with the basic principles of linguistics. You must know that the above-quoted phraseology is misleading because it perpetuates the myth that language and writing are one and the same. Shouldn't you have written: "The explosive quality of the sound represented by the letter p"? or perhaps ". . . of the /p / phoneme" or ". . . of the sound of p"? I don't think it is useful for the mavens (or is it mavinim?) of our language to preserve the misleading fiction that the written symbol is the linguistic reality rather than its reflection. You did make the point, true enough, that misuse of a term tends to canonize the misusage. Nonetheless, this particular carelessness transcends simple lexical peculiarities because it blurs nicely made distinctions honed out by meticulous linguists who labored long and hard to delineate and develop the concepts that you so easily ignored.

Jeff F. Segall
New York, New York

Rethinking Reclama

The caller must have set off all the recording machines in the Central Intelligence Agency by dialing my number at the Washington Bureau of *The New York Times.*

"*Reclama,*" the voice said, "as both noun and verb. Drives us crazy. And all you hear these days is the adjective *feckless.*" He hung up before the whirring machines could get a usable voiceprint or the vectoring sound trucks could close in.

This was the latest burst from my Spookspeak Mole. Although he clams up on the dull, classified stuff, he (or she—the word-maven-in-place is not necessarily male) can be depended on to report the most sensitive information of all: the latest lingo in the corridors of power.

Reclama is a word used by people who leak to, and write for, publications such as *Aviation Week* (which in 1958 added "Space Technology" to its title, lest readers think it still wore goggles and a silk Amelia Earhart neckerchief). "Navy and Army officials are now in the process of preparing *reclamas* on the LAMPS and aerial scout helicopters," it wrote in 1975. Six years later, in the same publication, an irate defense official complained of "zero time available to . . . accept *reclamas* from the services."

The word is hot in diplomacy, too: Prime Minister Margaret Thatcher, wrote James R. Schlesinger in *Foreign Affairs* magazine in 1986, "appeared at Camp David to deliver a *reclama* on Reykjavik." Mr. Schlesinger, it will be remembered, has been both Director of Central Intelligence and Secretary of Defense. In 1984, Secretary of State George P. Shultz explained how government differed from business: "In business you had to be very careful when you told somebody that's working for you to do something, because the chances were very high that he'd do it. In government you didn't have to worry about that, because if he didn't like it, there'd be a *reclama.*"

The word is gaining in highest-level usage: "Cheney had done a *reclama,*" Brent Scowcroft, the national security adviser, was overheard saying about a request from Defense Secretary Richard B. Cheney for a review of some decision. Another member of the National Security Council, whom I cannot identify for fear of burning a source, was responsible for turning the noun into a verb at a meeting in which the President participated: "I'd like to *reclama* that." Because nobody corrected the functional shifter, his verbification was tacitly adopted without a finding or Senate notification or anything.

Reclama is not in the general dictionaries, and has yet to appear in the *Oxford English Dictionary,* but is defined in the 1978 *Naval Terms Dictionary* as "a request to superior authority to reconsider its decision or its proposed action." The synonyms are *review* and *appeal,* both of which do double duty as verb or noun, so I suppose we cannot get upset at the verb form of *reclama* in the National Security Council.

My guess is that the word is a clip of the noun *reclamation,* from the verb *reclaim.* Both are rooted in the Latin *clamare,* "to cry out" (same root as *clamor,* the noise raised by grammarians at the first hint of functional shift).

From the Latin came the French verb *réclamer,* which means "to complain, protest, object, appeal," and spawned a noun, *réclame,* "publicity, notoriety"; the early meaning of a cry of protest led to the English *reclaim,* which began by meaning "to recall from improper conduct" and "to bring back from error" and now has a generalized meaning of "to recover," as in the reclamation of waste.

Let us now reclama the overuse of *feckless.*

Robert C. McFarlane, a former national security adviser, told *The New York Times* that the Iranians first sent a "feckless functionary" to meet him at the airport in Teheran in 1986.

Defense lawyers for former Arizona Governor Evan Mecham tried to discredit a police witness by claiming he had been "a feckless employee."

Ed Meese's lawyers said last year that a government prosecutor's report was a "mammothly feckless venture." Another Meese supporter was quoted as saying that the former Attorney General had been made to "look like a feckless hick."

Feckless, like its synonym *ineffective,* is short on *feck,* which used to be a word meaning "vigor" and is still with us in the form of *effect.*

To be *feckless* is to be a washout, a nebbish, a loser; although the word now has a connotation of "careless, irresponsible," it remains an umbrella term for "weak, spineless, inadequate, helpless."

Come to think of it, the hard-sounding *feckless* is a lot more effective than the soft-sounding *ineffective. Reclama* denied. Anybody for *feckful*?

Dear Bill:

Let me push back the date on "reclama." The word was in common usage when I was at the Pentagon from 1953–55 in the Office of the Labor Advisor to the Assistant Secretary of the Army for Logistics and Research and Development (a very grand name for an office that consisted of a lieutenant colonel, a secretary and me). The meaning was as you describe today: an appeal to a higher authority to reconsider.

> *Bill Green*
> *Member of Congress*
> *15th District, New York*

At Dartmouth, certain "feckless" souls—those lacking in social graces; the snivelling and cowardly; the brown-noser; any and all others perceived to lack backbone—are referred to singularly or collectively as "lunchmeat." I suppose that the explanation for this is self-evident; the hapless loser, like a piece of bologna or Oscar-Mayer ham, simply doesn't "stand up." Example: "All the girls left the party because there were so many lunchmeats there." A person who is deserving of the title is also apt to be "squashless"—meaning without "squash" (i.e., referring to a man's genital area, supposedly a source of masculine power).

There is a stronger form of the term, which can, in extreme cases, be applied to particularly pathetic types—"pimento loaf"—although not many merit this degree of universal condemnation.

Brian H. Corcoran
Charlottesville, Virginia

Wanna Buy a Ductile?

You can always tell when Sahabzada Yaqub-Khan, Foreign Minister of Pakistan, has been in town: The national security establishment and its hangers-on begin dropping unfamiliar English words.

As previously reported here, *feckless* is the vogue word in the spook-speakeasies for "ineffective, helpless"; now the word on everybody's lips in Foggy Bottom is *otiose,* "idle, indolent, lazy."

I confronted Mr. Yaqub-Khan with this suddenly with-it word and asked if he was the source; he demurred (a verb in diplolingo that means "denied, purring"), adding, "Americans are not so ductile."

O.K., you guys in the interagency task forces working on a succession of summits, this week's adjective is *ductile:* "easily molded; tractable; pliable." Any *otiose* sherpa who cannot use it in a sentence about arms negotiations is *feckless.*

On the chance that I'm stating the obvious: The words negotiations and otiose, which you used in the same sentence, come from the same source. NEGOTI-ATE NEG—OTIUM NOT—LEISURE.

Martin Meyers
New York, New York

Rot at the Top

Ἰχθὺς ἐκ τῆς κεφαλῆς ὄζειν ἄρχεται.

"There's an old Greek saying," said Michael Dukakis, responding to a question about whether President Reagan and Vice President Bush could be held personally accountable for their Administration's ethical lapses, "a fish rots from the head first. It starts at the top."

This scrupulously bipartisan column takes no position on the accuracy of any political accusation, but is ready to examine the roots of all colorful adages used in campaigns.

First, the wording: It appears that Governor Dukakis deliberately chose a euphemistic verb. Although *rot* is sometimes used, most citations of the proverb read, "The fish *stinks* from the head." While *rot* sounds less offensive, it means "decay, deteriorate, decompose, putrefy." *Stink,* on the other hand, does not necessarily impute decay; a healthy skunk in the process of defending itself will stink, as may the emission from the smokestacks of an operating factory.

Maybe the alliteration "Something is stinking in the state of Denmark" came to Shakespeare's mind when writing *Hamlet,* and the poet was not reluctant to use that verb on other occasions. He chose, however, to have the character Marcellus say, "Something is rotten in the state of Denmark"; it was not the way the political situation smelled, but the way it was decaying and becoming corrupt as the result of a secret crime, that was the point being made by that line in *Hamlet.* In more general terms, that was also the point Mr. Dukakis sought to make.

Now to the source. Italian proverbialists are familiar with *Il pesce comincia a puzzare dalla testa,* and the saying is also frequently identified as Turkish and Russian. The Dutch scholar Desiderius Erasmus mentioned this proverb in Latin early in the sixteenth century (*Piscis primum a capite foetet*), but the words are found earlier in Greek. It is, as the Massachusetts Governor claimed, an ancient Greek saying.

Finally, to the question rarely asked: Is it literally true? According to Jeff Clayton of the Smithsonian Institution's division of fishes (*fishes* is the plural for different kinds of fish—let's hold down the irate mail), "There is no biological evidence to support the proverb. Everything would decompose at about the same rate, though probably the stomach—or any injured part of the fish that led to its death—would start to smell first."

To defend Erasmus, Dukakis et al., let me say that it is common knowledge when checking fish for freshness to smell the gills. The proximity to the head might justify the piscean caveat.

John R. Shields
College Point, New York

As an old fish "peddler," I would suggest that the traditional and surest way of detecting a problem is to open the fish and smell it at the head, i.e., where the gills are located, because that is the area where bacteria is most likely to fester. (Naturally, if there is an injury, that would make a difference, but that should not be a factor in the discussion.)

My suggestion is easy to verify: Take a morning off, go down to the commercial fisheries and "nose" around. Just ask anyone in the business how they check for spoilage. You'll learn that you don't have to be a scientist. All you need is experience.

Jacob Levine
Danvers, Massachusetts

Certainly Mr. Clayton didn't mean to say that "any injured part of the fish that led to its death would start to smell first." I think it was G. K. Chesterton who solved the smell-stink distinction. When a society woman told him, "Mr. Chesterton, you smell," he replied, "No, madam, you smell, I stink."

Ann E. Kuzdale
Toronto, Ontario, Canada

Rumpelstiltskin Lives

Journalists tired of receiving heavy persuasion from political partisans called for a *spin moratorium.* The word appeared also as part of *spin doctors,* who formed a *spin patrol* and operated in a theater called *spin valley.*

That word—one of the oldest in English, dating back as a verb, meaning "to whirl," to circa 725—was introduced as a noun by the poet Thomas Moore, who wrote in 1831 of "A glorious spin, and then—a tumble."

In a piece titled "Calling Dr. Spin" in 1986, I examined the new *spin doctor* and alerted you to "a locution we must keep our eyes on for 1988." Would that my political prognostication had reached this level of prescience. The word and its associated phrases are used, without anger or contempt, by the targets of this media persuasion; rather, an amused toleration reigns.

Spin doctor was coined on the analogy of *play doctor,* but the noun *spin* gained its curvy connotation more than a century ago from the twist put on a ball in the game of cricket. In billiards, the spin put on a ball was known as *English;* Mark Twain wrote in 1869, "You would infallibly put the 'English' on the wrong side of the ball."

By figurative extension, this led to a twisting of truth, influenced by the old expression *spinning a yarn*—in which *yarn* played on the double meaning of "fiber" and "tale," and *spinning* carried meanings of "twisting" and "telling."

We are not finished with this metaphor. As yet unused in politics are such refinements as *backspin,* perhaps for candidates who want to undersell expectations, *topspin,* for a story planned to drop unexpectedly, and *sidespin,* for a use to be determined by future spin doctors. We can look forward to the Rumpelstiltskin Award for creative opinion-manipulation, named after that dwarf of folklore who helped a king's young bride to spin straw into gold.

With respect to Rumpelstiltskin, you missed an opportunity to be truly <u>au</u> <u>courant</u> in not including as a use of "spin" its use in physics to further distinguish between quarks (in addition to such terms as "up," "down," "top," "bottom," "strange," "charm," "free," and their color).

> Daniel S. Knight
> Philadelphia, Pennsylvania

Secretary of Synonymy

Don't you like to watch important people grope for the right word? There they are, certified big shots, going through the same mental process of elimination that all of us do all the time.

Whenever I see a power player on television saying, "I wouldn't call it (whatever), it was more like, um (grope, grope) . . . ," I shout out the synonym I think he's reaching for. Most of the time, it's not the word he ultimately chooses.

There was Samuel K. Skinner, our Transportation Secretary, facing the press about the Alaskan oil spill. Asked about the initial attitude of those responsible, he replied, "I wouldn't call it *callous.* I'd say it was, uh (grope) . . ."

It had to be something on the arrogant side, but slightly less hardhearted than *callous.* Quick—this was a job for Supersynonyman.

"*Insensitive!*" I hollered at the screen. "*Uncaring, heartless, aloof, thick-skinned!*" Maybe in the direction of "slow to react": "*Sluggish, apathetic, lethargic, foot-dragging!*"

Then the Secretary found the word he wanted: "*Cavalier.*"

Gee, that was a good word, worth reaching for. *Cavalier* is not as cruelly benumbed as *callous;* it means "offhand," with possible connotations of "supercilious" and "disdainful."

The Latin root is *caballus,* "horse." The word *cavalier* as a noun came to mean "horseman," and later any Royalist associated with Charles I in his dispute with Cromwell's Roundheads. The free-and-easy connotation of the adjective gained a sinister connotation of "indifferent, overly casual about important matters," the way a man on the ground views a man on his high horse.

Let's keep an eye on the Secretary-Synonymist. Unlike his boss, he seems inclined to want to finish his sentences.

You mentioned the Latin word "caballus" as being the root of the word "cavalier" and I think you might be interested in reading of another word stemming from the same "caballus." It is the Italian word "cabaletta."

If you are a regular opera-goer, you probably already know that a cabaletta is the second part of a two-part aria. I assume, however, that your time is taken up almost entirely with dealing in words, leaving little time for words and music and I shall, therefore, explain that the first part of the aria is slow or moderate in tempo; and then the cabaletta is sung, and it has a quick tempo, the rhythm being somewhat like a horse trotting, which explains its name.

Cabalettas occur mostly (only?) in Italian operas and Verdi used them quite often in his works.

Julius Heller
Forest Hills, New York

Shades of Gray/Grey

How do you spell the color (achromatic, but it's still a color) created by mixing black and white? Is it *grey* or *gray?*

"Both spellings are correct and common," advises the new *Webster's Dictionary of English Usage,* which at $18.95 is one of the great bargain books of our time. "In American English, the preference is for *gray,* but *grey* is also widely used. The British have a very definite preference for *grey.*"

Preference is fine in discussing pronunciation ("PREF-er-a-ble" is preferred to "pre-FER-a-ble," but the latter isn't a mistake), but I don't go for that preferential wishy-washiness when it comes to spelling. Here's how tough-guy orthographers, unafraid of taking black-and-white positions, handle the shade in question: If you're American, spell it *the color gray;* if you're British, spell it *the colour grey.* That's my *judgment;* if I were British, that would be my *judgement.*

Of course, I'm being prescriptive, laying my opinion on you because we have this tacit agreement that I know best about usage. The reason you go along with my ukases, diktats and pronouncements—most of the time—is that you don't have the time to break your head over what's the latest trend on the spelling of *grey*. Nor do you have the inclination to agonize over the worthiness of preserving a distinction between *masterful* (domineering) and *masterly* (skillful), or to puzzle out why *the reason is that* is In and *the reason is because* is Out. You figure we language mavens are paid to have our shootout at the Correct Corral and then to pass along the words and spellings left standing.

That's not the attitude at Merriam-Webster, where they've been publishing since 1831. Those guys are reporters of language, not columnists about language—descriptivists, not prescriptivists. They know that Noah Webster tried to straighten out the inconsistent and confusing spelling of the English language in his early nineteenth-century works, and remember that he failed miserably. Like good democratic politicians, these lexicographers and usagists have learned that the best way to get along in the language dodge is to go along with the native speakers. They're in love with Norma Loquendi.

This is by way of introducing you to the best-researched, most readable, illustrative, sensible but often wrongheaded book about the choices we make in the way we use the language since Henry W. Fowler's classic *Modern English Usage.* Frederick C. Mish, editorial director of Merriam-Webster, and E. Ward Gilman, editor of *Webster's Dictionary of English Usage,* have produced one of the great books on language in this generation, but in so doing frequently raise a standard to which all those who hate standards can repair.

The *anxious/eager* distinction, for example, is dismissed as "a shibboleth." Although some of us like to use *anxious* to signify "worried" and *eager* to mean "desirous," *W.D.E.U.* (along with Fowler) pooh-poohs this. "Anyone who says that careful writers do not use *anxious* in its 'eager' sense," it opines, "has simply not examined the available evidence," which it amply lays out.

I accept the evidence and reassert the shibboleth. If you're hot to trot and express this as "anxious to go," you'll have a lot of company, but many of us who will refrain from correcting you won't respect you in the morning. Certainly many people, and many good writers, use *anxious* when they mean *eager;* I say when you mean *eager,* use *eager,* and save *anxious* for when you're worried.

How do you like your *media*—singular, "media is," or plural, "media are"? According to *W.D.E.U.,* "The collective use . . . seems to be following the direction of development of *data,*" which is tending toward singular. But the roundheels have not yet won: "*Media* is still being construed as a plural more often than it is either as a singular count noun or as a collective noun with a singular verb."

Why do you suppose that bastion has not been overrun? Because some die-hards among us insist that when you speak of one medium, like "the damnable scriveners" of the press or "the sensationalist boob-tubers" of broadcast news, you are not speaking of all the media; *media* are multifarious, and "is" not monolithic. I get the feeling that Mr. Gilman expects us to lose this one in the end; we'll show 'im.

Between v. *among*? Say it isn't so: "We suggest that in choosing between *among* and *between,*" writes the usagist-reporter, using *between* correctly in choosing between two, "you are going to be better off following your own instincts than trying to follow someone else's theory of what is correct." *W.D.E.U.* cites the sainted Sir James Murray and Noah Webster as two of its authorities in this opinion, shows the mistake made by good writers throughout history and concludes: "The unfounded notion that *between* can be used of only two items persists, most perniciously, perhaps, in schoolbooks."

Thank heaven for those pernicious schoolbooks. Hold the fort with Samuel Johnson, Goold Brown and me: *Between* two, separating sharply, and *among* many, dividing loosely. It's cleaner. (Sell me one of those T-shirts that say, "I'm the Mommy, that's why.") (That *say,* not that *says.*)

Masterly v. *masterful*? "This distinction, however neat and convenient, is entirely factitious," declares the weathervane grammarian, using the forty-dollar word for "artificial," condemning the nice distinction as "the invention of H. W. Fowler in 1926." Ah, Fowler! Thou shouldst be living at this hour: Usage hath need of thee. A parade of citations showing no distinction proves only that many users have not caught on to the improvement he suggested. This one is worth fighting for.

On pronunciation, I am more of a roundheel, and go along with allowing such variants approved by Mr. Gilman and crew as "air" for *err* and "TEM-pe-cher" for *temperature*. However, the notion that *government* and *environment* pronounced without an *n* "must be considered standard" goes overboard. "Guvvamint" is prevalent, but *standard* implies approval; next we'll be accepting "gummint." Not in my liberry.

However, I find myself agreeing with many of the descriptive (I almost wrote "permissive") positions taken, such as allowing sentences that start with *however*. The exhaustive entry on *ain't* is masterly (nothing in this dictionary is masterful), and concludes: "at times you will probably find *ain't* a very useful word despite (or even because of) the controversy that surrounds its use." That's true, and my hat is off to the willingness of Merriam-Webster to refer to the uproar caused by the decision of the editor Philip B. Gove in 1961 to accept *ain't* as standard in the Third Edition of their unabridged dictionary. (A cartoon of the time had a receptionist saying, "Dr. Gove ain't in.")

Hopefully is approved by the editors; I've caved in on that, leaving Jack Kilpatrick about the only defender left on the ramparts. And *It's me* is considered "reputable"; I'd say it has become preferred to the grammatically perfect "It is I," which has become pedantic and stuffy. (The editors flirt with, but do not recommend, *it's* as a possessive pronoun; I believe it has long been settled that *its* is the only correct form.)

The attitude in this major work is consistent: Common usage dictates its recommendations for standard usage. My own attitude is inconsistent: I'll defend some distinctions, abandon resistance to new uses for old words (*contact* as a verb is punchier than *get in touch with*) and go into contortions to avoid *whom*. As a result, I find *W.D.E.U.* a valuable and often wryly amusing reference to help me work out my own decisions.

Take its information, but don't necessarily take its advice. Usage ain't style.

Is it grey or gray? You could have spared yourself the extended exercise if you had simply followed the dictum of Andrew Jackson: "It is a damned poor mind indeed which can't think of at least two ways of spelling any word."

> *Sid Esterowitz*
> *Brooklyn, New York*

In discussing the usage of <u>between</u> and <u>among</u>, Mr. Safire again offers his support for those teachers of grade-school English whose rules reach back to the conceit that only the Latinist has the right to prescribe the rules of English grammar. My own teacher, I suspect, would have had us write that Pennsylvania is situated among New York, New Jersey, Maryland, West Virginia and Ohio.

Hillel A. Fine
New York, New York

Short Grows the List

"How come," a lady asks her husband in a James Stevenson cartoon in *The New Yorker,* "you're never on anybody's *short list?*"

At the start of a new Administration, the *short list* is the place for an officeseeker to be. It is a kind of honor to be on the lips of the Great Mentioners of the media, enabling the mentionee to bask in the attention without having to fill out the onerous ethics forms.

A synonymous phrase for *on the short list* is *among the final contenders,* each meaning "small group of those under consideration," though *contender* imputes to the mentionee his or her active solicitation of the job. Although *finalist* is sometimes used, that word carries too much of a beauty-contest connotation, and *competitor,* even more than *contender,* shows not the proper deference to the fiction that "the office seeks the man."

When Alexander M. Haig Jr. told the 1988 Republican National Conven-

tion that the Democratic ticket could be characterized as "blind as a bat
... hanging upside down in dark, damp caves up to its navel in guano," the
convention chairman, Robert H. Michel, remarked of his heated rhetoric:
"That's probably why Al Haig is not on the *short list* for Vice President."

To those on the *short list* actually lusting after the appointment or nomination to whatever office is open, it can be a nerve-racking and humbling
position. And in politics, the listing never ends: Newly elected Senator
Charles S. Robb, Democrat of Virginia, was identified by the Associated
Press recently as "on most *short lists* of potential presidential candidates in
1992 or 1996."

The phrase is originally British. The earliest print citation is from *Contemporary English: A Personal Speech Record,* by William E. Collinson, in 1927:
"Selection committees to University posts first familiarized me with the
meaning of the *short list,*" suggesting the term had been used earlier. In
Britain, it is also used for the list of suspects in criminal cases. *The Economist,*
a weekly edited in London, has been its most frequent user, helping to
popularize the noun phrase across the Atlantic.

O.K., how do we write it? *Webster's New World* hyphenates the phrase, as
short-list; Merriam-Webster's *Ninth New Collegiate* makes it a single word,
shortlist, like *shortbread* and *blacklist.* I prefer two words, *short list,* like *sick
list* and *wait list* (airlinese for *waiting list*). I resist with temporary resolution
the verb form, *short-list,* as in "Lucky me, I've been short-listed."

What about the opposite of *short list*—is it, as logic might suggest, *long
list*? No. That phrase is not used in this specific context of job selection. The
"long" list is called *everybody else.* A rundown of legislative desires is called
a *wish list,* and an enumeration of goals in an inaugural address is called,
often derisively, a *laundry list.* These are never short lists.

Now we're down to the word *list* itself. In Old English, it meant "hem,
border, narrow strip at the edge"; influenced by the French *liste,* it gained the
sense of a strip of paper with the names of soldiers on it, a meaning that is
preserved in "entering the lists" against a political foe.

In the opening scene of Shakespeare's *Hamlet,* Horatio informs Marcellus:

> ... young Fortinbras,
> Of unimproved mettle hot and full,
> Hath in the skirts of Norway here and there
> Shark'd up a list of lawless resolutes. ...

The "list" was an army. I like that line, complete with vivid verb. Shark
me up a short list of candidates. ...

*The term "short leet" has been in common use in Scotland for several hundred
years, particularly in matters ecclesiastical and educational. Here are extracts
from three dictionaries.*

Chambers Dictionary, 1902 Edition:

> _Leet (Scot), a selected list of candidates for an office. Short leet, a small list of selected candidates, out of whom the final choice is to be made. (Ice. leiti, a share; cf. A.S. hlet, hlyt, forms of hlot, lot.)_

Chambers Scots Dictionary (1911), 1987 revision:

> _Leet, n, a lot, portion, a separate division; a nomination to office by election; a selected list of candidates or nominees; v., to nominate, to make a select list of candidates; to enrol, establish._

Chambers Dictionary, 1965 Edition:

> _Leet, n. (Scot) a selected list of candidates for an office. Short leet, a select list for the final choice. (perhaps élite; but cf. O.E. hlet, lot.)_

The Scots had close ties with France before the union with England in 1603 and there are hundreds of Scottish words which are phonetically related to French. (e.g., "ashet" from "assiette," a plate; "aumrie" from "armoire," a cupboard.) Being an expatriate Scot, I'm inclined to believe that the English (who never could understand Doric Scots) thought that "leet" was the Scots pronunciation of "list"!

David B. Buchanan
Victoria, British Columbia,
Canada

With regard to the word "list," I believe the expression "entering the lists" refers not to enrolling in an army, but to entering a jousting arena to try oneself in single combat against other knights. The "list" in this usage doubtless derived from the long rail or hedge along which the combatants, on opposite sides, rode toward each other. I always feel more noble when I enter the lists in some cause than when I am simply enlisted.

Interestingly, the words "list" and "tilt" share common double meanings of "joust" and "leaning." My guess would be that this also came from the tournament, since the knights must have had to lean over the "list" to strike their opponents riding on the other side.

William F. Linke
East Brunswick, New Jersey

Every English schoolboy knows (and I was one) that to enter the lists refers to the jousting tournaments of medieval times, and means to accept a challenge to engage in combat. The "lists" presumably referred to the fence bounding the *jousting field. Thus to enter the lists has the same broad meaning and derivation as to "pick up the gauntlet."*

These terms carry with them, of course, the idea of combat conducted with honor and constrained by rules of engagement. Thus they would seem appropriate in principle, if not always in practice, when discussing political battles.

Stuart M. Butler
The Heritage Foundation
Washington, D.C.

In discussing the word <u>list</u> itself, you say, "it gained the sense of a strip of paper with the names of soldiers on it, a meaning that is preserved in 'entering the lists' against a political foe." I beg to differ.

The "lists" which <u>you</u> want refer to a physical location, not a piece of paper. As a lifelong lover of the medieval, something in your explanation hit me as amiss. Off to the books . . . !

On page 3477 of my <u>Century Dictionary of the English Language</u> (1890) the sixth definition of <u>list</u> (noun): one of the barriers enclosing the field of combat at a tournament, used in the plural.

> *No man therfore, up peyne of los of lyf,*
> *No maner shot, polax, ne shorte knyf*
> *Into the lystes send ne thider brynge.*
> *—Chaucer's Knight's Tale (1687)*

Or how about

> *To the lists they came, and single sword and*
> *gauntlet was their fight.*
> *—Beaumont and Fletcher, <u>King and No King</u>*

My Bailey's (25th ed., 1790) says: "LISTS (<u>lice</u>, F.) a place enclosed in with rails for tournaments, races, wrestlings and other exercises."

And Zieber's <u>Heraldry in America</u> (1909) defines "Lists—a space enclosed for a tournament."

So, young Fortinbras may indeed have "shark'd up a list of lawless resolutes" as you say, but if he then "entered the lists" with them, they would be about to joust, not sign up.

JoAnne Fuerst
Mount Desert, Maine

I thought you might like to know that in the architectural and engineering world, "long list" denotes an initial group of professionals identified by a corporate, institutional, governmental or other client out of the universe of professionals to be considered to provide services for an upcoming project. The "short list" designates those few, usually three to six, remaining to be considered after the "long list" is culled after submission of credentials, proposals, interviews or other means.

Getting on the "long list" is a necessary first step; making the "short list" is better; being selected is best.

Peter Piven
Philadelphia, Pennsylvania

There is such a thing as a short list and also, in the horse world competition, at least, there are also long lists. These are the competitors who might be later selected for the short list and must keep their horses fit and conditioned in case they get lucky or in case some other horse or contestant is unlucky. Horses are mortal, athletes often suffer injury. No one can make up a matched competitive harness pair fit to do the world driving games on short notice, for instance. I believe other sports which must provide a specific number of players also have both long and short lists. The Olympic Committee long-lists people.

Mary Jean Vasiloff
Old Lyme, Connecticut

Sine-off

"Sino-Soviet Summit" was the way I slugged my thumbsucker about the meeting of Deng and Gorby in Beijing. "Frowned on," was the response of my editor, who pointed to *The New York Times Manual of Style and Usage:* "*Sino.* Avoid in adjectival references to China. Use *Chinese-American, Chinese-Russian,* etc. But: *Sinologist.*"

That was curious; *Sinologist,* which was O.K. in the stylebook, is a term I would never use for "student of China." *Pekingologist* would be my preference for "pundit analyzing the machinations of the People's Republic of China" (except it would now be written *Beijingologist*). Contrariwise, *Sino-American* and *Sino-Soviet* are proscribed by the stylesters, but are my preference. I wheedled a one-time-only pass out of the editors on the basis of alliteration: *Sino-Soviet Summit* had a ring to it.

The *Sino-*no-no crowd probably thinks the Latin form is not only old-fashioned but is less easily understood than *Chinese-.* But on that analogy, we would be saying farewell to *Anglo-,* and British-American relations would never be the same; same with *Franco-* and *Italo-*, and what about the most important combining form in linguistics, *Indo-*?

Some people feel that making the name of the culture into a prefix ending in *o* weakens or demeans that culture or country; Jesse Jackson, for example, rejects *Afro-American,* preferring *African-American,* which treats both cultures equally. The *o* ending is typical of the first elements of compounds of Greek origin, as in *Greco-Roman,* though *Greco-American* relations are usually called *Greek-American.* The stylebook is winning that one.

For guidance on *Sino-,* I turned to the Reverend Paul Chan, secretary general of the Sino-American Amity Fund in New York City, an unsung hero who has been making possible the education of Chinese students in the United States for a generation.

"*Sino-* comes from a Latin root meaning 'Chinese,' " says Father Chan, who is learned in Latin and pronounces the term "SEE-no"; he is an old friend of mine and never corrected my Anglicization to "SY-no." "At one time, the Europeans thought of China not as a separate country but as many countries joined together, so the root *Sinae* is plural."

Is he sticking to *Sino-* in his title? "Perhaps we should use *Chinese,* which is easier for many Americans, but 'Sino-American Amity' is how we're known, and the form is not incorrect."

Stick with it, sez I; Why do we feel the urge to simplify everything? The "Save *Sino-* Society" has just been formed and welcomes members around the world. Just be sure to capitalize the combining form; the lowercased *sino-,* as in *sinorespiratory,* means "sinus-related."

You wrote: "I wheedled a one-time-only pass out of the editors on the basis of alliteration. . . ." On first glance, the sentence suggests that you wheedled a "pass out." Furthermore, your printer placed "out" as the last word on the line, compounding the ambiguity. Recommended revision: "I wheedled out of the editors a one-time-only pass because of alliteration. . . ." or "Because of alliteration, I wheedled out of the editors a one-time-only pass. . . ."

Thomas Michael McDonnell
University of Florida
Gainesville, Florida

Want to get even with that editor who referred you to The Times's Manual of Style and Usage *on "Sino-Soviet Summit"?*

Advise (not "address") him and his colleagues to refer to the manual on the subject of American vice presidents. Since the Inauguration, almost without fail, The Times *has called the veep "Vice President Dan Quayle." If I remember rightly, that breaks precedent and the rules set down in the manual.*

From the moment of his swearing in, shouldn't Mr. Quayle have become simply "Vice President Quayle"? Wouldn't he be "Vice President Dan Quayle" only if he were vice president of another country, or still just Vice President-elect?

I have a theory about this: Either The Times privately wishes he were vice president of another country, or it delights in the application of his sobriquet in the same way it would if he were Vice President Charlie Brown.

In its quirky way, the editors of The Times are trying to damn the Vice President with first names.

Tom Dunlop
New York, New York

Sit on My Laptop

Time was, the sexist male boss dreamed of inveigling his female secretary to sit on his lap. Today, male and female executives dream of using their laps as launching pads for brainy little machines called *laptops.*

Wait—how can a lap have a top? A lap is already a top—a seated person's thightops—which can be more laboriously defined as "the horizontal area from knees to waist formed in the sitting position by a lascivious boss of either sex." (The word is rooted in the Latin *labi,* "to slide," and if you have ever had anyone slide off your lap as you rose, surprised by an unwelcome office boy, you can imagine how some embarrassed Roman senator might have coined the term.) But whence *laptop*? We cannot say "in the laptops of luxury" or "in the laptops of the gods" or even "sit on my laptop, dearie"—it sounds silly.

This new word is on everyone's lips, and has even made it into the new unabridged *Random House II Dictionary,* because as an adjective or attributive noun modifying *computer,* it gives us "a computer small enough to be rested on the user's lap," presumably when the user is traveling and no desk is available.

The desk is the clue to the formation of *laptop.* The earlier word was *desktop,* which was coined on the analogy of *tabletop* by Dashiell Hammett in 1929: "He . . . returned his feet to the desk-top." Other mystery writers, such as Rex Stout, picked up the word (it was a favorite area for activity by private eyes), and it was adopted in the late 1960's to describe computers then on the drawing boards that could be used in homes as well as offices. Today, it describes computers that are not as portable as laptops and is gaining frequency in the phrase *desktop publishing.*

As computers proliferated on the tops of desks, the smaller size reached for an extension of the analogy. The first citation in Nexis, the computerized clip service, comes from 1984: David Winer, the founder of a computer software firm, Living Videotext Inc., and his brother Peter, used the word *laptop* in *Byte* magazine. Reached at his headquarters in Palo Alto, California, David Winer said, "I wish I could say I coined the word *laptop,* but I didn't. It was already in common use in the industry. We tried various plays on the term, including *floortop, beachtop* and *bedtop.*"

Because *desktop* had already lost its hyphen, *laptop* was born without a hyphen; both words are now more often used adjectivally, but the phrase *laptop computer* is dropping the final word, and *laptop* will probably soon most often be used in its noun form: "I'm working on my 20-megahertz *laptop* with its 40-megabyte hard disk, General, which is why it is not advisable for me to stand and salute."

We should not be surprised by the appearance of *laptop;* the idea of a working surface on the lap dates back to 1804 with *lapboard.* The current combination has the added advantage of consonance, which is the technique of repeating a consonant sound—such as the *m* as in *time frame,* or *dim sum,* or, in this case, the final *p* of *lap* and *top.* (Alliteration deals only with the beginnings of words; consonance deals usually with the middles and endings. Only the most subtle speechwriters try the latter.)

A dependent of my acquaintance recently submitted a list of expenses including one item spelled "underware." I was about to chastise her for this apparent misspelling, but now it occurs to me—could this be what fashionable hackers wear beneath their *laptops*?

In French there is no word for lap, which Webster defines as "the front part of the lower trunk and thighs of a seated person."

A Frenchman takes his wife, child, secretary, mother, cat, or whatever on his knees (genoux), although thighs would seem more apt.

The French language, long admired for its logic, purity, and refinement, does not waste a lexical label on an anatomical area that ceases to exist when one stands up! Nor does it have need of neologisms to keep pace with technology. The device you describe will in all probability be known in France, not as a dessus-de-genoux (which suggests a lap rug or blanket), but as—what else?—a laptop. While the borrowed term works fine, it loses the visual associations that English speakers enjoy.

Hilda Tauber
Maywood, New Jersey

Although you may know it already, you did not mention to the reader that a computer software company by the name of "Underware" exists. Not coincidentally, they sell a PC text editor called "Brief."

Kim Moser
New York, New York

Slinging Muddle

"Albert Gore's analysis of the Democratic race has become received wisdom," wrote Michael Kramer in *U.S. News & World Report* early in the primary campaigning. "Iowa and New Hampshire have produced a 'muddle.' "

The Tennessee Democrat probably picked up that word from a piece in January by the *Washington Post* writers Paul Taylor and David S. Broder, in which the word was used three times. The G.O.P. race was described as "a picture of clarity alongside the anything-goes Democratic muddle." The Democratic race was likened to a show on the way to Broadway "after a long and bumpy road tour during which it lost its leading man. The plot's a muddle." Finally, "Gore is hoping that the Democratic muddle persists through the early calendar. . . ."

After the Southern regional primaries on Super Tuesday, *The New York Times* put the newly voguish old word in a headline: 3-WAY MUDDLE, and the political reporter R. W. Apple Jr. later described the result as "a muddle . . . for the Democrats."

If you are not intimately conversant with the etymology of *muddle,* you obviously cannot analyze the absence of a shoo-in in the Democratic race. (Watch out for *shoo-in,* too: *The Wall Street Journal* recently spelled it *shoe-in,* as if the slang term were rooted in the action of a shoehorn. In fact, the meaning comes from horse-racing lingo: Corrupt jockeys form a ring and agree to hold back their mounts and to "shoo in," or urge forward, a slow horse on which they have bet. In such a phony contest, the *shoo-in* is the only horse in the race that is trying to win, which is why the term is now applied to George Bush in the Republican race. But I run off the track.)

Muddle began as a verb, derived from the Middle Dutch *modden,* "to dabble in mud"; mud pies were apparently popular with children in the Netherlands in the sixteenth century, unless the verb was coined to describe some of the less light-filled paintings of the pre-Vermeer era.

By the 1600's, the verb's meaning had been extended by drinkers unhappy with the sediment in their favorite beverage: They grumbled that their wine was made to look muddy, or turbid, when the sediment was stirred up by a bumbling predecessor to today's smoothly decanting sommeliers. That led to the use of the past participle, *muddled,* meaning "dazed, confused, stupefied," as in the Scottish author John Arbuthnot's 1712 usage: "I was for five years often drunk, always muddled."

The noun is relatively recent. Henry J. Todd, a lexicographer who revised Samuel Johnson's dictionary in 1818, added "*Muddle,* a confused or turbid state: a vulgar expression." (*Turbid* is from the Latin for "disturbed, troubled," and would be useful in political discourse, but speechwriters stick with *muddled.*) The phrase *in a muddle,* meaning "in a mess or jumble," was added in 1833 by the English painter John Constable, who was not afflicted by a lust for tidiness: "Still it's a good thing to be in a muddle."

In verb form, the word made its appearance in politics as a famous utterance circa 1864 by the British statesman John Bright, a free-trader and anti-imperialist friendly to Lincoln and the Union: "My opinion is that the Northern States will manage somehow to muddle through." (That was not quite Albert Gore's point more than a century later, but not all that dissimilar.) The phrase means "to succeed ineptly," implying a courageous, if bumbling, determination; in the Stephen Sondheim lyrics for the 1959 musical *Gypsy,* the song "Together Wherever We Go" contains the lines "With you for me and me for you, / We'll muddle through whatever we do / Together, wherever we go!"

Muddle, as a noun, has no edifying or uplifting connotation. The word is stronger than *mix-up* or *hash* and weaker than *shambles* or *chaos;* the central meaning is "state of confusion," and its closest synonyms are *jumble* and the ever-popular *mishmash,* which is a fifteenth-century English word and not, as often considered, a Yiddishism. (But as copy editors say of *mishmash,* "Funny, it doesn't *look* English.")

The English have used *muddle* to powerful political effect. Edward Stanley, Earl of Derby, told the House of Lords in 1864—even as John Bright was predicting the Union would muddle through—that "The foreign policy of the noble Earl [Russell] . . . may be summed up in two short homely but expressive words: 'meddle and muddle.' "

Republicans today love to meddle in Democratic muddle. But though *muddle* was created out of *mud,* let there be no mudslinging; as Adlai Stevenson advised, "He who slings mud generally loses ground."

You discuss the various uses and meanings of the word "muddle." Your report was fairly exhaustive, but one slightly different meaning you didn't touch on exists. Having tended bar for ten years, I've read a number of bar manuals and drink recipe books. In every recipe for an Old Fashioned that I've ever read, the mixologist is instructed, after combining granulated sugar, bitters and an orange slice, to "muddle well." Better bar supply stores even sell a "muddler," which looks like a large pestle and is made of wood. In this sense, I've always expected that what was meant was to mash, mix, and generally turn the ingredients into a fine muddle. A few cubes, a couple ounces of bourbon, and Voila. (However, the secret to my really fine Old Fashioned, a drink hopelessly out of fashion, is a small, quick dollop of sweet vermouth.)

Timothy J. Johnson
Empire, Michigan

I was disappointed that you omitted the "Old Fashioned" cocktail and its complex recipe. This always begins, "Muddle 1/2 lump of sugar saturated with 1 dash Aromatic Bitters, etc. . . ." There was even a special bar utensil called a <u>Muddler</u> which was used for that drink alone. A status piece of equipment for any Art Deco bartender, the muddler (rather resembling the pestle of an under-endowed bull), was often fashioned from crystal, Laliquely frosted or clear, or, for the less opulent, from hardwood. Of course, soon, many began ordering <u>double</u> Old Fashioneds since, that way, the poor barman was saved the rather absurd task of trying to cut a sugar cube in half. This naturally led to the appearance of the Double Old Fashioned glass, which is now the standard for "On-the-Rocks." But I digress: The actual act of <u>muddling</u> consisted of thoroughly smashing the Bitters-soaked sugar cube in the bottom of the glass with the muddler. No, a simple spoonful of bar sugar would not do, for the ritual of assembling an Old Fashioned had acquired deep subliminal meanings, akin to the formalism of the Japanese tea ceremony.

Robert O. Vaughn
West New York, New Jersey

The Smartest Word

What idea is it that comes to mind when you hear the noun *intelligence*?

Brains? Wit? Perception, understanding, ability to figure things out, to reason abstractly? If that's your first reaction, you are in the center of six centuries of the meaning of the word, and may be using it as an attributive noun to modify *tests* and *quotients*.

You are also behind the times. The sense that has more frequently sprung to mind in this generation deals with "the gathering and evaluation of information, especially about an enemy." This brand of intelligence has agents, agencies, officers, operatives, committees and a community all its own.

The Latin *legere* is the root, and with elections impending, may be the root of the year: "to select, gather, catch with the eye." This choosy verb gave rise to a classy family of words, from *elegant* to *legend,* and none more elegant or legendary than *intelligence* in its sense of "data drawn by derring-do."

That espionage-product sense surfaced in the sixteenth century with the use of *intelligencer* as a synonym for "spy"; diplomats were sources then, the historian Abraham Fleming reported in 1587, praising the Queen's "intelligences from hir ambassadors." The diarist Samuel Pepys wrote of a House of Commons member who complained "that he was allowed but £700 a-year for intelligence," and in 1799, the Duke of Wellington's dispatches cautioned, "If our intelligence is true . . ."

So, if your first reaction to the word called up the cloaks of John le Carré and the daggers of David Wise, you think you are entitled to a semanticist's satisfied smirk?

Forget it. Not even spooks use the word to mean the product of spying anymore. "In the real world," writes Herbert E. Meyer in his book *Real-World Intelligence* (the hyphenated noun phrase used attributively means "practical, neither abstract nor academic"), "*intelligence* . . . has come to mean information that not only has been selected and collected, but also analyzed, evaluated and distributed to meet the unique policymaking needs of one particular enterprise. . . . In short, intelligence has become a management tool."

Gee, there goes the fun; no sooner does the combative sense of the word gain dominance than it is being replaced by a more diffuse, sophisticated sense. Change in language is inexorable, but it seems to be speeding up.

Mr. Meyer, who was vice chairman of the National Intelligence Council in William J. Casey's Central Intelligence Agency, holds that the word's meaning is now understood in a wide-ranging, beyond-spying sense as it is being absorbed into the everyday life of strategic planners in business: "It is this broadening of the concept of intelligence—from stealing secrets . . . to 'organized information'—that has freed business to leap forward in the use of intelligence."

If his intelligence is true, as we used to tell the Duke of Wellington, business budgets for detecting the influence of economics, science and politics on what used to be simple commerce will soon exceed £700 a year—without so much as a Pepys out of any oversight committee. And so to bed.

In one part of the world, an associated noun has not changed its meaning at all. Muscovites still use the word *intelligentsia.* That word means "intellectual elite, cultural vanguard," and carries a connotation of snobbery in the United States but is not pejorative in the Soviet Union for good political reason. Mikhail Gorbachev is appealing to those writers and artists to help him oust party members from power. The word was first recorded prior to 1907 by the English journalist Maurice Baring, who wrote in *A Year in Russia* about the fear professed by some revolutionaries of "a general massacre of the educated bourgeoisie, the so-called 'Intelligenzia.' " *The Economist* of London has popularized a spinoff to describe the perk-happy party elite: *privilegentsia.*

Smiles of a Moscow Night

"You said you were for *peaceful coexistence,*" Mikhail Gorbachev was reported by *Time* magazine to have told Ronald Reagan. "Then why not put [those words] in the communiqué?"

I don't know if that's exactly what he said. *Newsweek* quoted the Soviet leader directly as saying, "You told me last Sunday you were for peace. Then why are you against using this language in the final statement?" Both newsmagazines were relying on reports of a translation, and perhaps relied on different interpreters or different secondhand accounts. But the gist was the same, and both referred to a document, which the Soviet leader pushed across the table to the United States President, that contained the phrase *peaceful coexistence.*

"Why not, Mr. President, why not?" *Newsweek* said he insisted.

"Well," said Mr. Reagan (and there is a strong likelihood that he used that word, which he uses to start many sentences), "we don't think this language is right."

"What about you, George [Shultz]? What about you, Frank [Carlucci]? Why not this language?"

After a five-minute recess in which the Americans conferred about the phrase suggested by Mr. Gorbachev, the President returned to the table to say, "I'm sorry. This language is not acceptable." That, presumably, is exactly what he said; both accounts have it that way, suggesting that the room was wired, or that reporters were briefed by the same background source, or that the sources were different but relied on the same notes.

When the epochal meeting of true minds is troubled by the impediment of language, that is a matter for close examination in this space. What, indeed, was bothering Mr. Reagan's advisers in the seemingly innocent phrase suggested by the Soviets?

"This is the détente language of the 70's," Secretary of State Shultz said, according to *Newsweek,* in the five-minute caucus, explaining his opposition to the words. "This is the Kissinger talk that didn't get us anything. We're beyond détente now."

Kissinger talk? No. Lenin talk, perhaps. In 1920, the founding father of the Soviet Union spoke glowingly of what was translated as *"peaceful cohabitation* with the peoples, with the workers and peasants of all nations"; two years later, at the Ninth All-Russian Congress of Soviets, that phrase was translated as *peaceful coexistence,* roughly synonymous but a tad less intimate—suggesting living alongside but not necessarily together.

Nikita Khrushchev picked up the phrase in the 1950's and made it his own, calling it in 1961 "a form of intense economic, political and ideological struggle of the proletariat against the aggressive forces of imperialism in the international arena." After the "kitchen debate" with then-Vice President Nixon in 1959, the Soviet leader had written: "The states which decide to adopt the path of peaceful coexistence repudiate the use of force in any form. . . ." He accused Mr. Nixon of attempting "to find a contradiction between the Soviet people's professions of their readiness to coexist peacefully with the capitalist states and the slogans posted in the shops of our factories calling for higher labor productivity in order to insure the speediest victory of Communism."

Trusting Americans soon interpreted the phrase as meaning, "Live and let live"; Adlai Stevenson called *peaceful coexistence* an alternative to "coextinction."

When the party line turned to sweetness and light in the détente of 1972, those of us who went with Mr. Nixon and Mr. Kissinger to Moscow were alert to the history of the phrase. If I recall correctly, we went wacky over *détente,* a French diplomatic term for "relaxation of tensions," one long step short of *entente,* "agreement," but generally steered clear of what the Russians were calling *peaceful coexistence.* (We fell for plenty that year, but we were linguistically skeptical.)

In the mid-1970's, as the Soviets moved to take advantage of a Watergate-weakened United States, the Nixon *démarche,* or beginning step (not to be confused with *gambit,* "tricky opening move"), lost its charm; President Ford officially expunged *détente* from his speeches. Then came the Afghanistan invasion, the evil empire and a derogation by right-wingers of the Nixon-Kissinger era of détente as too trusting.

Ironically, when the Reagan-Shultz policy zigged, the Nixon-Kissinger view zagged; in 1988, the détenteniks of the early 70's were cautioning the evil-empiricists of the early 80's to slow the movement toward deep cuts in strategic arms without sufficient verification, conventional-arms reduction and "linkage" to Soviet behavior.

If Secretary Schultz did characterize the use of the old Leninist language as "Kissinger talk," that was the new détentenik calling the old détentenik foolable. If that was a fanciful description of what Mr. Shultz said, the mood in that five-minute caucus was still ironic: There were the President's advisers saving him from the presumed language, but not the policy, of the Nixon era.

At least, so goes my linguistic-strategic thesis. It is reinforced by the refusal of the Reagan advisers in Moscow to go along with a pledge not to "interfere in the internal affairs of others," which Americans used to think meant invading or subverting foreign governments, but which the Soviets read as meddling in the field of human rights.

Most significant, the Reagan summiteers eschewed any general statement of principles, issued in lieu of a specific agreement, that could be called a *framework.* The phrase *conceptual framework* was pure Kissinger, and statements of principles in the past that could be interpreted in several ways were the source of much right-wing criticism when Reagan was Reagan (in the current right-wing vernacular). And George Shultz, who wisely stopped the President from using a Lenin phrase, most especially did not want anybody to use a Kissinger word.

President Reagan was lucky that he didn't accept the insertion of that polysemantic concept—"peaceful coexistence"—into the bilateral statement issued at the end of the Moscow summit. Mr. Gorbachev was obviously disappointed that he failed where Mr. Brezhnev succeeded. It is true, unfortunately, that during his 1972 Moscow visit Mr. Nixon signed an Executive Agreement called "Declaration of Basic Principles of Mutual Relations between the USA and USSR," where both parties agreed that "in the nuclear age there is no alternative to conducting their mutual relations on the basis of peaceful coexistence."

> Charles T. Baroch
> Chevy Chase, Maryland

Recalling the Summit of 1972, you said, "Those of us who went with Mr. Nixon and Mr. Kissinger to Moscow were alert to the history of the phrase. If I recall correctly, we . . . steered clear of what the Russians were calling peaceful coexistence. (We fell for plenty that year, but we were linguistically skeptical.)"

Unfortunately, you do not recall correctly. President Nixon and General Secretary Brezhnev signed the "Basic Principles of U.S.-Soviet Relations," which stated that there was no alternative to peaceful coexistence. The ambiguity of that principle was used by the Soviets to justify military intervention in Angola, South Yemen, Ethiopia, Cambodia and Afghanistan. Secretary of State George Shultz was on the mark when he advised President Reagan not to repeat the error of Nixon and Kissinger.

> Arthur Macy Cox
> Secretary to the American
>   Committee on U.S.-Soviet
>   Relations
> Washington, D.C.

Back in the 30s Christian fundamentalists would have referred to philosopher John Dewey as the "evil empiricist," without the hyphen, but in this happy time of glasnost *"evil-empiricist" is simply a solecism.*

There is no etymological linkage between "empire" and "empiricist"; the former comes from the Latin "imperium" and the latter from the Greek "enpeira," to experiment. The words look alike only in English.

> Richard Akagi
> New York, New York

I hope "evil-empiricist" is a joke. Isn't "empiricist" related to "empirical" rather than to "empire"?

> Ivan V. Klumpar
> Lexington, Massachusetts

Sound Bite, Define Yourself!

When, weeks from now, the hurry-up "definitive" history of the 1988 campaign is written, what word or phrase will emerge as the favorite locution of the election? What short, punchy sound bite most helps this campaign to define itself?

It's a tie. Sorry, Mr. Bush's *furlough* and *I am that man* are fading fast, though we may hear more from *a thousand points of light;* Mr. Dukakis's *tough choices* and *competence, not ideology* are down the memory drain; among pundits, the *polling bounce* or *post-convention bump* faded fast, while tired *spin doctors* have long ago thrown their *spending caps* in the air.

The joint winners of cliché of the election year are *sound bite* and the reflexive use of *define.*

A *sound bite,* as every news junkie and couch potato knows, is a snippet of film that catches the rhetorical highlight of a speech, a quotation that is bright, snappy and memorable, and never mind the boring profundity. The campaign was summarized in a headline over an essay by David R. Gergen in *U.S. News & World Report:* THE POLITICS OF SOUND BITES.

Who coined the phrase and when? I am distressed to report that my fellow etymologists are at a loss for words (good title for a book on uncertain etymology).

I ran a search of the computerized files to get some clues on usage in the 1970's. Curious; no luck. The first citation is dated June 22, 1980, in a piece by Sandy Kyle Bain in *The Washington Post* reporting on the education in television being given candidates by William F. Rhatican.

"Remember that any editor watching," said Rhatican to a pin-striped political hopeful, "needs a concise, 30-second sound bite. Anything more than that, you're losing them."

That was not the sound of a phrase being coined; it was the sound of a locution known to insiders and experts being spoken to outsiders. For an earlier citation, I reached over to London, to the newly computerized *Oxford English Dictionary.* Surely, that venerable but vital institution, on the verge of publishing an updated amalgamation of its masterpiece and its supplements, would have a trade-press use.

No luck; the best their editors could offer was Rhatican in 1980. I called Bill Rhatican, now senior vice president for public affairs of the Advertising Council. "I remember you from the Nixon Administration," he said cordially. "You used to leave every meeting after thirty minutes, saying that either the problem was insoluble or the wrong people were in the room. Speeded things up."

Hastily, I put it to him about *sound bite;* did he claim it for his own? "I doubt that I coined it," said Rhatican, obviously a believer in truth-in-advertising. "The phrase was in the air. I used it in a lecture I gave in the mid-70's advising political candidates on the use of television: If you wander all over the place in your statements, you won't provide pithy sound bites for TV."

That puts us in the mid-70's; to reach back further, I called Dan Schorr, now senior news analyst for National Public Radio, who remembered its use in the early 1960's when he was with CBS News. "It came out of the editing room, in the days before videotape. When the producer saw the excerpt he wanted, he'd tell the film editor, 'Take that bite'; out of longer interviews, the bite would be thirty to forty-five seconds."

But why *sound* bite? If it was film, why not *sight* bite, which was also a rhyme? Would it not, as some have guessed, have come out of radio?

Sid Davis, a veteran NBC radio newsman who is now with the Voice of America, waves me off that line of folk etymology. "In radio, we called the short live takes *actualities.* I think *sound bites* came in during the early 70's, in the transition from film to tape. A piece of film was a *clip,* but a piece of tape was a *bite.*" But why sound, not sight? In composite film, the sound ran twenty-eight frames behind the picture; on videotape, the sound and picture are on the same frame. Maybe that's significant; I'll entertain mail on this subject from Lexicographic Irregulars, Film & Tape Editing Division.

Avoid orthographic confusion: Spell it *bite,* the sort you would take out of an apple or a piece of tape, and not *byte,* a computer term, of uncertain origin, for "character" (and send that etymon in if you have it, too), which in turn is confused with *bit,* a smaller unit of information, coming from a shortening of *binary digit.*

The term may be used affectionately by news editors, but is often used derisively by sit-down commentators. In 1984, television's Roger Mudd denounced a campaign he felt was made up of "sound bites and photo opportunities" (the latter, a Ron Ziegler coinage). In 1988, when Senator Lloyd Bentsen savaged Senator Dan Quayle with his "you're no Jack Kennedy" riposte, ABC's Jeff Greenfield used the term with a neutral connotation: "the biggest sound bite of the night." But print journalists, who have been using shorter quotes themselves, like to sneer at television coverage as a collection of inconsequential, sensationalistic, sloganeering *sound bites.*

Now to the cowinner, the reflexive use of *define.* A reflexive verb takes both a subject and object with the same referents, as when a winning debater tells his handlers, "I defined myself," and the loser admits in private, "I clobbered myself."

"The new President ably and attractively defined himself," wrote *The Washington Post* about Jimmy Carter's inaugural address in 1977. *The New York Times,* exactly four years later, wrote of Ronald Reagan, "But in defining himself to the world, the 40th President of the United States chose the role of moderate in a script of gradualism." Evidently the titans of editorialism like to apply the verb to public figures making self-introductory speeches, and its use blossomed in 1988.

"This convention," wrote John Balzar of the *Los Angeles Times* from Atlanta in July 1988, "has had the purpose of introducing Dukakis to the public." Then the reporter showed his sensitivity to cliché: "Defining himself, as they say in political argot." A refinement came in defining oneself *against* or *relative to* someone else: "Michael Dukakis has been allowed to define himself relative to Jesse Jackson," complained New Hampshire's Republican Governor John H. Sununu to the newsman Jim Lehrer that summer.

The vogue *define* is not always used reflexively. The Democratic pollster Peter D. Hart used its present participle, *defining,* to modify *event,* thus describing a major change that produces political results.

And George Bush, in debate, held that "what I've had to do is to define not just my position, but to define his."

What does the word mean? ("O.K., lexicographer, define *define.*") One sense is "to state the meaning of"; another is "to characterize, to describe the essential quality"; a third is "to delimit, specify, fix the boundaries, make clear the edges." In its reflexive political use, *to define yourself* means "to set forth your goals and values vividly," or in less idealistic terms, "to sharpen the impression of your personality and approach in a way that is memorably appealing to most voters."

Nobody ever said such self-portraiture was easy. While Mr. Dukakis failed to define himself until the last stages of his campaign, Mr. Bush redefined himself—from wimp to tiger—in what must have been a wrenching psychological effort. Alan Watts, the American philosopher and writer on Zen, was quoted in 1961: "Trying to define yourself is like trying to bite your own teeth."

I am a television reporter and producer, have been since the age of film.

About sound bites . . . or sometimes "sound pops" (an NBC usage, I think) . . . the striking thing to me is how quickly they are shrinking. I have heard bites as brief as four seconds in network reporting of political stories this year, and the average is probably not much more than 10 seconds. The 30-second bite your friend Rhatican was recommending in 1980 is extremely rare these days.

The convention of television sound is three words a second, so at ten seconds the typical tidbit of information is 30 words, perhaps as little as 12. This gives the advantage to people who speak quickly while articulating each word. I sometimes think successful politicians will begin to speak in condensed forms, like the old telegrams and cables, the better to exploit their alloted time.

I have also had successful experience with using very long passes of sound in big-time TV. It works when a person has something interesting to say and says it with some conviction, even passion. It is possible to trust a long sound bite when the speaker seems actually to mean and feel what he is saying. Sometimes the people who do that are politicians, most often they are not. The shrinking time given to politicians to talk on the air may reflect their failings as much as the medium's.

> *Tom DeVries*
> *Oakland, California*

I can confirm my former CNN colleague Dan Schorr that the phrase was around in the 60's, before the advent of tape. When I joined the staff of WSB-TV in Atlanta as a part-time film editor in the early 70's, it was in common use, both as "sound bite" and, alternatively, as "sound pop."

Unlike today's videotape technology, where the editing process is electronic and the tape itself is not physically cut, the first step in the film editing process was to actually tear the shots apart by hand. Later the film was spliced cleanly.

Given the reputation of newsfilm editors, who spent long periods inside darkened rooms alone, wearing white cotton gloves dotted with bits of film emulsion scraped off the film stock and talking to a viewing screen as they cut, it may be that, in primordial editing times, one used his teeth to split the film of the interview apart from the rest of the reel. A bite.

It was not a "sight bite" because the filmed interview was most generally a _talking head_, and the bite looked the same as that which preceded and followed it and eventually wound up unused on the original reel as _trims_. It was marked on the _sound reader_ (a device that read the magnetic sound track recorded 28 frames behind picture), with masking tape, until the reporter or producer would verify that what the editor had marked was, indeed, the sound bite.

At that point, the editor would physically cut the film at the tape mark, and hang it on the rack like a smoked eel, to await final splicing.

As part of the final splicing process, the magnetic audio track was _wiped_ using a small magnet passed over the film, erasing sound while picture remained. Improperly done, this process led to an audible crackle on the sound track, hence the term "sound pop."

Since the audio track was always 28 frames behind the picture, 28 frames, or about one second, of picture stayed behind so that the final audio selected could be heard, this effect, where the subject could be seen talking but not heard, was referred to as _lip flap_. For the technically sophisticated, a _lip flapper eliminator_ was available, a piece of equipment that displaced the audio track before editing so that cuts in the film were synchronous to both picture and sound, then replaced the audio track to its 28-frame lag after editing was complete and before broadcast. We didn't use those in day-to-day news in Atlanta, generally completing the reel with about enough time for the projectionist to thread it up on the _film chain_, the movie projector that faced into a television camera. Broadcast snobs would call the film chain a _telecine_. Anyone who did that in Atlanta was obviously a foreigner.

On a big story, or one where the sound bite was actually two bites edited together, producing a _jump cut_, we'd put a _cutaway_ shot on a _B-Roll_, a separate reel of film that ran in another film chain. The director would cue the B-Roll to cover the jump cut, eliminating the twitch of the interviewee's face where the edit took place. Cutaways persist with us even in the age of tape, as the movie _Broadcast News_ pointed out with phony dramaturgy. B-Roll is still with us as well, though there are probably few stations that still have the old B-projector still hooked up, as a term for the footage that goes around the talking head; Boston Harbor was George Bush's B-Roll. I can't recall what Michael Dukakis's B-Roll may have been, which may be one reason he's back in Boston. But it's been a long campaign, it may just be me.

John D. Hillis
General Manager
Rainbow News 12 Company
Woodbury, New York

A soundbite is called a soundbite because the term refers <u>only</u> to the audio contents of the bite. In other words, it relates to what the subject is saying— what the print media call a quote.

The video counterpart of a soundbite is generally called a shot.

Spanish is a language with a tradition of convolutions, and some of our interviewees show a penchant for never-ending phrases rich in connectives, clauses and subclauses.

Fortunately, in the past few years, some Hispanic leaders, especially the younger politicians, have understood the value of brief, to-the-point answers. The advent of the Spanish language soundbite (no translation for the term so far) has made editing easier and faster and our political coverage more agile.

As for the print journalists who sneer at soundbites, they should be reminded that they are the electronic version, albeit reduced, of the excerpts and quotes the newspapers have been using for centuries. Whether shorter is better than shortest can be a matter of argument, but the difference is relative, at best.

Diego Olive
Executive News Producer
WNJU–Channel 47
Teterboro, New Jersey

True, interviews or comments from "real" people in the audio world are called "actualities," which unintentionally casts a rather suspicious light on the rest of the program and its participants. Be that as it may, an excerpt from an "actuality" might still be called a "bite." A "bite" is a brief excerpt that either contributes a pithy point, sets up a straw man to be swept away by an upcoming segment or comment, or puts a dramatic or humorous button on a segment or story.

That sound on film is 26 frames ahead (not 28 frames behind) of its picture, whereas on video it occupies the same "frame" although a separate "track," also has nothing to do with the term. A red herring heading down a primrose path. "Bite" describes only the quality of being an excerpt whatever the medium, and, at least in my work, an excerpt which rarely exceeds thirty seconds in length. After thirty seconds, a bite becomes a full-fledged "interview."

Why "sound bite" and not "sight bite" is self-evident if you're talking about radio, and equally self-evident in film and video, when you think about it. The value of the particular piece of film or tape (audio or video) lies in what is being said by whom. To paraphrase the master: "The say's the thing."

It should also be noted that in documentaries the "sound bite" is often used to "voice-over" other scenes, a further demonstration of the dominance of sound over its accompanying visual, typically a dull "talking head." A "sight bite," if there were such a thing, would be Michael Dukakis riding the tank; George Bush sweeping his granddaughter into his arms; Dan Quayle looking cool in his

National Guard uniform. Up to now, film and video editors would refer to such visual moments as "cuts," "clips," "snips," shots," "scenes," or "cutaways" (referring to the act of cutting away from the master scene and not to any resemblance to formal dress), but having tossed "sight bite" onto the jargoning table, you may be seeing and hearing more of it.

Ed Schultz
New York, New York

As a television reporter who has been singling out sound bites for fifteen years, I always assumed we called them "bites" because the good ones had *bite. You might want to chew on that for a while.*

Lynn Cullen
Pittsburgh, Pennsylvania

When we first began using videotape in the late sixties (at the CBS News Bureau in Washington), no one ever said tape clip, *even though in the beginning tape, too, was actually cut, with a razor blade. For a while we used a lot of different words to describe an excerpt taken from a news event. Excerpt itself was one word used, or chunk, or bit. I think bits and bites were both used for a while. Then, with no vote, it just became sound bite.*

As to the big question—why sound *bite, not sight bite or some other visual reference—there's a very simple explanation. Television news uses these excerpts two ways—* with *sound, that is, you hear George Bush say "read my lips—no new taxes," and* without *sound, that is, you see George Bush, but the reporter or anchor does a "voice-over," telling you about the event and just using the picture of George Bush talking to illustrate it. In the days of film this differentiation was sound-on-film (SOF) versus voice-over film (VO or VOF).*

Sylvia Westerman
New York, New York

I should point out that I never seriously thought about the origin of sound bite *until I read your piece, but to me its meaning suggests the part of a videotape segment that is highlighted or justified by the sound. Sound bites are also called* sound on tape *in media jargon.*

In television news, videotape segments are regularly run silent, or with ambient or background sound, as a reporter or anchor person talks from the studio. (Such a technique is called a voice-over *in the industry.) An anchor would talk about President-elect George Bush appearing somewhere as viewers see him appearing there. Then, after a few moments, the anchor would stop talking and Mr. Bush would say, "Read my lips." "Read my lips" would be the sound bite, when the sound from the videotape becomes the focus.*

A reporter or producer would usually only choose to run a sound bite if it was interesting, significant or memorable, hence the term's evolution to its current definition. Sound bites are now, as James M. Perry wrote in The Wall Street Journal of September 23, "the carefully rehearsed zingers that get on the evening news and leave a lasting impression in the minds of the voters," or, I should add, any other viewer.

Beyond the concerns of rhetoric, there is a very practical reason for identifying a sound bite as such: The name lets the audio engineer know that he or she will have to raise the sound level of the videotape at the appropriate time, when the primary sound source changes from voice-over to sound on tape.

I imagine a sound bite could indeed be called a sight bite, as you suggest—since television is nothing without images—but in this case, for editorial as well as practical reasons, sound seems more germane to the concept.

Gerard Harrington
Kingston, New York

You ask, "Why sound (bite), not sight?"

Because the bite is selected for the sound heard, usually spoken words, and not for the pictures seen. In the mid-60s, when I worked as a writer and producer for the Huntley-Brinkley Report, it was called a sound cut. Bite became common at NBC some time later.

In radio, it was common in the 70s to refer to a cut or a bite without preceding it with sound, for the obvious reason that there was no need to make a distinction because radio has nothing but sound.

The difference of 28 frames between the sound track and the picture is accounted for by the distance between the lens aperture and the sound-recording head on the Auricon camera, which was standard in news film operations. It was corrected by transferring the sound from a magnetic strip (called a stripe) on the edge of the film to a magnetic tape of the same width as the film. That was called fullcoat. The film and the fullcoat were then marked for synchronization in the projector.

The Times and many other publications persist to this day in referring to the pictures seen on television news programs as film or film clips. It is, of course, videotape, and has been since the mid-70s, when nearly all TV news organizations switched to what many of them call E-N-G, for electronic news gathering.

Richard P. Hunt
New York, New York

I can offer the following guidance on two issues raised in your sound-bite piece:

• "Sound"-bite is used rather than "sight bite" because in tape/film editing, it is the audio component that generally determines the segment to be selected. To make sense and not to be discordant, the audio must begin and end at a coherent point. The video does not have such constraints and can simply tag along. In "sight bites," cases where the video determines the segment as in the <u>Challenger</u> disaster or Greg Louganis bumping his head, the audio is turned down or edited out. We care not what the NASA engineer or Jim McKay were babbling about when these events occurred. So "sound bite" seems right for composite video/ audio.

• The term "byte," a unit of random access memory composed of eight bits, was introduced by IBM in the mid '60s in connection with their computer series, System/360. Professor Frederick Brooks now at the University of North Carolina was associated with the development of this machine and can probably give you information as to byte's origins.

*Larry Snyder
Department of Computer
    Science
University of Washington
Seattle, Washington*

Nothing uncertain about the origin of byte. It was unleashed on 7th April, 1964, by IBM in its announcement of the 360 computer. It was already in use within IBM as it developed the architecture and software of the system. The man in charge was B. O. Evans, but the term was coined a little lower down in the organization, possibly by Larry Cantor.

Until the 360, computers consisted either of 6-bit characters, or of words of anywhere from 36 to 72 bits. IBM needed a standard 8 to replace the wide spread of grouped bits.

*Norman Sanders
Drammen, Norway*

While the origin of the term "byte" may be uncertain, there is an explanation for the variant spelling. As you pointed out, "bit" is a contraction of "binary digit." A "byte" is a collection of bits, often 8, which are dealt with collectively by some portion of a computer's hardware a bite-at-a-time. Fearful that the "e" in "bite" might get lost or, worse yet, be deleted by some editor somewhere, it was decided to substitute the "y" for the "i." I don't know where or when that decision was made, but probably it was done by a committee of IEEE (Institute of Electrical and Electronics Engineers) or its predecessor, the IRE (Institute of Radio Engineers). Note the "s" on "Electronics"; some engineers under-stand how the language is supposed to be used!

Additional trivia: A half a byte, usually 4 bits, is called a "nibble"; a computer with 640K bytes of memory has 655,360 bytes, not 640,000 because, in this usage, a K is 1024; a byte is 8 bits, but the memory in an IBM Personal Computer has 9 bits per byte to allow for error checking.

Arthur I. Larky
Professor
Lehigh University
Bethlehem, Pennsylvania

As you correctly note, a bit is a binary digit. It's, of course, a little thing, but it is also the past tense of bite. It is a pun on this sense of the word that led to the coin-age byte. Any doubts on this etymology should be laid to rest by the evidence of another neologism, nybble (I'm not making this up, so help me). A nybble is, as it should be, smaller than a byte. In fact, it's half the size—four bits.

The word "nybble" was introduced with the IBM 360 family of computers in the early seventies to describe the way that they perform "packed" decimal arithmetic.

I'm a little less certain about the word "byte." It was certainly already in use around 1960, having arisen with the first "big" IBM scientific computers. All did pure binary arithmetic and one bit was an impractically small unit of data to talk about.

Although it remained in use, the word "byte" didn't really catch on for 15 years. The reason is probably just an accident of taste. One byte can be written with 8 binary digits or, more economically, with two hexadecimal (base 16) digits. The latter is universally preferred today but, in the old days, computer people always used octal (base 8) representations when writing out the long binary numbers they dealt with. One octal digit corresponds to three binary digits so the octal representation of a long binary number doesn't mesh at all with its division into bytes. The preference for octal over hexadecimal probably resulted from the fact that the octal system is written with the digits 0 through 7, whereas the hexadecimal system requires not only the digits 0 through 9, but six additional digits, now always A through F. (It's a long time ago, but I seem to remember that those "big" machines handled their numbers in 36-bit chunks. That also might account for the bias toward octal and away from bytes.)

Nowadays, the big computers use 64 bit numbers and whatever generation of PC you're using, its microprocessor is 8-, 16- or 32-bit. The byte is unequivo-cally the right unit to use, and despite the discomfort we all feel with the digits A through F, we've all learned to "talk hex."

Michael Engber
New York, New York

The term BYTE was suggested first by Dr. Werner Buchholz of IBM Pough-keepsie during the development of the 701 series of computers.

> Richard G. Counihan
> Boulder, Colorado

As for the term bit *for binary digit: Claude Shannon (in* The Mathematical Theory of Communication, *University of Illinois Press, 1949, p. 32, itself a reprint of Shannon's article in* Bell System Technical Journal, *July and October 1948) attributes the word to be a suggestion by John W. Tukey (Emeritus Professor of Statistics, Princeton University).*

> Stefan Shrier
> Alexandria, Virginia

To those of us in the nerd biz (otherwise known as the computer industry), the origin of the word "byte" is not at all uncertain: It is a contraction of "BinarY TErm," as "bit" comes from Binary digIT." More interesting is the origin of "nybble," a term sometimes applied to half a byte. I suspect this is purely fanciful.

> Grant E. Hicks
> Newton, Massachusetts

Special Relationship

Special Relationships (Atheneum, $19.95) is the title of a book of memoirs by Henry Brandon, long of London's *Sunday Times,* now dean of the corps of foreign correspondents who make Washington their home.

I peruse memoirs like these for clues to today's diplomatic or bureaucratic language. Sure enough, Henry has a beaut: the transmission from American to English of *cost-effective,* brought to the Pentagon by Robert McNamara and his "whiz kids" of the Kennedy era.

Members of the British defense staff who were visiting Washington needed to know the latest lingo; John Thompson, a defense aide to the British Ambassador, realized he had to impart the meaning of this hot new hyphenated phrase to his colleagues.

"At a dinner he gave for them," writes Mr. Brandon, Thompson "therefore served three different red wines and asked them to tell him how, according to their taste, they rated each. After they had done that he told them how much each cost and then he asked them which, taking the cost into consideration, they would buy." Concludes the eminent reporter: "The wine samples did what wine does not always do, it cleared their minds, and thus *cost-effectiveness* entered the English vocabulary."

What about *special relationship* itself? That phrase is trotted out every time a new American President meets a British Prime Minister. The source is Winston Churchill.

"We should not abandon our special relationship with the United States and Canada," the wartime leader told the House of Commons on November 7, 1945, "about the atomic bomb." The following March, at Westminster College in Fulton, Missouri, he sealed the phrase into diplolingo with this passage: "Neither the sure prevention of war nor the continuous rise of world organization will be gained without what I have called the fraternal association of the English-speaking peoples. This means a *special relationship* between the British Commonwealth and Empire and the United States of America."

With most speakers, that would have become known as "the special relationship speech." In fact, it was buried in what is known as "the Iron Curtain speech"; Churchill had coinages to spare.

Stab in the Back

Familiar phrases can have hidden resonances; a figure of speech can be innocent to me but drive you right up the wall. Take *stab in the back*.

London's *Sunday Telegraph* quoted an unnamed American official (actually an unidentified official—the person has a name) criticizing an alliance-straining policy of West Germany's Chancellor Helmut Kohl in these words: "We are used to such NATO antics from the alliance's wets like Belgium and the Netherlands, but to experience a stab in the back like this from the Germans really does shake my faith in NATO. . . ." The headline in the paper WAS A "STAB IN THE BACK" BY NATO'S NEW WETS. (*Wets* is British for *doves;* our *superdoves* are their *wringing wets.*)

To most Americans, a *stab in the back* is merely a dirty double-cross from an unexpected source. To Soviet officials, it is also used in that neutral way: Reuters reported recently from Moscow that "official spokesmen have said the Georgian affair"—a nationalist demonstration that provoked a police riot—"was 'a stab in the back for perestroika.' " The infinitive phrase *to stab*

in the back was first used figuratively by George Bernard Shaw in a *New York Times Magazine* article in 1916.

But to Central Europeans, especially Germans, that phrase has far more sinister reverberations.

When Italy attacked France at the start of World War II, French Premier Paul Reynaud cabled President Franklin D. Roosevelt for help, with a message that was translated by our State Department in these words: "This very hour, another dictatorship has stabbed France in the back." The French leader, furious at Mussolini's duplicity, used "stab in the back" to describe the type of action that Americans would later characterize as a "sneak attack."

The State Department submitted a draft paragraph about the Italian attack to be added to a speech F.D.R. was making that day to a graduating class at the University of Virginia in Charlottesville; the President (probably without the help of speechwriter Archibald MacLeish, and hours before he received the cable from Reynaud) accepted the bland insertion but added a memorable line about a "stab in the back."

Democratic political leaders suggested, however, that such an inflammatory phrase might alienate Italian-Americans in that fall's presidential election, and Under Secretary of State Sumner Welles recommended against it as well, arguing that a chance still existed to separate Mussolini from Hitler.

According to William R. Emerson, the director of the F.D.R. Library in Hyde Park, New York, the reading copy of F.D.R.'s speech is missing; we do not know whether the President considered those objections and modified his line to use *struck* instead of *stab.* Using a dramatic date-first construction (a rhetorical device he would repeat in his call for a declaration of war after the attack on Pearl Harbor), he said: "On this 10th day of June, 1940, the hand that held the dagger has struck it into the back of its neighbor."

What was so inflammatory about this phrase, even if *struck* slightly softened *stab,* to cause such hesitation among Roosevelt's political and diplomatic advisers?

Dolchstoss in den Rücken was the German version of the phrase, used by Prussian officers to explain their defeat in 1918; the phrase and the charge were revived by Adolf Hitler in the 1930's, assigning the cause of Germany's World War defeat to German Jews.

Hitler knew that the phrase had special meaning to Germans: In the medieval legend of the *Nibelungenlied,* the hero, Siegfried, exhausted from being pursued, stopped to drink at a spring and was murdered by a villain thrusting a spear into his back.

This spawned the *Dolchstosslegende* and made Germans culturally sensitive to the duplicity of a stab in the back. (To a lesser degree, Americans remember the shooting in the back of the romantic desperado Jesse James.)

What's in a phrase? Plenty; if your purpose is to roil an opponent, go ahead and squeeze your verbal trigger, but be sure you know the size of the gun you're shooting.

You state that "the infinitive phrase was first used figuratively . . . in 1916."

Not true. The Century Dictionary (Vol. V, p. 5883) cites the usage of this phrase. While no date is mentioned, it must be long before 1916, since, as you well know, the Century was published in 1890.

Charles F. Gill
Williamsburg, Virginia

Why don't you hyphenate stab-in-the-back as Fowler tells you to? He says: "It (the hyphen) is always used in such phrasal compounds as stick-in-the-mud, ne'er-do-well, happy-go-lucky."

Larry Churchill
Bernardsville, New Jersey

There is more to the Siegfried story. Siegfried had made himself invulnerable by bathing in the blood of a dragon he had slain, except that a leaf from a linden tree fell between his shoulder blades, leaving one vulnerable spot. Although

never attaining the same degree of proverbiality, that was Siegfried's "Achilles'
heel." All this was confided to treacherous Hagen by Siegfried's wife Kriemhild,
who went so far as to sew a mark in his clothing for Hagen's special protective
care, thus creating a perfect target for his murderous spear. After marrying
Attila the Hun, Kriemhild slew Hagen with Siegfried's sword at Attila's court,
before being herself slain by Hildebrand. A bloody mess, if ever there was one!

Louis Marck
New York, New York

Suffer, Fool; Gladly!

"Susan Harris, who created *The Golden Girls,*" writes Carolyn See in a *TV Guide* article about the actress Betty White, "a woman who doesn't suffer fools gladly, says, 'I'm afraid I'm going to have to give you a cliché. Betty's wonderful.' "

In fact, the cliché was *suffer fools gladly.* An irate Lex Irreg writes: "Every profile about Governor John H. Sununu claims that he *doesn't suffer fools gladly.* The phrase seems to be replacing 'Have a nice day.' Where's it from?"

Sometimes you can get a straight, specific answer in this space.

Suffer is rooted in the Latin *sufferre,* meaning "to hold up, to support," but in the thirteenth century the verb's meaning shifted from "support" to "endure," especially "to endure pain"; it also had a milder sense of "to put up with, permit."

The authors of the King James translation of the Bible in 1611 used the milder sense in a couple of famous lines: "Suffer the little children to come unto me," goes Mark's gospel in quoting Jesus, "and forbid them not. . . ." They also took II Corinthians 11:19 (shorthand for the chapter and verse in the Apostle Paul's second letter to the church at Corinth) and Englished it thus: "For ye suffer fools gladly, seeing ye yourselves are wise."

For the meaning in context, let's use the New English Bible's clearer if less poetic translation: "Let no one take me for a fool," writes Paul, "but if you must, then give me the privilege of a fool, and let me have my little boast like others." In his view, bragging is foolish, and he lashes his readers with sarcasm: "How gladly you bear with fools, being yourselves so wise!" Those who put up with foolish braggarts, he is saying, are fools themselves.

Paul's point about boasting in this passage has been worn away with time. The expression *suffer fools gladly*—always put in the negative—now has to do with "the high-minded refusal of the person of integrity to deal with the world's jerks." However, the cliché also carries a different, antielitist sense:

"the imperious impatience of the powerful and learned toward those less gifted."

Summit Practice

Russian words that become well known in America reflect the geopolitical realities.

Nyet was the word popularized by Andrei Gromyko in the 1950's. Then, in 1957, *sputnik* streaked across the lexicon, the little fellow traveler in space giving birth in Khrushchev's time to dozens of -*nik* coinages. In the Brezhnev era, Americans learned the Russian acronym *gulag.* The favorite newsmagazine word for Organization Man in the 1970's was *apparatchik,* and the word most pounced upon by right-wingers was the K.G.B.'s *dezinformatsiya,* which we Anglicized to "disinformation."

Enter Mikhail Gorbachev with his *glasnost,* which is most often loosely translated as "openness," but has a meaning closer to "controlled publicity." No sooner had we become confirmed glasnostics than we were hit with *perestroika,* "restructuring." According to high-level Soviet informants, Mr. Gorbachev considers *glasnost* the sizzle and *perestroika* the steak.

Keep your eye on the *pere-* prefix, which means "re-" (*pere-,* "re-," and *stroika,* "structure"). When Richard Nixon was asked if he thought that the new détente was a sincere effort at peace or a desire to gain a breathing space, he replied in a kind of international shorthand: "You mean *peredyshka.*"

If you want to be hip to summit lingo, get with *peredyshka,* which means literally "rebreathing" or "respite" or, in the American idiom, "the catching-your-breath theory." In political terms, it means "the time needed to regain the strength to dominate the world," which hard-liners and other suspicious souls think is the plan of the perestroikaniks. If *peredyshka* is indeed the secret strategy of Mr. Gorbachev, then it would not be in our interest to help him salvage his floundering economy. (Do I mean *floundering,* "flapping or twisting" like the fish, or *foundering,* "sinking or collapsing"? I think both.)

Now we are ready for a Russian joke. What comes after *perestroika* and *peredyshka*? Answer: *perestrelka.* Tell that to a Russian dissident and you will get much thigh-slapping hilarity followed by a sad nod; *perestrelka* means "crossfire" as in "shootout" or "reshoot" and is not a cameraman's term but a reference to the same kind of crackdown that followed Mao's deceptive call to "let a hundred flowers blossom, let a hundred schools of thought contend." Then, whammo—for the newly noisy glasnostic perestroikanik, it's *perestrelka.*

Dear Bill,
It's not completely accurate to say that the Russian prefix pere- means "re-."
Its basic meaning is "across" or "trans," as in perevod, "translation," pereexat,
"to cross [e.g., a border], to run over [e.g., a pedestrian]." The derived
meaning that you translate as "re-" is itself a derived meaning of "re-," which
basically means "again" (as in "He reloaded his gun") but is often used to
mean "revise, improve" (as in "He rewrote his novel"). You in fact illustrated
the "across" meaning with perestrelka.

Jim [James D. McCawley]
Department of Linguistics
University of Chicago
Chicago, Illinois

Take That Decision

To arms, to arms, the Britishisms are coming!

During the past decade, lexicographers began breaking out the Revere bowls because American usage was acquiring a British flavor.

One sees it everywhere: *at the end of the day* is replacing *when all is said and done;* the *marquee* has replaced *the tent in the backyard* at fashionable social functions; *fridge* is now the name for *refrigerator* or *icebox*. The British *mixed bag* has been adopted in the United States for any assortment of people or inconclusive result; *smarmy* has overwhelmed *unctuous,* and *trendy* has bypassed *chic.*

American academics now *speak* to what they used to *address.* The formal pronoun *one* is substituted for *you,* as in "One sees it everywhere." We have dropped *expensive* for the British *pricey,* and rejected our *chancy* for their *dicey. Early on* now gets the worm, and hardly anybody now uses *in the beginning* ("Early on, God created the heavens and the earth").

"Commentators, politicians and, most recently, a Harvard economist on ABC News," writes Emily Wolfe of West Hartford, CT (under the new postal designations, residents of that state are no longer Conn. men), "are now referring to decisions being *taken* rather than *made.* Have you noticed people are taking more decisions? It sounds extremely affected to me."

Let's look through the clips: "The State Department said no final decision had been taken," goes an Associated Press report from Washington by Barry Schweid. A Tass correspondent in Havana covering a "deep socio-political crisis" in El Salvador reports, "No final decision has yet been taken." And Secretary of State James A. Baker 3d avoided the appearance of disagreement with Bonn during his first trip to West Germany in his new job with "This was not a decision-taking meeting."

With the exception of Foggy Bottom, where British English has long had a foothold, the sources of most of the citations are foreign. Reuters, Tass, *The Economist,* the BBC and quotations from foreign leaders all tend to use *take* instead of *make* at decision-time. Norman W. Schur, in his *British English, A to Zed,* confirms that *take a decision* is the British equivalent of *make a decision.*

The American use, however, is not as new as it seems. Thanks to Terrence J. Gough, a United States Army historian, I have a message dated 18 December 1951 (that's the way the military does dates) from Colonel George A. Lincoln in the Paris delegation of the North Atlantic Treaty Organization to his superiors in Washington, in which he notes the proposal of "a manageable paper on which to take decision."

The British like the verb *take.* We say, "I *get* your point"; they say, "I *take* your point," as if accepting a serve in tennis. In what must be a related development, Hollywood moguls for more than a decade have been *taking a meeting,* probably rooted in the Britishism *taking lunch,* an offshoot of *taking tea.* A good topic for a doctoral thesis would be the connection that may exist between *taking a decision* and *doing lunch.*

Although *take a decision* is not yet in the dictionaries, the fifty-sixth sense of the verb *take* in the *Oxford English Dictionary* is "to lay hold of, raise, put forth, make (an objection, an exception, a distinction, etc.)." That definition suggests a connection of the rhyming *take* and *make.*

The term *decision maker,* in frequent use by lobbyists in Washington, has not yet been replaced by *decision taker,* but give the unspoken locution time.

It seems to go with. Why? Brits, and now the Americans, say: *I haven't the foggiest.*

Dear Bill:
Even if you don't revere the idea that the Britishisms are coming, my advice is not to worry.

> Ed [Edward Bleier]
> New York, New York

The meeting-taking of Hollywood moguls is probably not rooted in a Britishism, but in the American practice of taking a bath or even a haircut. The British have a bath, or they simply bath—sometimes transitively, as when one baths the baby. (I once told an English friend I was going to Bath; she, deliberately misunderstanding, asked, "Why, is it somebody's birthday?")

> J. B. Handelsman
> Hampton Bays, New York

On the increasing use of "take a decision" for "make a decision": The situation is not a simple one of imitating a British usage. It is more a syntactic back-formation from the use of "take" in the passive with "decision," in contrast to the far more frequent use of "make" when the sentence is in the active. Thus, you make a decision, but a decision is taken. To say, then, "take a decision" suggests itself naturally given the ordinary use of "take" with direct noun objects that are really the verbal element of the sentence, such as "take a look."

I have what amounts to rock-hard evidence for this. I don't know if you have seen the new Collins COBUILD dictionary, but in addition to its innovative style of definition, it was based on a frequency study of English words in 18 million words of text. Definitions were then given in order of relative frequency of meaning for each word. The definition of "take" starts out this way:

> *The most frequent use of take is in expressions where it does not have a very distinct meaning of its own, but where most of the meaning is in the noun that follows it (i.e., its direct object).*

The examples include: take a look, take a nap, take a shower, take a deep breath, take a walk, take a risk, take a chance. Further down in the definition of senses it gives the example: Certain decisions had to be taken. Note the passive.

The word decision itself is defined as: A decision is a choice that you make . . . This is followed by the following examples: I think I made the wrong decision. The actual investment decisions are taken by boards of directors. To wrap up the case, the entry after decision is decision-making!

Now, the Collins COBUILD database was overwhelmingly British. In addition, you cite American usage of "take" with "decision" going back many years. So what we have here is a natural idiomatic development of the language with fortuitously different degrees of visibility in the various parts of the English-speaking world, and not a snobbish imitation of a supposedly "British" usage.

> *Joseph A. Reif*
> *Senior Lecturer in Linguistics*
> *Bar-Ilan University*
> *Ramat-Gan, Israel*

Not long ago I had a fortuitous experience: One of our ophthalmologist's assistants had just completed the preliminary eye exams for me and asked whether I was a Canadian. I told him that I was American and inquired why he asked. His reply: "When you read the eye chart you said 'zed' for 'zee.' I explained that I'd lived in Trinidad. It turned out that he was Canadian but had gone to live in Trinidad at age four and had lived there until recently when he took up residence in the U.S. Of course there was the time, when we had only been here a few months and I had made some chicken liver spread and decided to share it with an elderly neighbour. I had to explain to her what it was and told her it was very good when spread on biscuits. I'm afraid she probably used soda biscuits.

> *Isabel Allen*
> *Valrico, Florida*

Talk of the Town

In 1928, when the Ivory Soap slogan "It Floats" was being drilled into the American consciousness, *The New Yorker* magazine ran a cartoon by Gluyas Williams of a bunch of harried executives and hair-pulling copywriters running around a pool; it was captioned "The day a cake of soap sank at Procter & Gamble's."

The same image strikes me now (writing in 1989) in reading the copy in the

new *New Yorker*. That citadel of style, that fortress of proper prose—now under new management—has become an open house of grammatical laxity and with-it usage.

This is not all bad. I spotted two sentences beginning with *This is* in recent pieces for "The Talk of the Town," which caused me to turn to a little book called *The Elements of Style* by William Strunk Jr., which was revised and transformed into a best-selling guide by *The New Yorker*'s E. B. White. "The pronoun *this*, referring to the complete sense of a preceding sentence or clause," wrote the stylistic gurus, "can't always carry the load and so may produce an imprecise statement." This is sometimes true, but the Strunk-White warning about beginning with *this* has been carried out too strictly, and it's good to see *The New Yorker* copy editors eschewing rigidity.

But some of the usage now tolerated, even encouraged, sends some of us to a shockery. (You've never been to a *shockery*? In the "Goings On About Town" department, which bids fair to become the "How's-That-Again?" department, we find the phrase "sixties antiestablishment shockery." Far be it from me to knock neologisms, but it was never a staple of *New Yorker* style.)

For example, the noun *venue* is a favorite: "In choosing this *venue*, the inscrutable Dylan had again put his followers to the test"; in "Goings On," a number of actors are said to "do that *venue* proud." The word means "place of action or occurrence" and is best known in law when defendants ask for a *change of venue;* the use of the term as a synonym for *locale* or *site* is not incorrect, but a strict stylist would resist the frequent use of an archaic term in an unfamiliar sense.

Take *schmooze*. "Then he bounded off to *schmooze* among the guests. . . ." This is a Yiddishism for "chat," rooted in the Hebrew *shemu'oth*, "news, rumors." The verb has a nice flavor of "shoot the breeze," less formal than *converse* and more sensible than *prattle*, but somehow I never expected to encounter Yiddishisms outside of quotation marks in the publication symbolized by Eustace Tilley.

The breezy acceptance of verbification is also a departure for the magazine. For instance, two people in a picture being described "are *bookended* by two pieces" of statuary. "An attempt to *travesty* a whole Zeitgeist or narrative mode" in a play review really seems to make a travesty (much more frequent as a noun rooted in a sense of *vest*, "to dress in disguise") out of stylistic standards.

As for *really*, the magazine's prose is studded too often with this la-di-da qualifier. "Avoid the use of qualifiers," advised Strunk and White, who were really right. *The New Yorker*'s drift into this kind of voguish laziness is what has language mavens running around the pool as if the soap sank.

Kind of is another example: "The decorator went kind of hog-wild. . . ." Strunk-White urges restriction of this to the literal sense, as in "Editors detest this kind of criticism." The exception comes when "familiar style" is used. Some elements of style such as punctuation can be argued about—*Felliniesque*, along with *antiestablishment*, seems to me to call for a hyphen, though it's not settled law in this venue—but the editorial decision to change to a familiar style does not justify a descent into sloppiness.

Outright mistakes are too easy to find. In a recent issue: "It is only those drugs which are illegal that inspire the present public furor. . . ." The *which* is wrong; the absence of a comma in front of it should have sent a warning signal to the writer. *That* is defining or restrictive; *which* is not. The writer probably wanted to avoid two uses of *that* so close together, as in "those drugs that are illegal that inspire . . ." Yes, that's confusing; he or she should have recast the sentence. "It would be a convenience to all," wrote Strunk-White, "if these two pronouns were used with precision."

Another sin is the act of dangling: "Given the lack in the American mind of a subsoil of details about life in China, it seems . . ." Strunk and White's eleventh rule of usage is "A participial phrase at the beginning of a sentence must refer to the grammatical subject." This participial phrase, which strings together prepositional phrases, positively dangles.

Add to these clunkers the use of *respectively*, an unnecessary word; the frequent acceptance of *arguable*, a verb-based adjective whose meaning is swinging wildly from "defensible" to "questionable" to "debatable" and should therefore be avoided; the repeated use of the bureaucratic passive voice, and the lazy "despite *the fact that*," a phrase Strunk-White called "especially debilitating. . . . It should be revised out of every sentence in which it occurs."

Why am I casting obloquy on this literate publication? (Producers cast shows; fishermen cast lines; lovers cast glances; pop grammarians cast obloquy.) The same reason leads the Gotcha! Gang, shock troops of the Nitpickers' League, to gleefully circle mistakes in this column (I'll get postcards about splitting "to circle"): There lurks within each of us a desire to take the custodians into custody. And for decades, *The New Yorker*—usually wittily, often snottily—put down the dolts who misused the language.

Now the publication's writing style is changing, in many ways for the better: "Any horseshoed clump of dough is now called a croissant. . . . Time for a Baked Reality Check." I wouldn't compress "in the shape of a horseshoe" beyond "horseshoe-shaped," but *reality check* is a psychological term on the tip of cognoscenti tongues; the phrase comes from Freud's *reality testing,* "to separate the real from the imagined," influenced by *gravity check,* literally "the scientific test for the presence of gravity" but used facetiously since the early 1980's in response to defiance of logic or sanity.

Because the language used by the literate is moving more toward what William Hazlitt called "the familiar style," editors who closely observe language fashions, like those at *The New Yorker,* do not want to be left behind; that accounts for their tolerance of swinging verbification of nouns and the new breeziness in usage.

But breeziness ain't laxity. God knows how much money, effort and discipline Ralph Lauren spends trying to make his products look relaxed and informal. Those of us who try to be crossover writers—trying to bridge cultures and generations—want to attract a new audience without losing the aging regulars, but we have discovered that adopting anything-goes lingo does not do the trick. Many codgers feel awkward in straining to sound sloppily modern; many children resent having to call their parents by their first names.

There was a cartoon many years ago of a monkey cage at a zoo; the monkeys had stolen the hat of the confused keeper, who was helplessly trying to get his hat back; a lady called into the cage with the immortal question, "Who's in charge here?"

You have to tighten up to effectively loosen up. Editors and writers, redefining their audience and their times, are obliged to separate what is freshly permissible from what is supinely permissive. Then, to paraphrase Lenin—power to the copy editors! Adapt your style, if you wish, to admit the color of slang or freshness of neologism, but hang tough on clarity, precision, structure, grace.

I, too, deplore the laxity of The New Yorker *these days; its grammar and syntax are both slipping, but the sentence containing "those . . . which" was correct. The matter of restrictive versus nonrestrictive is not at issue here. "Those" is the plural of "that." As you would not say, "Is that a dagger that*

I see before me," so you would not say, "Are those daggers that I see before me." The correct pronoun to refer to "that" or "those" is "which"—always! It is that distinction which lends clarity to a sentence that might otherwise be unclear.

> Frances Apt
> Belmont, Massachusetts

Strunk & White is a useful guide for developing an inoffensive personal writing style; it reminds me of the rule never to wear stripes with stripes. But Strunk just isn't sufficiently exhaustive to use as a sourcebook in analyzing the writing of the more adventurous, and you shouldn't encourage such a thing.

Take Fowler's Dictionary of Modern English Usage down from the shelf instead, and you'll see that "Given the lack in the American mind of a subsoil of details about life in China, it seems . . ." isn't a "dangling participle" at all, but an absolute construction, identical in function to "hostages having been exchanged, the armies . . ." found so often in stiff translations of Caesar. Rewrite it in stock form and it would go: "The lack in the American mind of a subsoil of details about life in China being given, it seems . . ." which is perfectly respectable, if a bit turgid. (The elegant variation, of course, does not change the thing's basic nature.)

The proof of this pudding is in the fixing: All of Strunk's examples of dangling participles can be corrected by changing the subject. Since an absolute has no relation to the subject of the sentence, this cannot be done in the New Yorker sentence, can it?

> Michael Taglieri
> Flushing, New York

You wrote: ". . . schmooze . . . This is a Yiddishism for 'chat,' rooted in the Hebrew shemu'oth, 'news, rumors.' " I am not a member of the Gotcha! Gang nor of the Nitpickers' League but the Yiddishism derives from—it is not rooted in—the Ashkenazi pronunciation of the word, which is shemu'ose. In Hebrew, the accent is on the last syllable. In Yiddish the accent is on the penultimate, as in German. The word in Hebrew is used only in its noun form, and it means rumors. In Yiddish, the word took on the verbal shemu'osen or the past tense of ge-shemu'osed. In the United States the Germanic forms were modified to conform with English formation, leaving us with to shemu'ose or schmooze.

Actually, the derivation is a good example of how many English words developed out of non-English words.

> Arthur Centor
> Richmond, Virginia

You overlooked something more important than the absence of quotation marks around "schmooze." "Bounding off to schmooze" is probably an oxymoron. It's like sauntering into a firefight. Schmoozing is easy, soft, light, of little consequence, a way to pass the time. One doesn't bound into such an activity.

Edward Peizer
Pinehurst, North Carolina

True to its name, the apostrophe has a way of "turning" on you when you least expect it. Hebrew news or rumors are shemu'oth, not shemu'oth. The letter represented is not aleph but the more guttural ayin.

Merriam-Webster's Ninth New Collegiate is my dictionary of choice, and I recognized the lapsus calami immediately as their own, having spotted it on an earlier occasion. But the Third New International (unabridged) sets the record straight.

Todd Shandelman
Monsey, New York

That *New Yorker* Which

In taking a pop at the new style at *The New Yorker* recently, I argued that the following sentence was incorrect: "It is only those drugs which are illegal that inspire the present public furor. . . ."

Loosey-goosey grammarians from all over the country have taken issue with my stricture, sending citations—from Jane Austen to A. J. Liebling—to show how good writers have paid no attention to the difference between *that* and *which*.

However, here is a letter from Jacques Barzun, defender of the stern grammarian faith and the teacher who usually can be found on the burning deck after all the rest of us have fled: "Your general principle is right," writes Professor Barzun—"*which* is nondefining and the other defines. But Fowler, who invented the rule, makes clear that following it should not take precedence over other considerations and he mentions euphony."

Uh-oh. Does this mean that the new *New Yorker* style can be defended in this case? "In the use of *which* that you jumped on, I think euphony called for the disregard of the rule. Besides, many excellent writers in England pay no attention to it, being guided by those 'other considerations.' "

Gee. This deck is getting both hot and lonely. I think that the distinction between *that* and *which* helps the reader to know immediately whether the clause that follows is the restrictive kind, one that is necessary to meaning, or the nonrestrictive kind, which simply adds information.

For example, in "stylebooks *that* let writers get away with syntactical murder," the *that* restricts the meaning to only those stylebooks that are loosey-goosey. But "stylebooks, *which* let writers get away with syntactical murder," doesn't restrict the meaning to those particular stylebooks—on the contrary, it makes a blanket statement about the permissiveness of all stylebooks.

So here I stand, without support from Fowler or Barzun (O Captains! my Captains!) or the *New Yorker* editors, which I wish I had but that I can do without. (*That* I wish I had but *which* I can do without? No; "I wish I had" is a nonrestrictive comment about the "support," so *which* is correct, and "I can do without" is also nonrestrictive, so *that* is incorrect. Following my own anti-euphonious and inflexible rule, the clause should read: "which I wish I had but which I can do without.")

But who wants two *which*'s in one sentence? Recast to avoid the whole problem. I wish I had the support of the great grammarians, but I can do without it; here I stand.

Dear Bill:
It was gracious of you to quote me at such length on <u>which</u> *and* <u>that</u>. *But I have the feeling that you're not convinced, so I can flog the half-dead horse a little more.*

A further objection to making the largely useful rule absolute is that, quite apart from the writer's choice, it is not usable in two situations. One is the <u>that</u> <u>which</u> *construction: "Of the various toys, the boy chose that which was the least expensive." The rule would require* <u>That that</u>. *In the plural,* <u>those that</u> *is available, but it creates the excess of* <u>thuh</u> *sounds I am sure you find as disagreeable as I do.*

Again, when a preposition is required, <u>which</u> *is alone possible: "This is the toy to which he pointed." All those* <u>whiches</u> *are restrictive and your Salem-inspired urge to hang them all is condemned by enlightened opinion.*

Jacques [Barzun]
New York, New York

You, the estimable Jacques Barzun and everyone else, including the "loosey-goosey grammarians," are all wrong (if the latter can be said to be wrong about <u>anything</u>) *regarding the relative pronouns in the sentence "It is only those drugs which are illegal that inspire the present public furor. . . ."*

As given (that is, without knowing the preceding sentence), both clauses are clearly restrictive and both pronouns should therefore be that. Consider: It is not all drugs that inspire public furor, but only those that are illegal. That settled, It is only those drugs that are illegal would be meaningless unless followed by the second clause, making this clause restrictive also, and therefore requiring another that to introduce it.

Finally, the sentence could easily be recast to avoid the repetition of two which's or two that's, or any combination of them, by simply dropping the It is. Thus, "Only those drugs that are illegal inspire the present public furor"; or, alternately, "The present public furor is inspired only by those drugs that are illegal."

Logic, old boy, logic!

Leonard M. Friedman
Professor of French
Salem State College
Salem, Massachusetts

Reading your piece on the New Yorker that-which dilemma, I concluded that that that that that editor used, rather than which, was essentially stronger.

Robert C. Snider
Chevy Chase, Maryland

Tergive and Take

"His pomposity and tergiversations on every issue," seethed the conservative columnist William F. Buckley Jr., "make his running as a Republican an anomaly we ought to correct."

Senator Lowell P. Weicker Jr., Republican of Connecticut, the object of this blast from the right, limited his initial response to "What did he say?"

In reporting this story of a split in Republican ranks, Clifford D. May of *The New York Times* at first defined *tergiversations* as "apostasies"; the copy desk thought that was a bit high-hat, too, and the article appeared with the definition "repeated changes of opinion."

Tergiversate comes from the Latin for "to turn one's back on," and most often means "to desert a cause, to become a renegade." It has a second meaning of "to evade, equivocate," which Francis R. Erville of New York City informs me is the present sense of *tergiverser* in French; this alternative meaning fuzzes up the definition in English and is perhaps why the word has fallen into desuetude. ("Disuse" is the word I would ordinarily use, but I'm in a Buckley mood.)

A satirical crossline (or boldface subhead) called Buckley's use of this unfamiliar word an *animadversion,* which means "criticism." When we animadvert the tergiversators, we know the campaign is heating up—and we haven't even dealt with the irregularity or incongruity that the Buckley clan calls an *anomaly.*

You quote William F. Buckley, in his reference to Senator Weicker, to the following effect: " 'His pomposity and tergiversations on every issue,' seethed [my underscoring] the conservative columnist William F. Buckley Jr., 'make his running as a Republican an anomaly we ought to correct.' "

Though Buckley may have "seethed" in the process of criticizing Weicker, he could not actually "seethe" the utterance. It is not a veridical statement. Neither, for that matter, may one "fume," or "laugh," an utterance. This is not to say that one may not be fuming or laughing while in the act of speaking or writing; only that it is incorrect to conflate these actions simultaneously into these verbs. As an editor I would suggest the following: "Buckley wrote, seething: 'His . . . ,' " Or, alternatively, after "issue," you could have written "—the conservative columnist seethed—." The dashes are necessary to separate Buckley's sentence and sense from your interpolation. Of course, there are still other solutions.

Milton Eder
New York, New York

There was a lacuna in your exagimation of William Buckley's animadversion of Senator Weicker.

Not only did he denounce the Senator's "pomposity and tergiversations," the elegant Buckley also called the honorable gentleman a "horse's ass" (see Daily News clip).

Since this is a linguistic breakthrough, it does seem worthy of comment in your column. For instance: Is this the first time the Daily News has printed that phrase? Did The Times quote it, or will it? How many of the papers that syndicate Buckley ran that article, and did they use blanks, or what?

William S. Wallace
New York, New York

NOTE FROM W. S.: *The only ass to appear in The New York Times is a donkey.*

When we venture into new (to us) polysyllables, we must have sensitivity to their transitivity (or intransitivity). Thus your clause: "when we animadvert the tergiversators" is a glitch or lapsus, because "animadvert" is intransitive. We do not animadvert somebody or something, we animadvert <u>upon</u> him, her or it.

Arthur J. Morgan
New York, New York

While on the subject of TERGIVERSATION, you missed the chance of a lifetime to point out it is the longest well-mixed common desk-dictionary anagram: Voilà INTERROGATIVES!

Ralph G. Beaman
Boothwyn, Pennsylvania

Title Search

Titles are important to novelists and should be important to the readers of novels.

Set aside, if you will, the catchiness of a title. That's a matter for marketing people, formerly known as salesmen. A significant title goes beyond attention-arousal; it whispers a mysterious message to the reader during the reading, and reverberates with a clue to the novel's meaning long after the book is put down.

"While reading Thomas Mann's *Doctor Faustus*," writes Paul B. Bergman of New York City, "I came across this: 'some wandering lunatic with communistic visions, preaching a bonfire of the vanities . . .' Is this where Tom Wolfe got the title for his book? Is it an expression more common than it would appear?"

To get the right stuff, I went directly to the author. This technique infuriates deconstructionist critics, but it saves time. "Both Mann's narrator and I," responded Mr. Wolfe, "are alluding to the bonfires of the vanities of Savonarola toward the end of the fifteenth century."

A-hah. Remember the carnival of Florence in 1497? Girolamo Savonarola, an uncompromisingly ascetic Italian friar, had been preaching in plain, hard words his vision of moral reform in the teeth of the elegant humanism of the powerful Medici family. The teaching of Savonarola led, after the Medici rule, to a wave of austerity, sobriety and spiritual fervor, which kind of put a damper on the swinging good times of the Renaissance.

The 1497 whoop-de-do turned out to be no fun at all. At the Florentine carnival, where revelers liked to display their finery, the followers of the no-nonsense friar gathered in the Piazza della Signoria and engaged in the *bruciamenti delle vanità,* the "burning of the vanities." Books considered immoral were tossed in the flames, along with elaborate masks, paintings of nudes and "frivolous objects," which I suppose were the glitzy pants and sequined T-shirts of the time.

"This burning of the vanities," says Professor Roberto Severino of Georgetown University, "was to show the decadence of the period, a symbolical renouncement of luxuries."

"Savonarola," he adds, "was a fundamentalist in that sense, condemning even the Pope for his earthly interest. The word 'vanities' probably came from the Bible's use." (Here it is: "Vanity of vanities, saith the Preacher, vanity of vanities; all is vanity." That's from Ecclesiastes 1:2, meaning that material or earthly things have no value, from the Latin *vanus,* "empty.")

When was the first such repressive bonfire? "There are records of earlier *bruciamenti delle vanità,*" says Piergiuseppe Bozzetti, cultural attaché of the Italian Embassy in Washington. "They were apparently quite common at the beginning of the fifteenth century throughout Italy." He points out that the first word in the Italian phrase ends in *i,* a plural, to be translated "burnings." He adds, "Be sure to spell *delle* with a final *e,* not *a,* because *vanities* is plural, too."

Savonarola had been excommunicated by an angry Pope, and was later tortured and hanged, his body then burned at the stake. The etymology of *bonfire* is apt in this case; although Samuel Johnson derived the first syllable from the French *bon,* "good," most other etymologists see its origin in *bone fire,* an open-air burning of bones.

Did Tom Wolfe see himself as a modern Savonarola, or was he satirizing others in that hot-eyed reformist role who would be burned one day themselves? That's for the author to know and readers to guess, but a knowledge of the title helps.

A brief tangent: Professor LeRoy L. Lamborn of Wayne State University Law School in Detroit (there is no state named Wayne) has sent me two instances in the above book by Mr. Wolfe in which the author uses *podium* when he means *lectern.* "Are the two words now synonymous for the educated person," he asks, "as my Merriam-Webster's *Ninth New Collegiate Dictionary* contends?" No. A *podium* is an elevation to stand on; a *lectern* is a high desk to lean on and hide behind. Those knuckling under to other usages are the pleasure-seeking Medicis among dictionaries, and I'm with Savonarola on this.

Back to the title search. I wish we knew more about the origin of *The Satanic Verses,* a novel by Salman Rushdie that caused Ayatollah Khomeini to demand the author's murder. It is supposedly an allusion to an episode in Islamic mythology, when the prophet Mohammed was said to have been visited by Satan, disguised as the Archangel Gabriel, who presented to him verses of false religious belief.

Is there any allusion to English literature in the title? Maybe; in his circa-1833 *Sartor Resartus* (Latin for "The Tailor Retailored"), Thomas Carlyle listed three things a put-upon character could do: "Establish himself in Bedlam; begin writing Satanic Poetry; or blow out his brains." In 1821, the English poet Robert Southey had referred to the impious poetry of Byron, Shelley and their imitators as the *Satanic school.* Or, perhaps, the powerful monologues of Satan in Milton's *Paradise Lost* qualify as "Satanic verses."

Mr. Rushdie is understandably in hiding and unavailable for explication.

Your piece indicated that you were unaware of a state named Wayne in connection with Wayne State University. The institution to which you refer was named after General "Mad" Anthony Wayne and functioned as a private college until the early 1960's. At that time, it was incorporated into the Michigan statewide university system and renamed as Wayne State University.

> *Barry G. Smiler, M.D.*
> *Wayne State University, 1965*
> *Sarasota, Florida*

"Books considered immoral were tossed in the flames." Or were they tossed first into *the flames and then, perhaps,* in *the flames? Savonarola himself may have*

been tossed <u>by</u> flames <u>in</u> the flames, but only after he had been tossed onto and <u>into</u> them.

Just as a podium is defined essentially as a base to <u>stand</u> (pous/podos) upon, so a lectern is defined essentially as a stand to <u>read</u> (legere/lectus) from.

You write, "I'm for holding on to the difference . . . because it sharpens meanings." Me, too.

Edward J. Fischer
Jersey City, New Jersey

Title Search Follow-up

Authors of books sneak messages to their readers in titles. So do authors of columns (this one, at least); the double meaning of a pun in a headline can direct readers to an underlying message. In "Peking Too Soon," a pundit was hinting at a domestic political motive in President Bush's recent visit to the Chinese capital, just as in a piece some years ago about the predations of Sheik Ahmed Zaki Yamani, then-Saudi oil minister, a holdup warning was contained in "Yamani or Ya Life."

This draws moans from newspaper readers, but a pun can be catnip to a book reviewer: "The pun in the title 'The Lyre of Orpheus,' " writes Phyllis Rose in *The New York Times,* "suggests the donnishness of the wit in Robertson Davies's new novel. The play on 'lyre' underscores Mr. Davies's delight in art's proximity to fakery." (Orpheus, the mythic Greek poet, played the lyre so sweetly that it soothed the savage beasts; William Congreve wrote in 1697 that "Music hath charms to soothe a savage breast," forever confusing *beast* and *breast,* but I digress.)

More book reviewers are taking note of the allusive use of language in titles. Sometimes a reviewer objects to what may seem an unintended allusion. Caryn James, in a *New York Times* review of John Boswell's *The Kindness of Strangers,* about the pre-Renaissance care of abandoned children, took umbrage at "his bizarrely chosen title, with its inevitable echo of Tennessee Williams. In his preface, Mr. Boswell explains how he translated a problematic Latin phrase as 'the kindness of strangers' but does not seem aware that his readers, at that very moment, are probably struggling to dispel Blanche DuBois's famous phrase, 'I have always depended on the kindness of strangers.' "

I checked with Mr. Boswell, who teaches history at Yale: "Of course I was familiar with the use of that phrase as the last line spoken by Blanche in *A Streetcar Named Desire.* But Tennessee Williams wasn't the first to have that idea. The Latin phrase is *aliena misericordia,* which may seem at first to mean 'strange mercy,' but when you transpose the order, it means 'the kindness of strangers,' the theme of my book."

The playwright Williams was no stranger to allusions in his titles, either; an ancient idiom appearing in John Ray's seventeenth-century *A Collection of English Proverbs* was "to go like a cat upon a hot bake-stone." That became the heroine's feeling of being like a "cat on a hot tin roof" who did not know which way to jump.

Perusing the best-seller lists, we find George Bernau's *Promises to Keep*—an easy one, a phrase from the most famous Robert Frost poem, "Stopping by Woods on a Snowy Evening," with its implicit contemplation of suicide. A blockbuster paperback about personal inspiration, *The Road Less Traveled,* by M. Scott Peck, takes its title from Frost's "The Road Not Taken," which concludes:

> Two roads diverged in a wood, and I—
> I took the one less traveled by,
> And that has made all the difference.

Jack Higgins's *A Season in Hell* draws its title from the 1873 work by the French poet Arthur Rimbaud (pronounced like Rambo, but with the accent on the second syllable: "ram-BO"). Mr. Higgins substitutes suspense for despair in his own season down there. That scene is also recalled by the naturalist Peter Matthiessen in his collection of short stories titled *On the River Styx,* the border of Hades. Big year for hellish titles.

On the other hand, the Bible is a hot source for the latest titles. *The Book of Ruth* is Jane Hamilton's novel about domestic violence, and readers should remember that the biblical Ruth (1:16) refused to depart from her mother-in-law ("whither thou goest, I will go . . .").

In *Balm in Gilead,* Sara Lawrence Lightfoot's biography of her mother, the first black woman to gain fame as a child psychiatrist, the reference is to the metaphorical question by the prophet Jeremiah (8:21–22): "For the hurt of the daughter of my people am I hurt; I am black; astonishment hath taken hold on me. Is there no balm in Gilead; is there no physician there?"

The theater critic John Simon, a prince of prescriptivism when he writes about language, collected his literary essays under the title *Sheep from the Goats.* That's from Matthew 25:32, the warning by Jesus of future judgment, in which the good shall be separated from the evil "as a shepherd divideth his sheep from the goats." The sheep are to be rewarded and the goats cast into everlasting fire, a place familiar to some of Mr. Simon's targets, as well as to Orpheus, that lyre.

Still Small Voices, by the journalists John and Janet Wallach, is a moving series of profiles of the human beings who strive to make their lives amid the violence of the West Bank and Gaza.

The expression is in 1 Kings 19:11–12, when the prophet Elijah is visited by God: "And, behold, the Lord passed by, and a great and strong wind rent the mountains . . . but the Lord was not in the wind: and after the wind an earthquake; but the Lord was not in the earthquake: And after the earthquake a fire; but the Lord was not in the fire: and after the fire a still small voice."

That is especially appropriate to the turmoil of the intifada, but the phrase was also picked up in a despairing sense by Tennyson:

> A still small voice spake unto me,
> "Thou art so full of misery,
> Were it not better not to be?"

It had been used in a more uplifting sense by Thomas Gray in a 1769 poem:

> Sweet music's melting fall, but sweeter yet
> The still small voice of gratitude.

Today's reportage on the heavenly and hellish metaphoric sources of titles is a follow-up to a recent piece in which I advertised for the Islamic origin of the title of Salman Rushdie's *The Satanic Verses.*

The Islamic division of the Lexicographic Irregulars came through. Scholars at Columbia University and the University of New Hampshire call my attention to *Muhammad at Mecca,* a 1953 book by W. Montgomery Watt, which explains the incident that generated the now-world-famous phrase. In the seventh century, early in Mohammed's career as a preacher and "warner" in Mecca, the Prophet seemed to make his message more palatable to the

Meccans by accepting local cult idols with the words "These are the swans exalted / Whose intercession is to be hoped for."

According to Islamic tradition, when the angel Gabriel came to Mohammed and showed him his error, the Prophet recognized the words as inspired by Satan. These *Satanic verses* were then abrogated or nullified by God.

The specific verses have long been a source of controversy. John O. Voll of the University of New Hampshire wrote that "the historicity of the incident and its significance have long been debated among Muslims." Pierre Cachia of Columbia University added that "the story has nothing to do with the Prophet's wives. What Rushdie makes of them no doubt falls under the heading of the license generally conceded to writers of fiction."

Mr. Rushdie's choice of the phrase as a title was intended to be either self-mocking or provocative—or perhaps something else. In all cases, the double meaning is for authors to know and readers to noodle around.

You appear to take the biblical "still small voice" addressing the prophet Elijah as a hopeful metaphor of something like calm courage and reason making their way against "the turmoil of the intifada." To the contrary, the biblical prototype in 1 Kings 19:12 was ominous, to say the least. As an instrument of divine revelation, "the still small voice"—literally, "a voice of thin silence"—represented the prophet's raised consciousness directed against a religio-political establishment—the house of Ahab. It mandated to Elijah a revolutionary agenda more like the intifada than unlike it.

> *Bruce T. Dahlberg*
> *Northampton, Massachusetts*

What's in a title? What's in a title search, for that matter? I thought you would like to know that in the title insurance business you do not get a "follow-up" to a title search (as your most recent title search headline suggested). No, you get a "run down" or a "bring down" but never a "follow-up." Why?

In the eastern United States, where computers have been slow to catch up to the rest of the country with respect to this particular application, a search is done by running your eyes down a long column of names all starting with the same three letters, or all having the same initial of the last name and the same key letter of the first name (depending on the indexing system used). The entries are made chronologically on a page. A searcher stops at the bottom of the page on the day the search is done. Between that date and the actual closing, several more entries might appear on that page, and the searcher then "runs down" the rest of the page to the current date.

By the way, every time you use <u>title search</u> in a headline, I <u>think</u> I'm catching a hidden meaning, but it never works out that way!

Lisa W. Fraebel
Stanhope, New Jersey

You failed to point out M. Scott Peck's mistake in his selection of a title for his book, <u>The Road Less Traveled</u>.

Frost's "The Road Not Taken" is an ironic poem, in which the speaker tells how he made an arbitrary decision as to which road to take. Now, years later, he likes to tell listeners (and perhaps himself) that he made a momentous decision, and "that has made all the difference." As the first three paragraphs of the poem point out, the speaker was not too aware of what the road less traveled held for him either. In the fourth paragraph, he boasts of his courage in choosing the course he followed.

As this poem is often misinterpreted and used as a source of inspiration, I usually don't point this fact out. But Mr. Peck should have known better than to use a poem about self-deception as a source for the title of his self-help book.

Jonathan Pelson
New York, New York

I once heard Robert Frost, speaking at Amherst, say that, if he were a professor giving grades to critics, he would give "a D for life" to the critic who wrote that Frost was contemplating death in the lines "the woods are lovely, dark and deep."

Since it's not often that a poet will say what he meant when he was writing a poem, I found it interesting to hear one say what he <u>didn't</u> mean.

Mary C. Crary
Northport, New York

The Unhappy Campers

In David Aaron's spy novel *Agent of Influence* (Putnam, $18.95), a group of Wall Street M.&A. men are about to lose a leveraged buyout deal to a competitor with better inside information and deeper pockets. What figure of

speech does the author (a former deputy national security adviser) choose to describe the infinite glumness on the greedy faces of his characters? Here it is, as *au courant* as a "poison put" bond: "Seldom had he seen such a group of *unhappy campers.*"

For the second time in this decade, a camping term has become camp. The first was the verb *to snake-check,* popularized by that king of the caveats, General Alexander M. Haig Jr. Its current meaning is "to avert unintended consequences by closely examining a plan." The etymon is obvious to anyone who has gone on bivouac: Upon rising, wise recruits will look through their socks and other belongings to see if any snakes seeking warmth have slipped in during the night.

"It is not a group of happy campers that gets off the bus," wrote David Bird about homeless men in *The New York Times* in 1981. Although that is the first use recorded in the Nexis morgue, the phrase must have had earlier currency among counselors at summer camps; obviously, the phrase *unhappy camper* refers to the homesick city kid who mopes about the countryside hating cows, cursing mosquitoes, refusing to make up a bunk, rejecting the hearty companionship of fireside storytelling and tossing his cookies with dismaying regularity.

The columnist Mary McGrory soon appropriated the phrase for political use. Writing in 1982 about a suspiciously upbeat Republican TV spot in an area of high unemployment, she noted, "The happy campers of the commercial have few counterparts in the Peoria area today."

Within a few years, *People* magazine was listing *happy camper* as current slang about attitudes; *tired camper* was its opposite, synonymous with *having a massive attitude problem.* (*Happy trails* was this genre's "goodbye.")

Politicians knew a good metaphor when they met one. "I want the authors of the bill to know," warned Representative Thomas J. Tauke of Iowa, on the subject of toxic-waste financing, "that I am not a happy camper." Representative Billy Tauzin of Louisiana agreed: "This is the most unhappy camp-site in America."

Although the phrase retained its direct camping association (the actress Pamela Springsteen starred as a psychotic counselor in a movie titled *Sleep-away Camp II—Unhappy Campers*), its extended use dominated the field. "You got a bunch of happy campers up here," an astronaut A-O.K.'d Mission Control. And when President-elect George Bush selected New Hampshire Governor John H. Sununu (I know how to spell Sununu, but I never know when to stop) to be his chief of staff, rejecting the younger Craig Fuller, Maureen Dowd of *The New York Times* wrote: "Mr. Fuller has fought hard for the chief of staff's job and was described by one friend as 'not a happy camper.' "

The expression seems to have temporarily done away with the need for the modifiers *disgruntled, dissatisfied* and *discontented,* and substituted for the nouns *malcontent, grumbler, complainer, sorehead* and the more general *grouch.* If you are displeased with this linguistic development to the point of holding your breath and not eating your veggies, you know what you are.

In the course of writing the above, I used three terms that call for explanation. *Camp,* in the sense of "stylized, sophisticated, teasingly theatrical," is probably rooted, according to the new unabridged *Random House II Dictionary,* in the name for brothels catering to male homosexuals. *M.&A.,* to move on quickly, means "mergers and acquisitions," a burgeoning field of financial play far more rewarding than building companies or producing goods. And *agent of influence* was defined by my old Nixon colleague E. Howard Hunt as "either a government official so highly placed that he can exercise influence on government policy or an opinion molder so influential as to be capable of altering the attitudes of an entire country."

When You Say That . . .

In a biography of Cary Grant, Gary Cooper—the embodiment of the taci-turn American hero—was besmeared as one who was "entertained by Hitler" in the late 1930's and whose "political leanings" were in the Nazi direction.

I saddled my rhetorical horse and rode to the rescue of the Cooper reputation. According to his widow, the Coopers toured Europe in 1939 with a banker friend of Franklin Delano Roosevelt and met some Germans but not Hitler. Although one of Der Führer's favorite films was Coop's 1935 *Lives of the Bengal Lancers,* I concluded, no evidence has been produced to substantiate the charge. "Gary Cooper a Nazi sympathizer? Like the villain in *The Virginian,* his defamers will tremble at these immortal words in Coop's unforgettable voice: '*If you want to call me that, smile!*' "

Be very careful when quoting famous movie lines. People remember them vividly, and many now have tape libraries of the classics to catch out misquoters. Humphrey Bogart in *Casablanca* never said, "Play it again, Sam"; try perpetrating that version of his line (which, to be accurate, was "Play it!"), and the Gotcha! Gang will be out in force.

First call was from an anonymous movie buff who vividly remembers the Virginian saying, "*When you say that, smile!*" (That was the extent of the caller's conversation.) Next was Senator Bob Packwood of Oregon, who just as vividly recalled, "*When you call me that, smile!*"

The Senator was partially right: Those were the words used in the 1902 Owen Wister novel, and repeated in the 1946 film version starring Joel McCrea. However, in the 1929 version starring Gary Cooper, the Virginian looked hard at the villain (played by Walter Huston), who had just called him a "son-of-a-B," and said, "*If you want to call me that, smile!*"

I am indebted to Thomas B. Morgan, the profilist who wrote a memorable *Esquire* article in 1961 about Cooper and the cowboy as American hero, for copies of advertisements quoting these lines in the various versions. Maybe the original line in the 1929 script was as written by Wister and Gary Cooper delivered it wrong, or maybe the screenwriter preferred words pronounced "Ef you wanta" at the beginning of the line; nevertheless, that is the correct quotation of the Gary Cooper version, and you're all wrong, but thanks for writing.

As for my *Lives of the Bengal Lancers,* as the entire Gotcha! Gang hooted, the correct title is *Lives of a Bengal Lancer.*

Gary Cooper saying, "If you want to call me that, smile!" never registered with me (I was born in 1922). From day one the saying was "Smile, when you say that!," which is in common use today.

My old favorite is Mae West saying to Cary Grant, "Why don't you come up and see me sometime." I recently discovered that she actually said, "Why don't you come up sometime and see me." That was on an old video on A&E. Nothing is sacred.

Larry Zastrow
Major, U.S.A.F. (Ret.)
Seabrook, Texas

Whoever Uses Whomever Is Nuts

"To whomever receives this message," I wrote in an essay on the Op-Ed page of *The New York Times,* thereby committing the gravest of solecisms to the Who-Whom Owls. Between editions, eagle-eyed Allan M. Siegal, an assistant managing editor to whom I forward dozens of corrections addressed to me but meant for others, called in the change: *whoever.* In the final edition, preserved for historians, I was thus saved from embarrassment.

Look: I've never pretended to have a handle on *who-whom.* In this case, as droves of members of the Gotcha! Gang have pointed out with their customary glee, I relied on what turned out to be my own tin ear.

In a phrase like *to whom it may concern,* the word *whom* is the object of *it may concern.* But in *to whoever receives this message,* the pronoun *whoever* is the subject of the clause *whoever receives this message* and is not the object of the preposition *to.*

Get it? I don't either. Let us resolve to follow Safire's Rule on Who-Whom: Whenever *whom* sounds correct, recast the sentence.

Your own camp has been heavily infiltrated. The eminent New York Times *ran a headline reading: "Hearings on Capitol Hill And Who They Attract." The most painfully obvious problem is the "Who," which of course should have been a "Whom." If that were fixed, we would be left to wonder why "And" should be capitalized but "on" should not.*

> Judith Friedlaender
> New York, New York

Who Is the Eptest of Them All?

Some Democratic members of the Senate Judiciary Committee suspected that the Bush Justice Department was applying an "ideological litmus test" to its judicial nominations, and demanded that several nominees 'fess up to the kind of questioning they had undergone before being offered the jobs.

The *litmus test*—originally a procedure using an organic dye that turns blue in alkaline solutions, red in acid—was popularized as a political term in the mid-1970's during the debate about the Panama Canal treaties. Those

conservatives supporting the ultimate turnover of the canal (including William F. Buckley Jr.) were seen to be apostate right-wingers, turning red in the acid of true belief, while those opposing the "giveaway" (like Ronald Reagan) were held to have proved themselves true-blue.

The litmus-test charge is good for a medium headline on a quiet news day, and required Justice to respond. Somebody in the Administration—nobody will say who—drafted a letter to the committee for three nominees for federal judgeships to sign that denied any litmus-testing. Democratic Senators Ted Kennedy of Massachusetts and Joseph Biden of Delaware humphed, which is not germane to this column's discussion, but Senator Patrick Leahy, Democrat of Vermont, called the Justice document "one of the most grammatically inept letters" he had ever seen.

A portion of the letter: "I am pleased to address the Committee that, with regard to interviews which I had with members of President Bush's staff and members of the Justice Department who serve Attorney General Thornburgh: (1) I did not make any commitments with regard to how I might rule on any specific case or issue nor were any such commitments sought."

Inept? Let's mark it: *Address* is the wrong verb here. You can address an issue or address an envelope, but when you deal with a group of people, you should be physically present to address them; the correct verb in this case is *advise* or *inform* or, alternatively, *notify*. A lawyer can surely come up with an archaic sense of *address* to mean "present a suit," but not the sort of lawyer who should sit in judgment in this day and age. (The letter also spelled *judgment* in the British style—*judgement*—but maybe the nominees hope to wear wigs.)

After the word *interviews,* Justice misjudged *that* and *which.* "Interviews which I had with members of President Bush's staff" is incorrect because a restrictive clause modifying a word should start with *that;* in this case, not even *that* is needed, as the sentence could easily read "interviews I had with . . ." or, even more gracefully, "my interviews with . . ." (The word *interviews* was not as responsive as the more inclusive *communications,* but lawyers are trained to be unresponsive.)

Two uses of *with regard to* in the same sentence are two too many. Boiler-plate prose is the mark of a lazy or terrified writer. In this case, *concerning* would have been usable once, but it's best to observe the rule in regard to *in regard to:* When in doubt, try *about.*

This controversy was brought to my attention by Anthony J. Hope of D.C. (I am going to stop using "Washington, D.C." because there is no part of the District of Columbia that is not Washington), whose objection was not to the Department of Justice letters but to Senator Leahy's criticism: "Isn't *most grammatically inept* grammatically inept?"

Turnabout is foul play. The argument is either that *inept,* like *unique,* should not be qualified by any adverb or that *inept* should not be separated from its modifier *most* by the adverb *grammatically.* Knowing full well that the entire Gotcha! Gang, led by its shock troops of the Nitpickers' League, lies in ambush for any language maven, I advise (not address) Senator Leahy to zap the next offender with ". . . grammatically one of the most inept letters I have ever seen."

Even as you read this, some vengeful prosecutor at Justice is saying, "Shouldn't he have put a comma after *grammatically* in that sentence? We ought to be able to get that wiseguy on something. . . ."

You anathematize the locution "Interviews which I had . . ." as "incorrect because a restrictive clause modifying a word should start with that." *Well, there is them as agrees with this curious prejudice of yours, but there are just as many who cock a snook at it. Here is a rundown of lexicographical and other opinion on the subject:*

Webster's New World Dictionary of the American Language and Webster III state flatly that which *can be used to introduce either a restrictive or a nonrestrictive clause.*

The American Heritage Dictionary of the English Language, in a usage note on that, *calls* which *"particularly appropriate for introducing nonrestrictive (nondefining) clauses" but goes on to say that "Many also employ* which *(for* that) *to introduce clauses that are clearly restrictive."*

Fowler is a doughty champion of the distinction which (aha!) you favor, but he is man enough to admit that "it would be idle to pretend that it is the practice either of most or of the best writers."

Wilson Follett (Modern American Usage) is in your corner, but he concedes that "Many writers begin such [i.e., restrictive] clauses habitually with which, *not* that; *and many use* which *and* that *interchangeably."*

Your present stance on this matter is too dogmatic by half. I suggest that, in the future, you employ the following formula: "Like many thoughtful commentators on English usage, I strongly recommend using <u>that</u> in restrictive clauses and <u>which</u> in nonrestrictive clauses." To paraphrase Mae West, correctness has nothing to do with it.

Louis Jay Herman
New York, New York

Who's in Those Details?

"There is an old German saying," a source in Bremen told *The Washington Post*'s Hobart Rowen in 1978, "that *the Devil is in the details.*"

Max M. Kampelman, the United States arms negotiator, told Reuters in 1987 that agreement was close on intrusive verification, but "you know *the Devil is in the details.*"

"The old arms-negotiation maxim, *'the Devil is in the details,'* rarely seemed as apt as it did last week," wrote Tamar Jacoby in *Newsweek* later that year, as "an excuse for voting against the President: the Devil in the details made them do it."

Gennadi I. Gerasimov, the dashingly handsome Soviet spokesman, spoke in 1987 of the "three problematical D's: Devil, diplomats and details. The diplomats must now chase the Devil out of the details."

From these citations, one may assume that the details are occupied by the Devil. But wait:

"Ludwig Mies van der Rohe, the German Bauhaus architect," wrote Sarah Booth Conroy in *The Washington Post* in 1979, "said, *'God is in the details.'* "

"This is definitely not an art," wrote Hilton Kramer in 1981 in *The New York Times,* "in which *God is in the details.*"

" *'God is in the details,'* Friedrich Nietzsche once said," wrote Harvey D. Shapiro in the financial pages of *The New York Times* in 1983.

Roone Arledge of ABC was described last year in *U.S. News & World Report* as a "hands-on executive" who "operates on the theory that *God is in the details.*"

Somebody is definitely in those details; is the force malign (the Devil) or benign (God)? And who said it first?

Let's turn to the man who is culling and updating the next edition of *Bartlett's Familiar Quotations:* Justin D. Kaplan, biographer of Mark Twain and a world-class scholar.

"We've had little success with *God* (or *the Devil) is in the details,*" says Mr. Kaplan. "We know that Mies van der Rohe used it in discussing architecture; Flaubert has been suggested, but nobody can find it in his writings. I think it may come from John Ruskin, because it sounds like him on the subject of workmanship, but we need the specific citation."

I tossed in Nietzsche and tried to disengage, but Mr. Kaplan is also on the hunt for the coiner of "No woman can be too rich or too thin" (Babe Paley? I dunno) and "No good deed goes unpunished." I hung up before he could ask about "The opera ain't over till the fat lady sings," which I happen to know was a 1975 comment from Dan Cook, a sports editor for the San Antonio *Express-News.*

Now to the details of the word *details:* the preferred pronunciation is "dih-TAILS." The root is the Old French *detaillier,* "to cut in pieces," related to our *tailor,* and the tailor's cuttings were *details,* the tiny bits and pieces in which God or the Devil is found. It first appeared in English in 1603 as *in detail* as opposed to *in gross,* from the French *en gros* for "wholesale."

The noun was snapped up by the military as "the distribution in detail of the Daily Orders first given in general"; a *detail* soon became a group assigned to a task.

Edward Bleier, president of Warner Bros. (don't write it as "Brothers"; he likes it their trademarked way) Domestic Pay-TV, Animation and Network

Features, points out that *detailing,* in California, is more than a car wash: "It's a comprehensive, painstaking cleaning, waxing and polishing of every surface inside and outside a car."

Further evidence of the rise of the word is its use in a magazine, published in New York City, aimed at a younger rich audience than *Vanity Fair* or *Town & Country.* The editor of *Details,* Annie Flanders, explains the choice of the word: "The name occurred to me about ten years ago. When I'd ask my daughter Rosie about, say, her friends and their families, she'd answer generally, but I wanted *details.*"

In the pharmaceutical world, *detail man* is a 1920's term for a salesman who introduces new products to pharmacists and doctors; in our nonsexist age, that term has changed to *detailer.*

Why do we philologists, concerned with the broad sweep of the language and the rich veins of dialect, concern ourselves with the origin of a specific phrase or the development of one word's new senses and meanings? Because we know where God and the Devil meet.

Some years ago I, too, was interested in tracking down that Flaubert remark. I recall finding it in his letters, I think, but I seem to have (maddeningly) lost the reference. Still, I can offer a little more help.

The words in French were not "God" but "the good God"—le bon Dieu est dans le detail. This small difference is interesting in the light of the diabolical version that you cited, which lands God's opposite in the details. I take that to be another illustration of the old rhetorical device by which identical meanings are attached to antithetical words (Freud has a paper on this). It may also illustrate the rhetorical device by which, say, "curse the king" becomes "bless the king," though for reasons not at all clear.

There is also another source that I know of. He is Aby Warburg (1866–1929), one of the most original historians of culture in this century, a pioneer in the study of the Renaissance whose extraordinary library was spirited out of Hamburg and away from its inevitable Nazi doom to become the foundation of the Warburg Institute in London. According to E. H. Gombrich, in his biography of Warburg, the adage Der liebe Gott steckt im Detail was given by the scholar as one of his mottoes at his seminar in Hamburg in 1925–26. Note, again, the "liebe Gott." The adage suits especially well an iconographer of images drenched in the neo-Platonic cosmology, in which "God" really does infuse every bit of the world.

Gombrich mentions (page 16) that a French equivalent of the adage has been attributed to Flaubert, and concludes: "The question of its origin is still open."

Leon Wieseltier
Washington, D.C.

Who Will Indict the Indicters?

Indict is a strange verb; it looks as if it should rhyme with *interdict*. The confusion is rooted in the Latin *in-* ("against") and *dictare* ("to dictate, order"); to *indict* is to speak against, to accuse. We would all be better off to spell it *indite* (as in "to write"), but not even Noah Webster could straighten out English spelling.

The writers of the King James Version of the Bible in 1611 avoided the word when they should have used it. In Job 31:35, the afflicted hero expresses the wish "that mine adversary had written a book." What the put-upon man from Uz was expressing was a desire that God, who had been giving him an inexplicably hard time, had issued an indictment—a written list of charges—which Job could then have intelligently answered.

Comes now the special prosecutor Lawrence E. Walsh with an indictment of John M. Poindexter, Oliver L. North, Richard V. Secord and Albert Hakim, the Iran-contra "gang of four." Some have read that 101-page document with shock and dismay, deploring what they saw as a kind of coup d'état in the White House; others read the indictment with anger, asking, "What's the big deal? What does this tell us that we did not know before?"

This department is above all that: I read it for the language. How does this indictment rate as legal prose?

1. *Verbosity:* The indictment refers to "covert action activities"; why "activities"? The use of "covert action operations" is not redundant, but "action activities" is a matter for the Squad Squad; it's like a weather forecaster talking about "precipitation activity" when he means "precipitation." (What he really means is *rain,* or if sporadic rain, then *showers.*) Whenever you see *activity* (or *situation*) in your prose, cut it out.

In the same way, a nonfoolish consistency is called for in the use of prepositions. On one page of the indictment is "concealing a program to continue the funding of and logistical and other support *for* military . . ." On the same page is "including the support *of* military . . ." I prefer *support for* in these instances because the support is material, not physical, but whichever you prefer, stick to one or the other.

2. *Detours from parallel construction:* "the defendant North had given military advice to the contras, had knowledge of specific military actions conducted by the contras, had had contact with John K. Singlaub within the previous 20 months, had raised funds in support of the contras, had advised and guided Robert W. Owen with respect to the contras, and had had frequent contact with Owen."

Although the document shows consistency in verb tenses through the most convoluted sentences, in this instance the series of past-perfect verbs has a sore thumb sticking out. The past-perfect tense uses *had* and a past participle to show action completed (or state reached) before a specific time in the past. Here we see *had given, had had, had raised, had advised, had guided*—all fine. But—clunk!—*had knowledge.* That should have been *had known.*

3. *The effect-affect trap:* High marks must be given the indicters for properly choosing the infrequently used verb *to effect.* This verb is not *affect* ("to act on, to move"), but "to bring about, to accomplish," as in "to effect the objects thereof." The prosecutors were probably affected by the police use of "to effect an arrest," correctly using *effect* as a transitive verb. Effective, though not affecting, use of a rare verb.

4. *Jargon:* "the defendant . . . created and maintained a logistical infrastructure for the enterprise." *Infrastructure* is one of those terms dear to the hearts of bureaucrats who don't know if they want to say *foundation, skeleton, framework, setup,* or even the mouth-filling but understandable *administrative organization.*

Winston Churchill derided an opponent's use of "the infrastructure of a supranational authority" by suggesting "it may well be that these words 'infra' and 'supra' have been introduced into our current political parlance by the band of intellectual highbrows who are naturally anxious to impress British labor with the fact that they learned Latin at Winchester."

5. *Agreement:* "the chairmen of the House Committee on Foreign Affairs and HPSCI [House Permanent Select Committee on Intelligence] each wrote . . . on behalf of his committee." When *each* is used alone as a pronoun, it is construed as singular, but when it is used before the verb, as it is here, as

an adjective modifying the plural *chairmen,* a plural construction—"their committees"—should follow.

"From early November 1986 to Nov. 21, 1986, to conceal and cover up their illegal activities, the defendant John M. Poindexter made false and misleading statements." The pronoun *their* has no antecedent. Elsewhere in the document, *their* is unclear: "Together with that official of the C.I.A., and in order to conceal their participation in these activities, the defendant North . . ." Who is involved in "their"? North and that official? North and the agency? A whole bunch of guys? Pronouns count; link them closely to their antecedents.

6. *That/which differentiation:* A restrictive clause begins with *that* and restricts the meaning, while a nonrestrictive clause begins with a *which,* coming after a comma, and is not essential to the meaning. But not in this indictment: "the President's approval for the shipment of Hawk missile spare parts which had not yet been delivered to Iran." That needs a comma before *which* to be nonrestrictive, unless other shipments of spare parts had already been delivered. In "a written finding by the President which authorized the transfer of United States weapons to Iran," *which* should be *that,* because the clause restricts the meaning to the specific finding involved.

7. *Synonymy:* "the defendant . . . and others known and unknown to the grand jury, unlawfully, willfully and knowingly did combine, conspire, confederate and agree together and with each other to defraud the United States of America."

That certainly sounds like legalese, as in those wills that say you "give, devise and bequeath" your old lawbooks to the baby who looks like William Rehnquist. But *combine,* which has a mostly neutral sense, is usually found in antitrust use; *confederate* denotes joining, perhaps as an accomplice in a mischievous or criminal activity, and *conspire* has the most criminal meaning. (And while we're at it, *devise* refers to real property; *bequeath,* to personal property.)

What about the indictment's catchall use of "false, fictitious, fraudulent and misleading"?

Each has a meaning of its own. "The word *false* means 'wrong,' " says James D. Boyle, professor of law at the American University, "but that can refer to a simple mistake or to an intentional untruth. *Fraudulent* suggests the knowledge that a statement is false. *Fictitious* involves telling falsehoods that form a pattern, as in telling a story; that pattern can create an alternative picture of reality."

How can you tell the truth while being *misleading*? "If you're asked whether you've been driving for a long time, and you have not been, a truthful but misleading answer would be 'Well, I got my license 15 years ago.' "

All four of those terms—*false, fictitious, fraudulent* and *misleading*—are said by many lawyers to trigger slightly different points of law. In this case, opines Professor Boyle, all were needed to cover what he calls "the spectrum of mendacity."

If you forget everything else about this indictment, remember this: Indictments are handed *up* (to the judge on the bench up there), just as judges hand sentences *down*. If you hear a commentator say, "Indictments were handed down," fry that solecist.

A quote from the indictment mentions the "Hawk" missile. It should have been HAWK—an acronym for "homing all the way killer."

> Edward Olshaker
> Sigrid Benson
> Redstone Arsenal, Alabama

Even if indict *were pronounced with a short* i *and an enunciated* c, *it still would not* rhyme *(as you put it) with* interdict. *The two words would have the same pronunciation on their accented syllables, but the consonant sounds beginning those syllables are the same. Any poet knows that true rhyme requires* different *consonant sounds preceding the similar sounds.*

*Thus—*indict *(if mispronounced with short* i *and pronounced* c*) would rhyme with* convict *or* inflict *but not with* interdict.

> Elliot Tokson
> Armonk, New York

Wiggle, Wiggle

Wiggle room is not a free-play area in an especially permissive child-care center, but a frequently used phrase that means "space in which to turn around; an implicit opportunity for later flexibility; a political position permitting interpretation leading to modification. Not quite an *escape hatch* or a *way out.*"

That's how it was defined in this column four long years ago. But some people never get the word.

The editorial page of *The New York Times,* exercising its diatribal rights, castigated Michael Dukakis for suggesting that the United States Embassy be moved from Tel Aviv to Jerusalem, which Israel has designated as its capital.

The editorialist disagreed, but found some satisfaction in the vagueness of the candidate's formulation: "He has thus left himself wriggling room should he be elected."

Wriggling room is at best a prescriptive improvement, at worst a genteelism, that the editorialist picked up from an eminent lexicographer who did not have citations on hand for the correct dialect phrase, *wiggle room.*

Let us play the language as it lays (*lays* is the idiom, not the grammatical *lies*). The term is *wiggle room.* No interpretations, no modifications, no slipping out of the commitment.

Winkle-Pickers of the Press

In his morning briefing, Marlin Fitzwater, the President's press secretary, was working his way through the intricacies of arms-reduction negotiations. The White House press corps was riddling his presentation with detailed questions. Finally, the mildly exasperated Mr. Fitzwater said to the assembled reporters, "As the lady who sat beside me at the luncheon with the Queen in Buckingham Palace says, ''We can't *winkle-picker* this anymore.' ''

As the briefing transcript shows, that triggered a burst of questioning from the press.

Q: We can't what? What?! Huh?!

(Federal News Service transcripts now include a combination of exclamation point and question mark, which may cause the rebirth of the long-forgotten *interrobang.*)

MR. FITZWATER: How about that!

Q: You're going to have to spell that.

Q: Is that hyphenated, Marlin?

MR. FITZWATER: It's all one word, thank you, and the *winkle* is capitalized.

(The press secretary was being jocular, but is in error; on the analogy of *nit-picker,* the compound is hyphenated and not capitalized. Also, the verb form is properly *winkle-pick;* the noun is *winkle-picker.*)

Asked for a definition of *winkle-picker,* Mr. Fitzwater helpfully provided a second usage in the nominative, quoting his British dinner partner as also having said, "Those press can be such a bunch of *winkle-pickers,* can't they?" He said he agreed completely, whatever the word meant.

Maureen Dowd of *The New York Times,* alert to the need for vocabulary enrichment at the highest levels, followed up afterward. Mr. Fitzwater recollected that his luncheon companion at the palace explained to him at the time that a winkle was a very small shellfish that required the use of a tiny fork to pick out the meat. By metaphoric extension, a questioner who tries with piddling little questions to extract the last shred of informational nourishment from a subject was a *winkle-picker.*

Further research shows *winkle* to be a shortening of *periwinkle,* which most of us think of as a flower or a light purplish color. However, the shortened word is also used for any of various marine snails with a conical shell; these long, thin mollusks or whelks of the genus Busycon prey on oysters and clams by drilling a hole in their shells and rasping the succulent flesh, much as journalists do to clammed-up sources. The root of *winkle* is the Old High German *winkil,* "corner," which would be the sharp point of the attacking snail's shell (and we *wink* out of the corner of our eye as we accept news on deep background).

As a verb, drawing on the shellfish trope, *to winkle out* began as British military lingo, first cited in 1925 with the meanings of "to capture individual prisoners by stealth" and "to steal."

The lexicographer Eric Partridge defined a *winkle-pin* as a bayonet. By 1958, the British critic John Press had adapted the phrase for a literary argument: "It is illegitimate to compare the farfetched conjectures of Eliot's commentators with the inside information we might have winkled out of Donne."

The image of a long, thin, pointed object—a winkle-pin served with shellfish, or a slim fork—was taken up in the British fashion industry to describe shoes. The *Oxford English Dictionary* supplement defines *winkle-picker* as "*slang,* a shoe with a long pointed toe," citing a 1960 *Spectator:* "The incredibly pointed custom-built shoes in which teen-agers keep other teen-agers at arm's length . . . The shoes, called winklepickers"—not hyphenated, Mr. Fitzwater will be pleased to note—"look like something out of Grimm's fairy tales."

A *winkler,* true to the original notion of prying out with difficulty, is also a British term for "one who helps to evict tenants." The trans-Atlantic babytalk *winkle,* a familiar nursery euphemism for a child's penis, has no apparent provenance in the periwinkle we have been studying today.

Who was the British lady to whom we are indebted for taking a figure of speech and turning it into a legitimate lexicographic citation? Pressed for his source, the White House press secretary shakes his head. "In the best traditions of English chivalry," he replies, hand over his heart, "I must protect the identity of my gracious luncheon companion. You couldn't pry it from me with a *winkle-picker.*"

Woman Trouble

"Could you please explain to someone on *The New York Times Book Review,*" writes Mrs. Romulus T. Weatherman of Lexington, Virginia, "why the apostrophe in the enclosed clipping is in the wrong place?"

The clip: "Concealed within these tales are the seeds of many conflicts that bedevil the womens' movement. . . ." The punctuation was repeated in "womens' novels."

Women is plural; the only correct possessive form is *women's.* A large number of female persons can form a *women's movement,* and a lone female person's lurch in any direction can be called a *woman's movement,* but the apostrophe always goes before the *s.*

Perhaps the confusion comes from *people;* when Mr. Reagan goes to Moscow, he will be reminded to eschew "the Russian people" for "the Soviet peoples," and in that case the possessive form would read "the Soviet peoples' hospitality." Another contributor to the confusion: *Mother's Day* is preferred, but it would be possible to write it as *Mothers' Day* without grave grammatical offense; not so with *women.*

I have erred recently on *woman,* too, using it as an attributive noun modifying another noun, as in *woman journalist.* I think that should be *female* journalist, to avoid the kind of confusion that comes with *woman doctor*—is the doctor a woman or does the doctor treat female patients? *Female* is the best modifier when you want to specify sex, just as *sex*, not *gender*, is the most direct word when you want to specify male or female.

In case you never noticed, the first syllable of *woman* and *women* is spelled the same and pronounced differently, while the second syllable is spelled differently and pronounced approximately the same. That's one of women's mysteries.

Writer vs. Robot

"Last week I received a 'Grammatik III' word-processing program," writes Gertrude M. Webb of Waltham, Massachusetts, "and have been using it to analyze my own written work. I thought it might be fun to 'Grammatik-ize' a few paragraphs of your column. I'm passing the robot's comments along to you. Enjoy."

The opening paragraph of my column, which had been passed through the software to check style and usage, was this: "Charles Dickens fuzzed up the meaning of a good word when, in 1865, he titled a novel *Our Mutual Friend.*"

"PROBLEM," registered the software. "One-sentence paragraph."

What's so terrible about a one-sentence paragraph? "ADVICE," barked the program: "Usually a paragraph should have more than one sentence."

That offended not only my pride but also my ear. So what if one-sentence paragraphs were infrequently used, or even a rarity, which I doubt—must every writer conform to the norm? More important, in the robot's advice, the sentence adverb *usually* did not quite fit with the verb *should have*. A native speaker would say descriptively, "Usually, a paragraph *has* more than one sentence," or prescriptively, "*Ordinarily,* a paragraph should have more than one sentence."

In explaining the difference between *mutual* and *common,* I wrote: "But when the intended meaning involves no reciprocity, and instead refers only to a feeling or relationship shared about a third party, purists insist on *common. . . .*"

"PROBLEM," snorted the program, "*but*—hackneyed, cliché or trite. ADVICE: Use *but* sparingly to start a sentence."

What should I have used—*however*? I prefer *but;* it rebuts sharply. Roy H. Copperud's consensus book on usage says, "There is no reason why . . . *but* (or any other conjunction) should not begin a sentence." And according to William and Mary Morris's *Harper Dictionary of Contemporary Usage,* "*But* may . . . be used to start a sentence, a practice deplored by Victorian grammarians."

The robot is a century behind the times. Its use of *sparingly* suggests that it thinks *but* can be used at the beginning of a sentence once in a while. Why doesn't the machine check through my column to see whether I've used it elsewhere and, if I did not, just shut up instead of giving me irrelevant advice? That's the sort of fast checking these programs are supposed to be good at.

In the column, I quoted Henry Fowler, author of the classic *Modern English Usage:* "*Our mutual friend Jones* (meaning Jones who is your friend as well as mine), and all similar phrases, are misuses of *mutual.*"

"PROBLEM: *as well as*—language weak or wordy. ADVICE: Use sparingly or use *and* or *also* if that's what you mean."

The computer program is not harassing me in this case; it is taking on Fowler. I will let the old boy defend himself: "*As well as* is a conjunction and not a preposition. . . . Its strict meaning is not *besides,* but *and not only.*" The robot is confused if it thinks that *and* or *also* will substitute adequately for *as well as.*

Ms. Webb further informs me that the average length of my sentences was twenty-four words, which on some "Fog Index" meant that only a college student could understand me. That's cool.

I roared out to my local software peddler to get my own robot for further research. The store did not have "Grammatik," but (the robot would let me use *but* here, where it's safe and warm) it did have the competition, "Right-Writer," for eighty dollars. Must be a swinger: permits a capital letter right in the middle of a proper noun.

"Read the manual"; O.K. "RightWriter does not understand the actual meanings of words or the exercise of literary license," it disclaims up front. "It also does not have a human ear to judge how things sound. This means RightWriter will not find all types of errors, and in some cases, RightWriter will point out correct (or at least allowable) phrases as errors."

Fair warning; unfortunately, most buyers will ignore that disclaimer and treat the corrections as gospel. Yet the warning illustrates the problem with programmed style and usage guides: They point with mechanical certitude to what may or may not be an error, and then expect the customer to know if it's a mistake or not, and—if a correction is indeed needed—to automatically know how to fix it.

Let's put that paragraph through the works. Uh-oh—that last sentence was altogether too complex. "SPLIT INTO 2 SENTENCES?" No, thanks— the colon and the dashes do the trick as far as I'm concerned. What about *to automatically know,* an infinitive I slipped in to see what the robot would say? "SPLIT INFINITIVE," says the program, wide awake, but directs you to good advice in the manual: "This is incorrect only when it makes the meaning of the sentence unclear. Sometimes, the only way to clearly convey the intended meaning is with a split infinitive." (Better advice would concern emphasis rather than meaning, and the comma after *sometimes* is unnecessary but the use of "to clearly convey" shows subtlety.)

Let's try the Kennedy inaugural: "Let the word go forth from this time and place, to friend and foe alike, that IS COMMA NEEDED AFTER 'ALIKE'? the torch has been passed PASSIVE VOICE to a new generation. . . ." (Yes, the comma is needed after *alike;* no, nothing is wrong with the passive voice here.)

"And so, my fellow Americans, ask not what your country can do for you; ask what you can do for your country. SPLIT INTO 2 SENTENCES?" (No; don't fiddle with that line.) The "strength index" of that powerful speech reads "WEAK," and the robot says, "The writing can be made more direct by using the active voice, shorter sentences."

Try this sentence from *The Elements of Style* by William Strunk Jr. and E. B. White: "No one can write decently who is distrustful of the reader's intelligence, or whose attitude is patronizing." Says RightWriter: "WORDS TO REVIEW: Review this list for negative words, jargon . . . or words which your reader may not understand: patronizing."

The programs dealt with here are intended both to instruct beginning writers and to help professional writers correct their own copy. In my judgment (a word RightWriter persists in spelling "judgement," British-style), the available software falls far short and, in its present state, may do more harm than good.

The beginner, despite the disclaimers in the manuals, is likely to be intimidated and forced into a short-sentence, simple-word mold fit for ten-year-olds or Ernest Hemingway, while many a pro will be rattled by the mechanistic carping at any expression of personal style.

Word-processor spelling checkers and computer thesauri offer great help to all writers; maybe a usage program to catch *uninterested/disinterested* or *eager/anxious* would be useful, too. But on style—expression in writing—the robots are years away from matching what the average teacher can offer. That's because the style-usage programming is primitive, inconsistent, unsophisticated—unable to tell when a sentence is a run-on (to be fixed) or gracefully lengthy (to be savored).

In time, computers will be able to deal with the lines of thought, a mental process at the heart of style. At present, if you take a sentence from the start of the manual and put it next to a sentence at the end, the program will stupidly overlook the most glaring error in the paragraph—failing to flash "TRANSITION?"—because it cannot yet understand what the writer is trying to say, and offers no help. (SPLIT INTO 2 SENTENCES? Leap in the lake.)

What you say about RightWriter and, by implication, about Grammatik is true; I know both programs well. But you miss the point: We are not meant to apply these tools to the writing of Strunk and White, or William Safire, or whoever wrote JFK's inaugural. Neither program understands English; more important, neither program has any feeling for rhetoric.

These products are for the benefit of <u>my clients</u>: managers, "administrators," engineers, programmers, scientists. . . . These folks have no idea when a passive voice is preferable, because they aren't altogether sure what a verb is. They are people with little grammar, less style, and a tin ear for the cadences of speech. They are the ones who write <u>should it prove to be the case that</u> instead of <u>if</u>, <u>make a selection regarding</u> instead of <u>select</u>, and so forth.

The mere fact that RightWriter tags most passives and that Grammatik scolds everyone who uses <u>prioritize</u> makes them veritable national treasures. Of course, both programs make mistakes; of course, both still contain some of Miss Thistlebottom's hobgoblins. But I tell you, after two decades of trying to teach America's best-educated professionals to write better—and seeing little progress—I've decided that "style checking" software is our last best hope.

For the overwhelming majority of business and government communications, I expect to see no improvement and, therefore, I've written off most humans as writers and editors. What we really need are better style robots.

Edmond H. Weiss
Cherry Hill, New Jersey

Unfortunately, many people need programs like RightWriter. Someday, because a bank teller understands a procedure and is able to serve you correctly, you may benefit from such a program. Your column was a cheap shot at a useful tool.

> *Geoffrey Brown*
> *New York, New York*

You write that programmed style and usage guides ". . . expect the customer to know if it's a mistake or not . . ." One would hope that, whether the guide is sophisticated or not, it would point out that what you should have said was ". . . expect the customer to know <u>whether</u> or not it's a mistake . . ." It's a common error, and I have no doubt that if "if" had six letters and "whether" had two, people would continually use "whether" when they should have used "if," instead of vice versa.

> *Frank S. Stein*
> *Kokomo, Indiana*

I am dismayed by the quoted material from Mr. Copperud. Is it possible that a usage book on which William Safire relies contains the horrible redundancy, "reason why"?

> *Holly S. Kennedy*
> *Hartsdale, New York*

INDEX

ABOUT THE AUTHOR

WILLIAM SAFIRE is a writer of many incarnations: reporter, publicist, White House speechwriter, historian, novelist, lexicographer, and essayist.

His primary occupation since 1972 has been political columnist for *The New York Times,* usually taking the point of view of a libertarian conservative; in 1978, he was awarded the Pulitzer Prize for distinguished commentary. His column "On Language" in *The New York Times Magazine* is syndicated around the world and has made him the most widely read and argued-with writer on the subject of the English language.

Mr. Safire is married, has a son and daughter, and lives in a suburb of Washington, D.C.

ABOUT THE TYPE

This book was set in Times Roman, designed by Stanley Morison specifically for *The Times* of London. The typeface was introduced in the newspaper in 1932. Times Roman had its greatest success in the United States as a book and commercial typeface, rather than one used in newspapers.